THE PARADOX OF ISLAMIC FINANCE

The Paradox of Islamic Finance

HOW SHARIAH SCHOLARS RECONCILE RELIGION AND CAPITALISM

RYAN CALDER

PRINCETON UNIVERSITY PRESS

PRINCETON & OXFORD

Published by Princeton University Press
41 William Street, Princeton, New Jersey 08540
99 Banbury Road, Oxford OX2 6JX

press.princeton.edu

All Rights Reserved

ISBN 978-0-691-25831-7
ISBN (pbk.) 978-0-691-25830-0
ISBN (e-book) 978-0-691-25832-4

British Library Cataloging-in-Publication Data is available

Editorial: Meagan Levinson, Rachael Levay, and Erik Beranek
Cover design: Katie Osborne
Production: Lauren Reese
Publicity: William Pagdatoon

Cover image: View of The Gate at DIFC Dubai International Financial Centre (free zone) in the financial district of Dubai United Arab Emirates. Iain Masterton / Alamy Stock Photo

This book has been composed in Arno Pro

10 9 8 7 6 5 4 3 2 1

For Elise

وَإِنَّ الْمَلَائِكَةَ لَتَضَعُ أَجْنِحَتَهَا رِضًا لِطَالِبِ الْعِلْمِ ... وَإِنَّ فَضْلَ الْعَالِمِ عَلَى
الْعَابِدِ كَفَضْلِ الْقَمَرِ لَيْلَةَ الْبَدْرِ عَلَى سَائِرِ الْكَوَاكِبِ وَإِنَّ الْعُلَمَاءَ وَرَثَةُ
الْأَنْبِيَاءِ وَإِنَّ الْأَنْبِيَاءَ لَمْ يُوَرِّثُوا دِينَارًا وَلَا دِرْهَمًا وَرَّثُوا الْعِلْمَ ...
سنن أبي داود ٣٦٤١ (كتاب العلم، حديث ١)

Verily, the angels lower their wings for the seeker of knowledge . . . for the merit of the scholar exceeds that of the merely devout just as the full moon outshines the stars. The scholars are the heirs of the prophets, who have left behind neither dinars nor dirhams, but knowledge.

—SUNAN ABĪ DĀWŪD 3641 (BOOK OF KNOWLEDGE, HADITH 1)
(AUTHOR'S TRANSLATION)

CONTENTS

PREFACE

IN JANUARY 2004, I was a twenty-five-year-old business analyst with the Dubai office of a name-brand international management consultancy. We had been retained by Saudi Arabia's National Commercial Bank (NCB), a state-owned behemoth hoping to become leaner and more profitable. I spent my weekdays in Jeddah at NCB headquarters and my weekends—when I got weekends—back in Dubai. As the consulting team's junior member and "Excel monkey," my job was to build a model estimating the profitability of every one of NCB's millions of customers.

It was Tuesday, so I was in Jeddah. And I was confused.

"Four billion riyals?" I asked myself, incredulous as I stared at the largest current account at the bank. That was over a billion dollars. Who in their right mind would park that much money in an account that earned no interest? A current account, often called a checking account, accrues no interest because one uses it to pay bills. Any self-respecting Saudi billionaire with four billion riyals on hand, I figured, would ship that kind of money off to an investment vehicle in the Cayman Islands, or buy a soccer team with it, or at the very least deposit it in a savings account to earn interest.

There had to be a glitch in the model that I had spent the past month building. Crestfallen, I searched for someone who could explain.

I had stayed up past 2:00 a.m. for two weeks straight to finish the labyrinthine model, fueled by energy drinks and room-service hummus at the Inter-Continental Hotel Jeddah. Once my precious model was complete, I linked it to a database that contained account information for each of NCB's millions of customers. I sorted the customers by the deposits they held, and although I couldn't see their names, I knew they reflected Saudi Arabia's social hierarchy: at the bottom, janitors and construction workers from South Asia and maids and nurses from the Philippines, most of whom kept a few hundred riyals in the bank and remitted the rest home; in the middle, legions of Saudi civil servants and teachers; and at the top, the kingdom's royals and elite business families. At the apex sat this baffling customer, whose interest-free account held ten times more than anyone else's. "It has to be a glitch," I sighed again.

xi

I hunted down Khalid, a senior manager at NCB who always had answers. I pulled out my laptop and jabbed at the offending four-billion-riyal account.

"Oh, that's the king's account," Khalid said casually.

"The king . . . of Saudi Arabia?" I asked, instantly realizing how stupid that sounded. What other king could it be?

"Yes, King Fahd."

"But . . . why does King Fahd keep four billion riyals in an account that earns no interest?" I asked. Current accounts are where most people keep as little money as possible: whatever they need to pay imminent expenses. Was His Majesty about to buy dozens of French châteaux at once? Did he run a *really* high weekly grocery bill? I kept these ruminations to myself.

"It has to do with religion," Khalid explained. "With Islam."

"I see," I muttered, though I didn't. What did avoiding interest have to do with Islam? Khalid's response only made me more curious. Yet it was time to leave: Khalid was too genteel to tell me he was busy, and brief answers were his way of nudging me along. I returned to my hotel room and passed out on the bed.

———

Dubai, where our consulting teams serving NCB were based, felt in 2004 like the Wild West. The Arab Gulf states were booming, and Dubai's go-go real-estate market and permissive social mores made it a magnet for investors, professionals, and tourists. I had spent two years in our firm's Boston office, which was stately but staid by comparison. The Boston analysts and associates were polished, predictable Ivy League go-getters. Eight o'clock was a late night, since the partners wanted to get home to their families in the suburbs. The Dubai office, by contrast, recruited math prodigies from Turkey, elegant literati from Sudan, and the occasional scion of an Emirati cabinet minister. (My first ride in a Maserati was with one such scion, a national-champion jet skier.) We worked until midnight, then migrated to nightclubs.

After discovering the king's huge interest-free account, I started asking my colleagues at our Dubai office about it. "A lot of Saudis don't want to earn interest on their bank deposits," explained Aydın, a burly Turkish earthquake engineer.[1] "Well, not only Saudis—but especially Saudis." Why not? "The Quran says you'll burn in hell if you deal in interest," he replied matter-of-factly. So receiving *and* paying interest were off-limits? "Yup. A lot of Saudis just leave their money in current accounts." This was a great deal for Saudi banks, which ranked among the world's most profitable for decades as a result. Thanks to their millions of pious customers, Saudi banks could accrue large quantities of deposits without paying much in interest. They then turned around and lent those deposits out as interest-bearing loans, just like any other bank.

However, a new game in town threatened these Saudi banks' free lunch: Islamic banking. My colleagues mentioned it every time I brought up King Fahd's interest-free account. "Islamic banking is booming now," said Aydın. "So a lot of those interest-free deposits at the conventional Saudi banks will migrate over to Islamic banks." There, they could earn a positive return for the depositors—but a return that the bank described as profit on an investment, not interest on money lent to the bank.

I threw Aydın a quizzical look. "You're Muslim, right? So do *you* bank Islamically?" I asked.

"I don't," he replied. "I'm kind of a 'Muslim lite.' But not a light Muslim!" he chuckled, patting his gut.

I took Aydın's "Muslim lite" comment to mean that Muslims who patronized Islamic banks were especially religious—though I discovered years later that wasn't always true, and that what it means to be "especially religious" is hard to define anyway. The fear Aydın mentioned of burning in hell, while very real for some Muslim customers, belied much diversity: for every Islamic-banking customer I have interviewed who mentions hellfire, several assert that Islamic finance is "more ethical" or "better for society," like organic fruit or electric cars. Others offer simpler reasoning: "I'm Muslim, so of course I should bank Islamically!" For the time being, though, I accepted Aydın's hellfire theory.

So how did Islamic banks make money if they didn't receive or pay interest? Most banks live on interest: they pay low rates on deposits, charge high rates on loans, and pocket the difference.[2] "Do Islamic banks just charge fees instead of interest?" I asked Gabriel, an American with a PhD in economics from Northwestern. "Not exactly," he replied. Gabriel explained that Islamic banks trade and lease assets, and that the profits from those trades and leases take the place of interest. "It's all back-office operations," he concluded. I pursed my lips and nodded pensively, as though I knew what back-office operations were. (Gabriel meant that these trades and leases happen out of customers' sight.)

"But from a customer-facing perspective, the products Islamic banks offer are basically the same," he went on. "Islamic car financing, Islamic mortgages, Islamic savings accounts—to the customer, banking Islamically is pretty much the same as banking conventionally."

"Conventional" is what people involved with Islamic finance call ordinary non-Islamic finance.

There were, Gabriel conceded, some minor differences in the customer experience. "Sometimes there's more paperwork. And Islamic banks advertise 'profit rates' instead of 'interest rates.'" "Is that just to keep Muslim customers happy?" I asked. "Well, yeah—but also because the bank or customer is technically earning a profit on an asset trade or lease, not interest."

Guy, a tall, baritone Lebanese Christian, confirmed that Islamic banks trade and lease assets instead of lending and borrowing money. "Islamic banks trade all kinds of stuff so they can provide financing without charging interest. Cars, washing machines, metals, you name it." Guy dragged on his Gauloise cigarette and continued. "Some Islamic banks in Kuwait even pile stacks of iron and copper in front of their headquarters to prove they don't charge interest."

My head was swirling. I didn't understand this business about back-office trades and leases, nor about washing machines and piles of iron—things explained in chapter 2 of this book. Islamic banking sounded different from anything I knew.

"Look, it's all the same shit. It's all about making money," declared Abderrahmane, piercing like a balloon my naive impulse to exoticize Islamic banking. A debonair Moroccan of Berber descent, Abderrahmane was brash and sarcastic, and made a sport of charming everyone. He had worked for years at European luxury-goods conglomerates, and the cost of his hefty Swiss watch probably exceeded my monthly salary.

"You think being an Islamic bank means you don't want to make money?" he growled, growing even more animated than usual.

If Aydın didn't patronize Islamic banks, surely Abderrahmane didn't either. It was Abderrahmane who had counseled me to quaff my fill of whisky at the Emirates Airlines business-class lounge before we boarded our weekly flight from Dubai to Saudi Arabia, a dry country.

"Do Islamic banks charge more than conventional banks?" I asked. "Sometimes," Abderrahmane replied. "They used to, back in the 1980s and 1990s." But by 2004, Islamic banks in the Gulf were pretty price-competitive. "In Malaysia too," he added, referencing another major market for Islamic finance.

"Even when they charge a little more, Islamic banks are growing their assets at 30 percent CAGR,"[3] he went on. That was consultantese for "Islamic finance is growing really fast."

"Forty percent CAGR, 50 percent. I tell you, Ryan: Islamic banking is hot right now. Really, really hot. Everybody wants to get in the game."

And how exactly was this growth in Islamic banking happening? New Islamic banks were opening, but that wasn't all. Much of the growth was coming from conventional banks that had opened Islamic teller windows or Islamic branches. Some conventional banks were even converting entirely into Islamic banks. "NCB keeps opening new Islamic branches, and they're talking about going entirely Islamic. Some of the Emirati banks may convert in the next five or ten years too," Abderrahmane continued, using the Arabic demonym for someone or something from the United Arab Emirates.

"Speaking of which, doesn't 'Emirati' sound like a name for a Prada bag?" he riffed. "'Look at my beautiful new Emirati!'"[4] He dangled an invisible evening bag from his shoulder.

Handbag hijinks aside, what was Abderrahmane talking about? How could a conventional bank have an Islamic branch? I envisioned separate Islamic ATMs at Islamic bank branches that dispensed holy money, just as Mecca's Zamzam well and the fonts in a Catholic church dispense holy water. And how could a conventional bank possibly "convert" into an Islamic one? Did the CEO recite the *shahādah*—the profession of faith that one utters when embracing Islam—and, poof, "convert" the bank? (None of my musings were accurate. Chapter 3 explains what really happens.)

Abderrahmane's grin abruptly turned into a steely stare. "So Ryan: The profitability model is finished?" "Yes. Uh huh. Well, yeah, mostly." I replied unconvincingly. My laptop had been overheating and seizing up when I plugged NCB's massive customer database into my Excel model. "So go buy a better laptop! We need the model output by Wednesday morning," Abderrahmane declared. "It has to be perfect. Fucking perfect, ok? We present to the CFO on Thursday."

No more explorations into Islamic finance for me—and no more sleep.

———

I completed my consulting stint and left for graduate school in sociology a few months later, but Islamic finance stayed in the back of my mind. Increasingly, it appeared in the news too. Abderrahmane was right: Islamic finance was booming.

Meanwhile, my academic interest turned to Islam, and by the late 2000s, I was hunting for a dissertation topic. Like many in the same boat, I was indecisive. I studied Chinese for a summer, planning to study political Islam in Xinjiang and return to my roots as a Central Asianist: for my undergraduate thesis, I had interviewed Islamist politicians in Tajikistan. Yet the study of political Islam was crowded in the long shadow of September 11 and the U.S.-led invasions of Afghanistan and Iraq. I found it emotionally draining too. So many people I encountered in the United States seemed glued to the premise that Muslims were ontologically different from the rest of humanity. Talking heads on CNN presented bullet-pointed primers about Sunni and Shia Muslims, claiming that a seventh-century succession dispute meaningfully explained neighborhood killings in twenty-first-century Baghdad. The same talking heads treated the recent U.S. invasion as a footnote.

Even in Berkeley, allegedly the capital of Left Coast leftism, nearly everyone found it natural to speak of the "Muslim world," or of Iraq, Afghanistan, Somalia, and Iran as "Muslim societies":[5] regions whose political and cultural dynamics were somehow unitary and stamped indelibly by something coherent called "religion." Yet it would never cross their minds to speak of a twenty-first-century "Christian world," or to lump the United States together with the Philippines and Russia as inherently similar "Christian societies." Well-meaning friends, family members, and even those most enlightened of beings—my professors—took for granted that being Muslim meant Islam governed behavior in every domain of life: eating, drinking, dressing, childrearing, ruling, voting, protesting—and oppressing, fighting, and killing.

Every domain, that is, except finance. Somehow, the idea that there could be an Islamic way of dealing with money struck many of my interlocutors in the United States as ersatz to the point of being paradoxical. Their reflections boiled down to the following observation: "Money is just money; there can be no 'religious money.' Therefore, finance is just finance; there can be no 'religious finance.'" At best, anything calling itself religious finance had to be ordinary "secular" finance in religious robes, and at worst, it was Pharisaic legerdemain. When I explained that the Islamic-finance industry adhered to Islamic scholars' interpretations of shariah, these observers grafted Islamic finance onto their conception of halal and kosher food: curiosities governed by rules whose logic was lost to time immemorial, persisting as pure custom and tradition, dogmatically followed, and distant from commonsense modern concerns like food safety and animal welfare. Yet somehow, while religious strictures about food seemed perfectly natural to everyone—especially in California in the late aughts, when elimination diets and the "gluten-free lifestyle" enjoyed near-biblical authority—religious strictures about finance smelled deviant and dubious. It didn't help that whenever the word "Islam" appeared near the word "finance," non-Muslim neurons fired their way to "terrorist funding."[6] Throw in the word "shariah," and entire amygdalas lit up.[7]

I started to wonder what was going on here: not just with Islamic finance but with knee-jerk reactions to it. In assuming Islamic finance to be irrational and atavistic, my conversation partners drew on the Enlightenment conceit that religion is antithetical to modernity. They associated religion with backwardness: religion in general, Islam in particular, and shariah most of all. But that was hardly news; Edward Said had been saying it since 1979.[8] What piqued my interest was how they unwittingly conceived of finance. In insisting that money is money and finance is finance, they began from the premise that capitalist finance is strictly the domain of universal calculative rationality. To them, finance was void of culture and social structure: a pure modern terrain. People clung to that image of finance; it was sacred to them. That they could not think outside it was to me the true paradox.

After some hemming and hawing, years learning Arabic, a detour to Egypt, Bahrain, and Libya during the Arab Spring, and some sage advice from my advisors, I decided to focus on the Islamic-finance industry. Since then, I have attended trainings on the application of classical Islamic law to modern finance, internalized the structure of complex Islamic financial instruments, conducted fieldwork around the world, interned at an Islamic-finance law firm, and spent years conducting hundreds of interviews. I have never regretted my decision, because Islamic finance is simultaneously so many different things that interest social scientists: a social and intellectual movement, a capitalist industry, a system of voluntary religious certification, a collection of national markets shaped by regional and global political-economic forces, a transnational field of technical expertise and private regulation, an epistemic community, a space of debate and dissent, and, as I argue to close this book, a new way of seeing and being in the world.

The study of Islamic finance therefore has something to captivate everyone. It invites us to ask big questions: What is the relationship between religion and capitalism? How can twenty-first-century finance—the bull in the China shop—be corralled and regulated? And, most provocatively, what does it mean to be modern?

Islamic finance is many things. But most curiously of all, it is a mirror. How you understand Islamic finance says something about you. It reveals how you see the world.

TRANSLATION AND ROMANIZATION

THIS BOOK CONTAINS some Arabic and a bit of Urdu. Many of the Arabic words are terms of Islamic law, such as the names of nominate contracts used widely in Islamic finance (e.g., ijara, mudaraba, murabaha, tawarruq). It was hard to decide whether to use these terms or their translations (e.g., "murabaha" or "markup sale"). On the one hand, everyone in the Islamic-finance community uses the Arabic terms, whether they speak Arabic or not. Using the Arabic terms therefore allows readers to connect what they read here to other conversations about Islamic finance. On the other hand, using English translations improves comprehension for those who do not know Arabic. To address both concerns, I adopt an inelegant convention: I use the Arabic term throughout, but occasionally—usually at the word's first appearance in a chapter or chapter section—I remind readers of its meaning by including the English translation in parentheses. Readers can refer to the glossary too.

I use ALA-LC Romanization conventions for Arabic and Urdu and indicate them using italics (e.g., *muḍārabah*). However, when using Arabic terms common in Islamic finance, I generally drop the final "h" representing *tā ʾ marbūṭah* (ة), the marks for *ʿayn* (ع) and *hamzah* (ء), and most or all diacritics. *Muḍārabah* becomes "mudaraba" and *bay ʿal- ʿīnah* becomes "bay al-ina." For Arabic terms widely used in English-language news and literature, including the names of places and public figures, I adopt the most common Romanization: "ulama" instead of *ʿulamā ʾ*, "King Faisal Al Saud" instead of "King Fayṣal Āl Saʿūd," "Riyadh" instead of *al-Riyāḍ*. I Romanize my interviewees' names however they do on their business cards or personal websites.

In this book	Arabic script	ALA-LC Romanization	Definition
alim (pl. ulama)	عالم (ج. علماء)	ʿālim (pl. ʿulamāʾ)	scholar of classical Islamic studies; scientist
faida	فائدة	fāʾidah	interest (in a generic, non-normative sense)
faqih	فقيه (ج. فقهاء)	faqīh (pl. fuqahāʾ)	scholar of fiqh; Islamic jurist
fiqh	فقه	fiqh	Islamic jurisprudence, or the science of Islamic law; the human endeavor to study and implement God's normative system (shariah) on earth by combining revelation and reason
gharar	غرر	gharar	uncertainty in contract; transactional ambiguity
haram	حرام	ḥarām	Islamically unlawful; sinful
ijara	إجارة	ijārah	lease
ijtihad	اجتهاد	ijtihād	formation of new law through independent reasoning by qualified jurists
ina (aka bay al-ina)	عينة (بيع العينة)	ʿīnah (aka bayʿ al-ʿīnah)	sale followed by buyback
istisna	استصناع	istiṣnāʿ	contract in which a buyer pays an agreed price for future delivery of specific assets once they have been manufactured
maqasid al-sharia (sometimes just "maqasid")	مقاصد الشريعة	maqāṣid al-sharīʿah	the higher objectives of shariah (defined variously by different jurists)

(*Continued*)

In this book	Arabic script	ALA-LC Romanization	Definition
maysir	ميسر	*maysir*	unlawful speculation, including gambling
mudaraba	مضاربة	*muḍārabah*	silent partnership
mufti	مفتي	*muftī*	one who can issue fatwas; a shariah scholar
murabaha	مرابحة	*murābaḥah*	markup sale (used to simulate secured loans and other interest-bearing transactions)
musharaka	مشاركة	*mushārakah*	joint venture
riba	ربا	*ribā*	usury (interpreted by industry scholars to include all interest)
salam	سلم	*salam*	forward sale
sood	(الأردية) سود	(Ur.) *sūd*	interest (can have neutral or normative connotations in Urdu depending on context)
sukuk	صكوك (مفرد: صك)	*ṣukūk* (Ar. sg. *ṣakk* rarely used in English)	Islamic "bonds" (technically, securities representing individual ownership interests in a portfolio of eligible assets)
suq al-sila	سوق السلع	*sūq al-sila'*	the commodities market
takaful	تكافل	*takāful*	Islamic insurance
takhayyur	تخير	*takhayyur*	selection of a ruling from a different school of Islamic law than one's own
talfiq	تلفيق	*talfīq*	patching together of legal opinions, often from different schools of Islamic law
taqlid	تقليد	*taqlīd*	conformity to legal rulings by prior jurists within one's tradition without full understanding of the bases of those rulings
tawarruq	تورق	*tawarruq*	"cashification" (used to simulate unsecured loans)
ummah	الأمة الإسلامية	*al-ummah al-islāmīyah*	the community of all the world's Muslims

(Continued)

In this book	Arabic script	ALA-LC Romanization	Definition
usul al-fiqh	أصول الفقه	*uṣūl al-fiqh*	classical Islamic legal discipline that concerns principles and methodologies for deriving valid legal opinions
wakala	وكالة	*wakālah*	agency contract (the principal deposits cash with an agent, who invests the funds in a pool of assets and then returns the profits to the principal, minus a fee)
waqf	وقف	*waqf*	Islamic endowment of property, such as a building or plot of land, held in trust and to be used for educational, religious, or charitable purposes
zakat	زكاة	*zakāh*	Islamic alms tax (typically 2.5% of taxable wealth)

THE PARADOX OF ISLAMIC FINANCE

Introduction

MUSIC HUMMED FROM the speakers. It was time for the rock stars.

Rock-star shariah scholars, that is. To the deep, chant-like strains of devotional music,[1] three experts in Islamic law[2] walked on stage to address a convention hall packed with finance professionals at the sixth annual Kuala Lumpur Islamic Finance Forum. The scholars—one Bahraini, one Malaysian, and one Saudi—drew a larger crowd than any of the other VIPs, including bank CEOs and the prime minister of Malaysia. These three were among the international scholarly elite of Islamic finance: around a dozen experts in Islamic law most sought after to sit on the shariah boards of financial institutions around the world and dubbed "rock-star scholars"[3] by reporters and bankers.[4] Shariah boards are panels that certify that Islamic financial products adhere to Islamic law. Without a shariah board's fatwa of approval, firms cannot market their financial products as truly Islamic.

Elite shariah scholars get celebrity treatment at conferences. During the question-and-answer period at the Malaysian event, audience members addressed the august scholars deferentially, using the honorific "sheikh" or, to the panelists with PhDs, "doctor." After the panel ended, small crowds thronged the scholars. Bashful attendees settled for a handshake; bold ones proffered a business card, though they rarely received one in return. Some asked to snap selfies with a scholar. Queues formed as people sought the scholars' opinions on finer points of Islamic commercial law and business ethics. The scholars chatted with their questioners politely but expeditiously before walking briskly to business meetings or hopping in a black car to the airport. Top-tier shariah scholars are busy people. They log a lot of frequent-flyer miles.

Shariah scholars set the rules for what counts as Islamic in Islamic finance. To be Islamic, or "shariah-compliant" in industry lingo, financial transactions must avoid things the scholars deem sinful or unethical. This includes alcohol, pork, pornography, tobacco, weapons, the sale of debt (as in bond trading), the sale of risk (as in derivatives trading), payouts based on an uncertain future event (like insurance and options), and selling something you don't own (short selling). The scholars also ban ambiguous or poorly understood contracts, like the arcane, dubiously structured collateralized debt obligations that helped trigger the 2008 global financial crisis. Most consequentially of all, they ban interest: both receiving it and paying it.

While these rules may sound straightforward in theory, applying them in the twenty-first century can be challenging. Shariah scholars navigate the ever-increasing complexity of contemporary finance. One day they scrutinize a billion-dollar initial public offering (IPO), and the next day a syndicated Islamic financing involving investors from five countries and a special-purpose vehicle in the Cayman Islands. They also evaluate the byzantine methods Islamic bankers devise to make their transactions interest-free. For example, since shariah, as the scholars interpret it, requires all financial transactions to be based on an underlying asset, shariah scholars inspect intricate systems for electronically trading vast quantities of palm oil, palladium, mobile-phone airtime, and even seating capacity on airlines. Vetting such products and transactions is not just a matter of applying settled rules, either. If law is philosophy applied to changing times, Islamic law is no different. In evaluating financial instruments, the shariah scholars of Islamic finance ask questions that experts in religious and secular law have posed for centuries: "When does the public interest impinge on contracts freely entered into?" "When may lawful means be used to contravene the apparent spirit of the law?"[5] and even "What is money?" The scholars' judicial decisions, known as fatwas, authorize transactions that earn bankers millions. Yet the scholars' fatwas also impose shariah-compliance requirements that can cost the bankers millions to meet (see chapter 6).

Elite shariah scholars' certification authority stretches across borders, regulating some of the most powerful financial institutions in the world. The most prolific scholars sit on dozens of shariah boards around the globe, earning millions of dollars a year in honoraria and advisory fees. They oversee firms from Kuwait to Kazakhstan and from Singapore to South Africa, from domestic Islamic banks and boutique investment houses to titans of international finance like HSBC and Deutsche Bank. They advise Dow Jones and Morgan Stanley on which stocks are Islamic enough to be included in their Islamic stock indexes. They also sit on government shariah boards at central banks and securities commissions, issuing rulings that regulate entire countries' financial sectors. The top shariah scholars in Islamic finance are powerful ethical arbiters of a booming global industry.

Not everyone appreciates the shariah scholars, however. Some Muslims assume all shariah scholars are priggish and pushy, whether they work in Islamic finance or not. "Whatever the [scholars] say to do, I'll do the opposite," sneered Mahira, a twenty-five-year-old fashion-magazine editor in Karachi

wearing ripped jeans and Converse sneakers. "It's my life, not theirs." I asked
Mahira how Islamic banks avoid interest. "They don't," she retorted. "They
lie."[6] Other Muslims simply find Islamic finance perplexing. No matter where
I go, when new Muslim acquaintances hear that I study Islamic finance, they
ask me one question more than any other: "What do *you* think? Is Islamic
finance really Islamic?" (Non-Muslims ask, "What's Islamic finance?" or,
occasionally, "So you study how terrorists move money using hawala?")[7]

The biggest source of confusion and critique is that from an economic perspective, Islamic finance overwhelmingly simulates "conventional" (i.e., non-
Islamic) interest-based finance.[8] The shariah scholars facilitate this "interest
simulation" because of the way they interpret Islamic law. They authorize combinations of trades and leases that allow financial institutions to reproduce
most economic characteristics of interest-bearing products. In the language of
economist Al Roth, the Islamic-finance industry constitutes an attempt to circumvent the constraints that repugnance imposes on markets.[9]

As a simplified example of interest simulation, imagine that you want
$10,000 to remodel your kitchen. You don't have the money now, but you
know you'll have it in a year, once you've received your annual bonus at work.
You go to a conventional bank, which offers you a one-year loan at 10 percent
interest, meaning you would owe the conventional bank $11,000 in one year.
However, for religious reasons, you don't feel comfortable taking an interest-
bearing loan. So you turn instead to an Islamic bank, which arranges an alternative (see figure 6.3). First, the Islamic bank buys an asset from a broker for
$10,000. (The asset can be nearly anything worth around $10,000, so long as
it meets some conditions.) Second, the Islamic bank sells the asset to you for
$11,000 on credit: you receive the asset now and will owe the Islamic bank
$11,000 in one year. Third, you sell the asset for $10,000 to a different broker
from the first.

The result of this transaction, known as *tawarruq* (which I ungracefully
translate as "cashification"), is that you now have $10,000 in your pocket and
will owe the bank $11,000 in a year. From an economic perspective, this
arrangement simulates the $10,000 loan at 10 percent interest that the conven-
tional bank offered you. However, from a religious perspective—at least
according to shariah scholars who permit tawarruq—you and the bank have
avoided sin. For technically, the Islamic bank has not charged you interest.
Instead, it has earned a *profit* of $1,000 by buying a product at a lower price
($10,000) and selling it to you at a higher price ($11,000). And as the Quran
states, "God has permitted trade but prohibited usury."[10]

By designing techniques similar to this, automating them using the electronic infrastructure of commodities markets and stock markets, and stringing
them together in serpentine combinations, firms can engineer Islamic

financial products that simulate the effects of most major types of interest-bearing financial products. These include Islamic analogues of unsecured loans (like the above), secured loans[11] (such as mortgages and auto loans), savings accounts, time deposits (also known as certificates of deposit, or CDs), trade finance, commercial paper, money-market funds, bond funds, index funds, leveraged real-estate funds, project finance, convertible bonds, forwards, options, swaps, asset-backed securities, mortgage-backed securities, and credit enhancement, among others. From household banking to investment banking, from trade finance to mergers and acquisitions, most of the bestiary of conventional financial services is now available in Islamic form.

Interest simulation is only the most prominent example of an anxiety-inducing convergence[12] between Islamic finance and conventional finance that has transpired in the half century that the Islamic-finance industry has existed. Many Islamic banks are subsidiaries or divisions of conventional banks, which leaves potential customers wondering how Islamic they could be. Moreover, Islamic products often cost the same as their conventional analogues. It is not uncommon to find a conventional bank that offers a five-year auto loan at a 4.5 percent interest rate and an Islamic bank in the same country that offers a five-year Islamic auto financing at a 4.5 percent profit rate. The difference in terminology—profit rate versus interest rate—signals to some believers that the Islamic bank, instead of lending money directly to the consumer at interest, profits through less sinful means. But to others, the similarities smell fishy. In Lahore, prospective customers ask: "If Islamic banks offer the same prices as conventional banks, and link their profit rates to KIBOR [Pakistan's national benchmark interest rate] just like conventional banks do, aren't they just charging interest?"[13] Shariah scholars respond that price is just a number: if I sell grape juice at the same price at which my neighbor sells wine, my juice does not suddenly turn into wine. While such logic makes sense to some, it seems casuistic to others. An Egyptian cartoon captures this cynicism (figure 0.1).

This example of KIBOR and grape juice throws into relief a tension fundamental to Islamic finance. Evaluating the ethical valence of a financial transaction is a subjective and philosophical venture, a sketch necessarily executed in shades of gray. If I sell an investment product that pays investors a guaranteed return, and then each day, I set that return equal to a benchmark interest rate, am I effectively paying interest to the investors? There is no sure answer. The answer we choose depends on how we define interest and usury, which in turn depends on our conception of money and our vision of the good society.[14] Yet rulings in religious law, like rulings in secular law, are written in black and white. They carry the weight of moral certitude, and the more widely they are applied, the more indelible they become. They get written into state

FIGURE 0.1. On the right, above the caption "usurious bank" (*bank ribawī*, referring here to a conventional bank), the banker says "10 percent interest." On the left, above the caption "Islamic bank!" he says "10 percent interest, with God's permission [*bi-idhni-llāh*]!" The Islamic banker sports a beard, holds prayer beads, and has a prayer bump (*zabībah*) on his forehead, suggesting an ardent and perhaps ostentatious performance of piety. Credit: Abdul-Rahman Najmuddin.

regulations, into the design of financial products, into algorithms that screen stocks for shariah-compliance, and into Islamic-finance textbooks. Thus, the moral reasoning of elite shariah scholars on subtle philosophical problems crystallizes into the ethical blueprint for an entire global industry and becomes a taken-for-granted part of the financial ethics of millions of Muslims who take Islamic finance seriously. The Islamic-finance industry is institutionalizing and normalizing industry shariah scholars' financial ethics.

Yet the tension between the formal rules demanded by states and markets on the one hand and the complexity and contingency of jurists' hermeneutic work on the other never disappears completely, for there is never agreement on what the good society is. Each Islamic financial instrument becomes a microcosm of debate about the nature and ethics of money, credit, and prices. This makes Islamic finance fascinating.

Opposition to the Islamic-finance industry does not arise only from people like Mahira, the Converse-wearing fashion-magazine editor, who do not want Islamic law anywhere near their financial lives. The industry and its powerful shariah scholars also face opposition from quarters that *endorse* Islamic governance of the economy. This includes a vocal contingent of religiously minded academics, known as moral economists or Islamic economists, who sometimes chide the scholars for allying too closely with the banks they certify and for squandering Islam's potential to foment economic development. Most moral economists feel interest simulation in Islamic finance has gone too far and that a different Islamic practice called profit-and-loss sharing holds more promise for promoting equitable growth and building a just and morally upright Islamic society. Many of the moral economists believe free-market capitalist finance in Muslim-majority regions would benefit from Islamic brakes, but that bankers and lawyers are engineering their way out of these brakes with the shariah scholars' permission.

The shariah scholars respond that they are defending the "Islam" in "Islamic finance" by respecting the classical legal tradition while adapting to the challenges facing twenty-first-century Muslims. To justify interest simulation, they turn to a classical maxim of Islamic law, which states that if transactions are not clearly Islamically unlawful (i.e., *ḥarām*, sinful), no human may ban them in the name of Islam: only God may do so. While some shariah scholars working in the industry concede that interest simulation has become excessive, they often say it is up to states and firms to reform laws and corporate behavior. The scholars consider themselves theorists of sacred law, not policymakers. They assert that they cannot do in God's name what God has not explicitly authorized—though state regulators may and should do so in the name of good policy, and corporate boards in the name of corporate social responsibility. In practice, this means the shariah scholars circumscribe the "Islam" in "Islamic finance" mostly to the contractual form of a transaction.

Interest simulation lies at the heart of debates and struggles that recur throughout this book: debates about what it means to be financially pious. Some defenders of Islamic finance support the measured use of interest simulation because it puts Islamic finance on a playing field more level with conventional finance. Others insist that widespread interest simulation is a social boon, for it grants pious Muslims access to the fruits of financial modernity instead of shackling their capital to sin or keeping it out of circulation. Yet most Muslims who patronize Islamic banking did not keep their money under the proverbial mattress before they opened an Islamic account. Instead, they switched over from conventional interest-based banking. Whether this means Islamic finance is unnecessary or essential for Muslims depends on your point of view.

In addition to being influential certification agents, the shariah scholars have rejuvenated an entire branch of classical Islamic law. For a millennium, Islamic transactions law[15]—the study of commercial and civil obligations under shariah, including business, trade, and finance—had been a thriving sphere of Islamic legal theory and practice that adapted to changing economic conditions and needs.[16] Until the eighteenth and nineteenth centuries, Islamic transactions law resolved business disputes, structured long-distance trade, and governed financial affairs (even if not universally or consistently).[17] However, once European colonial administrators and indigenous modernizers decided that commercial law and financial law were too important to leave to religious scholars, Islamic transactions law lapsed. Now, thanks to the shariah scholars of Islamic finance, Islamic transactions law suddenly matters again after a century of lassitude. Knowing this branch of law now offers a path to a professional middle-class lifestyle for thousands of shariah scholars who, without the Islamic-finance boom, might have become workaday imams preaching in the local mosque and teaching schoolchildren to recite the Quran.

Criticism and cartoons notwithstanding, the shariah scholars have remained for half a century the supreme ethical gatekeepers of Islamic finance. Indeed, as this book shows, they have grown more powerful as more capital has flowed into the industry and an emerging epistemic community has entrenched their interpretations of shariah. The market acknowledges their influence: elite scholars can receive honoraria and advisory fees of as much as $300,000 a year for sitting on one financial firm's shariah board, and the world's most prolific elite scholars have been known to sit on as many as 85 shariah boards.[18] Moreover, they have helped establish Islamic finance as one of the most active domains of research and debate in influential international forums of Islamic law, alongside other hot areas such as Islamic bioethics.[19] While cynics accuse industry scholars of "selling out" as money pours into Islamic finance, there is evidence that the scholars are now imposing *more* restrictions on capital than they did before and scrutinizing shariah-compliance *more* scrupulously than in the past. Pithily: More capital, more shariah.

———

This book tackles two paradoxes. First, hundreds of millions of Muslims consider interest repugnant and sinful—and yet patronize Islamic finance, which simulates interest. To be sure, religious institutions have long dealt in interest. Temples, monasteries, and churches lent at interest in ancient Babylon and Rome, medieval Christian Europe, and early modern China, Japan, and south India.[20] And religious authorities have often promised that sums donated will come back multiplied, as do Prosperity Gospel televangelists who solicit "seed money."[21] Many others have portrayed finance as a road to godliness; the inventor of the limit order book[22] thought stock markets would instantiate Calvinist moral perfection. Nonetheless, interest simulation in Islamic finance is especially baffling. If something looks and acts like interest, how are so many convinced it is not? After all, interest simulation is no secret: Islamic banks explain openly how they do it. And the industry serves not just ordinary consumers, who could in theory be duped, but sophisticated corporations and savvy billionaires. So how have they all come to patronize it? What leads them to "buy" it—in both senses of "buy"?

Second, there is a multi-trillion-dollar Islamic-finance industry present in over 100 countries—but no Christian-finance industry," "Hindu-finance industry," or "Buddhist-finance industry" of comparable scale. Admittedly, Islamic finance has its cousins: Christian mutual funds screen out sin stocks just as Islamic mutual funds do, and a Jewish contract[23] designed by Talmudic scholars redefines all bank loans in Israel as joint ventures. But there is no true analogue to Islamic finance: no cohesive, technically sophisticated, global religious-finance *industry*. So what's the deal with Islam? Is something about it singularly simpatico with contemporary finance?

My answer to both questions is the same: it's the shariah scholars.

It is the shariah scholars, I argue, who are most responsible of all stakeholders for making Islamic finance a commercial success in the late twentieth and early twenty-first centuries. It is they who make contemporary religion compatible with contemporary capitalism. They do so in part by advancing practical interests: they make Islamic finance profitable for firms, affordable for consumers and investors, and politically palatable to states. While the bread of the Islamic-finance industry has many ingredients, the shariah scholars are the yeast: without them, the industry would not have risen as it has. It might still be religious finance, just as unleavened bread is still bread, but it would be very different: less profitable, less global, and less capable of offering Muslims a vast palette of financial products as convenient and price-competitive as those available in conventional finance.

Yet the shariah scholars do not simply facilitate interests; they *intellectualize* Islamic finance, making it a spiritually meaningful universe that is not governed by magical forces[24] but by rules that humans have the ability to comprehend.[25] Thus the sacred canopy[26] the scholars weave is of a unique sort. It is not transcendent and mystical, like the worldview of Sufi poets and adepts. Nor is it charismatic, held together by fiery sermons or toothy televangelism. Nor is it ritualistic or magical. Rather, the scholars' conception of religious virtue is theoretical and analytical. The shariah scholars endow capitalist finance with religious meaning by embedding it in expertise: specifically, expertise in classical Islamic law and their capital-friendly readings of it. Theirs is a cool, academic, and highly technical piety, a law professor's way of seeing and being in the world. Yet it is religious nonetheless, for it leaves no doubt that our financial behavior in this world will shape our futures in the next, and our fates on the Day of Judgment.

As decision makers, agenda setters, and gatekeepers of legal knowledge, the shariah scholars make capitalist Islamic finance more than just an industry or a certification system. Islamic finance has become an epistemic community—in business lingo, an "ecosystem"—that produces and enshrines a capital-friendly form of Islamic expertise. Yet it is even more than that. Islamic finance has become a *social world* whose diverse elements work together to make contemporary financial markets morally and spiritually meaningful spaces. In this social world, one can be more religious by being more economically modern, and more economically modern by being more religious. Under the shariah scholars, Islamic finance is a religious capitalist modernity.[27]

Face-to-Face with the Scholarly Elite

When I showed up at the Kuala Lumpur conference, none of this was in my head: I was just trying to get shariah scholars to talk with me. After the crowd around Sheikh Nizam Yaquby dissipated, I saw my chance. I speed-walked toward the bespectacled Bahraini scholar, intercepting him as he was strolling out of the conference hall in his white ankle-length *thawb*. "Sheikh Nizam, *al-salāmu 'alaykum*," I said, greeting him politely in Arabic. I proffered the Arabic side of my business card—the card that introduced me in two languages, with strategic ambiguity, as a "graduate researcher" rather than "graduate student." "*Wa- 'alaykum al-salām*," he replied, before continuing in flawless English: "How can I help you?"

To my amazement, the sheikh and I sat in the hotel lobby and talked for over an hour.

I pushed Yaquby, asking him tough questions. How did he justify the millions of dollars that elite shariah scholars earn each year? He asked why this should be a problem when highly paid corporate lawyers and business executives make millions more than leading shariah scholars do. And he noted that as the son of a Bahraini merchant family, he could have made more staying in the family business.

I had reason to listen to Yaquby with a critical ear. I had spoken with many people who found fault with the scholarly elite, accusing them of profiting excessively from their certification work, of arbitraging their big names, and of playing fast and loose with Islamic law. One industry-veteran-turned-critic compared the elite scholars to medieval Catholic priests who sold indulgences, offering "get-out-of-jail-free" cards to believers who engaged in the sin of usury but didn't want to go to hell. In this critic's mind, industry shariah scholars authorize financial practices that are dubious from a shariah perspective. To him, the scholars lift the anxiety of financial sin off Muslims' shoulders while allowing them to enjoy the profit and convenience of modern interest-based finance. "Everyone wants to go to heaven, but no one wants to pay for the ticket," he inveighed.[28] The industry veteran had especially choice words for Nizam Yaquby, in whom he saw all that was wrong with the scholarly elite.

Yet I admit that getting so much time with Yaquby lifted my ego, which had been clobbered by rejection after rejection when I requested interviews with less prominent scholars. I felt like a small-market sports reporter who had tried to squeeze in a question edgewise for an NBA superstar, then scored an hour-long sit-down. Everybody in international Islamic finance knows who Yaquby is. He sat on the most shariah boards of any scholar in the world when I spoke with him: by one count in 2010, eighty-five boards—and probably more today. He certifies sukuk (Islamic "bonds")[29] and syndicated loans worth billions of dollars. His time, like that of a top international lawyer or consultant, was worth thousands of dollars per hour. As a graduate student doing fieldwork, mine was worth approximately zero.

Yaquby has mastered the art of making his interrogators laugh. "Some people claim that Islamic finance imposes extra costs and conditions just to produce outcomes identical to those of conventional finance," I pointed out. "What do you say to them?" He responded to my question with a question: Had I noticed that most of these people were economists? "You see, the economists who say this, they want to reduce everything to economics: to transaction costs. But that's not how religion works."

Yaquby persisted with the Socratic method. "Which costs more: Being married or paying someone for sex?" Having never experienced either, I was still muddling through the math when he gamely answered his own question. "Being married, of course! You pay for a house, and a car, and clothes, and your children's school—for years and years! Honestly, it never ends. But if you pay someone for sex, you pay for one night, and *khalāṣ*."[30]

By that logic, he continued, religion should promote sex work over marriage. "But no religion in the world says that. Why not?" he asked.

I was starting to catch up with this lightning-fast game of call-and-response. "Because there are other benefits to marriage that can't be measured in transaction costs," I replied.

For a second, I found myself wondering whether Gary Becker would agree, and whether Becker applied rational-choice theory in the bedroom.

Yaquby flashed an impish grin. "Yes," he said, satisfied that we had both arrived at a rational conclusion about the suprarationality of religion, and had fun in the process. "You see? So if everything is about transaction costs, then you can come to all kinds of conclusions."[31]

However one feels about the elite shariah scholars of Islamic finance, one thing is clear: their prominence as regulators of a young, fast-growing industry is curious and unusual. But do they really matter as much as the celebrity treatment makes it seem? How exactly have they, and the hundreds of less prominent shariah scholars, contributed to the industry's growth? And what does all this tell us about the relationship between religion and modern capitalism? These questions lie at the heart of this book.

A Young, Booming Industry

The breadth of Islamic financial products is remarkable. Around the world, ordinary households save money in Islamic savings accounts. When they need credit, they turn to Islamic credit cards, Islamic mortgages, and Islamic auto financing. Islamic insurance[32] covers their homes, cars, health, and lives. They buy stocks using Islamic mutual funds, Islamic micro-investing apps, and Islamic indexes like the Dow Jones Islamic Market and the S&P 500 Shariah. The wealthy place their millions in Islamic private equity and invest in land through Islamic real-estate trusts. They retain Islamic wealth-management advisors to manage their money and Islamic estate planners to convey it to their progeny. Corporations raise funds via billion-dollar Islamic "bonds" and Islamic corporate financings, structured and underwritten by global banks like Goldman Sachs, Morgan Stanley, and Credit Suisse. They manage risk using complex Islamic derivatives such as profit-rate swaps and Islamic cross-currency swaps, designed by Islamic-finance specialists at some of the world's largest law firms. And governments rely on Islamic project finance to ensure that highways, airports, and power plants get built. In short, everyone from middle-class families to billionaires, corporations, and governments can now be financially Islamic in myriad ways.

This proliferation of Islamic products and services has been matched by spectacular growth. As of 2022, the Islamic-finance industry comprised just over $3 trillion in assets, and around 0.65 percent of world financial assets. This makes it larger than the entire financial sector of Eastern Europe,[33] South America, or India, and comparable in size to the U.S. Social Security trust fund ($2.9 trillion) and the global hedge-fund industry ($4 trillion).[34] World Islamic financial assets have grown even faster than world financial assets in general (figure 0.2 and table 0.1). Even during the 2008–9 financial crisis, Islamic finance kept growing fast while conventional finance faltered.

Islamic finance has a global footprint too. The industry is well-developed in the Arab Gulf states of the Gulf Cooperation Council (GCC),[35] as well as in Malaysia—a world leader in the issuance of sukuk (ṣukūk; Islamic "bonds")—and its tiny hydrocarbon-rich neighbor Brunei (figures 0.3 and 0.4). However, Islamic financial institutions operate in over 105 countries. Dubai, Kuala Lumpur, Riyadh, and Bahrain have been Islamic-finance hubs since the 1980s, with international financial centers such as London, Singapore, and Geneva vying to join them. Offshore-finance jurisdictions such as Jersey and Luxembourg have long attracted Islamic finance, since their laws and regulations favor the complex special-purpose vehicles and asset flows that Islamic-finance lawyers design to comply with shariah (figure 0.5). Iran

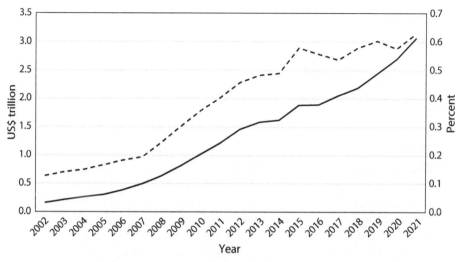

FIGURE 0.2. Global Islamic financial assets, 2002–21. Author calculation.

——— Global Islamic financial assets (left axis)

- - - Global Islamic financial assets as a share of total global financial assets (right axis)

TABLE 0.1. Islamic Financial Assets by Region and Sector, 2021 (US$ billion)

Region	Islamic Banking Assets	Sukuk Outstanding	Islamic Funds Assets	Takaful Contributions	Total	Region as Share of World Total (%)
Gulf Cooperation Council	1,212.5	332.3	46.0	12.7	1,603.5	52.4
Southeast Asia	287.5	390.3	37.5	4.7	720.0	23.5
Middle East and South Asia	477.1	26.9	22.0	5.6	531.6	17.4
Africa	58.2	1.8	4.0	0.6	64.6	2.1
Others	68.8	24.4	45.1	0.7	139.0	4.5
Total	2,104.1	775.7	154.6	24.3	3,058.7	100.0
Asset Class as Share of World Total (%)	68.7	25.4	5.1	0.8	100.0	

Source: Islamic Financial Services Board 2022.
Note: Region shares sum to 99.9 percent instead of 100.0 percent due to rounding.

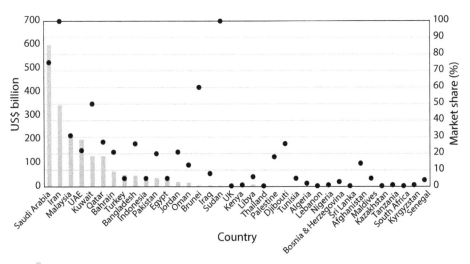

FIGURE 0.3. Domestic Islamic banking assets by country and their share of all domestic banking assets, 2021. *Source*: Islamic Financial Services Board 2022, 17.

and Sudan are special cases, as governments there outlawed conventional banking in the 1980s and 1990s, respectively, making their domestic banking sectors fully Islamic. State leaders from many other countries—including Nigeria, Kazakhstan, Oman, Indonesia, Australia, and Japan, to name a few—have arrived later to the game. For governments with substantial domestic Muslim constituencies, promoting Islamic finance serves to communicate religious bona fides. But even for countries without many Muslims, Islamic finance can be a lucrative on-ramp for Arab Gulf capital. Thus the globalization of Islamic finance proceeds due to a blend of economic, political, and religious motivations.

Interest Simulation

Interest is the lifeblood of modern capitalism, so doing finance without it sounds well-nigh impossible. At the small scale, I have trouble imagining how my wife and I would get by without our credit cards, car loan, and mortgage. At the large scale, a world without bonds seems alien too, for the bond market shapes every aspect of the global economy. How would companies raise money to grow? How would governments afford to build bridges and schools? The folksy Washington political consultant James Carville once reflected on

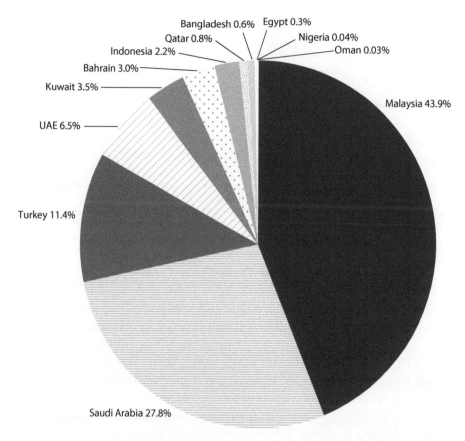

FIGURE 0.4. Corporate sukuk issuances in 2021 by jurisdiction of originator: share of world total. *Source*: Islamic Financial Services Board 2022, 28.

the ubiquity and power of bonds. "I used to think if there was reincarnation, I wanted to come back as the president or the pope or a .400 baseball hitter," Carville mused. "But now I would like to come back as the bond market. You can intimidate everybody."[36] Bonds are everywhere, after all. Interest is everywhere.

Yet maybe a world without interest wouldn't be so bad. As Carville claimed, and as David Graeber has shown,[37] interest is inseparable from intimidation. Do we want a world that runs on intimidation, where investors bully national governments and moneylenders drive families into misery? In Argentina, public spending has been held ransom for over two decades by U.S.-based "vulture" hedge funds, which bought Argentina's bonds on the cheap in the early 2000s and have since threatened to ruin its credit rating if

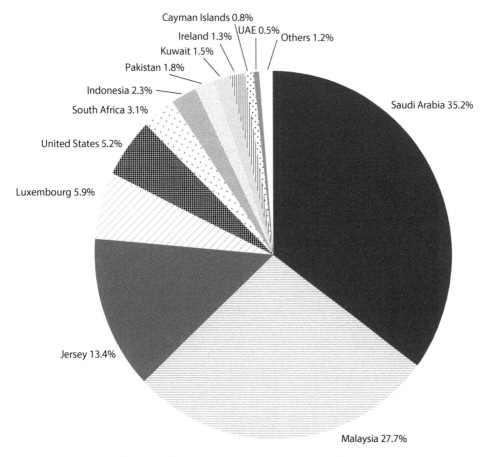

FIGURE 0.5. Islamic fund assets by domicile: share of world total, 2021.
Source: Islamic Financial Services Board 2022, 43.

they do not get their pound of flesh. From Thailand to Greece to Ecuador, debt crises have ushered in the International Monetary Fund's austerity chemotherapy, which treats the cancer of insolvency by slashing welfare nets and sacking teachers and nurses. In India, ten thousand farmers commit suicide every year when harvests fail, buried in mountains of interest-bearing debt they have taken to buy fertilizer and genetically modified seed.[38] And in the United States, twenty years after starting college, half of student borrowers still owe more than $20,000.[39]

The metaphor "falling into debt" speaks volumes: debt is a hole, and interest is the shovel we get to dig ourselves out. Loans are ostensibly tools that will allow us to better our condition, investing in fertilizer, seed, or a college education. But loans come with interest, and as that interest compounds, we get mired further in debt. And as our financial position worsens, the interest rate we must pay in the debt market rises, for lenders consider us a riskier proposition. The "tool" becomes a trap, and the more we rely on it, the deeper our difficulty and more hopeless our condition.

So does Islamic finance offer an interest-free alternative that humanizes capitalism? Naturally, the answer depends on how Islamic financial institutions go about avoiding interest. They do so in two main ways. From an economist's perspective, the first way differs radically from interest-based lending, while the second approximates interest-based lending closely. I limn them here in broad strokes, as I do when discussing my research with a stranger next to me on an airplane.

The first way to extend financing while avoiding interest is *equity-based*. People in the Islamic-finance industry call it "profit-and-loss sharing" (PLS). Imagine that you need $1 million to launch and run a pizzeria. I give you the $1 million, and then you and I split any profits according to a formula we have agreed upon in advance: 60 percent of profits to me and 40 percent to you over the next five years, for example. If at the end of this period the pizzeria has lost money, I, as the investor, bear all the losses. You lose nothing but the time and effort you have put in. This is basically how private equity and venture capital work.

When my airplane seatmates learn how the equity-based approach works, they immediately see how it differs from interest-based lending. "It kind of seems more fair," they reason. The promise of profit motivates the entrepreneur to work hard. Yet if the pizzeria fails due to an unexpected circumstance like a pandemic, liability falls entirely upon the party that has money: the investor. This logic ostensibly favors entrepreneurship and innovation while having a socially progressive cast. Since the early twentieth century, proponents of a modern Islamic economic system have supported the equity-based approach to Islamic finance, with many today still considering it an ethical holy grail.

The second way to avoid interest is *debt-based*; it is what I call "interest simulation." Imagine now that you want to buy a car that costs $50,000. (For simplicity's sake, let's pretend there is no down payment.) If you had no qualms about paying interest, you could approach a conventional bank and request a $50,000 car loan, to be paid in 60 monthly installments of $1,000 each over the next five years. Thus, you would pay a total of $60,000 to the conventional bank, which works out to an interest rate of 7.42 percent. However, an Islamic bank offers you interest-free shariah-compliant financing instead. There are several interest-simulating techniques Islamic banks use for auto financing. In one technique (figure 0.6), the Islamic bank buys the car

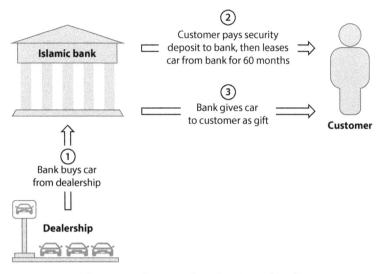

FIGURE 0.6. Islamic auto financing based on lease (ijara) contract.

from the dealership for $50,000, then *leases* it to you for the next five years for $1,000 per month. After five years, the Islamic bank gives you the car as a gift or sells it to you for a nominal amount, like $1.

In another technique (figure 0.7), the Islamic bank buys the car from the dealership for $50,000, then *sells it to you on credit* for $60,000, which you pay in 60 monthly installments of $1,000 over the next five years.

Whichever of these interest-simulating techniques you choose, the Islamic auto financing's impact on your pocketbook is identical to that of the conventional bank's interest-bearing auto loan: you end up paying $60,000 across 60 monthly installments of $1,000 for a car that costs $50,000 now.

When I explain the interest-simulating debt-based approach, using cocktail napkins and airline snacks as props, my seatmates react differently. "Wait . . . how is that not interest? That's totally interest!" many exclaim. Some, including Muslims, conclude that Islamic finance is a scam. Some people even grow indignant, like Larry, a financial advisor from Connecticut who banged his meaty fist on his tray table, sprinkling me with Biscoff dust.

The shariah scholars who work in Islamic finance certify both approaches to avoiding interest as shariah-compliant. Some industry scholars assert that the equity-based approach is ethically preferable to the interest-simulating debt-based approach, even if both are Islamically lawful. Others consider them equally virtuous. But what really matters for the industry's commercial success is that the shariah scholars permit interest simulation at all. Interest simulation

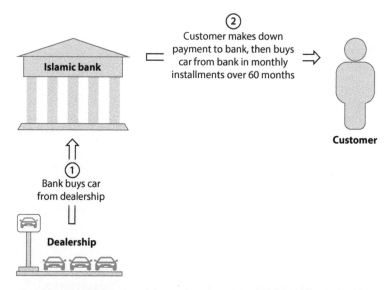

FIGURE 0.7. Islamic auto financing based on markup-sale (murabaha) contract.

has proved far more convenient and cost-effective for banks, more appealing to customers, more workable for government regulators, and better able to keep the fledgling Islamic-finance industry afloat than the equity-based approach. As chapter 1 relates, interest simulation therefore won out in the late 1970s and 1980s, becoming the business paradigm for Islamic finance, even if many shariah scholars hoped it would be only a stopgap before Islamic finance could move earnestly toward equity-based finance. Today, firms overwhelmingly practice Islamic finance using interest simulation.

Fiqh-mindedness

To understand the context in which interest simulation may make ethical sense for some Muslims, it helps to understand "fiqh-mindedness," a concept central to this book. Fiqh-mindedness[40] is not an organized movement, a sect, or an official creed. Rather, it is a way of being religious and a conception of legitimate authority about religious knowledge. It exists around the world, among both Sunni and Shiʿa Muslims, and in Muslim-majority and Muslim-minority societies. Since the 1970s, it has grown more prevalent with the worldwide Islamic revival.

Fiqh-mindedness is a mode of piety that takes Islamic law seriously as a normative ethical code governing everyday life. (By "mode of piety," I simply mean a way of striving to act in a religiously virtuous manner.) Fiqh-minded believers see religion not just as faith, community, big abstract principles, and ritual but also as a vast matrix of formal rules derived through systematic juristic methodologies. It is the interpretation of Islam embraced by the ulama (religious scholars) and those who consider them authoritative. Contemporary fiqh-minded believers (a) turn for guidance about religious virtue to Quranic revelation and to the hadith literature, which comprises thousands of records of sayings and deeds attributed to the Prophet Muhammad; (b) hold scholarly training in the classical Islamic sciences in high esteem and consider it vital for accurate interpretation of those sources; (c) engage with scholarly knowledge through modern institutions such as universities, shariah courts, mass media, and social media; and (d) consider scholarly knowledge normative in many spheres of everyday life. Fiqh-minded Muslims might consult scholarly opinion on matters ranging from correct prayer, pilgrimage, and dress to business dealings, inheritance, family life, education, and grooming.

Fiqh-minded piety does not encompass all of contemporary Islam. In the fiqh-minded conception, knowledge of Islamic jurisprudence or access to knowledgeable jurists' opinions is indispensable for adopting shariah as a normative framework for daily living. Fiqh-mindedness therefore parts ways with much Islamic-modernist thought, which tends to treat Islamic jurists and their scholarship as legalistic, obscurantist obstacles to piety and progress.[41] Although the world's fiqh-minded Muslims cannot be counted precisely, Rumee Ahmed estimates that they represent 15 to 20 percent of all Muslims.[42] Fiqh-mindedness is better understood as an orientation toward particular sources of scriptural authority and exegetical expertise than as a clear-cut membership group.

Regardless, a significant percentage of Muslims today refer, at least occasionally, to the views of Islamic jurists (also known as "shariah scholars") for guidance. These scholars participate in contemporary social and political debates,[43] and some have millions of social-media followers. According to the *Muslim 500*, compiled by a Jordanian think tank, six of the world's ten most influential Muslims are Islamic jurists.[44]

Yet incorporating fiqh-mindedness into one's religiosity does not necessarily mean accepting interest simulation as Islamically lawful or Islamic finance as superior to conventional finance. One reason is that there are some shariah scholars outside the Islamic-finance industry who do not endorse interest simulation or particular forms of it. In Egypt, several of the most prominent shariah scholars have publicly asserted in the past several decades that Islamic finance is no better than conventional finance, including two grand muftis of Egypt—a grand mufti is the highest government-supported shariah scholar in a country—and two rectors (shaykhs) who have led al-Azhar, one of the most storied Islamic universities in the world.[45] Being fiqh-minded also does not mean turning into an automaton who does not reason on one's own or no longer sees the world through the filter of "common sense."[46] For some fiqh-minded Muslims, that can mean embracing Islamic interest simulation for offering convenient yet pious financial alternatives incomparably more virtuous than the anxiety-inducing sin of usury. For others, it may raise serious doubts about Islamic finance, which is endorsed by some shariah scholars but criticized by others.

Methods

This book draws on extensive field research. At its core are 291 interviews with a total of 303 people based in 20 countries, with most interviews conducted between 2013 and 2023 (but some as early as 2009) and 2023 (but some as early as 2009). Most interviewees were based in—but sometimes not citizens of—the five countries where I spent the most time: Pakistan (114 interviewees), Saudi Arabia (76), Malaysia (37), the United Arab Emirates (26), and the United Kingdom (18). Other interviewees were based in Australia, Bahrain, Canada, Curaçao, Indonesia, Iran, Japan, Jersey, Kuwait, Luxembourg, Oman, Qatar, Turkey, the United States, and Yemen. The methodological appendix describes the interviewees in more detail, as well as why and how I secured interviews with them.

Sixty percent of the interviews for this book were expert interviews: semi-structured conversations with people I targeted for their knowledge of Islamic finance. The experts fell into four categories, in descending order of frequency. The first and most numerous were "practitioners," such as bankers, lawyers, management consultants, shariah consultants, shariah auditors, accountants, fund managers, commodities brokers, fintech entrepreneurs, representatives of credit-rating agencies, and Islamic-microfinance managers. Second, there were shariah scholars, including some who sit on shariah boards (the panels overseeing Islamic financial institutions), some who work in the internal shariah departments of Islamic financial institutions or as independent shariah advisors, and some who were outside Islamic finance altogether and opined about it. I interviewed a significant portion of the internationally elite "rock-star" shariah scholars; those who work in Islamic finance will recognize their names in the text and the endnotes. I also interviewed many other shariah scholars, ranging from those renowned in particular national markets to those just starting their careers in Islamic finance. I also heard most of the world's dozen or so international elite speak at conferences. The third group comprised representatives of government organizations (mostly central banks and securities commissions) and multilateral organizations. These interviewees mostly represented Saudi Arabia (where I spoke with the governor of the central bank), Pakistan, Malaysia, Oman, and Iran; I also interviewed officials at the Islamic Development Bank in Jeddah and attended a World Bank conference in Washington on Islamic finance. The fourth were observers who sat outside or adjacent to the industry, such as moral economists, other academics, and journalists. With most interviewees, at least part of the conversation concerned shariah scholars.

The other 40 percent of the interviews for this book were with customers at Islamic banks and other members of the general public. All of these interviews took place in Pakistan or Saudi Arabia, the two countries I compare in chapter 7. The interviewees' familiarity with Islamic finance ranged from technically knowledgeable to clueless, and their attitudes toward Islamic banks and the shariah scholars who certify them ranged from strongly supportive to ambivalent to deeply cynical.

I also engaged in many activities beyond interviews that augmented my expertise in Islamic finance. During graduate school, I interned at the Islamic-finance desk of a leading Malaysian law firm. Over the subsequent years, I attended over 80 talks and panels about Islamic finance and Islamic commercial jurisprudence at conferences, training courses, and workshops held in Pakistan, Saudi Arabia, Malaysia, the United Kingdom, Qatar, the United States. To understand Islamic education in Pakistan better, I toured two of the country's most prominent madrasahs. Further details appear in the methodological appendix.

I also conducted site visits to branches of Islamic banks in Pakistan and Malaysia, and had my research assistants do the same in Saudi Arabia and the United Arab Emirates as per my training. In all four countries, our activities included "mystery shopping": asking questions of bank staff as if we were potential customers interested in opening an account. I have also reviewed documents extensively and even examined the marketing strategies that appear in Islamic banks' television commercials. These too are described in the appendix.

Through this range of activities, I developed a thorough understanding of Islamic finance's technical mechanics, contractual structures, shariah regulation and certification by shariah scholars, "secular" government regulation and legislation, sectoral segmentation (across capital markets, retail and commercial banking, corporate banking, insurance, wealth management, risk management, and other domains), organizational structure, business strategy, profitability drivers in major national markets, and marketing. I have also come to understand the cultural and intellectual world of the shariah scholars, and while I would never purport to possess the depth of expertise in the classical Islamic sciences that they accumulate over many years of study, I can speak with them comfortably about the technical details of their work and judicial decisions. Just as importantly, I have learned how ordinary people who do not work in the industry talk and think about usury, Islamic finance, and shariah scholars.

Structure of the Book

Each chapter of this book answers one or more questions about a different way that industry shariah scholars make Islam and capitalism compatible. Chapter 1 ("Origins") opens by observing that from the late nineteenth century through the late twentieth, Muslim intellectuals and leaders harbored many different visions of what an Islamic financial system could look like. Yet today, the term "Islamic finance" refers singularly to the capitalist Islamic-finance industry. So what happened? What exactly is this "capitalist Islamic finance" that became dominant? Why did it appear when and where it did—in the Arab Gulf region in the mid-1970s—and then succeed in spreading worldwide?

Chapter 1 identifies scholar certification, interest simulation, and a liberal mode of state involvement as the defining features of the new form of Islamic finance that appeared in the midst of the 1970s' oil boom and that differed from past attempts to build Islamically inspired systems of savings and credit. I call this trio of features the "Gulf model" of Islamic finance because it originated in the hydrocarbon-rich Arab Gulf economies. The unique economic, political, social, and world-historical circumstances of these countries—especially Saudi Arabia, the United Arab Emirates, and Kuwait—in the 1970s and early 1980s explain how the term "Islamic finance" became synonymous everywhere with the Gulf model. Instead of emerging out of crisis, as many financial trends did in the latter half of the twentieth century,[47] the Islamic-finance industry grew out of a condition of political stability (underwritten by U.S. political and military hegemony) and unprecedented wealth (serviced by bankers and brokers from New York, London, and Western Europe hunting abroad for returns). The simultaneity in the 1970s and early 1980s of the oil shocks, global Islamic revival, the inception of global financial expansion,[48] and a "spatial fix" in labor[49] sending bankers of the Global North toward the Global South accounts for the liberal cast of the Islamic-finance industry.

So does the Islamic-finance boom merely represent the triumph of northern capitalist ethics over southern religious ethics—with the scholars' complicity? Chapter 2 ("Ethics") argues no. It asserts that the scholars' Islamic finance, although thoroughly intertwined today in capitalist institutions and interests, is grounded in an Aristotelian-scholastic view of money that differs radically from the dominant modern view. Religious jurists in Judaism,

Christianity, and Islam shared this Aristotelian-scholastic view throughout the medieval and early modern periods, coming to remarkably similar conclusions about what kinds of transactions were sinful and what kinds were religiously acceptable. All three arduously defended a strict ban on non-zero interest while authorizing various accommodations that allowed merchants to conduct business. However, Jewish rabbinical authorities and Christian scholastics and reformers eventually jettisoned or "accommodated away" the red-line ban on interest. This explains why a large, distinctive "Islamic finance" sector can flourish on the basis of an easy-to-understand ban on interest, whereas the marketing case for a "Jewish finance" sector or "Christian finance" sector is harder to make.

How do Islamic banks and other firms practicing Islamic finance make money? Chapter 3 ("Profitability") demonstrates how shariah scholars have applied the scholastic conception of money and usury to twenty-first-century finance, authorizing various forms of interest simulation that make Islamic finance profitable. The chapter opens by walking the reader through a branch of a hypothetical Islamic bank: a composite of the many Islamic bank branches I have visited around the world. The guided tour highlights similarities with, and differences from, conventional bank branches. The Islamic bank's advertising and aesthetics position Islamic finance as subtly and ambiguously Islamic; the authority of shariah scholars is almost invisible. Nonetheless, the scholars' interpretations turn out to be tremendously consequential for the bank—in the back office, where the structuring and execution of financial products happen. The chapter proceeds to describe the most common Islamic financial products, highlighting ways in which their interest-simulating structures facilitate profitability and allow Islamic banks to claim ethical superiority over conventional banks—but trigger moral debates too. Ultimately, interest simulation and the system of certification by shariah boards also advance profitability by affecting corporate strategy. The chapter identifies three self-reinforcing circuits at the level of strategy that have spurred the dramatic growth of capitalist Islamic finance: the "cost loop," the "conversion loop," and the "technocratic loop." Without the shariah scholars, none of these loops would function as well.

Why do people "buy" Islamic finance, both in the literal sense of paying for Islamic financial products and in the metaphorical sense of considering it superior to conventional finance? Who takes the scholars' opinions about finance seriously, and why? Chapter 4 ("Legitimation") tackles these questions by showing how shariah scholars legitimate Islamic financial products and institutions. The shariah scholars' legitimacy stems partly from their classical religious training, their professional and educational pedigrees, their skills in Arabic and English, and their ability to present a "business habitus." However, the way they transfer their own legitimacy to the products they certify differs in different segments of the market for Islamic finance. In "low" Islamic finance, which serves ordinary households and small businesses, shariah scholars provide moral legitimacy,[50] reassuring customers that they are avoiding sin. In "high" Islamic finance, which caters to large corporations, governments, and the ultra-rich, scholar certification provides pragmatic legitimacy[51] by reducing the risk of disagreements over shariah in big-ticket transactions. The growth of international high Islamic finance since the late 1990s has amplified the power of around a dozen scholars, the so-called "rock stars" who form the international scholarly elite, cementing their status as "super-legitimators" atop the scholarly pyramid.

How do the shariah scholars who work in Islamic finance adapt Islamic law to capitalists' financial needs? Chapter 5 ("Justification") explores the range of techniques scholars use to justify interest simulation, some of which stretch mainstream convention in classical Islamic law. Industry scholars' fatwas achieve two outcomes. First, they minimize otherworldly risk:[52] by taking interpretive responsibility on their own shoulders, they lift it from the shoulders of clients. Some Islamic-banking customers feel that if they go to an Islamic bank and buy a product that turns out not to be halal (Islamically lawful), "the shariah board will go to hell" in their stead.[53] Second, shariah scholars minimize disruption to capitalists. They do so by coding capital[54] in the language of Islamic law: that is, they protect the rights of firms and families with wealth to invest it and preserve it as they wish.

The shariah scholars who work in the Islamic-finance industry can achieve these outcomes not only because Islamic law has a history of adapting to changing economic circumstances but also because industry scholars' close relationship with capital has entrenched them as the dominant experts in the Islamic law of finance. In countries where Islamic finance is popular, shariah scholars outside the industry may disagree with some of the industry insiders' interpretations, but they tend to avoid criticizing the insider scholars vociferously in public. Instead, the outsider scholars defer to the insiders as subject-matter experts within the increasingly autonomous subfield defined by Islamic financial expertise. In this way, the growth of Islamic finance as an industry has strengthened the authority of shariah scholars who specialize in it, granting them the space to "do their own thing."

The wide, malleable range of interpretive logics and techniques applied by shariah scholars speaks to Islamic law's flexibility in protecting the industry as a project—and not just the interests of individual firms. For example, shariah scholars' interpretations occasionally take into account what "looks bad" or "looks good" in the eyes of laypersons who know little about shariah. They are aware that scrupulous adherence to the law will not suffice to maintain the reputation of Islamic finance if the average Aishah or Ahmad on the street considers it bogus. Moreover, shariah scholars tolerate certain instruments they might otherwise consider Islamically dubious so as to meet the Muslim ummah's[55] need under modern economic conditions for easily accessible, sin-free financing. While Islamic law has long demonstrated an ability to code and preserve capital reliably,[56] this ability reaches new heights of technical complexity and accommodation to modern financial markets in contemporary Islamic finance.[57]

If shariah scholars do so much to align Islamic law with the interests of firms, investors, and customers, are they merely agents of capital? In other words, has religion in Islamic finance capitulated to market forces? Chapter 6 ("Restriction") argues no. Although they legitimate and justify capitalist Islamic finance, shariah scholars also impose constraints on it that cost capitalists real time and money. They intervene in centimillion-dollar transactions, occasionally just days before they are to be executed, frustrating partners at the world's largest investment banks. Shariah scholars who sit on shariah boards also oversee a bureaucratic apparatus of shariah-compliance officers and shariah auditors who serve as the long arm of their law, monitoring products, transactions, customers, and even sales staff for shariah-compliance. All this restriction keeps Islamic finance Islamic. Without it, capitalists could push the shariah envelope as far as they wanted. Islamic finance would go the way of scholastic Catholic finance and scholastic Jewish finance, effectively permitting nearly any transaction and ceasing to have a distinctive, marketable religious identity. Instead, as in some other sectors such as kosher foods that are certified by religious scholars,[58] the shariah scholars' authority and the bureaucratic apparatus beneath them produce real consequences for violators.

Yet there is a twist: when shariah scholars reject certain arrangements as noncompliant, entrepreneurial product engineers stand ready to address the scholars' concerns. As the epistemic and business community surrounding scholar-certified Islamic finance has grown, legions of start-up founders, app developers, commodities brokers, and other innovators have designed platforms and services to apply and monitor shariah-compliance ever more minutely and efficiently, hoping to meet powerful shariah scholars' expectations. Thus the scholars' imprimatur does restrict capital, but eventually, it also creates new business opportunities for nimble innovators and generates new and more efficient platforms for interest simulation. The logic of shariah-compliance and the logic of capital's relentless creation of new market possibilities reinforce each other.

What shapes country differences in the development and character of Islamic finance? Chapter 7 ("State and Society") argues that the prestige of shariah scholars in a country, their social standing, and the degree of consensus that they are legitimate experts in *fiqh* (Islamic jurisprudence) explain much of the difference in the success of Islamic finance in Saudi Arabia and Pakistan. Building on the notion that stable and contentious politics produce different outcomes for private ethical-certification regimes,[59] and that the country-specific dynamics of political competition shape the development of Islamic finance,[60] this chapter shows how widespread fiqh-mindedness among the populace, a political culture amenable to pragmatic-juristic interpretations of usury, and state and corporate institutions that stabilize and reinforce the pragmatic-juristic perspective paved the way for capitalist Islamic finance to blossom in Saudi Arabia. There, usury is widely understood first and foremost as a problem of individual piety. The Saudi state treats it as such, taking a hands-off approach that allows the banker-scholar alliance to proceed smoothly with interest simulation. By contrast, in Pakistan, where fiqh-mindedness is less widespread, the authority of shariah scholars as a group is regularly challenged and even disparaged. Usury is widely perceived to underpin inequality and subjugation, from the village to the capitalist world-system. The political culture situates welfarist-economistic understandings of usury within contentious Islamist politics, and judges, legislators, and financial regulators sometimes seek to curtail interest simulation. Capitalist Islamic finance therefore faces headwinds. Chapter 7 thus melds cross-national comparison with the globally oriented historical sociology presented in chapter 1 ("Origins").

Does capitalist Islamic finance change the way people see and behave in the world religiously? Often, it does not. In fact, as this book reveals with interview data, most customers patronize Islamic banks when they happen to be a good option for the usual nonreligious reasons, such as low price and efficient service. Likewise, sovereign and corporate issuers of Islamic "bonds" (sukuk) around the world, including in countries like Germany, the United Kingdom, and Japan, are motivated almost entirely by the desire to tap deep pools of Middle Eastern capital cheaply and quickly. That said, there are also many customers who turn to Islamic finance because it alleviates their anxiety about the sin of usury.

Yet beyond these two sets of participants—the "secular" ones and the "sin-avoiding" ones—lies a core constituency for whom engagement with the Islamic-finance industry foments a novel form of fiqh-minded piety. For this dedicated few, I argue, Islamic finance has become a "form of life."[61] Most are employees of Islamic financial institutions, but some are customers. In their eyes, practicing capitalist Islamic finance scrupulously according to industry shariah scholars' prescriptions offers a way of striving to being religiously virtuous in the financial world. The book's conclusion describes my encounters with these believers. Crucially, their devotion does not manifest as slavish repetition of the scholars' fatwas. Instead, they become eager students of cap-italist Islamic finance, training effortfully to grasp its legal principles and to apply its methodologies. They report being motivated not so much by fear of sin but by the joy of learning and self-improvement. Theirs is a cerebral, scho-lastic form of piety, one consonant with the technical and theoretically rational world of capitalist finance. And because of this dedicated core, I argue, Islamic finance is more than a successful industry: it is a way of being in the world, as well as a community of people who inhabit that way of being. In this form of life, capitalist finance is allowed to exist, but it must continually, in every process, submit itself to a fiqh-minded Islamic way of being and to the author-ity of the scholars.[62]

1

Origins

ON WINTER mornings in Dubai, the weather is so perfect you forget about the weather. Eight months of the Dubaian year, I would sweat through my suit under the punishing sun, then shiver in glacial air conditioning, my wet shirt clinging to clammy skin. But it was December, and strolling through Old Dubai was a joy. After watching Indian merchants and laborers file up and down the narrow stairs of the Shiva Temple, I strolled on to the textile souq, where Uzbek shuttle traders negotiated for bolts of shiny cloth. For one dirham, the venerable, rickety ʿabrah ferry took me across Dubai Creek. Upon alighting at the spice souq, wafts of cardamom and saffron greeted me.

I ambled on through Deira, one of the few neighborhoods that appears in sepia-toned maps of pre-independence Dubai, to the offices of Hajj Saeed bin Ahmad Al Lootah's charitable foundation. The simple decor there reminded me of my middle school's in New Jersey: all linoleum tiles and thin brown carpeting. Just as at my middle school, girls and boys ran excitedly around, tinkered in the metal shop, and pored over their textbooks. "They learn science and they study Islam," Al Lootah explained matter-of-factly.

Everything about Al Lootah was matter-of-fact, from his direct speech to his unadorned robe—everything except his nonagenarian eyes, which twinkled like the pearls his family had plucked from the ocean floor and traded in his childhood. In 1975, when oil had long displaced pearls as the Gulf's moneymaking natural resource and Al Lootah had become a prominent Dubai merchant, he founded Dubai Islamic Bank (DIB). It is now the world's second-largest Islamic bank, with divisions in eight countries; its headquarters sit next door to Al Lootah's foundation. But in 1975, DIB was just an audacious experiment: the first for-profit Islamic bank. Back then, "it was easier to say 'Islamic whisky' than 'Islamic bank,'"[1] recalled the elite shariah scholar Hussein Hamid Hassan (1932–2020). No one knew how a bank could possibly be Islamic.

Al Lootah died in 2020 a widely admired billionaire and a hero in the history of Islamic finance. However, he felt ambivalent late in life about the direction taken by the industry he had helped found. His main concern was that Islamic bankers today are too busy trying to make a profit for their shareholders. Therefore, he explained, bankers neglect or fail to internalize the fundamental ethics[2] of Islamic finance, which to him included the humane treatment of debtors, the avoidance of usury, and reliance on straightforward Islamic contracts. Secondarily, Al Lootah allocated industry shariah scholars some blame, albeit less than he allocated to bankers. "When [the bankers] run into problems," Al Lootah lamented, "they try to get the [shariah scholars] to cover for their mistakes."[3] In DIB's early years, Al Lootah also saw little need for shariah scholars to serve as formal certification agents. Between 1975 and 1989, DIB had no shariah board: Al Lootah felt he knew all the shariah needed to make the bank flourish. And after we had spoken for a while, Al Lootah obliquely questioned the high remuneration that elite shariah-board members earn today. Since those scholars work on behalf of shariah, "personally, I think they should do it for free. But that's just my opinion," he conceded.

As our meeting ended, Al Lootah handed me a book of religious thought he had written, looked me in the eye, and said gently: "I hope you establish an Islamic bank in America."[4] At age ninety-three, despite all he had seen, he still believed that Islamic finance ought to spread far and wide.

———

The arc of this chapter takes us from Old Dubai to New Dubai. Old Dubai is centered on the crowded warrens of the spice souq, textile souq, and gold souq. Now a working-class and petit bourgeois area, it is home to traders of many nationalities, as well as to migrant workers from South Asia, the Philippines, and non-oil Arab countries who squeeze into crowded apartments. Since the nineteenth century, Old Dubai's trade and cultural interchange have been oriented toward the Subcontinent, Iran, Central Asia, and East Africa. In Old Dubai, I found the merchant ethos of a pre-oil Gulf entrepôt alive in the sparkling eyes of Al Lootah, who thought Islamic finance would surely advance human welfare if it stuck to the basics of scholastic Islamic law.

"New Dubai" refers to the rest of the city, especially the neighborhoods of glitzy skyscrapers, mega-malls, special economic zones, flyovers, office parks, cookie-cutter mansions, and manicured lawns lining the fourteen-lane Sheikh Zayed Road artery and extending into land reclaimed from the desert and the Gulf. New Dubai's over-the-top reputation is not unwarranted: more than once, while waiting at a stoplight, I have turned my head to find a live cheetah or tiger in bejeweled collar looking back at me nonchalantly from a Lamborghini's passenger seat.

New Dubai is home not only to big cats but to big finance. Its clout is symbolized by the Dubai International Financial Centre (DIFC), a special economic zone housing thousands of foreign finance professionals and an offshore financial hub that enforces the rules of private international finance. Envisioned by a ruler[5] keen to make Dubai a world city, the DIFC had established Dubai as the leading financial hub in the Middle East and North Africa (MENA) region and a top-20 global hub as of 2022, ahead of venerable Frankfurt and Zürich.[6] Even the DIFC's architecture invokes the financial might of the Global North and the symbolic power of an imagined Western rationality: its main building, which appears on the cover of this book, looks like an angular Arc de Triomphe on steroids. In the DIFC and its environs along Sheikh Zayed Road, the artery of New Dubai, I interviewed investment bankers, finance lawyers, commodity brokers, management consultants, and others who make the business of Islamic finance whir. One afternoon, I even made it my task to count the cars in the parking garage attached to a major Islamic bank's DIFC office. Late-model luxury cars such as Mercedes-Benzes, BMWs, and Porsches outnumbered mass-market marques like Toyotas and Hyundais almost two to one. Islamic high finance travels in style, just as conventional high finance does.

Most of this book shows how shariah scholars make capitalist Islamic finance work. This chapter sets the stage. It begins by highlighting the diversity of Islamic financial possibilities that Muslims envisioned from the late nineteenth through the late twentieth century as they grappled with the problem of financial piety under modern conditions.[7] Against the backdrop of such historical diversity, Islamic finance in the twenty-first century looks remarkably homogeneous. When people say "Islamic finance" today, they mean the capitalist Islamic-finance industry. So how did many possibilities narrow down to one? To explain convergence toward the Gulf model of capitalist Islamic finance, I emphasize a combination of macroeconomic and cultural trends, market competition, and organizational dynamics, bridging "the 'macro' and the 'micro' by taking the interests, ideas, and agency" of actors in the Global South seriously.[8] This chapter traces how the unique conditions of the Arab Gulf economies and societies in the 1970s and early 1980s left an indelible imprint on the Islamic-finance industry, setting the path that it would take thenceforth. Today, the model of Islamic finance that is nearly universal worldwide is what I call the "Gulf model." The Gulf model is based on scholar certification, relies heavily on interest simulation, and involves a liberal mode of state involvement (as opposed to state imposition of Islamic finance by fiat). The Gulf model originated in the Arab Gulf states in 1975 and was swiftly exported to other regions with start-up capital from Arab Gulf investors.

Possibilities and Precursors

It is hard to define what is and is not Islamic. The difficulty stems partly from the ummah's vast diversity: as Marshall Hodgson notes, Islam "is unique among the religious traditions for the diversity of the peoples who have embraced it."[9] The long shadow of Orientalist scholarship amplifies the challenge, for it has left us with the conventional wisdom that everything Islam touches becomes Islamic: that Islam pervades all of social life and individual behavior in a way that other faiths do not.[10] Thus contemporary Bangladesh, Egypt, and Turkey are regularly called "Islamic societies" or "Muslim societies"[11]—even in studies of party politics, economic development, and demography—whereas Brazil, France, and the United States are rarely described as "Christian societies," or Korea and Japan as "Buddhist societies," except in comparative scholarship on religion.

Trying to define the Islamic by nailing down some theological or scriptural kernel of Islam does not get us far. As Shahab Ahmed observes, the Islamic philosopher par excellence Avicenna conceptualized Divine Truth in ways that directly contradicted the Quran; the Sufi devotional poetry of Ḥāfiẓ's *Dīvān*, for centuries the book second only to the Quran in popularity between the Balkans and Bengal, overflows with lush allusions to wine and erotic love; and museum collections devoted to Islamic art are full of figural representations of humans and animals, even though many of the canonical scholars in Islam's classical juristic tradition have advocated aniconism.[12] So in nearly any sphere of human activity, we encounter adjectival ambiguity when it comes to "the Islamic."

What makes Islamic finance Islamic, then? Until the late twentieth century, there was rarely consensus, whether among laypersons or religious scholars. Twentieth-century Muslim intellectuals, activists, and state leaders envisioned wildly different projects in "Islamic finance" avant la lettre. They shared a stated commitment to elevating the economic, political, moral, and spiritual condition of Muslims and to dismantling the Euro-American metropole's control over domestic capital. They also sought to theorize an Islamic economy: a system that avoided laissez-faire capitalism's cruel disparities but granted more liberty than state socialism, while cultivating morality and integrity.[13] However, they diverged on basic issues such as the permissibility of interest and the appropriate role of shariah and shariah experts in an Islamic system of finance. Three types of Islamic financial visions were especially prominent: Islamic-modernist, Islamic-statist, and grassroots-developmentalist.

Islamic Modernism

Many influential Islamic modernists[14] asserted that not all interest counts as Islamically forbidden usury (riba). Instead, they interpreted Islamic usury as interest that exploited the vulnerable, distinguishing it from interest that can serve the public good. Some of these Islamic modernists were themselves prominent shariah scholars, such as Egyptian reformer Rashīd Riḍā (1865–1935). In 1904, Riḍā issued a fatwa declaring Egypt's postal savings fund Islamically lawful, partly because it channeled capital into infrastructure.[15] The fund issued savings certificates to individual depositors and paid them a fixed, predetermined return.[16] Although this smelled like interest to many Egyptians, Riḍā argued that depositors were in fact investment partners with the government, not recipients of interest. He justified the decision by asserting that the rationale[17] behind the Quranic ban on usury is to eliminate oppression and preserve the virtues of compassion and cooperation,[18] and to prevent the rich from exploiting the poor.[19] Other Islamic modernists did not involve shariah scholars extensively in their Islamic financial projects. Mohammad Hatta (1902–1980), an economist and anticolonial activist who became independent Indonesia's first vice president, argued for the elimination of Islamic usury both to respect Islamic principles and to ameliorate the chronic indebtedness of the Indonesian peasantry.[20] An ardent supporter of cooperatives, Hatta envisioned usury-free banks owned and operated by cooperatives or the state. But he did not consider all interest to be usury, and expected that these banks would charge some interest on loans to fund their operations. Moreover, he believed banks could not survive if they did not pay interest to attract deposits.[21] Likewise, Egyptian magnate Talaat Harb (1867–1941) despised Islamic usury, lamented peasants' perpetual debt peonage,[22] and decried the inflationary effect of interest-bearing foreign capital[23]—but rejected the premise that interest is un-Islamic. Harb dealt little with religious scholars. He founded Banque Misr, which in the 1920s and early 1930s spurred Egypt's industrialization and is today Egypt's second-largest bank.

Islamic Statism

Other attempts to integrate Islam into finance deployed state power to suppress interest in some form. These statist projects yielded mixed results. In the 1970s and 1980s, for example, Libya's Muammar al-Gaddafi synthesized what we might call socialism, Third Worldist nationalism, and his own idiosyncratic, mercurial conception of Islam. Gaddafi instituted laws in 1972 that suggested an awareness of classical shariah, declaring interest "absolutely prohibited" and forbidding lotteries and wagering for their excessive uncertainty (*gharar*; see chapter 3 of this book).[24] While lotteries and sports wagering remained prohibited across Libya under Gaddafi,[25] interest-based banking and finance persisted. In the wake of the 1969 revolution, the country's banks—which had mostly been Italian, British, and American—were nationalized and given Arabic names but continued to charge interest on loans. The catch was that

Gaddafi's 1972 law banning interest referred only to transactions between individual people, not to transactions involving institutions. So in theory, it became illegal for one neighbor or family member to lend money to another at interest, but it remained legal to pay interest to a bank or accept interest on deposits. In practice, the ban on interest was completely ineffectual.[26]

In more dramatic manifestations of financial Islamic statism, Islamist governments in Iran, Pakistan, and Sudan in the 1980s and early 1990s attempted to eject interest entirely from their national economies by state fiat. These efforts formed part of large-scale attempts to Islamize the economy from above. The Iranian government promoted significant state intervention in economic affairs in the name of Islam and justice,[27] while the Sudanese government under the Muslim Brotherhood proved more interested in financing its supporters in the merchant class by controlling Islamic banks.[28] The Pakistani case fell in between (see chapter 7). In all cases, shariah scholars helped design official financial policy. However, government industrial and developmental policy, foreign relations (especially embargoes on Iran and Sudan by the United States and its allies), and the imperative of keeping national economies running during crisis situations (such as the Iran-Iraq War) tended to supersede scrupulous avoidance of interest in Iran and Pakistan, and eventually destabilized Islamist rule in Sudan.

Grassroots Developmentalism

In the 1950s and 1960s, pioneers in Egypt and Malaysia launched experiments in social welfare–oriented interest-free banking. These projects avoided interest and invested in local businesses but did not focus on maximizing profit. They were only weakly embedded in Islamic jurisprudence, and in the Egyptian case, the institution's Islamic character was concealed.[29]

Egypt's grassroots-developmentalist experiment in Islamic banking occurred in the rural Mit Ghamr area of the Nile Delta in lower Egypt, where Ahmed al-Najjar founded nine branches of a mutual-savings bank between 1963 and 1967.[30] The MGSB was effectively an experiment in microcredit embedded in the traditional authority structures and practices of rural Egypt. In the 1960s, Egyptian peasants lacked access to development-oriented credit. Moneylenders existed in rural Egypt but generally charged exorbitant interest rates. Pawnshops were widespread, but they hardly served to improve the condition of the rural poor. Al-Najjar sought to address this gap. The MGSB neither charged nor paid interest, but rather made its profits by investing on a partnership basis in commercial and industrial ventures[31] and with craftsmen and small entrepreneurs.[32] It used these profits to provide interest-free loans. It did not offer current accounts or checking services,[33] and therefore its appeal to commercial- and retail-banking customers in middle- and upper-income brackets was limited. Branches were spartan; one was a Volkswagen bus. Al-Najjar also advocated a moral reconstruction of the peasant mind, a reorientation toward individualism and thrift. An effective mutual-savings scheme, he thought, would not only elevate the economic condition of the peasantry collectively but would also produce economic individuals acclimated to private-property ownership, habituated to individual saving, and inspired to become small entrepreneurs whenever possible.[34]

The MGSB reflects al-Najjar's syncretic intellectual background, which combined Western development economics with Islamic approaches to the economy. He grew up in Egypt but earned a PhD in social economics in West Germany in the 1950s and worked at a savings bank in Cologne before returning to set up the MGSB.[35] The unique German system of savings banks (*Sparkassen*) served as the primary model for al-Najjar's vision of Islamic finance,[36] which he is said to have crafted largely while sitting around the dinner table of his advisor, a German economics professor.[37] The Sparkassen are independent, locally managed institutions defined by their mandate to develop the regions in which they are located by helping a wide range of social strata save money and launch small businesses while adhering to social, environmental, and governance ethics. Yet al-Najjar also had connections to a different economic tradition. His maternal uncle was Muhammad Abdullah al-Arabi, "a renowned professor of economics in Egypt and the first Arab professor to write on the Islamic economic system."[38]

The Malaysian experiment was called the Tabung Haji (Hajj Fund). When it formed in 1963, "its purpose . . . was simply to mobilize Malay peasant small-scale savings, according to Islamic principles, in such a way as both to benefit the Malay economy and to facilitate performance of the hajj" pilgrimage to Mecca.[39] Tabung Haji held its clients' deposits and invested them in industrial, agricultural, and construction projects that did not deal in interest and that Tabung Haji deemed Islamically acceptable.[40] By all accounts, Tabung Haji was quite successful, and in 1969 it merged with the Malaysian government's Pilgrims Affairs Office to become the Pilgrims Management and Fund Board, a state organization.

Tabung Haji still exists today. It has expanded its remit somewhat but still focuses on savings for hajj. It has become a relatively small but diversified financial and administrative organization that collects the savings of Malaysian Muslims, invests them Islamically, pays dividends, provides interest-free pilgrimage loans to the needy, and extends Islamic home loans and car loans to its members. Tabung Haji also manages the travel and visa requirements of hajj pilgrims.[41] Some contend that Tabung Haji's own success set the stage for the founding of Bank Islam in 1983,[42] Malaysia's first Islamic bank.

Oil Bonanza: The Arab Gulf States in the 1970s

More than any other driver, the oil boom of the 1970s set Islamic finance on a fiqh-centric, compliance-oriented path. With the oil boom, a handful of wealthy, pious Gulf Arab entrepreneurs launched commercial Islamic banks that competed in existing national banking markets against conventional interest-based banks. While these entrepreneurs admired the grassroots Islamic-developmentalist experiments of the 1960s and had ties to some of their founders, conditions in the Gulf Arab societies in the 1970s led the Gulf entrepreneurs to instantiate a more fiqh-centric and profit-oriented model of Islamic banking that could offer shariah-compliant products functionally similar to those that their interest-based competitors sold. In these societies, especially Saudi Arabia, Kuwait, and the United Arab Emirates, merchant families had long been powerful economic actors with strong ties to rulers. A compliance-oriented mode of Islamic finance found influential supporters and ready customers. In Saudi Arabia particularly, jurists were socially and politically influential, and fiqh-centric conceptions of piety were widespread among the masses and the wealthy alike.

The oil boom's effect on the Arab Gulf countries in the 1970s and early 1980s cannot be overstated. Almost overnight, they became the wealthiest countries in the world—a sudden rise in fortunes unmatched in modern history before or since. In real terms, the world oil price nearly doubled between October 1973 and January 1974, and doubled again between April 1979 and May 1980, remaining elevated until a precipitous drop in 1985–86. Over the course of the 1970s, oil production also more than doubled in Saudi Arabia and the UAE.[43] Moreover, governments wrested control over production from the Western oil majors.[44] As a combined result of high oil prices, rising production, and nationalization, government revenues increased dramatically in Saudi Arabia, the UAE, Qatar, and Kuwait. Government spending grew concomitantly, increasing about tenfold between 1970 and 1982 in Saudi Arabia, for example.[45]

The oil bonanza gave rise to a rentier political economy in which authoritarian royal dynasts perpetuated stable rule by funding high standards of living for the citizenry and distributing lucrative market opportunities to core elite families.[46] Gulf Arab governments spent heavily on public goods such as defense, subsidized housing, education, health care, social security, infrastructure, subsidized utilities and fuel, and policing. They also transferred wealth to their citizens by offering them well-paid public-sector jobs, driving consumer demand upward. New middle classes emerged, comprising civil servants, professionals, skilled technicians, teachers, and petty bourgeois entrepreneurs and shopkeepers.[47] States also injected hydrocarbon revenues into the economy by establishing secondary rents. They issued government contracts (e.g., for construction and service delivery), import and sales licenses (e.g., to become the sole authorized importer and dealer of Toyotas), and executive managerial positions in state-owned or state-linked enterprises either in sectors connected to oil or, chasing the dream of economic diversification, in sectors such as aluminum and dairy. These market-mediated forms of patronage became paths to rapid enrichment for elite merchant families—"the aristocracy of the Gulf"[48]—as well as for penumbral royal princes and others outside the immediate dynastic line.

Economic growth following the oil boom spurred the rapid development of domestic financial institutions in the Arab Gulf countries. Circa 1950, just as Saudi Arabia and Kuwait were beginning large-scale oil exports (and over a decade before Abu Dhabi began them),[49] "banking in the Arab Gulf was insignificant."[50] A few foreign banks specializing in trade finance and serving expatriates operated a smattering of branches. Aside from the moneychangers that served the pilgrimage circuit of western Saudi Arabia (see chapter 7), domestic banks or bank-like financial intermediaries were rare. Subsistence agriculture, animal husbandry, fishing, and date farming were economic mainstays, and exchange was carried out on a cash and barter basis, requiring very little formal financial intermediation.[51] Even the maritime trading houses based in entrepôts like Dubai, Bahrain, and Kuwait financed themselves mostly through cash, retained earnings, and informal non-bank lending.

The oil boom in the Arab Gulf economies meant that there, unlike in other Muslim-majority regions in the 1970s, the structure of financial institutions could be divorced from the developmental problem. Elsewhere, policymakers either concluded that a truly Islamic financial system was one that would generate equitable growth and improve social welfare or that subordinated Islamic finance to industrial policy and the economic survival of the state. In either case, developmental imperatives were paramount. But in the Arab Gulf states in the 1970s, the central question driving financial innovation was not how to create wealth but how to save and invest it. With banks mushrooming, business opportunities proliferating, incomes rising, and new homes and consumer goods available, millions of ordinary citizens now faced the question of whether they should deal with conventional interest-based banks. Cash transactions no longer sufficed for everyday financial needs. Many Gulf Arabs happily turned to interest-bearing banks. Many others, particularly in Saudi Arabia, used banks merely as safe-deposit boxes, refusing to accept interest on their savings. Naturally, the banks loved this, for it lowered their cost of funds. Yet it suggested that there was a mass constituency for Islamic banking, so long as it could present itself as reliably shariah-compliant.

At the level of haute finance too, Arab Gulf societies became newly implicated in the problem of usury. The Arabian Peninsula had long been an irrelevant backwater for big international banks. With the oil boom of the 1970s, however, the region's petrodollars could not find enough investment or consumption opportunities at home. The obvious solution was for the oil-producing countries to lend to the oil-consuming ones, and at the market-friendly Nixon administration's insistence, private-sector banks—rather than intergovernmental Bretton Woods institutions—were allowed to handle this process. Bankers from Wall Street and the City of London flocked to Jeddah, Riyadh, Abu Dhabi, and Kuwait City, contrast-collared incarnations of a "spatial fix"[52] at a moment of stagnation back home. They negotiated to soak up governments' petrodollars and recycle them as loans to governments and corporations in oil-importing countries, including infamously the "Baker 15" developing economies.[53] The majority of the Arab Gulf governments' funds were quietly placed in highly liquid short-term interest-bearing instruments on the newly formed Eurodollar market in almost inconceivable amounts. Yet despite their vast scale, government placements in interest-bearing instruments remained a sensitive issue at home, particularly for the Saudi, Qatari, and Kuwaiti governments. Privately, some religious scholars rebuked the royal houses for placing oil wealth, which the scholars saw as a gift from God, in usurious instruments.[54] Meanwhile, some religiously conservative high-net-worth businesspersons, as well as some religiously oriented government institutions (such as national ministries of religious affairs and religious endowments), continued to avoid interest.

The Birth of Commercial Islamic Banking

The First Commercial Islamic Banks

The Arab oil embargo of October 1973, initiated in response to Western support for Israel in the Arab-Israeli war, pushed commercial Islamic finance into the world.[55] Not only did it trigger the oil boom, but in the same year, with Saudi Arabia leading the way, the finance ministers of the member countries of the Organisation of the Islamic Conference launched the Islamic Development Bank and established in its charter that its operations would conform to shariah. The petrodollar boom also produced a stratum of elite capitalist families who enjoyed close personal ties to the ruling houses and came to dominate sectors such as construction, transport, retail, and oil-related downstream products.[56] Together, these elites and the royals capitalized and launched the first wave of Islamic banks in the 1970s and 1980s (table 1.1).

In 1975, when Saeed Al Lootah launched Dubai Islamic Bank (DIB), he merged religion and finance in a novel way. The bank was explicitly Islamic: it

TABLE 1.1. The First Wave of Major Islamic Commercial Banks (1975–1984; excludes investment banks and funds)

Islamic Bank	Country	Year Established	Lead Founder(s) and/or Lead Provider(s) of Startup Capital (with Nationality)	Source of Wealth of Lead Capital Provider(s)
Dubai Islamic Bank	UAE	1975	Saeed Al Lootah (UAE)	Construction, trading
Kuwait Finance House	Kuwait	1977	Ahmad Bazi' al-Yasin (Kuwaiti), consortium of Kuwaiti merchants, government of Kuwait	Trading, government
Faisal Islamic Bank of Sudan	Sudan	1977	Mohammed bin Faisal Al Saud (Saudi), Sudanese economic and political elites; Saudi and other foreign investors	Real estate, trading, construction
Faisal Islamic Bank of Egypt	Egypt	1978	Mohammed bin Faisal Al Saud (Saudi), Muhammad Mutawalli al-Shaʿrāwī (Egyptian)	Real estate
Jordan Islamic Bank	Jordan	1978	Sami Homoud (Jordanian), Saleh Kamel (Saudi), Saʿd al-Din al-Zumeili and Misbah al-Zumeili (Jordanian)	Infrastructure contracts, pilgrimage services, media, trading
Al Rajhi Bank	Saudi Arabia	1978	Sulaiman al-Rajhi (Saudi)	Moneychanging and remittances
Bahrain Islamic Bank	Bahrain	1979	Abdul Latif Janahi (Bahraini), Abdul Rahman bin Mohammed bin Rashid Al Khalifa (Bahraini)	Trading, insurance
Egyptian Saudi Finance Bank (later Al Baraka Bank Egypt)	Egypt	1980	Saleh Kamel (Saudi)	Infrastructure contracts, pilgrimage services, media
Islamic Bank for Western Sudan	Sudan	1981	Faisal Islamic Bank, Kuwait Finance House, Dubai Islamic Bank, Bahrain Islamic Bank	Islamic finance
Qatar Islamic Bank	Qatar	1982	Government of Qatar; Qatari investors	Government, other
Al Baraka International Bank	United Kingdom	1982	Saleh Kamel (Saudi)	Infrastructure contracts, pilgrimage services, media, Islamic finance
Faisal Islamic Bank of Bahrain	Bahrain	1982	Mohammed bin Faisal Al Saud (Saudi)	Real estate, Islamic finance
Faisal Islamic Bank of Cyprus	Cyprus	1982	Mohammed bin Faisal Al Saud (Saudi)	Real estate, Islamic finance

Bank	Country	Year	Founder/Investors	Activities
Al Baraka Bank Tunisia (formerly Saudi-Tunisian Finance House)	Tunisia	1983	Saleh Kamel (Saudi)	Infrastructure contracts, pilgrimage services, media, Islamic finance
Bank Islam Malaysia	Malaysia	1983	Abdul Halim Ismail (Malaysian), government of Malaysia, Tabung Haji (Malaysian), Muslim Welfare Organization of Malaysia	Government, pilgrimage savings fund, non-profit
Islami Bank Bangladesh Limited	Bangladesh	1983	Muslim Businessmen's Society (Bangladeshi); Al-Rajhi Company (Saudi), governments of Bangladesh and Kuwait, Islamic Development Bank, Kuwait Finance House, Jordan Islamic Bank	Trading, Islamic finance, government
Faisal Islamic Bank of Guinea	Guinea	1983	Mohammed bin Faisal Al Saud (Saudi)	Real estate, Islamic finance
Sudanese Islamic Bank	Sudan	1983	Merchants affiliated with the al-Khatmiyah Sufi order, including the al-Mirghani family	Trading
Tadamon Islamic Bank Sudan	Sudan	1983	Sudanese businesspersons affiliated with the Muslim Brotherhood; Gulf investors	Trading, other
Al Baraka Bank Bahrain	Bahrain	1984	Saleh Kamel (Saudi)	Infrastructure contracts, pilgrimage services, media, Islamic finance
Al Baraka Bank Pakistan	Pakistan	1984	Saleh Kamel (Saudi)	Infrastructure contracts, pilgrimage services, media, Islamic finance
Al Baraka Bank Sudan	Sudan	1984	Saleh Kamel (Saudi)	Infrastructure contracts, pilgrimage services, media, Islamic finance
Al Baraka Participation Bank Turkey	Turkey	1984	Saleh Kamel (Saudi)	Infrastructure contracts, pilgrimage services, media, Islamic finance
Faisal Islamic Bank of Senegal	Senegal	1984	Mohammed bin Faisal Al Saud (Saudi)	Real estate, Islamic finance
Faisal Islamic Bank of Niger	Niger	1984	Mohammed bin Faisal Al Saud (Saudi)	Real estate, Islamic finance

Sources: Abdul Alim 2014; Abdul-Rahman 2010; Ahmad Tajudin 2000; Camara, O'Toole, and Baker 2014; "Elenco degli istituti" 1988; Gelbard et al. 2014; Khan and Mirakhor 1990; Stiansen 2004; Warde 2010; Wilson 1983; correspondence with Prince Amr bin Mohammed al-Faisal Al Saud, 27 January 2024; company websites; news reports.

structured its products to comply with shariah, largely by avoiding interest. Indeed, religious virtue was DIB's biggest selling point. Yet it was unmistakably a profit-maximizing capitalist venture. Like its conventional competitors (i.e., non-Islamic banks), DIB profited from the spread between the deposits it took and the financing it extended, as well as from familiar trade-finance services such as letters of credit. DIB was also capitalized by investors. Like Al Lootah, these were largely leaders of the Dubai merchant community, though the governments of Dubai and Kuwait also took small equity stakes, demonstrating their friendly stance toward Al Lootah's project.[57]

Al Lootah recalled the early days:

RC: In the beginning, where did you get your ideas for how to run the bank?

AL LOOTAH: From the Quran, of course. And from my own experience in life—my knowledge about savings and my years trading pearls around the world. . . . When I went to experts in economics [for advice], I found they knew nothing about religion. And when I went to the religious people, I found they knew nothing about running a bank.

RC: And how did you decide what kind of products and services to offer?

AL LOOTAH: I tried to do the same thing the conventional banks were doing—but by taking away all the elements that included usury.[58]

Al Lootah saw financial piety through the lens of consumer choice. He wanted to provide Muslims with a banking option that conformed to shariah, not to overturn the capitalist financial system. Moreover, he tailored his product offerings to suit the market: he developed shariah-compliant solutions to the financing needs of customers, especially merchants and small businesses, as he went along.

Just four millionaires—Al Lootah, who is Emirati, and three Saudis—launched more than half the Islamic banks founded worldwide between 1975 and 1984 (see table 1.1). All four businessmen were wealthy from the oil boom and connected to the Gulf Arab regimes. Al Lootah hailed from a venerable Dubai pearl-trading family that had diversified into construction and government contracting and profited handsomely from the Gulf building boom of the 1970s.[59] Saleh Kamel, another of the four pious pioneers, made his fortune during the oil boom as a contractor for the Saudi government. He then channeled his profits into the fledgling Islamic-banking movement. Prince Mohammed bin Faisal Al Saud, a Swarthmore-educated son of Saudi Arabia's King Faisal (r. 1964–75) and quondam iceberg entrepreneur, launched two of the world's earliest Islamic banks in Egypt and Sudan, respectively, and like Kamel went on to launch

dozens more around the world. The fourth, Saleh Al Rajhi of Saudi Arabia—
founder of what is now the world's largest Islamic bank—began as a young, small-
time moneychanger in the 1950s. By taking deposits from pious Saudis who mis-
trusted banks, the Al Rajhi organization became one of Saudi Arabia's largest
financial institutions by the 1970s and an Islamic bank in the 1980s.[60]

Prince Mohammed bin Faisal and Saleh Kamel in particular were zealous
Johnny Appleseeds, planting the idea of Islamic banking in the minds of Muslim businesspersons and government leaders capitalizing Islamic banks
around the world. Prince Mohammed's son Prince Amr bin Mohammed al-
Faisal Al Saud recalls those heady days working for Dar Al-Maal Al-Islami
(DMI), the organization then led by his father—and now by him—that was
seeding the Faisal banks:

> The spirit in our group in the 1980s was a missionary spirit. We were . . .
> proselytizing [Islamic banking]. . . . Basically wherever anybody allowed us
> to, we'd set up a bank. . . .
>
> My father was traveling all over the Islamic world. One day he'd be in Mali,
> the next day in Morocco, the next in Sudan, going around trying to convince
> people to allow him to open an Islamic bank in his country. Some countries
> allowed it; some didn't. And even if they didn't allow an Islamic bank, he
> would give talks, meet with the regulators, talk with the business community—
> about what Islamic banking is, how it's different from conventional banking,
> and what are its benefits. Constantly traveling—a man on a mission!
>
> We established banks in many places, odd places; many of them failed.
> But the idea was to create this momentum, if you like. There was—there
> still is!—this huge demand, a hunger for a banking system that didn't make
> Muslims feel bad in dealing with it, that they felt . . . was not against their
> religious beliefs.[61]

These zealous pioneers not only capitalized and evangelized Islamic banking
but established and circulated templates for the shariah-compliant contracts and
instruments that Islamic banks would use. These templates were essential to the
young industry's survival, for without them, even the most enthusiastic convert
to Islamic banking would have no idea how to practice it. Alongside shariah
scholars sympathetic to their mission as well as auditors and lawyers they hired,
DMI staff studied how they might apply classical Islamic nominate contracts to
modern banking in ways that complied with secular law and regulation. Many
new Islamic banks around the world adopted DMI's templates—some so faithfully that "they even took the spelling mistakes" in them.[62]

The early Gulf-based pioneers of commercial Islamic banking brought together capital—their own and that of like-minded investors—with ulama
highly regarded in the Gulf. In the second half of the 1970s and the early 1980s,

these jurists advised the first-wave Islamic banks, often on an ad hoc basis, as to what financial products and procedures shariah allows. They also legitimated Islamic banking to members of the public and government figures. Some of the ulama who endorsed Islamic banking were Gulf-born. They included leading Saudi shariah scholars of the day, such as Saudi Arabia's first minister of justice Muḥammad bin ʿAlī al-Ḥarkān and ʿAbd al-ʿAzīz bin Bāz, Saudi Arabia's most widely respected shariah scholar of the last three decades of the twentieth century and a towering figure in Salafi jurisprudence.[63] Ibn Bāz publicly pressured King Fahd in 1987 to allow the creation of Islamic banks in Saudi Arabia. "The shaykhs are still receiving embarrassing written and oral inquiries which they are not able to answer" as to why there are no interest-free Islamic banks in Saudi Arabia, ibn Bāz lamented.[64] Ibn Bāz also issued fatwas legitimating some key contracts that Islamic banks use to simulate interest, such as installment sale on credit (murabaha).[65] Other ulama allied to Islamic banking were born outside the Gulf but moved there during the oil years, eventually joining the communities of mainstream ulama there and often establishing connections to state shariah institutions. The Egyptian-born Sheikh Badr ʿAbd al-Bāsiṭ, for example, moved to Kuwait in 1970 and advised the country's first and largest Islamic bank, the Kuwait Finance House, and became a prominent establishment scholar. Yet other ulama outside the Gulf advised Islamic banks in their own countries—banks that had been capitalized by the Gulf millionaires. They generally hailed from Arab countries that during the 1970s enjoyed warm relations with, and funding from, the Gulf states, and included Sheikh al-Ṣiddīq al-Ḍarīr of Sudan and the former grand muftis of Egypt and Jordan.[66] In sum, by funding Islamic banks around the Islamicate world, Gulf capital constructed a worldwide network of Islamic jurists friendly to Gulf governments, sympathetic to the belief that shariah is compatible with modern finance, and supportive of their conception of Islamic finance.

The Gulf Model

This conception was what we might call the "Gulf model" of Islamic finance, after the region from which it spread worldwide. The Gulf model has three defining features. First, it is based on *scholar certification*. Shariah scholars serve as the arbiters of whether finance is Islamic or not. Islamic banks and other financial institutions offering Islamic financial services are each governed by a shariah board composed entirely or mostly of shariah scholars. Because the scholars are experts in classical Islamic law, the fundamental feature of Islamic finance in practical terms today is that it is scholar-certified. The 1970s oil boom shunted vast wealth to the Arab Gulf states, where shariah scholars maintained significant prestige. In contrast to Islamists who sought to Islamize state and society, many scholars maintained stable, friendly relations with dynastic regimes. This facilitated what Monzer Kahf has dubbed the "banker-scholar alliance."[67] From the mid-1970s onward, as they sought to legitimate their fledgling industry, the bankers began enlisting scholars to help: first to advise them informally, and soon thereafter to certify their Islamic products formally.

Second, the Gulf model relies heavily on *interest simulation*. A large portion of Islamic financial products closely approximate the economic effects of interest while avoiding it in the eyes of the shariah scholars who certify those products. The most common Islamic financial products deploy and combine scholar-approved Islamic nominate contracts such as leases, asset sales on credit, and partnerships in ways that effectively apply a time value to money.

Third, the Gulf model is *liberal*. The state does not impose Islamic finance on firms or people in the country. Instead, Islamic financial institutions are free to compete against conventional financial institutions, and customers and investors may choose freely among these options. Shariah governance in the Gulf model is also liberal in the sense that it is voluntary and private. Financial institutions that want to be Islamic are free to retain shariah scholars of their choosing to monitor and certify them, merely with the proviso in most countries that the scholars meet certain minimum standards for education and training.

Ahmed Al-Najjar: A Bridge from Grassroots Developmentalism to Commercial Islamic Banking

No individual played a more central role in bridging the grassroots-developmentalist vision and Gulf capital than al-Najjar. Al-Najjar inspired and collaborated with the pioneering Gulf capitalists, Sheikh Saleh Kamel and Prince Mohammed bin Faisal Al Saud, who later launched world-spanning networks of Islamic banks. In 1970, the Organisation of the Islamic Conference (OIC)—the international organization of states with large Muslim populations—asked al-Najjar to explore the possibility of a development bank, which he did in a 1972 paper. With leadership from the Saudi state under Prince Mohammed's father King Faisal Al Saud, the OIC then founded the Islamic Development Bank (IDB) in 1973, which was mandated to operate in accordance with shariah and build the international visibility of the idea of Islamic banking.

Al-Najjar also helped Prince Faisal of Saudi Arabia establish the Faisal Islamic Bank of Egypt (FIBE), which began operations in 1977 as the world's second Islamic commercial bank after Dubai Islamic Bank (1975). Al-Najjar's connections to influential figures in the Egyptian government, especially the charismatic preacher-turned-government-minister Sheikh Muḥammad Mutawallī al-Shaʿrāwī at the Ministry of Religious Endowments, proved decisive in the drawn-out two-year process of gaining approval for the FIBE and passing parliamentary legislation to facilitate Islamic banking.[68]

The political and economic climate in Egypt in the mid-1970s also uniquely suited the merger of neorevivalism and fiqh-mindedness that the FIBE represented. President Anwar Sadat (r. 1970–81), who came to office upon the assassination of Gamal Abdel Nasser (r. 1954–70), had eliminated Nasser's one-party system in 1971 and granted the neorevivalist Muslim Brotherhood, severely suppressed under Nasser, room to operate in society. Also in the early 1970s, Sadat launched his massive liberalization of the Egyptian economy. One of its primary goals was to attract investment from the oil producers of the Arabian Peninsula, in part through Egyptian-Gulf joint ventures, and another was to liberalize the banking sector.[69] Thus when Prince Faisal, with Ahmed al-Najjar's help and connections, proposed a bank that would appeal to religious constituencies and would be 49 percent financed by Saudi investors and 51 percent by Egyptian ones, it seemed to fit the bill.[70] Sadat may have felt that the FIBE project would increase his legitimacy in the eyes of the Muslim Brotherhood's millions of sympathizers.[71] Indeed, the investors on the Egyptian side included the Ministry of Religious Endowments, various Islamic charitable organizations, and a number of influential businessmen, some of whom had direct ties to the Brotherhood (such as Youssef Moustafa Nada) and some who were sympathetic to many of the Brotherhood's social, religious, and economic goals (such as Osman Ahmed Osman).

Al-Najjar would go on to help Prince Mohammed launch more "Faisal banks" (named after the prince's father, King Faisal Al Saud [r. 1964–75]) in Sudan, Switzerland, Bahrain, Pakistan, and Cyprus.[72] The two also established the International Association of Islamic Banks, a group headquartered in Saudi Arabia that would coordinate and lobby on behalf of the infant industry; al-Najjar moved to Jeddah in 1977 and served as the secretary-general. On the academic front, al-Najjar and Prince Mohammed collaborated to found the International Institute of Islamic Banking and Economics in Cyprus in 1982.

In sum, the political climate of the 1970s and 1980s made possible a merger of fiqh-minded approaches aligned with the Gulf Arab royal houses and international Islamism, a development that would likely have been more difficult from the 1990s onward. As the center of economic gravity and political leadership in the Arab world shifted from Nasser's Egypt to the oil exporters of the Arabian Peninsula in the 1970s, it was easy for al-Najjar to transition smoothly from the realm of grassroots-developmentalist nonprofit Islamic microfinance that he inhabited in the 1960s to a leadership role in the emerging world of commercial Islamic finance.

Today, al-Najjar is sometimes remembered as "the father of modern Islamic banking." Yet his writings show that he retained a commitment to the core precept that profit-and-loss sharing (PLS) is central to the transformational potential of Islamic banking, particularly in the alleviation of poverty.[73] Toward the end of his life, al-Najjar lamented the industry's near-total turn toward murabaha-based financing for the wealthy and "fell out with some people who went on to found large Islamic banking groups, in part because they focused on the established merchant classes."[74] And shortly before his death in 1994, al-Najjar expressed to his mentee and translator Abdulkader Thomas his deep disappointment with Islamic finance as it exists today.[75]

The Gulf Model Crystallizes
The Difficulty of PLS

The Gulf model succeeded in large part because PLS proved hard to implement. In the mid- to late 1970s, when the first commercial Islamic banks were appearing, there was no consensus as to how they should operate. Those few people who spoke and wrote much about Islamic banking associated it largely with PLS, which was supposed to liberate Muslims from the shackles of debt and Western financial hegemony. But this was a hopeful prediction developed by Islamic economists, most of whom had never run a bank. Ahmed Al-Najjar's nonprofit MGSB experiment in Egypt in the 1960s had deployed PLS financing extensively, and it was one of the few existing precedents for modern Islamic banking that the Gulf Arab entrepreneurs took seriously. But it had shut down under government pressure after just a few years, before PLS had been tested seriously under competitive market conditions. Within less than a decade, commercial Islamic banks around the world would largely desert PLS-based Islamic banking. They turned en masse to a less radical, more commercially attractive alternative: interest simulation.

By the early 1980s, the actual functioning of Islamic banks had diverged sharply from the theoretical ideal of PLS. Islamic economists, who were still writing the most influential theoretical expositions of Islamic banking, continued to focus almost entirely on PLS methods when describing the distinctions between Islamic and conventional banking.[76] Even seasoned practitioners focused overwhelmingly on PLS when they described how Islamic banking works: Sami Homoud's 1985 book *Islamic Banking* devoted fifty-nine pages[77] to PLS-style financing and only three pages to *murabaha* (*murābaḥah*; markup credit sales). This was ironic given that Homoud, arguably more than any other individual, helped legitimize a working model for the use of murabaha credit sales in Islamic banking and put it into practice at Jordan Islamic Bank. Likewise, when introducing themselves to the Western business community in the early 1980s, some Islamic banks stressed their commitment to PLS techniques.[78] Yet the divergence between theory and practice was plain to all knowledgeable observers. By 1986, Volker Nienhaus, a German political economist who has followed Islamic finance closely since its beginnings, remarked soberly that "models presented by Islamic economics are practically irrelevant with respect to the explanation and evaluation of the business activities of Islamic banks. . . . One can leave aside academic models of PLS banking and interest-free economies when considering real Islamic banks."[79]

The first-wave commercial Islamic banks of the 1970s did invest significant portions of their deposits using PLS. However, unlike Ahmed al-Najjar's MGSB, which used PLS to fund small local enterprises, the new commercial Islamic banks tended to invest in large industrial and construction projects. During the boom years of the late 1970s in the Gulf, government or government-linked entities were developing many such projects; they reinjected oil revenues into domestic and regional economies and adapted to the new rentier economic model. For example, Dubai Islamic Bank invested in the world's largest single-site aluminum smelter, built in Dubai in 1979. Both Dubai Islamic and Kuwait Finance House also took stakes in the construction of low-cost residential housing complexes, built largely to house expatriate laborers.[80]

Once the oil boom subsided in the mid-1980s, Islamic-banking practice quickly diverged from the PLS-based vision, and large-scale PLS-based investments became a rarity. Attempts to instantiate PLS-based finance went against the grain of an entrenched interest-based capitalist financial system that was linked to nearly every part of the modern economy. Implementing a radically different way of banking is difficult, as Habib Ahmed, an Islamic economist at Durham University, notes: "Building an Islamic financial system is hard. You're like a gear trying to turn in one direction while the rest of the world economy is going in the opposite direction."[81] More specifically, Islamic banks attempting to implement PLS faced the following challenges.

INFORMATION ASYMMETRY, AGENCY PROBLEMS, AND MONITORING COSTS

In PLS-based financial arrangements, such as mudaraba (*muḍārabah;* Islamic silent partnership) and musharaka (*mushārakah;* Islamic joint venture), the parties agree in advance on the percentage of future profits that each will receive from a project. Losses will be borne fully by the provider of capital. Economists have noted that under such conditions, the interests of the principal providing capital (e.g., the Islamic bank) and the agent (e.g., the business receiving funding) may not be aligned.[82] For example, prior to the contract, a problem of moral hazard may arise: potential funding recipients might inflate the projected profitability of their ventures. Adverse selection may also become a problem: banks offering PLS-based financing may attract businesses and projects with low expectations of profit or high risk, because businesses confident of earning higher profits will be better served taking an interest-bearing loan, thus locking in their cost of funding and keeping a larger part of the profits for themselves. So low-quality clients may flock to PLS financing while high-quality clients may shun it. This situation is analogous to the one George Akerlof describes as a "market for lemons":[83] information asymmetry that protects the sellers of low-quality goods (or here, the managers of low-quality businesses) will drive the sellers of high-quality goods (here, the managers of high-quality businesses) out of the market.

In practice, attempts at PLS-based Islamic financing have indeed encountered problems of moral hazard and adverse selection. For example, a survey of potential customers of PLS-based Islamic financing in Australia in the 2000s found that many risky small businesses were attracted to PLS because it would allow them to share business risk with the lender.[84] Going back further, Prince Amr bin Mohammed Al Faisal Al Saud notes that national state laws and regulatory systems in the first two decades of Islamic banking were often unsuited to protect all parties adequately in a PLS partnership. Prince Amr worked in the 1980s and 1990s for the umbrella organization that launched the global network of Faisal Islamic banks, the Dar Al-Maal Al-Islami (DMI) Trust (which he now chairs). When I asked him if DMI ever implemented PLS in the early years of Islamic banking, he explained how badly it went:

> We did! But every time, we lost our shirts. In Saudi Arabia, for example. We [financed] real-estate projects and industrial projects [via PLS], and [in] most of them, we lost our money. Because the regulatory environment was weak.
>
> It was a catastrophe. The legal system was so bad. Mostly, there was fraud on the other side, and they could get away with it. In many cases, we had actual judgments from the court in our favor [but could not recoup our funds]. . . . That was a problem in Saudi Arabia in the 1980s and 1990s. Al-ḥamdu li-l-lāh, things have changed.
>
> Had we gone in [to provide capital] the conventional way, or even with murabaha, we would have been ok. We would have gotten our money back, because the legal system was designed for conventional banks.[85]

As newcomers whose business model was poorly understood by the public, Islamic banks were also often approached for funding by people who had been refused by conventional banks. Many potential clients wrongly believed that the new Islamic banks would simply offer them zero-percent loans—a confusion that persists today, as noted by Sulaiman Al Harthy, now CEO of Oman Arab Bank.[86] Finally, once the project is complete, moral hazard can arise again: the funding recipient has an incentive to under-report profits. All of these problems of information asymmetry are exacerbated by the fact that mudaraba and musharaka provide project-specific funding. Thus, the bank must evaluate not only the potential client but the details of the specific project. These various challenges made it very difficult for banks using PLS to price financing. Conventional banks can simply set an interest rate on loans to customers by adding a reasonable spread to the government benchmark interest rate. Banks usually know what their competitors are offering, and hence generally have little difficulty setting a competitive spread. In contrast, Islamic banks trying to implement PLS had to demand a particular percentage of future profit earned—an entirely different metric. The first Islamic banks in any national market had no obvious benchmark to use; they were flying blind.

In principle, such problems with PLS-based bank financing can be overcome, but in practice, solutions proved too complex or costly for the first-wave commercial Islamic banks of the 1970s and 1980s to apply. Similar agency problems also arise in conventional forms of profit-sharing or equity investment, such as private equity.[87] While the obvious solution is to reduce information asymmetry through extensive due diligence and ongoing monitoring, Islamic banks lacked such capacity. They were small institutions in relatively immature banking markets, not seasoned investors with deep experience combing balance sheets and inspecting projects. The computerization of finance was in its early years even on Wall Street; in the Middle East, banking was largely conducted and accounted for laboriously with pen and paper, and potential clients' account books were not always impeccable or systematic.[88] Moreover, the employees of the first Islamic banks mostly had backgrounds in retail and commercial banking, not investing and corporate finance. In theory, if extensive due diligence is too costly, information asymmetry can also be mitigated by arrangements that increase transparency, such as performance-linked bonuses, rebates, and other incentives.[89] However, such arrangements also require sophisticated staff capacities, and anyway would likely have driven away the Islamic banks' prototypical clients: pious petty entrepreneurs, traders, and shopkeepers. Legal penalties for misreporting or under-reporting risks can also reduce information asymmetry, but government regulators in the Middle East, North Africa, and Southeast Asia in the 1970s and 1980s lacked the capacity to implement such measures and were unfamiliar with Islamic banking to boot. More generally, property rights poorly defined or enforced under state law can undermine PLS.[90]

To make matters worse, there was a mismatch between theoretical models of PLS and the real conditions of its implementation. The Islamic economists

of the 1960s and 1970s had theorized PLS-based banking systems as components of a holistic, self-contained Islamic economy. Most had not modeled
PLS-based banking in competition against conventional banking. Many theoreticians had also assumed that Islamic banks' clientele would behave honestly
because they anticipated God's judgment in the hereafter.[91] Some used math-
ematical modeling to argue that PLS-based financing could be as economically
efficient as interest-based debt financing, or even more efficient—so long as
clients behaved honestly, which Muslims in "value-oriented society" would be
expected to do in the long run.[92] These Islamic economists predicted that in
the meantime, Islamic banks using PLS would learn through repeated interactions to identify trustworthy clients and avoid dishonest ones, thus reducing
monitoring costs.[93]

LIQUIDITY MANAGEMENT AND
ASSET-LIABILITY MISMATCH

The very earliest commercial Islamic banks—those that began operations in
the 1970s, such as Dubai Islamic Bank (1975), Faisal Islamic Bank of Egypt
(1977), Faisal Islamic Bank of Sudan (1977), Kuwait Finance House (1977),
and Jordan Islamic Bank (1978)—appear to have been quite successful in attracting deposits during their first years. The banks' founders and early employees paint a picture of pious depositors lining up around the block to place their
money in a shariah-compliant manner.[94] The banks' financial reports corroborate this account: customer deposits climbed fast at these banks in the late 1970s
and early 1980s. The worldwide Islamic resurgence was in full swing by this
point, and it "inspired Moslems' enthusiasm to abide by religious principles"
and patronize Islamic banks[95] just as the oil boom was fueling rapid economic
growth in the Arab Gulf states and much of the rest of the MENA region.

Public statements of support from leading ulama attracted depositors and
investors to Islamic financial schemes, too. For example, as soon as the grand
mufti of Saudi Arabia, Ibn Bāz, issued a fatwa approving participation certificates issued by the Sharjah (UAE)-based Islamic Investment Company of the
Gulf (IICG) in 1978, "People were filed up and queued up along the staircase
up to the first floor" to place their funds in the certificates, recalls Ibrahim
Kamel, who worked with Prince Mohammed bin Faisal Al Saud to establish
the IICG. "There were people all over the place handing out money, counting
money, stacks of money."[96] Similarly, deposits flowed into the Faisal Islamic
Bank of Egypt (FIBE) thanks in part to endorsements from leading ulama,
who attested to FIBE's bona fides and stressed that Islam prohibits interest.[97]
The Egyptian bank also sponsored public seminars and conferences on Islamic
banking and launched media campaigns rebutting the views of famous Islamic
scholars who argued that interest *is* permissible.[98] Kuwait Finance House

(KFH) likewise touted the merits of Islamic banking and publicly denounced Kuwait's usurious banks "for bleeding Kuwaiti consumers of limited income."[99] KFH's deposits increased dramatically.

However, deposit growth alone does not guarantee a bank's success. A fully PLS-based banking model poses serious challenges for treasury management— the task of managing a bank's liquidity and the risk-return profile of its balance sheet. All commercial banks, whether conventional or Islamic, must avoid skewing too heavily toward short-term or long-term liabilities and toward short-term or long-term assets. Having too many short-term liabilities or long-term assets increases a bank's liquidity risk (e.g., its exposure to a run on the bank or to a credit crunch), but having too many long-term liabilities or short-term assets reduces the bank's profit margin and competitiveness. To optimize their balance sheets on a daily basis, conventional banks buy and sell interest-bearing government bonds and paper; they also borrow from and lend to other banks on the interbank market using very-short-term (e.g., overnight) interest-bearing instruments.

However, structuring very-short-term PLS-based tradable instruments is difficult. It is not easy to arrange a profit-sharing joint venture that only lasts one night, for example, and that will likely generate a reasonably predictable positive return. Even most of the early Islamic economists conceded that treasury management in an Islamic banking system might have to employ very-short-term interest-simulating markup instruments (e.g., murabaha) instead of PLS instruments. Yet markup-based government-issued Islamic instruments were unavailable in most countries until the 1990s and 2000s. Likewise, since the first Islamic banks—such as Dubai Islamic Bank in the UAE and Kuwait Finance House in Kuwait—were alone in their national markets, there was minimal Islamic interbank lending before the late 1980s. Still today, only Malaysia has a robust Islamic interbank-lending market. Given the paucity of Islamic liquidity-management options, shariah scholars often provisionally allowed the early Islamic banks to deal in conventional interest-bearing money-market instruments. They quietly argued that a bank Islamic in its "front end" (products available to customers) but conventional in its "back end" (treasury management) was better than no Islamic bank at all.[100] Half Islamic was better than fully sinful.

OTHER CHALLENGES

PLS-based Islamic banking faced still more challenges. PLS contracts are not convenient for financing business activities that do not produce profits in themselves. This includes much government spending, such as on health care, education, infrastructure, and defense. During the boom years in the

Arab Gulf states, however, government spending was a huge component of GDP. PLS contracts are also not well-suited to provide working capital, inventory financing, and trade financing to businesses. Thus any Islamic bank offering only PLS would lose the ability to compete for a lot of banking business with government entities, corporations, and small businesses. Moreover, PLS-style finance products could not be resold above par[101] on a secondary market or securitized, so Islamic banks had to keep them on their own books.[102]

Finally, the state also sometimes made it difficult or impossible for commercial banks to engage in PLS-style investment partnerships with business or with their depositors. Even when Islamic banks could legally engage in PLS, tax laws often disadvantaged them. States often treat interest payments as an untaxed business expense, while taxing investments in partnerships. And later, by the early 1990s, central banks were growing increasingly concerned that some Islamic banks, especially in the Gulf, were engaged excessively in trading operations that posed unknown risks to the banking system. These concerns grew stronger as the banks (such as Kuwait Finance House) began to take significant shares of national banking markets. Central banks eventually passed regulations that forced Islamic banks to act more like conventional banks, which in turn pushed them toward banking instruments that mimicked conventional interest-based instruments.

When I spoke with the leadership of the Saudi Central Bank in 2019, they described the implementation of PLS in commercial banking as unrealistic and systemically risky. Fahad Ibrahim Alshathri, deputy governor for supervision, asserted that "musharaka is a form that we should encourage, but on the investment-banking side, not the commercial-banking side." Implementing musharaka aggressively in commercial banking would "run the risk of making commercial banks illiquid and exposing them to higher risk."[103] In short, moral economist Nejatullah Siddiqui's vision of commercial Islamic banking based on equity partnerships clashes in Alshathri's eyes with a sound, modern, well-regulated banking system.

Kuwait Finance House: The Islamic Bank as Trader and Developer

Today, PLS is no longer considered by most industry practitioners a defining aspect of what makes Islamic finance Islamic. To be sure, some reformers and industry critics still consider PLS a holy grail of Islamic finance, but they have largely been sidelined from the business practice of Islamic finance, in part because their view is not amenable to the predominance of interest simulation, which the managers of today's Islamic financial institutions consider essential to their viability and profitability. But how did this ethical transition happen? How did prevailing wisdom about what counts as Islamic finance change in the 1970s and 1980s? One way involved the replacement of the belief that an Islamic bank should act like an investment house (i.e., using PLS finance) with the belief that it could act as a trading house instead. And trade-based Islamic finance, as we will see, is many steps closer to interest simulation than investment-based (i.e., PLS-based) Islamic finance. The trading-house model of Islamic banking served as a bridge to today's Gulf model.

Not all of the early Islamic banks emphasized PLS. In the Gulf entrepôts of Dubai, Bahrain, and Kuwait, oil windfalls did not supplant traditional merchant communities so much as enrich them. Trade finance—in which, for example, banks provide or guarantee payment on behalf of buyers before goods are shipped—quickly became central to early Islamic banks' operations. PLS is usually ill-suited to such functions. Instead, Islamic banks used familiar trade-finance instruments, and wherever interest appeared as a component, they charged a fee or commission instead, sometimes employing markup contracts like murabaha. Saeed bin Ahmad Al Lootah, founder of Dubai Islamic Bank (DIB), describes this:

> What we did, basically, was to take the system of the conventional banks, and we cleaned it of all that go[es] against Islamic teachings and principles. Essentially we removed all the riba and the processes that included riba.[104]

Al Lootah also explains that while DIB accepted deposits and offered Islamic investment accounts, it focused more on trading facilities such as letters of credit and letters of guarantee. It also financed commercial agriculture and industrial projects, and engaged in the sale and purchase of commodities.[105]

Some Islamic banks went further, not just financing trade but becoming heavily involved in it themselves by maintaining large inventories of goods such as cars and homes. In this "trading-house" model, the Islamic bank helps end users acquire goods from suppliers in a shariah-compliant manner, with the bank providing financing. For example, a consumer who wants a particular model of car could approach the Islamic bank, which would either (a) order, buy, and import the car from an overseas supplier or (b) offer the customer one of its own stock of cars for sale. The bank would then sell the car to the customer on credit, typically in installments, marking up to a price higher than what it paid. The Islamic bank would buy cars in bulk and establish relationships with overseas car suppliers, allowing it to negotiate good prices. It would also manage all import paperwork and logistics. Alternatively, a real-estate developer planning to build a residential complex might approach the Islamic bank. The bank would provide advance funding for construction using an istisna (*istiṣnā*ʿ; requesting manufacture) contract, allowing it to take ownership of the residential units upon completion. The bank would eventually resell those units, usually on credit and at a slightly higher price than it paid, to individual home-buyers. In the trading-house model, the Islamic bank takes on both business risk (as a buyer, seller, and holder of goods) and credit risk (as a financier). However, PLS is not central to the bank's mission. Instead, the fundamental characteristics that make the bank Islamic are that it (a) avoids interest and otherwise adheres to Islamic law and (b) links all financial transactions to the possession or production of real goods or services. Today, in Islamic-finance industry practice, it is these principles that make Islamic finance Islamic—not a logic of profit- and risk-sharing.

The trading-house model suited the social and economic conditions of the Arab Gulf states in the 1970s and 1980s, and no major Islamic bank embraced the trading-house model more thoroughly than Kuwait Finance House (KFH). By serving Kuwait's recently naturalized and socially conservative Bedouin population, it functioned as a counterweight against the country's conventional banks, which Kuwait's elite urban merchant families controlled and used to channel the profits from oil patronage to their businesses.[106]

During the boom years of the 1970s and 1980s, as the purchase of homes and imported commodities skyrocketed[107] and the urbanization of the once-nomadic Bedouin population drove demand for housing, KFH's trading-house model proved wildly successful. The bank built up inventories of homes and autos and marketed furniture, building supplies, and electronics. One KFH manager said the bank would import anything within the bounds of Islam, "from needles to aircraft."[108] By 1983, KFH had become Kuwait's largest landholder, and at one point, the bank's trading operations generated half its profits.[109]

KFH's historical significance extends far beyond the borders of the emirate of Kuwait. By 1981, it had become the world's largest Islamic bank, with subsidiaries all over the world. It remains large, as the world's third-largest today. For our story, KFH is central because it showed that the trading-house model can work. Specific conditions facilitated the model's success: a friendly Kuwaiti state granted KFH a monopoly on Islamic banking and regulated it leniently until the early 2000s, letting it conduct trading operations that other banks could not and exempting it from many of the prudential requirements other banks had to follow. The fast growth of consumer demand and housing demand in Kuwait's rentier economy also proved crucial.

Despite the uniqueness of its success in practice, KFH cemented in theory—in the consciousness of the Islamic-finance community worldwide—the trading-house model as a viable, pious, and distinctively Islamic mode of banking. Whereas the ideal of Islamic finance was once synonymous with PLS and the elimination of interest-bearing debt (and still is to some), many advocates of Islamic finance now assert that the essence of Islamic banking lies in its embedding of all financial activity in the ownership, possession, and movement of real assets. Indeed, even those first-wave Islamic banks that did not implement the trading-house model as thoroughly as KFH still tended to focus heavily on trade finance and real estate.

Getting from the trading-house ideal to the prevailing operating model of Islamic banking today requires far less of a cognitive leap than getting there from a PLS-based ideal. Consider these questions: In order to qualify as properly Islamic, how long does a bank, functioning as a trading house, have to maintain ownership of an asset (such as a car) before selling it on to the end user? Surely a month or a week would suffice. But what about an hour, a minute, or a second? Also, is the bank properly Islamic if it only buys the asset from the supplier on the condition that a consumer has already signed a binding promise to buy that asset subsequently from the bank (at a markup) and can be penalized if she does not? In other words, to what extent can the trading house minimize the risks of asset ownership that it faces, thus becoming closer and closer from an economic perspective to a conventional interest-bearing bank, and still be considered a trading house operating Islamically?

The Irresistible Appeal of Interest Simulation

MURABAHA (MARKUP SALE): SIMULATING AN INTEREST-BEARING SECURED LOAN

The earliest Islamic banks hunted desperately for banking techniques that were commercially viable yet shariah-compliant. Turning into investment houses by embracing PLS quickly proved unwieldy and risky, but the full trading-house model adopted by KFH could not work in all circumstances either. It suited Kuwait, a small nation that was experiencing insatiable demand for imported consumer durables and new homes thanks to its oil windfall. The founders of KFH had the large amount of capital needed to buy inventory. And Kuwaiti regulators permitted KFH to act in a very un-bank-like way—something most regulators would not do. In contrast, for most Islamic banks around the world, transforming entirely into a trading house was an untenable option.

Necessity begets invention, and since the late 1970s and early 1980s, all of the world's commercial Islamic banks have turned to interest simulation. Interest simulation embeds financial operations in the ownership, possession, and movement of real assets while minimizing (and usually transferring to the customer) the risks associated with such ownership, possession, and movement. ("Banks hate risk," remarks one Pakistani banking regulator, "and they're always trying to minimize it or pass it on to someone else.")[110] It was in the 1970s that this approach to Islamic banking was theorized, applied, and approved as shariah-compliant by leading Islamic jurists. A subset of these jurists agreed that a customer's promise to buy may indeed be considered binding under Islamic law. They also confirmed that Islamic law draws no distinction between a trader that holds an asset for a year or a second, so long as the various conditions for ownership, possession, and sale are met under Islamic law.

The Jordanian economist Sami Homoud[111] is widely regarded as having introduced murabaha financing to the world. In 1976, Homoud submitted his PhD thesis to the University of Cairo's College of Laws. For-profit Islamic banking was still in its infancy: Homoud began his doctoral studies in 1973. The thesis "was widely viewed as the most substantial academic piece on Islamic banking that had been written until that time"[112] because it provided a blueprint for how to develop a modern banking system that avoided interest and complied with other Islamic principles.[113]

Homoud's own background foreshadowed the mixture of expertise that would go on to underpin Islamic finance: he was influenced by both Islamic legal studies and conventional banking and economics. Having worked at a conventional bank in Jordan since 1956, he was familiar with modern banking techniques but was troubled to see that bank interest forced some customers into bankruptcy. He also noted that many Jordanians avoided depositing their money in banks because of the Islamic prohibition on usury. Homoud's father was an Islamic scholar and encouraged him to study the possibility of an interest-free banking system.[114]

Homoud's innovation was to repurpose a classical trade transaction into a modern financial transaction. Murabaha has a long history in Islamic jurisprudence; it is attested in the Muwaṭṭa' of Imam Mālik (711–795 CE), a seminal text in Islamic jurisprudence. Indeed, Homoud devised murabaha financing by revisiting the *Kitāb al-Umm*, the masterwork of another towering classical Islamic jurist, Imam al-Shāfiʿī (767–820 CE). In this original version of murabaha, Party B (a trader) buys a good from Party A (a supplier) and then resells it, at some stated markup on the purchase price, to Party C (a customer). In murabaha *financing* (see figure 0.7), Party C (the customer) promises, in advance of the sale by Party A to Party B, that she will subsequently buy the good from Party B. Industry shariah scholars consider the promise to be binding. Murabaha financing therefore allows an Islamic bank, acting as Party B, to finance the purchase of goods by customers at a predetermined markup without technically charging interest and without having to take on much of the business risk that a trader normally does. Islamic banks use murabaha to finance cars, homes, real estate, aircraft, raw materials, industrial equipment, and countless forms of retail and wholesale inventory. Murabaha financing also serves as a key component within complex products such as sukuk and Islamic derivatives. It is the bread and butter of the Islamic-finance industry. The amount changing hands in a murabaha transaction can range from a few dollars to a few billion. At the time, murabaha was quite controversial among Islamic scholars in Jordan and beyond as it clearly simulated the economic effects of conventional interest-based lending. However, Homoud used a strong hand to overrule the Islamic jurists on his Fatwa Committee.[115] Although he believed strongly in the risk-sharing vision for Islamic finance, Homoud saw that without offering some analogue to interest-based financing, the entire Islamic banking project would die a young death.

Like Ahmed al-Najjar, Homoud built strong ties to the powerful Gulf millionaires who were seeding Islamic banks worldwide. And like al-Najjar, Homoud went on to become a luminary in the world of Islamic finance. In 1976, Homoud suggested murabaha financing to the Islamic Development Bank and to the newly formed Dubai Islamic Bank. He also built support in Jordan for Islamic banking by appearing on a weekly Islamic television program in 1977, and in 1978 founded Jordan's first Islamic bank, where he applied murabaha financing. Homoud also proposed murabaha financing to Kuwait Finance House.[116] Moreover, he established relationships with Prince Mohammed bin Faisal Al Saud and Sheikh Saleh Kamel. Sheikh Saleh eventually became the largest shareholder of Jordan Islamic Bank; Prince Mohammed was also a major shareholder. These powerful Gulf connections helped win over the Jordanian royal family who, like many Arab rulers, feared that Islamic banking might build the influence of the Muslim Brotherhood and other Islamist groups. To mollify the Jordanian government, Homoud portrayed his model as a scheme for the financial inclusion of religious groups.

Murabaha financing spread quickly through the nascent Islamic-finance industry. Crucial to this spread was the first Islamic Banking Conference, hosted in 1979 by Dubai Islamic Bank. In attendance were representatives of the handful of Islamic banks that now existed: Dubai Islamic Bank, the Faisal Islamic Bank of Egypt, the Faisal Islamic Bank of Sudan, Kuwait Finance House, Jordan Islamic Bank, and a few others. Shariah scholars at the conference issued a fatwa endorsing the use of murabaha financing[117]—a seminal moment for the industry. This clarification gave banks the assurance that they could continue to use murabaha financing to mimic conventional interest-based banking without the fear that religious scholars would suddenly declare it un-Islamic. Murabaha financing quickly made its way around the world, being introduced by Bank Islam Malaysia in 1983, for example.[118]

A CONVERGENCE OF INTERESTS: HOW ISLAMIC BANKS ALIGNED WITH MARKET-MINDED SCHOLARS

While many critics disliked murabaha financing because it simulated interest-based credit and created debt, shariah scholars entered into a more legally minded dispute about murabaha financing. Consider this hypothetical situation:

An Islamic bank has agreed to finance a new truck for you using murabaha financing. It has ordered from the dealership the model you wanted and is ready to sell it to you at a markup. However, there is now the thorny problem of what happens if you decide, after the Islamic bank has ordered the truck from the dealership but before it has arrived, that you no longer want it. Shariah scholars agree that an Islamic bank may not sign a contract selling you the car before it has bought the car from the dealer: a hadith attests that the Prophet forbade selling things one does not yet possess, such as fish still in the sea. So if you change your mind during that window between order and delivery, the bank would be stuck owning a new truck. Indeed, in the eyes of the shariah scholars, the bank is only justified in charging a markup on the truck precisely because it is taking on liability for the truck it owns for some non-zero period of time. In theory, during the period when the bank owns the truck, the truck could be stolen, be damaged, or suddenly drop in market price. The bank would suffer the consequences.

Occasionally having to own automobiles unexpectedly when fickle customers change their minds might not be so bad if most Islamic banks wanted to be in the business of trading autos. As discussed earlier in this chapter, Kuwait Finance House and others have indeed functioned as trading houses at times, and some moral economists argue that the trading-house model is an ethically and economically desirable one for Islamic banking. But in practice, most Islamic banks do not want to carry inventory. Most countries' banking regulators prevent this anyway, fearing that if banks engage substantively in the trade of non-financial goods and services, their depositors' funds will be put at excessive risk. Government regulators keep commercial banks on a tight leash.

Fortunately, shariah scholars have found a solution that allows Islamic banks to minimize their ownership risk. Although shariah scholars prohibit you and the Islamic bank from signing a contract that binds you to buy the truck from the bank at the agreed-upon price, you may make a unilateral *promise* (*waʿd*) to do so (figure 1.1). In fact, the scholars allow banks to insist that the customers make this promise as a condition of entering into the murabaha contract. Crucially, Islamic banks treat that promise as a legally binding one. The industry's shariah scholars have followed the rulings of a subset of classical jurists who asserted that a promise may be considered legally binding on the promisor, and enforceable by courts. So you may not change your mind after the Islamic bank has ordered your truck; you must buy the car from the bank or suffer a penalty.

Since murabaha financing was already by that point the most common financing instrument used in Islamic banking, the ability of banks to impose such a condition on their customers was a make-or-break issue for the young industry. But does Islamic law allow banks to impose this condition? This was by no means a settled question at the dawn of commercial Islamic banking. (Indeed, it relates to a perennial question about financial ethics that arose again during the 2008–9

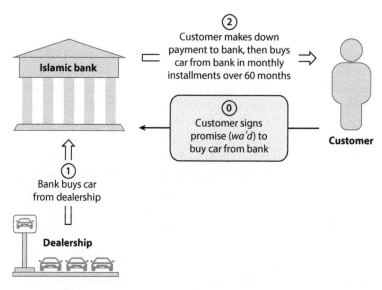

FIGURE 1.1. Unilateral promise (*wa'd*) in markup-sale financing.

global financial crisis: in the words of Marion Fourcade and colleagues, "is it *ethical* to protect the right of creditors to receive interest payments?")[119] Various classical scholars from the major Islamic juristic schools have taken differing positions on what a promise is and when it may be used. Sheikh Yusuf Talal DeLorenzo, an internationally elite scholar who became involved in Islamic finance in 1980 just as this debate was unfolding, describes what happened:

> Take, for example, murabaha. [Premodern] murabaha was a very simple instrument—the jurists[120] justified [it] for the reason that a lot of people are simply ignorant of market conditions. They come from villages to the town in order to purchase something, not knowing really what's going on in the market.
>
> That's all well and good, but what's the modern application of that? . . . Maybe Kuwait Finance House is buying a fleet of Cadillacs. You have to amend it a little: you need to say that . . . you, the buyer . . . must promise the seller that you're going to actually buy [the financed goods].
>
> [But] you had some scholars[121] at conferences in the 1980s and 1990s who would stand up and say, "that's not allowed!"[122] [DeLorenzo wags his index finger.] "You've added a condition[123] that was not there previously, that contravenes various interpretations of laws that we had previously."[124]

I asked DeLorenzo what set apart the scholars who accepted the business-friendly version of murabaha financing from those who didn't. He described how an elective affinity developed between business-friendly scholars and "Wall Street–type" bankers:

> Follow the money. When I think about the really outstanding scholars that I deal with—someone like Nizam Yaquby—his family is from the souq [i.e., bazaar], and they understand business. You really have to have that kind of mentality to understand business. . . . The ones whose motivation is to see business happen, to see business take place and work, to move the project forward—those are the ones that the Wall Street types latched onto, because they said "we need to move forward." If there's one that's just going to be an obstacle in our way, we don't need to talk to him; we won't hire him.
>
> So I guess—I won't call it natural selection, but—what is modern finance? It's greasing the wheels of business; it's providing capital for all this economic activity to happen. So obviously, [the Wall Street types'] interest from a shariah perspective is to have people who can work with them and be creative in finding solutions rather than standing back and saying, "No, there's no way you can do this."[125]

In short, the scholars who interpreted Islamic law in ways that allowed Islamic finance to flourish in capitalist economies were the ones who stayed in the industry. Those who were "obstacles" were not hired. There was a convergence of interests between the bankers and those shariah scholars with a business-friendly merchant ethos. The result was the hybridizing of the former's interests with the latter's interpretations of religious law, and the formation of what would go on to be the dominant institutional logic of Islamic finance thenceforth. This institutional logic justified interest simulation in the name of the industry's survival. The collective goal of keeping Islamic finance alive, which bankers and scholars alike could depict as a blessing for all Muslims, served to justify an interpretation of Islamic finance that would go on to serve handsomely the interests of individual firms.

Murabaha and similar markup structures also allowed capital that was leaving Saudi Arabia and other oil-rich countries to stay at home. In Saudi Arabia, for example, tight state control over the banking system and government anxiety about religious opposition to high interest rates led National Commercial Bank and Riyad Bank, the two dominant commercial banks in the 1980s (both majority-owned by the state), to offer very low rates on deposits. Wealthy Saudis sent their money abroad to earn a better return, either next door to the emerging offshore financial hub of Bahrain (where deposit rates were 10 percent higher) or to American and British banks and to other offshore banking centers. (Ultimately, the Latin American debt crisis was triggered by this flood of petrodollars back to Western banks.)[126] So the pump was primed for an Islamic option: somewhere people could place their money domestically, in good conscience and in ways that might not draw opprobrium from religiously minded relatives, friends, or business associates.

TAWARRUQ: SIMULATING AN UNSECURED
INTEREST-BEARING LOAN

Once murabaha became widespread in Islamic finance, *tawarruq* followed shortly thereafter. Tawarruq, sketched briefly in the introduction, means "conversion into silver/cash," and I translate it awkwardly as "cashification." Tawarruq (figure 6.3) is an application of markup sale that simulates the economic effect of unsecured interest-bearing loans (i.e., cash loans in which there is no collateral). Imagine that Party C (the customer) effectively wants to borrow $100 from Party B (the bank). In that case, Party B can buy a good for $100 from some unrelated entity (Party A), paying on the spot, and sell the good for $110 to Party C on credit (i.e., Party C pays Party B later, perhaps in installments). Then, Party C can sell the good on to another unrelated entity (Party D) for $100. Party C (the customer) now has $100 cash and owes Party B (the bank) $110 at some agreed point in the future.

Today, tawarruq is very widely used in Islamic finance, especially in the Gulf region. Its primary specialists in the Gulf are commodities brokers who work in the Dubai International Financial Centre and elsewhere in New Dubai. They draw on existing international commodities infrastructures to execute trades on behalf of firms offering Islamic financing (figure 6.4). Yet tawarruq seems to fly in the face of the idea proposed by early Islamic bankers in the 1970s and 1980s that Islamic finance should not simulate conventional interest-based lending. Even today, tawarruq remains controversial among many shariah scholars. "Many critics call it a paper transaction," notes Muzammil Kasbati, Ernst & Young's global Islamic-finance expert.[127] So how did this accommodation to capitalist needs become so widespread?

Tawarruq first became popular not as a way of making cash loans to bank customers but as a way for banks to lend to one another. When Islamic banks first appeared, there was no Islamic interbank lending market. (Even today, the weakness of the Islamic interbank lending market is a perpetual headache for the Islamic-finance industry.) Without recourse to some Islamic lending instrument similar to an interest-based loan, Islamic banks faced a huge disadvantage in liquidity management relative to their conventional competitors. In order to meet the government reserve requirement, they had two undesirable options: they could always keep on hand a large surplus of cash above the reserve requirement, which would make them less efficient than their competitors; or they could borrow and lend on the conventional interbank market, which would mean engaging behind the scenes in the sinful interest-based activity that it was their mission to avoid.

Tawarruq presented the ideal shariah-compliant alternative: Islamic banks could now structure an overnight tawarruq just as they would structure an overnight loan. This is so easy, in fact, that some conventional banks also do overnight tawarruq business with Islamic banks. The utility of tawarruq as a liquidity-management instrument shows how the rise of the risk-shifting model of Islamic finance and the decline of the risk-sharing model was largely a matter of survival. "Liquidity is the soul of the bank: if you don't have liquidity, the bank will collapse," remarked Malaysian shariah scholar Zulkifli Hasan.[128] The Islamic banks of the 1970s and 1980s faced a dilemma: compromise on their utopian vision of a risk-sharing economy or disappear in the Darwinian marketplace. Islamic bankers, against the wishes of some Islamic scholars and also the industry's early visionaries, self-consciously decided to adopt tawarruq widely even though it was a risk-shifting instrument. In order to survive, they made their industry more like conventional finance than the visionaries had ever expected it to be.

A striking but rarely acknowledged aspect of the turn toward tawarruq is the early involvement of Western financial firms and Western commodities markets in it. Western banks already had a history by the 1970s of serving the Gulf's commercial elite. I met with Stella Cox CBE, a thirty-year veteran of the Islamic-finance industry and managing director of DDCAP Group, a London-based firm that helps financial institutions facilitate shariah-compliant financial transactions via the London Metal Exchange—the dominant venue in which tawarruq is executed. Cox's technical expertise is so respected that veteran Islamic bankers call her simply "the Sister." Kleinwort Benson, Stella Cox's employer in the late 1970s and a leading London merchant bank at the time, already enjoyed relationships with leading Saudi, Emirati, and Qatari merchant families "going back absolute decades."[129]

As the price of oil skyrocketed in the late 1970s, Western banks promoted the creative use of tawarruq in order to service the nascent demand for Islamic finance. According to Cox:

> Led by the Saudis, and principally by . . . Sheikh Saleh Kamel, [these leading Gulf merchant families] came to Kleinwort in the late 1970s and said, "Ok—you've been a great relationship bank for us [over the decades], but . . . now we're going to be shariah-compliant."[130]

Seeking to retain its lucrative business with the merchant families at a moment when the region was awash with new wealth, a few of Kleinwort Benson's partners and associates taught themselves all they could about Islamic banking. A merchant bank since the eighteenth century, Kleinwort Benson had extensive expertise in structuring boutique trade finance. Its bankers were quick to realize that they could use tawarruq to keep doing the same merchant-banking business they were already doing with their wealthy Gulf clients, but in ways that conformed with those clients' new appetite for shariah-compliant contracts.

London grew into an international hub for Islamic interbank operations because in the 1970s and 1980s, banking markets were still overwhelmingly a national affair, especially in the developing world. If they had Islamic banking at all, most countries had only one Islamic bank: the UAE had Dubai Islamic Bank, Malaysia had Bank Islam, Saudi Arabia had Al Rajhi, Kuwait had KFH, and so on. These singleton banks had no domestic partners with whom to exchange shariah-compliant overnight loans. Hence, it was virtually impossible to set up an Emirati Islamic interbank market, a Malaysian Islamic interbank market, a Saudi Islamic interbank market, or a Kuwaiti Islamic interbank market. So to solve the ethical problem of liquidity management, the Islamic banks came to London, where Western banks were happy to help them develop shariah-compliant solutions to the liquidity problem—for a fee. Cox recalls:

> We had Islamic banks emerging in their national markets . . . but they were pretty isolated. . . . They had no interbank infrastructure to fall back upon whatsoever. So they came to London—a global financial center, a center for liquidity.

Once they came to understand tawarruq, Western banks helped spread its use as an interbank liquidity solution. Kleinwort Benson and a few of its Western competitors, such as Citibank and ANZ Bank, began providing interbank services to the emerging Islamic banks. For liquidity-management purposes, "[tawarruq] again became a contract that the bank could get comfortable with, because effectively, there are parallels between [conventional] interbank contracts . . . and [tawarruq]."[131]

The Birth of the Shariah Board

As Islamic banks began offering more interest-simulating products based on debt-based contracts such as murabaha and tawarruq, the need for formal legitimation grew. Widespread interest simulation was taking Islamic finance in a direction that some of its most zealous proponents, such as the moral economists, deemed potentially un-Islamic. Some shariah scholars too objected that murabaha and especially tawarruq entailed end runs around the spirit of the law.

The entrepreneurs who pioneered Islamic banking came up with a solution for legitimacy problems: the shariah board. This institution would formalize and systematize the unofficial advisory relationships that the early Islamic banks had established with shariah scholars. A shariah board is a panel of scholars charged with ensuring that the products, services, and operations of an Islamic bank (or other financial institution) comply with shariah. Nearly every Islamic bank today has one. The shariah board typically convenes every few months. At these meetings, its members sit with bank executives and scrutinize the bank's operations, paying special attention to new products the bank hopes to launch. If all members deem the new product halal, they issue a signed fatwa (Islamic legal decision) declaring this. The product may now be sold as "shariah-compliant" (i.e., halal). Shariah-board members are not employees, so they do not receive salaries. However, like members of corporate boards, they receive honoraria.

The shariah board is not a centuries-old feature of the Islamic legal tradition. Rather, it first appeared in 1977 at Faisal Islamic Bank of Egypt. Its appearance reflects ties that were strong at the time between Egypt's religious establishment and Prince Mohammed bin Faisal Al Saud of Saudi Arabia. Faisal Islamic Bank of Egypt's shariah board was headed by Sheikh Muḥammad Khāṭir Muḥammad al-Shaykh, who was then Egypt's grand mufti. Samir Abid Shaikh, who was active in Islamic finance in its earliest days and became general secretary of the International Association of Islamic Banks in 1993, believes the idea to establish shariah boards for Islamic banks was "most probably that of the Egyptian minister of religious endowments, Sheikh Muḥammad Mutawallī al-Shaʿrāwī . . . in conjunction with Prince Mohammad bin Faisal." Al-Shaʿrāwī, whom Samir Abid Shaikh describes as "an avid enthusiast for Islamic banking," had recently been a leading faculty member at two prominent Saudi universities, King Abdulaziz University in Jeddah and Umm al-Qura University in Mecca. As a result, Prince Mohammed knew him well already.[132]

The idea of the shariah board spread quickly. Many of the pioneering Islamic banks of the late 1970s and early 1980s then adopted it, including Jordan Islamic Bank, Kuwait Finance House, and the network of "Faisal banks" being seeded around the world by Prince Mohammed bin Faisal Al Saud.[133] By the 1990s, being an Islamic bank anywhere meant having a shariah board.

In sum, the shariah board has cemented certification by shariah scholars as the basic governance model of Islamic finance. In doing so, it has created a community of scholars with special expertise in, and commitment to, the Islamic-finance industry. These scholars universally accept interest simulation via murabaha financing and leases as shariah-compliant and hence play a major role in legitimating the Gulf model of Islamic finance. By providing a reliable and visible badge of certification in the form of the fatwa, the shariah board has also converted Islamic finance into a mode of certified ethical consumption, not unlike Fairtrade® bananas and coffee or socially responsible investing.

Abdul Halim Ismail and the Gulf Model in Malaysia

Interest simulation and the Gulf model came to have their own legitimating discourses and ideology by the 1980s. One of their staunchest defenders has been Malaysia's Abdul Halim Ismail (b. 1939), who is best known for having helped found Malaysia's first Islamic bank, Bank Islam Malaysia, in 1983 and for having served as its managing director into the 1990s. Ismail had a mixed educational pedigree: as a youth in Kedah state, he attended an Islamic school that has produced a number of well-known Islamic jurists, before transferring to an elite English-language high school that has produced two Malaysian prime ministers. He then became the first Malay to earn a PhD at Oxford and went on to serve, from 1974, as the first dean of the economics faculty at the National University of Malaysia (UKM).[134] Being trained in both classical religious sciences and Western economics, Ismail has much in common with the leading Islamic economists of his generation, such as M. Nejatullah Siddiqi and Umer Chapra.

Yet Ismail's fiqh-centric conception of Islamic finance broke sharply with that of the Islamic economists. The Islamic economists saw Islamic banks as functionally diverse institutions with social-welfare responsibilities: hybrid commercial banks *cum* investment trusts responsible for deploying depositors' funds in ways that would advance the public good.[135] In contrast, Ismail argued that Islamic commercial banks are responsible for maximizing returns for their shareholders and depositors. He drew a sharp tripartite distinction between (a) financial institutions in the government sector, in charge of regulatory oversight and domestic financial and monetary stability; (b) commercial Islamic banks, whose obligations were to maximize returns for their shareholders and depositors; and (c) the welfare sector, responsible for achieving societal well-being through the administration of zakat (*zakāh*; the Islamic alms tax), endowments, and charitable funds.[136] Ismail also directly rebutted the Islamic economists' claim that PLS is the essence of Islamic banking. In a monograph tellingly titled *The Deferred Contracts of Exchange: Al-Quran in Contrast with the Islamic Economists' Theory on Banking and Finance*[137] he wrote:

Shari'ah, as authentically derived from its sources of Al-Quran, Al-Sunnah, Al-Ijma' [consensus] and Al-Ijtihad [independent legal reasoning by qualified jurists], has ordained that both categories of Contracts of Profit-sharing and Contracts of Exchange are permissible. . . . Any bank or financial institution is free to choose to implement any form of contract from either categories [*sic*] for any of its operations in accordance with its own circumstances, and in keeping with the Quranic doctrine of "mutual willingness" of the two contracting parties as well as the doctrine of personal freedom of choice to enter into any form of contract . . . so long as the contract is allowed by Shari'ah. Any bank or financial institution that operates within these Limits of Allah is then in complete compliance with Shari'ah, and is "Islamic" irrespective of whether it liberally implements the contract of exchange.

Ismail's reasoning shows that the fiqh-centric Islamic financial thought of the Gulf model is compatible with free exchange in the credit market. Indeed, he effectively fuses the two. First, he aligns Islamic finance with microeconomic liberalism. So long as financial institutions remain within the formal limits of shariah-compliant contracts, they may be considered Islamic. They are free to enter into any shariah-compliant relationships they like with their customers. Second, Ismail proposes a societal division of labor that undergirds his liberal vision. He tasks the Islamic government sector and the Islamic welfare sector with the attainment of social objectives such as reducing inequality and caring for the poor. This leaves the Islamic commercial sector free to do what it does best: serve the common good through the competitive pursuit of profit.

Moreover, Ismail advances a fiqh-minded conception of shariah. In writing that shariah must be "authentically derived from its sources of Al-Quran, Al-Sunnah, Al-Ijma', and Al-Ijtihad," he implicitly critiques Islamic economists who, in his opinion, stray too far from canonical sources and classical exegetical methodologies in deciding what shariah demands and encourages. (The subtitle of his monograph makes clear whom he considers his discursive foes.) The Islamic economists invoke the higher objectives of shariah (maqasid al-sharia)[138] to justify their call for PLS-based Islamic finance, but Ismail and other advocates of fiqh-centric Islamic finance see this use of maqasid theory (they also make their own uses) as excessive and unscientific human editorializing on God's commands. Those commands, he feels, are communicated in sacred sources and should be interpreted by qualified jurists using appropriate exegetical methods. Crucially, Ismail does not deem murabaha and other deferred contracts of exchange that simulate the economic effects of interest to be unvirtuous end runs around the objectives of shariah, as the Islamic economists do. If God had considered them unvirtuous or off-limits, He would have said so. Ismail thus justifies the form of Islamic finance that by the mid-1980s had become completely dominant in Malaysia, the Gulf, and virtually everywhere else: one in which commercial Islamic banks were regulated by shariah scholars, allowed to deploy interest simulation, and freed from social-welfare obligations.

Indeed, Abdul Halim Ismail's Bank Islam Malaysia—and, following suit, most other Malaysian Islamic banks—went in the 1980s and 1990s even more aggressively down the road of interest simulation than Islamic banks in the Gulf did. At a 1992 international conference, Ismail stressed the importance of developing interest-simulating Islamic debt finance while his Egyptian peer, the governor of Faisal Islamic Bank of Egypt, advocated PLS as the best means to meet Muslims' economic needs.[139] Ismail and his staff at Bank Islam Malaysia also rejected Kuwait Finance House's model of the Islamic bank as trader and developer in favor of simply providing financing, as conventional commercial banks do.[140] As Hideki Kitamura explains, most of Ismail's hires at Bank Islam came from a conventional-banking background, and "they sought to pragmatically make the modern banking system permissible to Islam" instead of taking what one twenty-year veteran of Bank Islam called a "radical or disruptive" path. They did so not only to be profitable but also to demonstrate to the government that Islamic banking could be commercially viable and operate under the central bank's regulation.[141]

Driven by Prime Minister Mahathir Mohamad's pragmatic stance toward Islamic finance[142] and his goal of financial inclusion for Malaysia's Muslim ethnic-Malay community,[143] the Islamic-finance sector came to rely heavily[144] in the 1980s and 1990s on a particularly controversial interest-simulating financing mechanism. Ina, also known as bay al-ina (*bay ʿ al-ʿīnah*), is a sale-buyback transaction and perhaps the simplest way to simulate interest. Consider this example: C is a seeker of financing (e.g., a bank customer) and B a provider of financing (e.g., an Islamic bank). C sells an asset to B on credit for $1,050, and then B immediately sells it back to C on spot terms for $1,000. The result is that C has $1,000 cash on hand and owes B $1,050, to be paid at a future date. This simulates a $1,000 loan with $50 interest. Most Islamic jurists through history have disallowed ina on the grounds that it replicates interest too baldly, with the asset serving merely as a prop. However, some classical jurists of the Shāfiʿī school allowed it, and in the 1980s, Malaysian shariah scholars justified its use by citing them (the Shāfiʿī school predominates in Malaysia).[145] These contemporary scholars also argued that while ina might be contentious from a shariah perspective, it facilitated the growth of Islamic finance at a nascent stage. However, heavy reliance on ina led to criticism both from outsiders—especially those from the Middle East who looked down on what they considered Malaysia's playing fast and loose with shariah—and from domestic constituents. As a result, the central bank of Malaysia forced the country's financial sector to shift away from ina in 2012.[146]

Conclusion: To Capitalist Islamic Finance via Islamic Revival, Certification, Oil Rents, and Financialization

This chapter has argued that the unique economic, political, and social circumstances of the Gulf Arab countries in the 1970s and early 1980s explain how the term "Islamic finance" became synonymous everywhere with the Gulf model. The petrodollar windfall inclined wealthy members of prominent merchant families—and one Saudi royal prince—to entrench the Gulf model in their newly formed Islamic banks and funds and empowered them to spread it worldwide.

These early pioneers of Islamic finance were ambivalent about "Western" capitalist finance. On one hand, they portrayed themselves as an economic vanguard of the global Islamic revival and advertised their new financial institutions as Islamic antidotes to the godless, exploitative, interest-based international financial system. On the other hand, they were businessmen who saw no inherent conflict between Islam and private capital accumulation. They inhabited societies where the fundamental macroeconomic question was no longer how to alleviate poverty by distributing scarce capital but how to invest and circulate suddenly abundant capital. Moreover, the ruling dynasts in their countries were already enmeshed in the international interest-based financial system and were becoming ever more so as American and European bankers recycled their petrodollars.

Under these unique conditions, the pioneering financiers formed a decisive alliance with shariah scholars in the late 1970s and 1980s[147] that set Islamic finance on a capitalist path. While at first the financiers sought advice informally from shariah scholars, they quickly formalized the relationship by establishing the shariah board. This official certification body legitimated Islamic banks and funds to pious constituents. The alliance also led to the entrenchment of interest simulation. Not all shariah scholars considered interest simulation to be Islamically lawful. Yet in a sorting process driven by elective affinities, the early Islamic banks gravitated toward the scholars who authorized interest simulation. Interest simulation allowed the newly hatched Islamic banks and funds to survive in the liberal financial markets of the Gulf, where they had to compete against existing conventional banks and funds.

This chapter's journey began in Old Dubai with Saeed Al Lootah's vision of a pious, merchant-style, unbureaucratized Islamic finance. It ended, before the excursus to Malaysia, in the commodity-trading platforms of New Dubai and London. There, Islamic finance takes the form of a highly rationalized, capital-friendly, globally oriented certification system governed bureaucratically by powerful shariah scholars.

How are social scientists to think about this transformation? One approach is to think in terms of the political economy of the Arab Gulf rentier states. Political-economy literature highlights one path toward the unusual success of entrepôts like Dubai, and to a lesser but still impressive extent Bahrain, that have only limited hydrocarbon revenues. These city-states have benefited from the hydrocarbon wealth of their neighbors by becoming regional catchment centers that manage that wealth and link it to global circuits of finance.[148] American-aligned countries' financial centers, including Frankfurt, Geneva, New York, Singapore, and Zürich, have contributed financial expertise to this end, especially in the realm of capital markets. London, as home of the Eurodollar market since the 1970s and a hub for financial engineering, has been particularly important in providing expertise and trading infrastructure, as the story of Stella Cox and DDCAP showed. In the Arab Gulf economies, expertise and infrastructure from the Global North have paired with shariah scholarship from across the world, but most of all from Arab countries. Especially prominent have been business-minded, scripturally knowledgeable shariah scholars who, as subsequent chapters will show, tend not to be "political": that is, they do not publicly challenge the pro-United States political arrangements of Gulf dynasts.

Connecting too to the literature on financialization and world-systems theory, we see that the emergence of capitalist Islamic finance in the 1970s and its subsequent growth, especially from around the turn of the millennium onward, have depended on the integration of the Arab Gulf states into a global system of American hegemony during the age of financial expansion that has accompanied the end of the long American century.[149] Demand for oil, particularly from the United States and its allies, has generated the capital behind the global spread of Islamic finance. In particular, as Adam Hanieh has shown for the contemporary period and as this chapter showed for the early years of Islamic finance, wealthy elite Gulf families have been overrepresented among the founders and owners of Islamic banks.[150]

At the same time, there are crucial differences between the rise of Islamic finance and the turn toward finance in the Global North. As Greta Krippner has demonstrated in the case of the United States, financialization often transpires as the result of political responses to crisis.[151] Yet the birth of Islamic finance in the 1970s and its "financialization" from the mid-1990s onward—in the sense of a turn toward more intensive financial engineering, a growth in securitization, and greater detachment from economic activity such as industrial production and trade—did not emerge from economic crisis. Instead, they were largely the result of economic windfalls: the problem was not one of how to distribute scarce resources in a politically tenable way but of how to invest massive surplus wealth. In this regard, the rise of Islamic finance depicted in this chapter can contribute to the way we think about the expansion of finance, especially outside the Global North and the core of the world economy.

With regard to the genesis of the shariah board, literature in organizations and regulation points to two pathways along which voluntary private certification regimes like shariah-scholar certification emerge. In what Tim Bartley calls "Track 1," certification systems emerge as a result of information asymmetry and as a solution to collective-action problems, driven by both activists that "name and shame" firms and consumers who want to shop ethically. In "Track 2," they arise due to political challenges and social movements that politicians or others may deflect and channel toward non-state regulatory solutions.[152] Insofar as the birth of Islamic finance was an economic manifestation of the larger global Islamic revival that gained momentum in the 1970s, the emergence of Islamic finance itself is a Track 2 story, particularly given that Islamic finance has turned out to be a face of that revival much more palatable to stable authoritarian U.S.-aligned regimes than political Islam. But with regard to the rise of the shariah board specifically, a Track 1 story comes into view: the early pioneers of Islamic finance, with a few exceptions like Saeed Al Lootah, turned to shariah scholars to appease consumers who were suspicious and confused about this newfangled thing called Islamic finance. The combination of Track 1 momentum and Track 2 momentum helps explain how the shariah board became entrenched and "went global" so fast.

Competition among private governance regimes can lead to the convergence of rules over time.[153] This appears to have happened in Islamic banking in the 1970s and 1980s: the early Islamic bankers, shariah scholars, and economic thinkers first interested in the industry held a wide range of views about what it might mean for Islamic law and ethics to govern finance, but by the mid-1980s, the governance regime had converged toward the dominance of scholars and the acceptance of a few specific forms of interest simulation. A subset of shariah scholars with similar interpretations of Islamic law formed a "horizontal alliance" that excluded most non-scholars and all scholars who rejected interest simulation entirely.[154] Yet as the private-governance literature also notes, such convergence rarely results in complete harmonization of rules. Islamic finance was left by the 1990s with increasingly powerful elite shariah scholars who agreed on most governance rules that mattered substantively to the banks they governed but who disagreed on the margins.

Having traveled back to the previous century in this chapter, we will next travel centuries further back, to the forebears of today's shariah scholars. We will also consider the intellectual rivals of the shariah scholars: the moral economists, who offer an alternative reading of what Islamic finance should be.

2

Ethics

"FINANCE IS ALWAYS SOCIAL," writes Sarah Quinn. "It is social not just because it distributes profits and risks among people," but also because it distributes them "on the basis of understandings, usually unspoken, of what people can imagine owing to and sharing with one another." Quinn therefore strives to reveal "how competing moral visions . . . are written into specific ways" of practicing finance.[1]

Quinn's case is the American bond market, but her words and mission are just as apposite to the study of global Islamic finance. As the previous chapter showed, competing moral visions of an Islamic economy appeared in the late nineteenth and twentieth centuries. This chapter focuses on the two visions that became central to contemporary debates about Islamic finance: the moral economists' vision and the shariah scholars' vision. These visions evaluate financial owing and sharing differently, and each is written into specific ways of structuring and executing Islamic financial instruments. The two visions largely overlapped in the 1960s and 1970s, but by the 1980s they were diverging and clashing as Islamic banks struggled to implement the moral economists' utopian brand of finance while competing against conventional financial institutions. The scholars' vision proved more amenable to existing capitalist markets and market infrastructures, and today it dominates industry practice.

To understand the two visions, this chapter and part of the next chapter probe the moral logics that suffuse the moral economists' vision and the shariah scholars' vision. Whenever possible, I allow shariah scholars and moral economists to speak for themselves. I spoke at length with shariah scholars and moral economists in Saudi Arabia, Pakistan, the United Arab Emirates, Malaysia, the United Kingdom, and the United States. Many hailed from those countries, but others from Bahrain, India, Iraq, Morocco, Oman, Syria, Turkey, and elsewhere. To explain the two visions' content, the chapter also explores their historical roots. Toward the end, it tackles the following question: Why is there a huge Islamic-finance industry today but no Christian-finance industry or Jewish-finance industry enjoying comparable commercial success—even though the scriptures of Judaism and Christianity prohibit usury in the same vocabulary that Islamic scriptures do?

If Islamic finance replicates the economic effects of interest, does the Islamic-finance boom merely represent the triumph of capitalist ethics over religious ethics—with the scholars' and bankers' complicity? This chapter argues that this is not the case. It asserts that the scholars' Islamic finance, although thoroughly enmeshed in capitalist institutions and interests, carries the germ of a powerful ethical critique of financialization. The scholars' critique of conventional finance is far more compatible with existing capitalist financial markets than the moral economists' critique—yet it is a critique nonetheless, and one that invites us to rethink our contemporary definitions of money and credit and the moral meanings we attribute to them.

The Moral Economists in Historical Perspective

Shariah scholars are not the only technical experts promoting an interest-free, Islamically regulated financial system. Their ideological sparring partners, the moral economists (also known as Islamic economists), believe Islamic finance should focus more on social welfare and poverty alleviation than it does.[2] The moral economists insist that economic principles enshrined in shariah, such as the interest ban and the alms tax, are divinely inspired building blocks for a just and crisis-free moral economy.[3] Many therefore deem today's Islamic finance a "social failure."[4] Frequently cited publications whose titles offer a sense of Islamic economics' subject matter include "Application of *Waqf* [Islamic charitable endowment] for Social and Development Finance,"[5] "A Framework to Analyse the Efficiency and Governance of Zakat Institutions,"[6] and *Riba, Bank Interest and the Rationale of Its Prohibition.*[7]

Since the 1980s, Islamic economics has gradually gained prominence in both secular and Islamic academia in Muslim-majority countries and beyond. In Malaysia, Indonesia, the Arab world, Pakistan, and Bangladesh, university courses and degree programs in Islamic economics are now common. They are less common but on the rise in the United Kingdom, India, Central Asia, and West Africa. To be sure, some mainstream economists allege that its normative agenda—to prove the economic wisdom of shariah—casts doubt on its findings. Yet it has established beachheads in well-known "secular" academia. Durham University hosts an Islamic-finance summer school every year, while for many years, Harvard University hosted an annual Islamic-finance conference. The Society for the Advancement of Socio-Economics (SASE), an international conference popular with economic sociologists, now has an "Islamic Moral Economy" section.

Despite their foothold in academia, the moral economists' influence on the Islamic-finance industry remains weak. In addition to the traditional orientation toward waqf,[8] zakat, and riba that has dominated their work for decades, today's moral economists do offer technically novel proposals for increasing social welfare that could mesh well with existing capitalist financial markets, such as shariah-compliant crowdfunding[9] and commodity-linked sukuk.[10] However, Islamic banks and Muslim investors have yet to take interest, for Islamic economics lacks widespread legitimacy in business circles. Governments enlist secular economists as development advisors and industrial planners. Islamic banks overwhelmingly hire bankers from conventional banking backgrounds. And unlike rock-star jurists, Islamic economists rarely serve as brand names. So for now, they remain marginal to capital and have yet to implement their welfarist vision much in the real world.

The Moral Economists' Intellectual Lineage and Their Differences with the Shariah Scholars

The idea of a moral economy that establishes alternatives to market logic has a long history.[11] But the Islamic moral economists' intellectual lineage traces back to movements in the first half of the twentieth century to theorize an interest-free economy that would liberate Muslims from imperialist financial domination. At recently established Islamic universities in the Subcontinent, Muslim academics began blending the methodology of Western economics with the moral language and institutions of Islam. This environment was enlivened by debates in the Subcontinent's intellectual centers about the long-term viability of capitalism and socialism and about the relevance of religious knowledge in modern economies. Islamic economics as such was born at Osmania University in the princely state of Hyderabad,[12] taking shape in the period between the university's establishment in 1918 by the nizam of Hyderabad and freshly independent India's invasion and annexation of Hyderabad in 1948. Hyderabad, the "cultural metropolis of Muslim India,"[13] had been prominent for centuries in Islamic education and juristic scholarship, and in the nineteenth and early twentieth centuries was a thriving center of Muslim internationalism: a crucible for exchange among modernist and traditionally minded Islamic intellectuals from the Subcontinent, the Ottoman Empire, Persia, Central Asia, and Europe, thanks to its status outside direct crown rule (as a princely state, Hyderabad was formally distinct from India) and to its long-standing local stratum of lettered bureaucrat-intellectuals.[14] The language of instruction at Osmania until the 1948 Indian annexation was Urdu, and in the 1920s and 1930s, the university published a stream of Urdu translations of famous economics texts, including those of

J. S. Mill and William Stanley Jevons.[15] Osmania's faculty of Muslim theology
and its school of economics sat under the same roof, and one former Osmania
professor recalls that "whenever a student took a subject pertaining to economics from the Islamic point of view" in either of the two, the student received "double guidance"—from one theology professor and one economics
professor.[16]

According to Abdul Azim Islahi,[17] who has exhaustively chronicled the
contributions to Islamic economics of Osmania professor Muhammad
Hamidullah and other seminal figures, Hamidullah was the first person to use
the term "Islamic economics," which appeared in his 1936 paper on Islamic
perspectives on labor.[18] Starting with that work, there runs throughout
Hamidullah's oeuvre a conception of a modern Islamic economy as inherently
more egalitarian and stable than a laissez-faire capitalist economy, largely
because of its avoidance of interest. Hamidullah identified the capitalist credit
system as a major driver of speculation, of the funding of incompetent entrepreneurs and unnecessary business ventures, and of credit bubbles that inevitably end in busts.[19]

These pioneers of Islamic economics were the progenitors of Islamic neorevivalism as applied to the economy, and by the 1950s and 1960s, many of the
most prominent Islamic economists were members of, or allied with, major
neorevivalist political movements such as Jamaat-e-Islami or the Muslim
Brotherhood. From the beginning, the Islamic economists' motivation was
the belief that neither laissez-faire capitalism nor godless socialism had succeeded in improving the conditions of large numbers of people, including
most Muslims under British suzerainty, and that Islam—as both a divinely
inspired system of thought and a fundamentally rational one—contained, in
its institutions and in the rules of shariah, the kernel of a socially just and morally upright economic system. This "Islamic economy" would preserve private
enterprise while ensuring that the benefits of that enterprise extended beyond
the individual, increasing standards of living and promoting equity across society. This vision resonated powerfully among Muslim intellectuals living
under British domination, especially in light of the crises shaking British capitalist world hegemony in the early twentieth century, including anticolonial
revolts, World War I, the October Revolution of 1917, the Great Depression,[20]
and the crumbling of the sterling-centric global financial system.[21] The idea of
an Islamic economy that is neither capitalist nor socialist remains dear today
to many Islamic economists and helps explain their disillusionment with the
essentially capitalist Islamic-finance industry.

The Islamic neorevivalists advocated the revitalization of Islam through a
return to Islamic first principles. They found these principles in the Quran,
and often also in the hadith literature and other core scriptural sources.

However, they were less wedded to the classical Islamic sciences than most classically trained ulama—including shariah scholars—whom they viewed as either "buried in medieval texts" or "co-opted by the state."[22] Instead, the neo-revivalists interpreted scripture more freely and independently, often deviating from or jettisoning traditional exegetical methodologies.[23] Instead of building carefully on the edifice of juridical tradition, they focused on transforming contemporary societies in order to instantiate what they considered the ideal social, economic, and political characteristics of the Muslim community in the age of the Prophet, such as solidarity, social justice, and a collective commitment to alleviate poverty. As "lay activists and intellectuals," they saw themselves as the "vanguard class of public religiosity."[24]

As of the middle of the twentieth century, the neorevivalists differed from the classically trained ulama in crucial ways. Like the latter, neorevivalists typically took a socially conservative stance on morality and gender roles. However, they placed much more emphasis than most traditional ulama on modern forms of social engineering such as health care, job creation, minimum wages, state-controlled income redistribution, and public education. They embraced the forward-looking belief that Islam is "the blueprint for a total modern society, an ideological and political alternative to liberalism, socialism or communism."[25] They generally found Western influence imperialistic and corrosive, as many of the classically trained ulama did, but were more likely to accuse indigenous rulers of corruption and impiety, including not only secular modernizers but also authoritarians who stressed their Islamic bona fides. As a result, neorevivalists were far more likely than the traditional ulama to pursue political change through electoral contestation or even revolutionary struggle, particularly when mainstream classically trained ulama had been absorbed into state religious bureaucracies.

The neorevivalists' vision for Islamic finance was driven by an ethos of social engineering. Neorevivalists viewed shariah as a divine structure for a just, poverty-reducing Islamic economic system. In this system, debt's role in the economy would be radically limited. Banks would not only be governed by Islamic law but would also be driven by motivations other than profit maximization. In the 1950s and 1960s, neorevivalists theorized interest-free Islamic banks that would deploy profit-and-loss sharing (PLS; see chapter 1) to liberate Muslims from the yoke of interest-bearing debt and the hegemony of Western capitalist finance. They saw PLS-based Islamic banking as an integral component of a future Islamic socioeconomic system that would reduce inequality, exploitation, oppression, and immorality. The welfarists drew relatively little on the long tradition of classical Islamic jurisprudence, seeing themselves as economic revolutionaries advancing beyond the limits of what classical jurists imagined rather than scrupulous rule followers bound by classical tradition. The neorevivalists' epistemic framework was the emerging discipline of Islamic economics. By the 1940s, 1950s, and 1960s, neorevivalist social-welfarist intellectuals were using Islamic economics to draft ambitious blueprints for Islamic tax systems, Islamic monetary policies, Islamic institutions to channel investment capital, and Islamic banking systems. Today's moral economists are the intellectual descendants of these neorevivalist theoreticians.

The Moral Economists' Case for PLS

Equity-type partnership contracts provide financing by distributing risk and liability differently from debt. If I am an investor and you are an entrepreneur, we can form a partnership that grants me a share of any future profits in your venture but also places on me partial or full responsibility for any losses. In the moral economists' language, this partnership is a PLS arrangement. The moral economists consider it qualitatively more just than interest-bearing debt, which imposes costs on you—the requirement to repay both principal and interest—regardless of how well the venture performs. Equity-type PLS contracts have a long history in Islamicate societies. They were a crucial means of financing medieval long-distance trade. By the tenth century, partnership law was advanced in the Islamicate Middle East and among Muslim traders along the Indian Ocean littoral.[26]

Given their historical legitimacy and their stark difference from interest-bearing debt, it is no surprise that PLS is endorsed by both the moral economists and the shariah scholars. Applying a logic of divine command, both camps appreciate that it avoids sin. Applying a logic of transactional justice—that is, examining the fairness of exchange within the transaction—virtually all moral economists and some shariah scholars also consider it more just than interest-based lending because it requires that owners of capital share in the risk of a business venture. By tying the fortunes of the party that has capital (i.e., the investor) to those of the party that uses capital, it ostensibly gives everyone involved an incentive to work together, sharing knowledge and resources to achieve a common goal. By contrast, one who lends at interest stands to gain even if the borrower's venture fails—regardless of whether failure was the borrower's fault. Supporters therefore see PLS as being in line with principles of justice and beneficence.[27] More broadly, supporters consider PLS consonant with the concept of a *homo Islamicus* who acts not only to maximize personal utility, as *homo economicus* does, but also to advance collective well-being and moral virtue.[28]

Applying a consequentialist logic, moral economists have also advanced economic arguments in favor of PLS. They assert that it encourages innovation

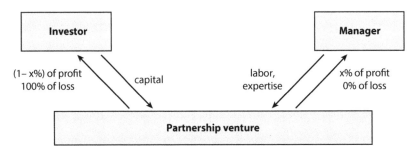

FIGURE 2.1. Islamic silent partnership (mudaraba).

and entrepreneurship, particularly in small- and medium-sized ventures. According to this logic, someone with a promising business idea and the skills to implement it might be overlooked by conventional banks for lack of collateral but might get financing from Islamic banks instead.[29] Some proponents also argue that widespread adoption of PLS could cure ills seemingly endemic to capitalism such as bank runs, credit crunches, cycles of debt poverty, and national financial crises—particularly when implemented as a form of banking, as discussed in the next section.

THE FUNDAMENTALS OF PLS: ISLAMIC SILENT PARTNERSHIP (MUDARABA) AND ISLAMIC JOINT VENTURE (MUSHARAKA)

One of the two most common equity-type PLS contracts is mudaraba. The investor contributes capital while the manager contributes work and know-how (figure 2.1). The investor bears any losses, while the investor and the manager split any profits according to a previously agreed ratio (e.g., 60-40, 50-50). Islamic silent partnerships function a lot like stock ownership or private equity, but unlike those arrangements, they are limited in time (though they can be rolled over into a new silent partnership).

The other major Islamic PLS contract used in Islamic finance is musharaka (figure 2.2). It too is a partnership, but it differs from mudaraba in that the manager may also be a capital contributor, so it is best described as a joint venture. Two or more partners each take an equity stake, and any of the partners may contribute capital, labor, or expertise. Profits are shared based on a pre-agreed ratio (often equal to equity participation), and losses are shared based on equity participation. Musharaka is similar to many conventional limited partnerships and joint ventures.

Islamic equity-style partnerships can be used in a manner fully consonant with the profit-maximizing tendencies of contemporary capitalists. Today,

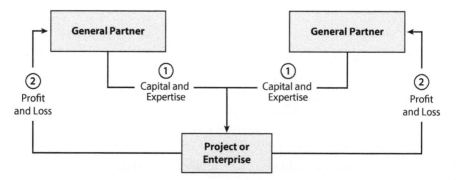

FIGURE 2.2. Islamic joint venture (musharaka).

shariah-compliant private-equity funds employ mudaraba and musharaka because they are similar to the secular contracts used in private equity and venture capital. Barrister Bilkis Ismail notes the parallels: mudaraba "is suited well for the general-partner/limited-partner fund model [of private equity]," in which the fund manager is liable only if negligent, whereas musharaka is well-suited to investment in underlying portfolio companies for it "encourages entrepreneurship and enables companies to obtain funding to generate internal growth without losing control."[30] Shariah-compliant venture-capital funds and mutual funds also use mudaraba and musharaka extensively.

Meanwhile, shariah scholars vary in their attitudes toward mudaraba and musharaka. They universally consider such partnerships shariah-compliant; but do they consider them ethically *superior* to debt-based modes of Islamic finance? Some shariah scholars do, acceding to the moral economists' principle that equity-based instruments represent an ideal form of Islamic financing. This concession is particularly common among shariah scholars in South Asia, where Islamic economics has its strongest roots, and in Southeast Asia. For example, the internationally elite Pakistani scholar Taqi Usmani avers that interest-simulating debt-based Islamic finance is "not ideal" and "should only be used in cases of need."[31] On the other hand, leading shariah scholars and bank executives in the Arabian Peninsula tend to downplay or even reject the assertion that equity-based modes are inherently superior to debt-based modes.

A VISION TO REINVENT BANKING: TWO-TIER MUDARABA

The fit between Islamic equity-type contracts and conventional equity-based forms of finance such as private equity is straightforward. But how might PLS principles be incorporated into commercial *banking*? Mohammad Nejatullah

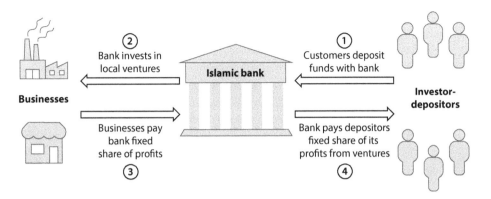

FIGURE 2.3. Two-tier mudaraba (theoretical model for interest-free PLS-based banking).

Siddiqi, a renowned moral economist, advanced a theoretical model called two-tier mudaraba (figure 2.3) in the 1960s to achieve this.[32] Siddiqi's goal was nothing less than to reinvent banking.

A bank based on two-tier mudaraba is structured much like a mutual fund. Depositors invest their money with the bank under a mudaraba contract (the first tier), placing it in a special mudaraba investment account. The bank then invests with promising businesses and projects as a silent partner using another mudaraba contract (the second tier), just as a mutual fund invests in corporations. Crucially, unlike a depositor at a conventional bank who knows in advance the interest rate she will earn on her deposits, the depositor-investor in an Islamic bank based on two-tier mudaraba will earn returns that vary based on the performance of the businesses and projects in which the bank invests. This is a riskier proposition. If the bank's portfolio of investments performs well, the depositor-investor will reap greater reward. But if they perform poorly, she will earn little or nothing.

Beyond religio-ethical concerns, some economists have argued that the two-tier mudaraba model could make banks less prone to going bust during crises. Whereas interest-based financial intermediation causes maturity mismatches for banks that can result in bank runs and collapses during uncertain times,[33] profit-and-loss-sharing capital, like private-equity capital, tends to be more patient and long-term. A bank that employs PLS on both sides of its balance sheet, as in the two-tier mudaraba model, also passes through part of the investment risk that it takes on its asset side to depositor-investors on its liabilities side, much in the manner of a mutual fund or private-equity fund.[34] In other words, if the economic environment turns sour and a bank's assets perform poorly, the bank will pay depositor-investors less, thus cushioning the blow to the bank.

Although some Islamic banks in the 1960s, 1970s, and early 1980s did attempt to implement the two-tier mudaraba model of banking, it failed to gain traction, largely because it proved riskier for banks, less popular among customers, and harder to regulate than conventional interest-based banking. The failure of this PLS-based banking model quickly set Islamic finance on a path toward greater acceptance of interest simulation: shariah scholars and early Islamic bankers conceded that if a completely revolutionary, equity-based system of Islamic banking was infeasible for the moment, then reliance on debt-based Islamic financial contracts—such as leases—was the next best thing, a shariah-compliant stopgap until PLS could be made to work.

INTEREST-SIMULATING ISLAMIC EQUITY FINANCE

Today, Islamic commercial banks do use silent partnership and joint venture, but mostly in ways that effectively guarantee a fixed or nearly fixed "profit rate" in advance, simulating a conventional interest rate. Thus they do not conform to the logic of PLS embodied in Nejatullah Siddiqi's two-tier silent-partnership structure. Instead, they specify in advance what each party will earn or pay. The reason for simulating interest-bearing debt is simple: banks want to minimize the risk and liability they bear. Moral economists are often uncomfortable with equity structured to act like debt, arguing that it undermines the spirit and purpose of PLS and the distinctiveness of Islamic finance. Industry shariah scholars, however, defend the practice, arguing that imperfect PLS is better than none. The lesson is that "real utopias"[35] in alternative finance can become compromised when exposed to unbridled competition, especially when the ethical valence of such projects is contested and state regulations are not amenable to their wide implementation.

PROFIT SMOOTHING: MAKING EQUITY-TYPE CONTRACTS ACT LIKE DEBT-TYPE CONTRACTS

Savings accounts based on mudaraba exemplify interest-simulating equity-type products. Technically, they offer a variable return. In practice, however, they advertise an "expected profit rate" or "expected return" from a pool of investments that the bank manages (see table 2.1, which is from an Omani bank but could be from an Islamic bank anywhere). Following the rules of Islamic silent partnership, Islamic banks also state in their marketing materials the profit-sharing ratio between the manager (i.e., the bank) and the investor (i.e., the depositor). Note that the profit rates the bank expects to pay in April 2023 are identical, down to one-thousandth of 1 percent, to the declared (i.e., actual) profit rates that the bank paid in March 2023, for every tenor. Only tenors of 1,

3, and 6 months are shown, but the equivalence holds all the way to 24 months, the longest tenor. In other words, the bank does not expect its yield curve to budge in the slightest.

When it comes time to pay out, the bank invariably manages to provide a profit rate that is very, very close to the expected rate. This raises a philosophical question. If I invest by earning a share of the profits from a pool of assets (as opposed to making a loan), but each month, my return on investment is precisely what the bank predicts it will be, is that interest? To Islamic economists, shariah scholars, and religiously minded customers, a return truly guaranteed in advance counts as the forbidden riba. Yet to customers who are accustomed to conventional savings accounts, an unpredictable return on a savings account sounds unattractive. Islamic banks therefore navigate gingerly between Scylla and Charybdis: telling customers that the return on their savings is technically not guaranteed to be predictable—but if asked by a nervous customer, offering the reassurance that no customer of the bank has ever received anything but the expected return. In a common response, one sales representative at Sharjah Islamic Bank in the United Arab Emirates told my research assistant "we cannot say with certainty"[36] what the profit rate will be but that it is "usually close to the market rate"—the market rate being the market *interest* rate at that tenor.[37]

Islamic banks also effectively guarantee that the depositor will not make a loss, excising the "loss" portion of the profit-and-loss-sharing formula. Shariah scholars and academics have justified this departure from the PLS principle on the basis of necessity, saying that without capital guarantees, "the majority of households would shy away from the [Islamic-banking] system," which "no country can afford."[38]

One strategy Islamic banks employ to ensure that they pay returns extremely close to the advertised expected return is to engage in techniques called "profit smoothing" or "income smoothing."[39] First, Islamic banks set a floor on the return paid to depositors using corporate accounts known as profit-equalization reserves (PER) and investment-risk reserves (IRR) that top up lower-than-expected returns so that the depositor receives at least as much as the "expected rate." Second, Islamic banks set a ceiling on the return paid to depositors by inserting language in its contract with the depositor stating that the bank's management fee may be up to some maximum percentage of the profit. The bank can adjust its fee upward so that the depositor never gets significantly more than the promised return. Effectively, the bank creates a very small collar around the expected return. Profit smoothing is widespread in major Islamic-banking markets, including the GCC economies and Malaysia.[40]

When it comes to interest-simulating equity contracts, the difference of opinion between the moral economists and the shariah scholars hinges on the

TABLE 2.1. Declared and Expected Profit Rates on Mudaraba Investment Accounts from an Islamic Bank in Oman

Mudaraba Investment Accounts Declared Profit Rates for March 2023		
Currency: Omani riyals	*Payout: Monthly*	
Amount Invested	**Participation Weightage**	**Declared Profit Rate**
Tenor: 1 month		
1,000–24,999 riyals	46.00%	1.354%
25,000–99,999 riyals	47.00%	1.421%
100,000–249,999 riyals	48.00%	1.426%
250,000–999,999 riyals	49.00%	1.431%
1,000,000 riyals and above	50.00%	1.436%
Tenor: 3 months		
1,000–24,999 riyals	51.00%	1.501%
25,000–99,999 riyals	52.00%	1.531%
100,000–249,999 riyals	53.00%	1.560%
250,000–999,999 riyals	54.00%	1.590%
1,000,000 riyals and above	55.00%	1.595%
Tenor: 6 months		
1,000–24,999 riyals	61.00%	1.796%
25,000–99,999 riyals	62.00%	1.825%
100,000–249,999 riyals	63.00%	1.827%
250,000–999,999 riyals	64.00%	1.832%
1,000,000 riyals and above	65.00%	1.837%

Source: Bank website.

way one defines interest, or more specifically, riba. If a deposit account estimates its profit rate in advance every quarter and then consistently comes extremely close to meeting it, are the returns on that account tantamount to interest, even if they flow from investment returns from a pool of assets (assets that do not appear on the bank's books as loans)? It is worth noting that while Islamic banks virtually always do end up paying the expected return on partnership-based savings accounts or something vanishingly close to it, they reserve the right to pay a lower—or higher—return. Anecdotally, Islamic bankers at one Pakistani bank proudly told me that their bank paid a significantly higher-than-promised return to depositors one month when unexpected movements in commodity markets produced bonanza returns on those

TABLE 2.1. (*continued*)

Mudaraba Investment Accounts Expected Profit Rates for April 2023

Currency: Omani riyals	Payout: Monthly	
Amount Invested	**Participation Weightage**	**Expected Profit Rate**
Tenor: 1 month		
1,000–24,999 riyals	46.00%	1.354%
25,000–99,999 riyals	47.00%	1.421%
100,000–249,999 riyals	48.00%	1.426%
250,000–999,999 riyals	49.00%	1.431%
1,000,000 riyals and above	50.00%	1.436%
Tenor: 3 months		
1,000–24,999 riyals	51.00%	1.501%
25,000–99,999 riyals	52.00%	1.531%
100,000–249,999 riyals	53.00%	1.560%
250,000–999,999 riyals	54.00%	1.590%
1,000,000 riyals and above	55.00%	1.595%
Tenor: 6 months		
1,000–24,999 riyals	61.00%	1.796%
25,000–99,999 riyals	62.00%	1.825%
100,000–249,999 riyals	63.00%	1.827%
250,000–999,999 riyals	64.00%	1.832%
1,000,000 riyals and above	65.00%	1.837%

depositors' assets. Yet everyone agrees that such cases are extremely rare. Indeed, these bankers told me this to illustrate that their Islamic bank was far more scrupulous than most.

DIMINISHING MUSHARAKA: AN EQUITY-TYPE CONTRACT WITH DEBT-LIKE CHARACTERISTICS

Diminishing musharaka (i.e., diminishing joint venture; *mushārakah mutanāqiṣah*) is another equity-type contract (figure 2.4) that Islamic banks and other for-profit Islamic lenders use often to simulate the economic effects of interest. It is used primarily to construct Islamic mortgages and finance real estate, and less often to finance other fixed assets, such as machinery and

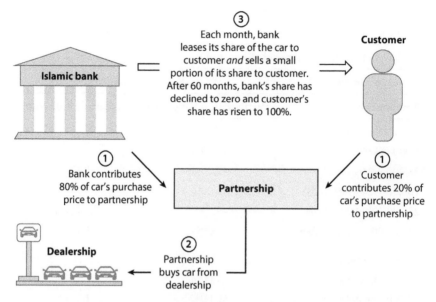

FIGURE 2.4. Auto finance based on diminishing joint venture (diminishing musharaka).

vehicles, as well as in project finance. However, it can also be used in a PLS-style manner. Debates therefore arise about the most Islamically virtuous and social-welfare-enhancing way to execute diminishing musharaka.

To understand diminishing musharaka's typical interest-simulating usage, imagine you are on a quest to finance a Toyota Prius. This book's introduction described lease-based (ijara, figure 0.6) and markup-sale-based (murabaha, figure 0.7) options, but your sales rep at this Islamic bank offers you something different. "We'll form a partnership with you to buy the car jointly," he says. The Islamic bank will put up 80 percent of the $25,000 equity needed to form the partnership. You will put up the remaining 20 percent, or $5,000. You and the bank will buy the car together from the Toyota dealership and become co-owners, with the bank owning 80 percent of the car at first. But since you will be the only one using the car, the Islamic bank will then lease its share of the car to you on a monthly basis. It will also sell you a small portion of its share of the car every month. Thus, diminishing musharaka is like a hybrid of lease-based financing and sale-based financing. Each month, your payment to the bank will remain steady, but the portion of this that counts as a lease payment will decline as the Islamic bank's ownership share declines, and the portion that counts as a purchase will increase. From an accounting perspective, diminishing musharaka is thus similar to a conventional mortgage, in which the homebuyer's interest payments decline over time as principal payments

increase. By the end of 60 months, you will have bought out the bank's ownership stake in the car, and it will be entirely yours.

From an economic perspective, the Islamic bank's auto financing is very
similar to a conventional interest-based auto financing. Even though musharaka is an equity-type partnership contract, the partnership here does not
exist to invest in a business venture that will pay unknown future returns. Instead, it exists to "invest" in a "venture" that will produce returns known in
advance: your use of the Prius.

People that side with the shariah scholars find diminishing musharaka
shariah-compliant and therefore fully Islamic. Their primary concern is that the
bank complies with all its responsibilities under Islamic law. One major responsibility is paying for insurance: as in the lease-based auto financing, the bank as
lessor must cover losses—prorated for its ownership percentage at a given
time—associated with theft, natural disaster, and defects. The Islamic bank
passes on the cost of insurance by raising the customer's monthly payments. To
shariah scholars, this is irrelevant to the virtuousness of the product. Moreover,
the bank may not charge a penalty if the customer decides to buy out the bank's
share (i.e., pay off the remaining balance) earlier than planned. This is particularly germane in the case of mortgages, since many secular jurisdictions allow
mortgage financiers to charge hefty prepayment penalties.

Indeed, if one is legally minded, diminishing musharaka does look quite different from a conventional interest-based financing or mortgage. An attorney at
a UK-headquartered firm found diminishing musharaka–based mortgages so
unique that they could appeal to non-Muslims interested in ethical finance:

> It is very clear that a Diminishing Musharaka mortgage is very different from
> a conventional mortgage and not just a "window-dressing" exercise as
> claimed by its detractors. . . . [P]erhaps Diminishing Musharaka is a "fairer"
> product for the customer (not taking into account pricing considerations)
> in contrast with conventional mortgages and as a consequence there may be
> a market for such products among the ethical non-Muslim market.[41]

To many moral economists, however, the interest-simulating form of diminishing musharaka is just more mimicry of conventional finance.[42] They
find it as problematic as financing based on murabaha (markup sale) or lease
(ijara) because it simulates a predetermined stream of interest payments. Used
thus, diminishing musharaka reproduces the economic problems associated
with interest-bearing debt: it allows people to spend beyond their means and risk
foreclosure while banks earn a predetermined profit from them.

However, some moral economists also see diminishing musharaka as a promising vehicle for a socially conscious and PLS-oriented type of Islamic finance—
if used the "right" way. One such approach is to make the financing entity a

cooperative, which means profit and loss from the diminishing musharaka part-nership are split between co-op members and the homebuyer. In fact, diminish-ing musharaka was invented as a form of nonprofit cooperative financing. In the late 1970s, a group of Muslim immigrants in Canada found themselves unable to buy homes because they did not want to take an interest-bearing mortgage. At the same time, Canadian landlords were hesitant to rent to them, partly because many had large families.[43] One member of this community, Pervez Nasim, es-tablished a co-operative in 1980 that implemented diminishing musharaka as a solution. Anyone can become a member of the co-op by purchasing a member-ship for $75 and at least six shares a year for $100 each. Members include pro-spective homebuyers, parents and grandparents investing for their children, charitable foundations that want to support riba-free community finance, and others investing for a halal return. Members who want to buy a home begin by making a down-payment-like investment. But unlike with a conventional mort-gage, this payment must remain in the general fund pool for six months before the co-op will acquire a home on their behalf. "We help one another. It's not just 'me, me, me—I have this money, so give me a house right away,'" Nasim explains, stressing the cooperative's preference for patient, solidaristic capital.[44] Then, the homebuyer moves in and begins paying rent to the co-op while buying more membership shares to pay the principal down eventually to zero. Today, Nasim's Ansar Financial and Development Corporation is a flourishing "real utopia" in the language of Erik Olin Wright;[45] it finances riba-free property acquisition all over Canada. Strikingly, Nasim's innovation was not inspired by moral econo-mists, shariah scholars, or the Islamic banks just emerging in the Middle East in the late 1970s (though it did receive a fatwa of shariah-compliance from the in-ternationally elite shariah scholar Taqi Usmani in 1989) but simply by the need for a practical solution to his immigrant community's problems.[46]

In sum, diminishing musharaka shows that what is technically an equity-type partnership contract can behave very differently in the hands of different users, and that it can manifest different ethical visions in each case.

The Shariah Scholars in Historical Perspective

The fiqh-centric vision of the shariah scholars, in contrast to the social-welfarist vision of the moral economists and "real utopian" innovators like Pervez Nasim, approached the Islamization of finance as first and foremost a problem of facilitating individual compliance: specifically, compliance with juristic decisions interpreted through the lens of premodern "Islamic merchant ethics." Fiqh-minded Muslims look to classically trained jurists as authoritative arbiters of what kind of activity counts as Islamically virtuous or permissible. Islamic jurists' influence in society shrank in most Muslim-majority societies through the nineteenth century and the first half of the twentieth, largely due to processes of state formation that eroded their autonomy. However, in a few places, particularly Saudi Arabia, classically trained jurists continued to have significant moral authority. The vast majority of these jurists had no background in economics, and they did not theorize a modern Islamic economic *system* the way the neorevivalists did. Instead, they focused on helping Muslims seek virtue and eschew vice through adherence to classical Islamic law in individual transactions. In the fiqh-centric conception of Islamically virtuous finance, pious Muslims focus on avoiding sins: most importantly riba, *maysir* (unlawful speculation), *gharar* (uncertainty in contract), and investment in prohibited sectors such as alcohol and pork. Whether sin-avoidance will transform existing configurations of power in society is of secondary concern, or of no concern at all. This fiqh-centric view of finance had long roots and particularly widespread credence in Saudi Arabia, as evinced by the persistence there of moneychanging houses, which functioned as an interest-free, shariah-compliant alternative to banks for huge portions of the Saudi population well into the late twentieth century.

The mechanics of interest-simulating debt-based instruments approved by shariah scholars—but often criticized by moral economists—are described in different parts of this book as they appear in context. Chapter 1 describes murabaha and its quick ascent in the 1970s and 1980s into the most popular contract in Islamic finance. Chapter 3 touches on ijara (lease-based) financing. Chapter 5 explains how sukuk ("Islamic bonds") work, and chapter 6 discusses tawarruq ("cashification"), a very common yet controversial contract that simulates unsecured interest-bearing loans. But why do shariah scholars certify these products as shariah-compliant when they simulate interest-bearing loans? While some critics interpret their certification as a capitulation of Islamic ethics to capital, I argue that these shariah scholars are defending an Aristotelian-scholastic critique of modern interest-based finance. The Aristotelian-scholastic view differs radically in its conceptions of credit and usury from the conventional capitalist economic view, and hence arguably holds the kernel of a fiqh-centric critique of modern capitalism. But at the same time, the scholars' Aristotelian-scholastic perspective can align with the interests of contemporary capitalist financial firms.

The Aristotelian-Scholastic Critique of Usury in Abrahamic Sacred Law

The shariah scholars are religious jurists, or experts in religious jurisprudence: the science and philosophy of religious law. They have historically had counterparts in the other Abrahamic religions. In Judaism, the religious jurists are the halakhists: sages and scholars versed in the Torah, the Talmud, and other sources of Jewish law (*halakhah*). In Christianity, they are the canonists (i.e., specialists in canon law), and specifically, in the medieval era, scholastic jurists and often also theologians. In Islam, they are the *fuqaha*: experts in fiqh.[47]

In premodern Judaism, Islam, and Christianity, scholastic jurists theorized and systematized religious law and ethics with previously unknown sophistication. They became the dominant theorists of economic ethics, including usury and just price. And in all three faiths, the scholastics shifted religious conceptions of usury dramatically from the simple conceptions that came before they arrived. Instead of understanding usury primarily as a failure of generosity, especially by the rich toward the poor, these scholastics conceived of it first and foremost as a defective and perverse *transaction*, regardless of the partners involved. To the scholastics, sin inhered not only in the unvirtuous actor (the wealthy and exploitative moneylender) or the consequences for the borrower (immiseration and tyranny under debt) but in the act of usury itself.

Rooted in an Aristotelian epistemology of finance, the scholastic analysis of usury is strikingly similar in Judaism, Islam, and Christianity. It has two interrelated planks. First, scholastics consider usury a violation of *commutative justice* because it involves taking something for nothing: effectively, theft (a deontological argument). Christian scholastics define usury explicitly as theft,[48] while Jewish and Islamic scholastics define it as something akin to theft. "It is a sin against justice, to take money . . . in return for lending money," writes Aquinas.[49] Likewise, the canonical Ḥanafī juristic commentary *Kanz al-Daqā'iq* defines usury as "a surplus of commodity without counter-value in a commutative transaction of property for property."[50]

The first plank of scholastic usury theory depends on the second: the Aristotelian belief that money is merely a medium of exchange, not a commodity with its own use-value. According to the Aristotelian-scholastic view, one may reasonably charge rent for lending assets with use-value: a plot of land that produces wheat, a horse that tills fields. But charging rent for money—sterile metal that produces nothing—violates money's natural function (a natural-law argument). "Money was intended to be used in exchange, but not to increase at interest," Aristotle explains.[51] Aquinas makes the same point,[52] as does al-Ghazālī.[53] The Talmudic analysis of usury is likewise profoundly Aristotelian.[54]

For readers accustomed to interest-based finance, it may be hard to grasp that taking interest on a loan could seem like an abhorrent violation of nature, especially when borrower and lender freely enter into it. Yet medieval subjects saw usury as something akin to incest: horribly perverse even if mutually agreed upon. Indeed, humans only came to view money as a tradable commodity after considerable socioeconomic upheaval. "Our" present-day view that money is a commodity, and that interest rates represent the "natural" price of it in a self-regulating market, is in fact a historical aberration.[55]

Scholastic Views of Money Survive in Islamic Finance

Today, the Aristotelian-scholastic epistemology of finance lives on in Islamic finance. Mufti Taqi Usmani, perhaps the most influential living shariah scholar in the world of Islamic finance, insists in his *Introduction to Islamic Finance* that money is not a commodity. After all, money "has no intrinsic utility" and "cannot be utilized for fulfilling human needs directly."[56] Islam, writes Usmani, therefore "does not recognize money as a subject-matter of trade."[57] Asif Iftikhar, a scholar of classical Islamic law and former shariah advisor to a large Pakistani bank, explains what this means for finance in terms reminiscent of Marx's *Capital*, volume 2. "When you charge a predetermined increment on circulating capital and not fixed capital, it's riba." Following the Aristotelian-scholastic line, he stresses that "the issue [with riba] in the Quran ... is the injustice!"[58] "*Lā tazlimūna wa lā tuzlamūn*," he continues, invoking the Quranic injunction on riba that states, "Deal not unjustly [by demanding more than your capital sums], and you shall not be dealt with unjustly [by receiving less than your capital sums]."[59]

Crucially, in the Aristotelian-scholastic view, riba's injustice cannot be measured by its social consequences. This is where it parts ways with the moral economists' assertion that "truly Islamic" or the "most Islamic" finance should advance social welfare by distributing risk to those with the means to bear it. Echoing Aristotle's famous distinction in the *Nicomachean Ethics*,[60] Iftikhar responds by arguing that riba violates commutative justice, not distributive justice. Riba is immanent in the transaction of interest itself, not in its consequences. Like failing to tell a used-car buyer about serious engine problems, a transaction stained with riba is prima facie immoral and Islamically unlawful, regardless of the relative socioeconomic position of the parties or the financial risk borne by each. The moral economists take too many liberties when interpreting scripture, Iftikhar insists:

> The whole field of Islamic finance has been diverted by the failure to look at the reasoning behind the prohibition of riba, which is not [the promotion of] risk-sharing. When modern spectacles are used to make modern analyses of [sacred] texts, we may come up with politically correct statements, but in the academic world, the analysis has to be far more rigorous.[61]

In this regard, scholastic riba is somewhat like child labor (as many people see it): regardless of consequences or consent, it is exploitative the moment it happens. And just as with child labor, laws must draw a sharp qualitative line between what does and does not constitute the unjust act. Such lines, such as setting sixteen as the minimum age for non-agricultural labor in the United States or zero percent as the maximum ethical interest rate, may seem arbitrary. But they establish necessary qualitative distinctions of exploitative and non-exploitative acts.

The idea that interest is fundamentally unnatural and transactionally unjust—and not only a transgression of divine command—has broad cultural credence in some societies, grounded in widespread popular sentiments about legitimate and illegitimate gain. Many Pakistanis, for example, find interest abhorrent not only because God prohibits it but because it involves earning a return without doing work or having "skin in the game." Anam, a thirty-eight-year-old conservatively dressed middle-class store clerk I interviewed in Karachi, did not know the word *riba*. When asked to define interest—sood (*sūd*), an Urdu word with strong negative connotations in Pakistan—she replied, "Well, it's earning money on money."[62] But she continued, "You know, it's when you get a return without doing any work."[63] Hamza, a twenty-three-year-old recent engineering graduate in Karachi hunting for a job, said, "Sood is wrong. It's anything extra on a deposit. And it's wrong to get [money] for free without putting in labor."[64] Zain, a pious forty-eight-year-old working-class guesthouse custodian who used to work at a bank, understood sood as the absence of both work and the shared liability for loss that characterizes equity partnerships:

> MY INTERVIEWER: Do you know what riba is?
> ZAIN: I've heard of it, but I'm not sure what it is.
> MY INTERVIEWER: What about sood?
> ZAIN: Sood is haram. It's when you get money without doing any work.
> RC: What about stocks, then?
> ZAIN: Well, they're good for the country.
> RC: But don't you earn money from stocks without doing any work?
> ZAIN (not missing a beat): Stocks are different because they involve risk. They could go up to one hundred or go down to zero.[65]

In sum, Islamic finance does not exist only because God prohibits interest (a divine-command logic) but because scholastic Islamic law preserves a conception of money and finance entirely different from the prevailing modern capitalist conception (a natural-law logic). The Aristotelian-scholastic epistemology of finance therefore necessitates a separate Islamic-finance industry.

The Scholastic Jurists: Preserving the Usury Ban while Accommodating Capitalism

Despite abhorring usury, scholastic jurists have always been central to devising contracts that resolve the conflicting value-orientations of capitalism and salvation religions. In Judaism, Christianity, and Islam alike, they preserved the usury ban as an inviolable tenet of religious doctrine while also authorizing legal innovations that accommodated capitalist financial needs. Most often, these innovations compensated providers of capital for investment risk in a time-dependent manner through the use of partnerships, asset sales, leases, and currency exchanges instead of loans. Scholastic debates about usury, and the resulting accommodations to premodern financial needs, were strikingly similar in premodern Jewish, Christian, and Islamic law. In all three legal traditions, for example, scholastic jurists authorized similar contractual structures to simulate the economic effects of interest-bearing loans: higher prices for credit sales than spot sales, bills of exchange, antichresis (sale and leaseback), and pawnbroking.[66]

From a modern economic perspective, these innovations appear to have constituted usury by another name.[67] Max Weber noted that economic needs may "make themselves manifest" through "casuistic by-passing" of sacred commandments.[68] In medieval Christendom, for example, "the prohibitions against usury generated legalistic circumventions of all sorts."[69]

Yet from the scholastic perspective, these solutions did not merely cloak the wolf of usury in sheep's clothing but identified through legal reasoning where to draw vitally important moral boundaries between good and evil, between natural and unnatural. Medieval scholastic debates were not simply attempts to bypass the spirit of scripture but efforts to plumb scientifically what exactly constitutes usury. Such debates were inseparable from other proto-economic investigations into the ontology and epistemology of markets: into the nature of money, credit, trade, prices, and wealth.[70] At the same time, debates about usury were profoundly moralized. For as Ebrahim Moosa observes, "[Muslim] legal theorists were primarily interested in formulating a legal-moral epistemology. This was accomplished by marshaling proofs for the various forms of rational discourse. It is through reason that one discovers what is good or bad."[71]

In fact, such debates about markets—simultaneously probing the nature of economic objects, their morality in social context, and their legal status—are not foreign to the modern condition. Life insurance, as Viviana Zelizer has shown, aroused considerable angst in the nineteenth-century United States, as it seemed to wager on human life.[72] Was it gambling, and therefore both immoral and illegal, or caring provision for the future needs of loved ones? Financial derivatives likewise suffered from definitional ambiguity—legal, moral, and economic—impeding their trading on exchanges in the United States until the 1980s.[73] Thus, the intertwining of legal, moral, and economic categories so characteristic of scholastic thought has not disappeared. Instead, it lives on in modern classification conundrums.[74] Like life insurance and derivatives, interest had to undergo a similar transvaluation for liberal credit markets and modern debt-based capitalism to become hegemonic.[75] Islamic finance attempts to roll back the clock on this transvaluation, questioning what the modern economic subject considers ineluctable laws of financial nature.

Islamic Derivatives: Dodgy or Essential?

A majority of Islamic jurists today, and the vast majority involved with Islamic finance, consider most conventional derivatives not to be shariah-compliant. Their objections typically center on transactional ambiguity (*gharar*) and gambling (*maysir*). Consider the most common types of derivatives: forwards, futures, options, and swaps. Jurists deem these contracts laden with ambiguity because the counterparties involved often cannot say with absolutely certainty that they will possess the assets slated for exchange, in agreed-upon condition, at the future date specified in the contract. Jurists also find most derivatives Islamically unlawful for other reasons too: interest-rate swaps, for example, violate the ban on riba. To make matters worse, there has historically been a subset of shariah scholars who do not understand derivatives and see them only as murky financial time bombs. In an amusing anecdote, Islamic financial engineer Humayon Dar described once proposing to a shariah board an Islamic hedge fund that used Islamic derivatives extensively. "I was so surprised," Dar recalls. "They didn't ask any tough questions. They just nodded, smiled, and said 'this is great!'" Unfortunately for Dar, the shariah scholars' goodwill evaporated when they realized he was saying "hedge fund," not "hajj [pilgrimage] fund."[76]

Despite their dodgy reputation among many shariah scholars and in the non-financial press, derivatives are used not just for speculation but very often to hedge against risk and diversify it. Commodity producers such as farmers and commodity users such as airlines use them to hedge against price fluctuations and exchange-rate fluctuations beyond their control. Shariah experts and academics such as Mohammad Hashim Kamali, Obiyathulla Ismath Bacha, Asyraf Wajdi Dusuki, and Muhammad al-Bashir Muhammad Al-Amine have therefore argued that certain conventional derivatives, if used only for hedging real-economy transactions instead of for speculation or leveraging, can reduce gharar and protect against the harm caused by speculation, and hence should be considered shariah-compliant.[77]

Efforts to distinguish between Islamically legitimate and illegitimate uses of derivatives raise thorny questions. "The whole concept of derivatives is a question mark [from a shariah perspective]," notes Sultan Al Nugali, who specializes in shariah-compliant asset management in Saudi Arabia. "Are they using [derivatives] for speculation or for hedging? And how are they useful for companies? For individuals?"[78] For example, is it acceptable for a shariah-compliant institution to engage in a derivative transaction, for hedging purposes, with a non-shariah-compliant counterparty (such as a conventional investment bank) if it does not know whether the counterparty is hedging or speculating? More generally, to what extent are Islamic financial institutions responsible for the actions of their counterparties? Such questions highlight the difficulties of applying of

Islamic merchant ethics in twenty-first-century financial markets that are dominated by sophisticated non-shariah-compliant institutions. The challenge for
Islamic financial institutions is that they cannot ring-fence and isolate themselves from conventional financial flows.

In sum, moral economists and others in the welfarist-economistic camp see
derivatives today much as most conventional economists do: as a powerful
tool that can be used for good or bad, requiring creativity and monitoring.
Shariah scholars and practitioners in the pragmatic-juristic camp, meanwhile,
are coming around fast to the possibility that derivatives can be shariah-
compliant. In particular, the handful of "rock-star" shariah scholars who sit on
dozens of shariah boards and regularly monitor transactions worth millions
of dollars are increasingly well-versed in the mind-boggling financial and legal
mechanics of shariah-compliant derivatives such as currency swaps and rate
swaps. According to some practitioners, these elite scholars are careful not to
approve shariah-compliant derivatives likely to be used for speculation or
other purposes widely considered un-Islamic. Richard Tredgett, a derivatives
expert and partner at law firm Allen & Overy who has worked extensively with
shariah scholars, makes this point:

> Scholars—certainly the more well-known ones that I've dealt with—do actu-
> ally question what is the ultimate purpose of the transaction. "What are you
> trying to achieve by putting in this type of structure?"—you know. So if it's
> funding the construction of a factory or funding the acquisition of a business
> or real estate they can understand that and they'll see the benefit of that, why
> people are doing it. But if it's a hedge fund, then they're sort of thinking, "Ok,
> I'll set this fund up, and I'll invest in some financial instruments, and do some
> short selling and I'll do this and do that"—and the scholars will say, "Hang on,
> what has that got to do with ethical or shariah-compliant financing?"[79]

Yet in some cases, innovation in shariah-compliant derivatives seems to
have pushed the boundaries of what could reasonably be called Islamic, leading to bouts of contention in the industry. The introduction of a derivative
known as the Islamic total return swap, discussed further in chapter 6, was a
dramatic example.

Christian and Jewish Finance Today as
Comparative Cases

To appreciate the importance of the scholastic analysis of usury in facilitating
modern religious finance, we can consider two comparative cases: the Christian and the Jewish. As discussed above, both medieval Christian and medieval
Jewish scholastic jurists theorized usury along Aristotelian lines. Yet between

the sixteenth and nineteenth centuries, the Aristotelian-scholastic analysis of usury disappeared from Christianity and became radically attenuated in Judaism. Today, therefore, there is no specialized Christian-finance industry or Jewish-finance industry on nearly the scale of Islamic finance.

How the Scholastic Usury Ban Disappeared from Christianity

The Aristotelian-scholastic epistemology of finance was a mighty centerpiece of medieval Western Christian thought,[80] but today it is absent from Christian doctrine and practice. It disappeared gradually from Christian concern along two routes: the Protestant and the Roman Catholic.

One decisive factor in the Protestant case, and eventually also the Roman Catholic, was the decline of religious jurists. Martin Luther despised religious jurists, calling them enemies of Christ and saying no jurist should speak "until he hears a pig fart."[81] He blamed them for authorizing circumventions of the usury ban's spirit, especially the Zinskauf land rents, which were sucking the German peasantry dry.[82] After Luther, scholastic jurists played a lesser role in Protestantism than they continued to do in Roman Catholicism for another two centuries, and legalistic accommodations of the sort found in medieval Christianity, Judaism, and Islam disappeared.

Another decisive factor in the Protestant case was John Calvin's reinterpretation of usury itself.[83] To him, usury meant not simply what we today consider interest but only interest that harmed the borrower. Surrounded by the bankers of Geneva, he also accepted that interest could have positive social consequences. Calvin thus shifted from a formal rationality of usury to a substantive one, opening the door to a gradual reconceptualization of usury in terms of harm caused—harm that could be theorized, as it was by Bentham[84] and Adam Smith,[85] and regulated in secular terms—rather than in terms of Aristotelian-scholastic natural-law conceptions.[86]

In the Roman Catholic case, usury never experienced an explicit redefinition of the sort Calvin enacted, but instead, permissible exceptions to the rule grew so large that they eventually justified what we today call interest. The term "interest" itself stems from id quod interest: in Roman law, "that which I have lost and would have gained."[87]

Following this logic, medieval Latin scholastics delineated "extrinsic titles": justifications for charging interest. Extrinsic titles were based on the idea of commutative justice: the notion that a lender, even if not profiting from a loan, should not suffer losses. Common medieval extrinsic titles included damnum emergens, charges to compensate for the expenses associated with lending, such as a charitable lender's operating costs; poena conventionalis, a late payment penalty, charged as a percentage of the principal, to compensate for losses and inconvenience caused by the lateness; and *lucrum cessans*, payment to compensate for opportunities the lender missed to invest elsewhere.[88] Aquinas recognized some extrinsic titles, but by around 1600, they had expanded to absorb new, modern conceptualizations of the time value of money: the Flemish Jesuit jurist Leonardus Lessius, observing the Antwerp Bourse, noted that exchange bankers "value more the lack of their money for five months than the lack of it for four."[89]

Eventually, these various Catholic exceptions came to justify most of what today is considered interest, and though the usury ban remained part of Roman Catholic doctrine until 1917, it was a dead letter by the eighteenth century.

"Christian Finance" Today: A Small Market for Funds Avoiding Abortion and Stem-Cell Research

Because the scholastic analysis of usury disappeared from Christianity, no robust Christian-finance sector analogous to Islamic finance can be said to exist. Five types of entities could hypothetically be candidates to carry the mantle.

The first comprises "Christian-affiliated" financial institutions: those founded by Christian churches or their members, owned by them, or targeting them as customers—but not practicing finance differently from "secular" financial institutions. This includes banks and credit unions (e.g., United Methodist Federal Credit Union) and mutual and fraternal insurance providers (e.g., Catholic Financial Life). But saying these organizations practice Christian finance would be akin to saying St. Jude's Hospital practices "Christian medicine."

The second encompasses "Christian financial counseling": small for-profit and nonprofit groups worldwide that offer Christian credit counseling, "biblical wealth management" and tax advice,[90] Christian life coaching for business owners, and spiritual support groups for Christian entrepreneurs.[91] Such organizations advocate some combination of thrift, charity, spiritual rebirth, hard work, giving to churches, and commonsense planning (e.g., "identify what you value most in life"; "set 1-, 3-, 5-, and 10-year goals") by invoking Christian scripture, values, and spiritual power. Prosperity-gospel ministries, also part of this group, assert that donors will reap manifold financial returns.[92] Again, however, calling such activity "Christian finance" seems questionable, as charity, donation, saving, and sound financial management hardly constitute a unique mode of finance. Analogous Islamic organizations, of which there are many, do not claim to practice Islamic finance.

The third category contains "gospel-spreading" Christian welfare organizations: financial charities and microfinance institutions that incorporate proselytization and Bible studies into their outreach (e.g., HOPE International, a Christian microfinance provider). Here, the connection between religion and finance is stronger.[93] However, this sector remains very small: the net global portfolio of such organizations is likely well under US$1 billion.

Church bonds and church loans constitute a fourth group.[94] The case for calling them "Christian finance" is reasonably strong given that spiritual interests often motivate investors to fund churches' construction, operation, or renovation, and that marketing for church bonds often includes religious themes. However, church financing occupies a minuscule part of the financial landscape and in practical terms does not differ from other modes of finance.

Finally, we find Christian investment funds, which do effectively constitute "Christian finance." These comprise mutual funds, exchange-traded funds, and other investment vehicles that apply Christian investment criteria. Just like Islamic investment funds, they apply negative sector screens, which depend on denomination—such as Roman Catholic, Lutheran, Presbyterian, Southern Baptist, Mennonite/Anabaptist, and Christian Scientist—and ideological orientation. Most avoid companies connected to abortion, contraception, stem-cell research, alcohol, tobacco, gambling, and arms. Some follow investing guidelines established by institutional bodies such as the United States Conference of Catholic Bishops[95] and German Bishops' Conference[96]—a clear parallel to Islamic funds' reliance on shariah scholars.

Yet the market for Christian investment funds is tiny compared to the size of Islamic finance, which is composed mostly of Islamic banking and the sukuk market: sectors based mostly on interest simulation, not equity investment. Christian investment funds totaled approximately US$30–40 billion worldwide in net assets under management as of February 2017,[97] or about half the total for Islamic investment funds worldwide, around US$65–70 billion in early 2017. However, Christian investment funds worldwide are a paltry 1.2 to 1.6 percent the size of Islamic finance, which comprised around US$2.5 trillion in worldwide assets in the same year.

"Jewish Finance" Today: A Piece of Paper on the Wall

Jews were long able—and often forced—to work as moneylenders among gentiles because early Jewish sources felt Deuteronomy's prohibition of lending "upon usury to thy brother" allowed Jews to take interest from gentiles.[98] Nonetheless, Jews still had trouble lending to one another profitably. Halakhic scholarship explored this problem in tremendous depth.

Like their Roman Catholic and Islamic counterparts, Halakhic jurists from the second to the sixteenth century developed a wide range of accommodations. These included allowing advance payments for goods, credit sales at a higher price than the cash price, and antichresis—"indirect usury" paid by pledging land as collateral for a loan, with the land's usufruct substituting for interest.[99] Sometimes, the diasporic condition and religious persecution made such accommodations imperative.[100]

These accommodations could have served as the basis for a modern Jewish-finance industry much like the Islamic, except one accommodation became so popular that it effectively obviated the need for a separate system of Jewish finance. This contract, the *heter iska*, acts like an interest-bearing loan but is technically a partnership.[101] (Today's Islamic banks structure their savings accounts and term deposits somewhat similarly.)[102] It emerged in late sixteenth-century Poland, as growing long-distance trade networks among Jewish merchants necessitated inter-Jewish credit mechanisms. Although initially controversial among some rabbis, it became a widespread boilerplate contract among European Jews by the seventeenth century.[103] In the nineteenth century, Eastern European rabbis began approving a variation known as the "general" *heter iska*[104] that, once written into a bank's bylaws or publicized in all the town's synagogues, ensured all interest-bearing "loans" in the bank or town were actually partnerships.[105] Today, every Israeli bank operates under a *heter iska*, sometimes found hanging on the wall.

In sum, a "Jewish-finance" industry does exist today to satisfy Orthodox Jews who concern themselves with halakhic observance in their economic lives. However, it has become generalized and standardized into a transparent wrapper around the "secular" banking industry in Israel.[106]

The Ethics of Usury, Marx's Formulas for Capital, and Performance Circuits

How can we understand this chapter's material with regard to the historical development of capitalism? While a detailed treatment is impossible here, it is worth highlighting a connection to Marxist and neo-Marxist formulas for capitalist exchange. In volume 1 of *Capital*, Marx describes various ways in which commodities and money can circulate.[107] As shorthand, he abbreviates money as M, more money as M,' and commodities as C. In premodern economies, some common forms of exchange were barter (C–C, where one commodity is exchanged for another), trade mediated by money (C–M–C), and usury (M–M'). To premodern economic subjectivities, such as those of Aristotle and medieval scholastics in the Abrahamic traditions, usury appeared as a fundamentally strange use of money: a way in which money would multiply itself incomprehensibly and without justification. From a modern perspective, it can be hard to wrap one's head around this "problem" with interest. To some economic historians, Aristotle's perception was based on an error: a mistaken belief that money's value inhered in the materiality of gold and silver specie. However, it was also because the M–M' circuit represented a ghoulish "second world" in which value seemed to multiply on its own, independent of any mediation by a commodity C, simply starting with money and ending with more money. Jacques Le Goff and David Hawkes, writing about medieval continental Europe and Elizabethan England, respectively, show just how macabre and loathsome usury seemed to premodern and early modern sensibilities, to the point where artists and theologians depicted in the most gruesome terms what fate awaited usurers upon their deaths—and what hate premoderns harbored even for priests who gave usurers last rites.[108] Usurers were not just exploitative people; they were practically non-human: aliens from another planet who threatened the existence of everything normal about economic life. Even the emergence of increasingly widespread credit markets in early modern Europe did not stanch this feeling that usury was bizarrely otherworldly, as Hawkes shows; it only exacerbated the problem.

With the rise of industrial capitalism, usury still had its detractors and those who advocated controlling its level, but the sense that it was incomprehensibly unnatural disappeared. Rather, it came to be understood simply as lending at interest, with that interest being a compensation for the other uses to which money could be put instead of sitting idle. If an interest rate was too high, perhaps it was greedy or pernicious, but the idea of interest itself was not macabre.

Consider the formula for industrial capitalist production: M–C–M'. Typically, theorists of capitalism focus on the surplus value extracted by the capitalist, which is (M' minus M). But when we juxtapose M–C–M' next to M–M', the formula for usury (i.e., lending at interest), we see that the cognitive leap from the former to the latter is not so great as from C–M–C to M–M'. In both M–C–M' and M–M', a capitalist begins with money and ends with more money. Indeed, there is an application of labor involved even in M–M' when it takes the form of modern banking, for banks require employees to operate them.

Today, then, we might think of the two ethical stances toward Islamic finance as the same solution to two different "problems." To the moral economists, with their economic stance, the biggest problem with usury—aside from the fact that God prohibits it—is that it generates social inequality. In this regard, (M' minus M), which is the surplus extracted by bankers when they lend money, accrues unfairly to them and sucks money from productive investment, which operates according to M–C–M'. The difference (M' minus M) is *too large*; it is too easy to make without the application of a lot of labor; it is "unearned"—a phrase that, as we saw, many ordinary consumers still use to describe why usury is wrong. But by this viewpoint, interest simulation—which inserts a commodity into transactions to "solve" the problem of usury—does nothing to diminish that difference (M' minus M).

To the scholastics, on the other hand, inserting a commodity is tremendously important from an ethical perspective. It reorganizes transactions to avoid the inherent repugnance of usury. It removes financial affairs from that ghoulish, macabre second world, one as utterly loathsome and foreign to explicable, proper human function as incest—an analogy that both Islamic scholastic and Christian scholastic sources drew. To say to a scholastic that interest simulation is just as unethical as interest because it "merely reproduces" the economic effects of interest is like saying that sleeping with someone who looks very much like your parent or sibling is just as unethical as sleeping with your parent or sibling. Once we grasp that deep and visceral difference, and view it not as an incomprehensible taboo specific to Islam but as the extension of what was once a very widespread logic of money—a logic that was only displaced globally by the spread of industrial capitalism—only then can we truly understand Islamic finance from the scholars' perspective. We enter what Fred Wherry has described as the "performance circuit" of an economic transaction: the space in which participants share cultural scripts and worldviews that allow them to make sense of a transaction in the same way, understanding it as one thing (a legitimately pious and ethical avoidance of something as viscerally awful as usury) and not another (usury dressed up in different clothes).[109]

Conclusion: The Moral Economists' Social Welfarism and the Shariah Scholars' Scholasticism

Chapter 1 presented a global historical sociology of the rise and spread of capitalist Islamic finance. This chapter has introduced a comparative perspective, but one that compares "in terms of new scales, units, and objects" besides the cross-national.[110] We have seen two ethical stances toward religiously embedded finance presented in this chapter. The first, which I call the *economic* or *social-welfarist* stance, is represented by the moral economists and their predecessors, who since the early twentieth century have envisioned an interest-free Islamic economic system as a road to anticolonial and postcolonial liberation from European, and later Euro-American, financial suzerainty. Although some contemporary Islamic economists take a neoliberal approach, and today's moral economists may not be as utopian as their predecessors in the 1970s and 1980s who aligned more closely with Islamist movements like the Jamaat-e-Islami, the intellectual thrust of the moral-economy movement in Islamic finance remains oriented toward the notion of building a cohesive, welfare-increasing, morality-maximizing Islamic economy—as opposed to focusing on individual transactions and their shariah-compliance. This stance is "economic" in a double sense. First, it focuses on building an Islamic *economy* in the sense of a system that includes Islamic labor, Islamically run firms, and Islamic government economic policy, not just a collection of halal sectors that adhere to Islamic law. Second, it considers an Islamic financial system that does not alter the economic consequences of usury hardly Islamic at all.

The moral economists sought to instantiate their vision largely by encouraging the implementation of profit-and-loss-sharing (PLS), which relies on equity-type partnership instruments roughly similar to mutual funds and private equity. However, as this chapter showed, Islamic banks have reconfigured these equity-type instruments to simulate conventional interest-bearing debt instruments. Islamic banks thus limit the risk and liability they face, allowing them to act—and be regulated by the state—much more like conventional banks. Yet this subverts the moral economists' goals of building a PLS-based Islamic economy and of radically reducing the role of debt in finance.

The second ethical stance, which I call *scholastic*, is instantiated by today's shariah scholars. It has its roots in the premodern Aristotelian view of usury, which portrays lending at interest not only as harmful to unfortunates and to social welfare but also as a transactionally unjust and fundamentally unnatural use of money. This Aristotelian conception was shared and extended by premodern Jewish halakhists, Christian canonists, and shariah scholars. As shown briefly here, and in more detail elsewhere,[111] all three of these premodern groups of scholastic intellectuals developed sophisticated legal theories of finance and endorsed (with a fair amount of internal debate) various types of accommodations similar to the interest simulation employed in the contemporary Islamic-finance industry. One crucial lesson is therefore that contemporary scholar-authorized interest simulation in Islamic finance has a lot of historical precedent in the three major Abrahamic religious traditions, even if it was never rationalized, bureaucratized, and applied with high-tech infrastructure the way it is in contemporary Islamic finance. Another lesson is that it has always been controversial and debated. A third important lesson is simply to understand that there is a fundamentally different premodern conception of money. As we will see at the end of this book, this difference is important because it serves as the kernel of "scholastic modernity" in Islamic finance: the way of being a financial subject that involves embracing and learning the shariah scholars' understanding of money and shariah.

3

Profitability

HOW DOES Islamic finance manage to be convincingly Islamic to millions of Muslims, yet profitable for capitalists and able to grow fast in capitalist markets? This chapter's first section, "Practice," illustrates the importance of interest simulation and shows how some of the most common Islamic financial instruments simulate interest. Even though industry shariah scholars sign off on these products, they are not without controversy; this section opens the technical "black box" to show how each of these common products remains a small universe of legal and philosophical contestation among industry commentators and stakeholders.

Scholarly approval of profitable interest-simulating products goes a long way toward explaining why Islamic finance has grown internationally, but as any business owner can attest, merely having the right products does not guarantee business success. The second section, "Three Feedback Loops," goes beyond products to identify three self-reinforcing tracks that have spurred the dramatic growth of capitalist Islamic finance. Without shariah scholars playing a central role in Islamic finance, none of these loops would function.

Practice

Simulating Interest: An Example

I have had the same conversation dozens of times, often in airplanes. When strangers outside Muslim-majority countries hear that I study Islamic finance, most ask the same question: What makes finance Islamic? I reply that Islamic banks avoid interest because some Muslims consider it sinful. (Islamic banks adhere to other rules too, but I keep these chats simple.) My interlocutor invariably then asks how Islamic banks avoid interest. I first sketch on a cocktail napkin PLS financing methods Islamic banks use that differ widely from conventional banking practices. But I quickly concede that the vast majority of Islamic financings closely approximate the economic effect of conventional interest-bearing financings. Using in-flight snacks as props, I show how Islamic banks combine techniques such as credit sales, lease-to-own contracts, and diminishing partnerships to simulate the economic effect of interest without technically dealing in it. Such products range from Islamic auto financings and mortgages to Islamic bonds and derivatives.

The response is consistent. "So, uh, how is that different from interest?"

Newbies often ask the best questions. How *is* Islamic finance, as currently practiced, different from "conventional" (i.e., non-Islamic) interest-based finance? Let's return to the hypothetical from chapter 2 involving First Islamic Bank: you'd like to buy a Toyota Prius that costs $25,000. You can afford the down payment of $5,000, but you'd like to finance the remaining $20,000. A conventional bank offers you a 60-month loan of $20,000 at an interest rate of 7.00 percent, which works out to 60 monthly payments of $396.02 each. Your 60 payments will total $23,761.20.

However, you'd prefer a shariah-compliant auto financing, so you walk into an Islamic bank, where an employee is happy to explain how the interest-free financing will work (see figure 0.6). "This is called our *ijara* auto financing," the employee says. Ijara (*ijārah*) means "lease" in Arabic. First, you make a security deposit of $5,000 to the bank. The bank then buys your chosen Prius from the Toyota dealership for $25,000. Next, you lease the Prius from the bank for an additional $396.02 per month for a period of 60 months. As in the conventional auto loan, these 60 payments total $23,761.20. Crucially, however, they do not constitute principal plus interest; they are rental payments. In other words, you are not paying off a car loan; you are leasing a car. This difference makes the transaction shariah-compliant in the eyes of the shariah scholars who sit on the bank's shariah board. At the end of the 60-month lease, the bank will give you the Prius as a gift. From the "formal" or contractual perspective of the back office, this lease-based Islamic auto financing is completely different from a conventional interest-based one. All Islamic financing must be linked to real non-financial assets or real non-financial economic activity. Money may only be paid in exchange for a good or a service—in this case, for the right to use the bank's car. Money may not be paid for the right to use money, for the shariah board considers that usury (riba). In the present scenario, the Islamic bank retains the car's title for five years, and you are paying the bank for the right to use its car during that period, not for the right to use its money. To a shariah scholar, this lease is utterly different from an interest-bearing loan.

From a "substantive" or economic viewpoint, however, the Islamic bank's product is very similar to a conventional bank's. In both cases, you are obligated to pay the bank $5,000 up front, and then to make a stream of 60 monthly payments totaling $23,761.20, after which you will have total unencumbered ownership of the car. And just like a conventional bank, the Islamic bank will first levy extra charges on you if you fall behind on payments. Both banks can and will repossess and sell the Prius if you fall too far behind. To an economist, therefore, this lease looks a lot like an interest-bearing loan. Indeed, secular tax laws often treat these types of leases, known as financing leases, like sales bundled with an interest-bearing loan.

Nonetheless, there are some substantive differences between the two product offerings that arise because classical Islamic jurisprudence imposes responsibilities on the lessor—in this case, the Islamic bank. First of all, the Islamic bank's shariah board prohibits the bank from profiting from you if you fall behind in your payments. In their eyes, that would constitute usury. So all late payment charges go to charity. They serve to discipline the customer but not to enrich the bank. Herein lies a clear ethical distinction between Islamic finance and conventional finance.

Moreover, there is the question of what happens if the car becomes inoperable. Islamic jurists agree that as the lessee, you are responsible for expenses associated with *use* of the leased item (e.g., gasoline, replacing worn-out tires, repairs in case of accident) and for any damage caused by negligence (e.g., you let your unlicensed teenager drive the car and she crashes it). However, they hold the lessor (the Islamic bank) responsible for expenses outside your control that are associated with *ownership*. If the car gets stolen, washes away in a flood, gets damaged by an earthquake, or turns out to have been defective from the start, the Islamic bank is on the hook. It must cover repairs or absorb the loss of the car's value and cannot collect lease payments from you while the car is unusable. No conventional bank would accept such liability, but it is precisely this taking of liability that makes the transaction shariah-compliant in the scholars' eyes. So in this regard, lease-based financing seems to differ substantively from a conventional auto loan. And finally, the financing imposes the additional burden on the lessee not to use the car for haram (*ḥarām*; Islamically unlawful) purposes: as a beer-delivery vehicle, for example.

Do these differences really make the lease-based Islamic auto financing ethically distinct from conventional auto financing? It depends whom you ask. Within the community of practitioners and shariah scholars active today in the Islamic-finance industry, lease-based auto financing is universally accepted as shariah-compliant. (Some widespread Islamic products arouse controversy even among a large percentage of industry shariah scholars, as I discuss later in this chapter, but this is not one of them.) In their eyes, dealing in interest is such a great sin that an interest-free auto financing is immeasurably better than an interest-based one, even if their economics are basically the same.

However, other voices inside and outside the industry—most prominently the moral economists—complain that the Islamic version mimics the conventional version too baldly. Many of these critics feel that the fundamental problem with conventional capitalist finance is that it preys on debtors and produces too much debt, which in turn generates social inequality and financial instability. Lease-based auto financing produces debt just as much as conventional interest-bearing auto financing does.

These critics also point to pricing practices. Islamic banks quote the price of lease-based auto financings (and other Islamic financing products) as percentages of the amount of the loan. In the scenario above, the bank would quote you a "7 percent profit rate." By using the term "profit rate" instead of "interest," banks highlight the arrangement's shariah-compliance. Indeed, Islamic banks take pains to avoid the terms "interest" and "loan" in their documentation and marketing. Yet no ordinary auto lease would be marketed as a percentage of the price of the car. Islamic banks present the product's math thus so that customers can comparison-shop against other financing offers, including conventional ones. In theory, this Islamic bank could advertise instead that it will lease you a Toyota Prius for $396.02 per month, but in practice, Islamic banks never do this.

Regardless of one's ethical perspective, the fact is that most Islamic banks today are profit-maximizing institutions competing in capitalist markets against conventional banks. They therefore do what they can to maximize their returns and minimize their liability—within the restrictions established by their shariah boards and state law. Consider, for example, the shariah scholars' aforementioned insistence that the Islamic bank take on liability for the theft of your Prius or its destruction by an act of God. The Islamic bank manages such risks by buying an insurance policy on the Prius and then adding the cost of it to your payments. It is as if a conventional bank required its auto-loan customers to buy comprehensive auto insurance. So while the Islamic bank does take on extra liability, it passes the cost of insuring this liability on to the customer.

Even this arrangement, however, has uniquely "Islamic" consequences. The shariah scholars who work in Islamic finance consider conventional insurance Islamically unlawful. This is because conventional insurance entails making certain premium payments now in exchange for a future payout that may or may not happen. Shariah scholars deem this a form of gharar and somewhat akin to gambling. They also object to conventional insurance because insurance companies invest large portions of their premiums in interest-bearing securities. Hence, the Islamic bank must buy Islamic insurance—known as takaful (*takāful*)—on the Prius.[1]

The example of Islamic auto financing illustrates one of the challenges—and opportunities—facing people who seek to build an Islamic financial system: the interdependence of all financial activity in a modern economy. If the project of Islamic finance is an effort to break free from the moral shortcomings of the conventional financial system and to establish a viable, self-sustaining alternative, practitioners are constantly reminded of the challenges they face.

The Fundamental Rules of Islamic Finance

The shariah board is, today, the consummate institution that makes Islamic finance Islamic. Much as a state shariah court deploys scholarly legitimacy for state ends such as the maintenance of public order, the private shariah board deploys scholarly legitimacy in the interest of capital by issuing fatwas that certify products as shariah-compliant.

Shariah boards focus mostly on enforcing three fundamental rules: the ban on usury, the ban on excessive transactional ambiguity, and the ban on dealing in immoral or dangerous goods and services. These fundamentals are essentially uncontested among industry stakeholders, including shariah scholars from different juristic schools and moral economists. Where individuals differ is on the details of what counts as usury, excessive transactional ambiguity, and immoral goods and services—and on whether there are other evils that the Islamic-finance industry can and should strive to eliminate, and other goods it can and should foster.

BAN ON USURY. The Quran clearly prohibits usury, stating that "Those who devour usury [riba] will not stand except as stand one whom the Evil one by his touch Hath driven to madness."[2] The Prophet Muhammad is alleged to have said that one dirham of usury consumed is more severe a sin than fornicating 36 times, and that even the least of the 72 types of usury is like committing incest with one's mother. Other records cite him as predicting that "there will come a time when there will be no one left who does not consume usury, and whoever does not consume it will nevertheless be affected by its residue."[3] Looking around today and seeing interest-bearing debt everywhere—from the mortgage payments and credit-card balances that bury families to the bond markets that topple governments—it is not hard to conclude that this time has come.[4] Usury-free finance may therefore be what this world needs. Yet what exactly constitutes usury has been debated since almost immediately after the Prophet died in 632 CE. So has the rationale behind the usury ban, and the extent to which humans might be able to divine it.

Today, just as they have done through most of the history of Islam in most places, the majority of Islamic jurists insist that any non-zero level of interest constitutes usury. In the world of Islamic finance, all jurists do. Quite a few shariah-minded Muslim thinkers throughout history have disagreed, saying interest under certain conditions does not constitute usury. And in practice, many Muslims have dealt in interest regardless of juristic opinion.[5] But in the Islamic-finance industry today, the interest ban is unquestioned. It is the industry's primary raison d'être. Shariah scholars therefore ban all interest-bearing products, including conventional loans, bonds, interest-bearing deposit accounts, overdraft products, credit cards, interest-bearing derivatives, and conventional insurance.

BAN ON MAJOR CONTRACTUAL INDETERMINACY AND GAMBLING. The term "gharar" does not appear in the Quran but was applied by early Islamic jurists to refer to a common feature of some activities and transactions, especially sale transactions, prohibited in the Quran and the hadith literature. The word implies risk, speculation, uncertainty, incomplete information, or sometimes deception. "Transactional ambiguity" begins to encompass its various meanings. When such ambiguity rises to a "major" level (*gharar fāḥish*), jurists ban the associated transaction. Thus the prohibition on gharar is often described as a divine injunction that ensures transparency and fair dealing and prevents exploitation and social disharmony in conditions of information asymmetry.

Examples are instructive here. In one hadith, the Prophet enjoins one of his companions: "Do not sell what you do not possess."[6] Likewise, other hadith prohibit selling birds in the sky, fish still in the sea, and escaped slaves. In all of these cases, the seller cannot guarantee that she will control an asset at the future moment when she will be obligated to transfer it to the buyer, or that it will be in sound condition.[7] Gharar can also arise when one or more transacting parties lack knowledge about the existence, genus, quantity, or other relevant characteristics of the asset being exchanged. For example, the Andalusian Mālikī jurist and polymath Ibn Rushd (1126–98) identified gharar in an alleged pre-Islamic practice called *mulāmasah* in which the buyer purchased a robe on the basis of touching it in the dark or while it was still folded.[81] The logic of an ethical framework to address social problems caused by information asymmetry in a pre-modern market economy should be clear.

Relatedly, all forms of gambling and lottery are consistently prohibited in juristic sources. The Quran itself explicitly bans *maysir*, a game of chance played in pre-Islamic Arabia that involved tossing unfletched arrows in order to win camel meat, calling it "Satan's handiwork."[9] Gambling and lotteries can be understood as extreme cases of gharar, since the entity to be received in return for a sum paid is indeterminate at the time of payment. Islamic jurists have also identified major gharar in insurance, short selling, forwards, futures, options, and swaps. Nonetheless, entrepreneurs have engineered shariah-compliant alternatives to all of these.

BAN ON INVESTMENT IN UNLAWFUL SECTORS. Islamic banks and funds avoid financing or investing in sectors that jurists deem haram or socially harmful. These include alcohol, pork, interest-bearing financial services, highly leveraged companies (because of the ban on riba), pornography, gambling, and often weapons and tobacco. Some industries fall into a gray area, being prohibited by some shariah scholars and permitted by others. These include aerospace and defense; hotels, resorts, cruise lines, and restaurants;

broadcasting and satellite movies; and companies involved in research on stem cells, human embryos, and genetic cloning.[10]

Like legal experts and ethicists operating in other settings (both religious and secular), shariah scholars in Islamic finance must draw sharp lines in gray areas. After all, weapons and tobacco kill people, but so do autos and sugary soft drinks. Should jurists prevent Islamic financial institutions from financing all of them? And if an airline or restaurant chain earns a small portion of its revenue from alcohol sales, but most of it from halal sources, should those companies be off-limits to Islamic investors too?

Three Feedback Loops

The Cost Loop and the "Kosher Coke Effect"

The scholars' acceptance of interest-simulating products was hugely important to the commercial survival and success of Islamic finance, but it could not have been sufficient. History is littered with the carcasses of entrepreneurial businesses that introduced compelling new products and yet failed to gain traction. Below, I argue that the Islamic-finance sector has benefited from three positive-feedback loops: self-reinforcing tracks to the commercial success of Islamic finance at both the global level and, in some countries more than others, the national level.

First, there is the "cost loop" (figure 3.1), which drives down the "cost of being Muslim": the extra cost that banks and other financial-services providers incur in producing and selling Islamic products instead of conventional ones. Economist Mahmoud El-Gamal and economic historian Timur Kuran have presented sophisticated analyses of the causes and complex consequences of transaction costs in Islamic finance.[11] My focus here is on processes that can push these transaction costs down. For example, electronic platforms for trading commodities (such as for palm oil or mobile-phone airtime) or commodities warrants (as at the London Metal Exchange) have reduced the cost of Islamic unsecured lending based on tawarruq to the point that conventional and Islamic unsecured lending to mass-market household customers cost the same. Secured financings too are rationalized to the point where they are extremely competitive in major markets with conventional products: table 3.1 shows that at Malaysia's CIMB Bank and its Islamic sister division CIMB Islamic, auto financing rates were the same in January 2024. Both move in parallel to the same benchmark interest rate from the Malaysian central bank.

Likewise, an analysis of retail rates paid on conventional and Islamic three-month certificates of deposit (CDs) by all institutions in Malaysia offering them shows that while the average conventional rate was slightly higher, the difference was not statistically significant, and that being Islamic or conventional

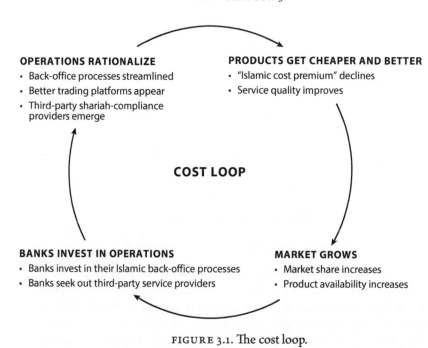

OPERATIONS RATIONALIZE
- Back-office processes streamlined
- Better trading platforms appear
- Third-party shariah-compliance providers emerge

PRODUCTS GET CHEAPER AND BETTER
- "Islamic cost premium" declines
- Service quality improves

COST LOOP

BANKS INVEST IN OPERATIONS
- Banks invest in their Islamic back-office processes
- Banks seek out third-party service providers

MARKET GROWS
- Market share increases
- Product availability increases

FIGURE 3.1. The cost loop.

explains virtually none of the variation in rates ($R^2 = .06$).[12] This equalization of costs for retail financial products reflects the maturation and deep rationalization of production-design and sales processes, as well as the expansion of scale in Islamic finance.

The "cost of being Muslim," distributed across the increasing scale of major Islamic banks in mature markets like the GCC and Malaysia, is also very low when it comes to the special personnel and monitoring that Islamic banks require. Every one of the ten management consultants I interviewed between 2020 and 2022 on this topic—consultants with a combined century of experience serving Islamic and conventional banks across Malaysia, Indonesia, Brunei, the GCC, the Levant, Egypt, and North Africa—insisted that shariah audits, personnel staffing the internal shariah department, and even the Rube Goldberg–style commodities-trading platforms are, in the 2020s, insignificant cost drivers at Islamic banks. Commodities trades, for example, typically cost only 25 basis points (0.25 percent) relative to the size of a financing, which Islamic bankers consider negligible, especially because the platform trades are structured to minimize commodity-price risk to the bank. And for all the uproar about elite shariah scholars' high pay, financial institutions do not consider this a burden either. Islamic banks have increased in scale and rationalized their "Islamic processes" to the point where they hardly suffer from being Islamic. As the literature

TABLE 3.1. Rates for Conventional Hire-Purchase Auto Financing at Malaysia's CIMB Bank and for Islamic Lease-Based Auto Financing at Its Sister Division CIMB Islamic, 29 January 2024

New Passenger Vehicles			
Conventional		**Islamic**	
Fixed Interest Rate	Variable Interest Rate	Fixed Profit Rate	Variable Profit Rate
National	3.75% p.a. flat	BLR minus 0.25%	3.75% p.a. flat	BFR minus 0.25%
Foreign	2.70% p.a. flat	BLR minus 1.75%	2.70% p.a. flat	BFR minus 1.75%

Used Passenger Vehicles			
Conventional		**Islamic**	
Fixed Interest Rate	Variable Interest Rate	Fixed Profit Rate	Variable Profit Rate
National	4.45% p.a. flat	BLR plus 1.70%	4.45% p.a. flat	BFR plus 1.70%
Foreign	4.00% p.a. flat	BLR plus 0.95%	4.00% p.a. flat	BFR plus 0.95%

Sources: CIMB websites; Bank Negara Malaysia.
Note: BLR (base lending rate at CIMB) is now 6.85% p.a.; BFR (base financing rate at CIMB Islamic) is now 6.85% p.a. BLR and BFR have both moved in parallel to the overnight policy rate (OPR) of Bank Negara Malaysia, the central bank. OPR is now 3.00%.

on certification shows, keeping the cost of private voluntary certification low relative to firms' profits in an industry can be crucial not only for those firms' survival but for avoiding ethical scandals that can arise when certification costs rise and create incentives for the direct bribery of certification agents,[13] or where certification agents compete heavily on price and seek market share by keeping the cost of certification cheap.[14] My interviews with boutique consultants who "supply" shariah certification by prominent shariah scholars on a one-off basis to firms likewise show that competition on price is not intense: they simply charge a flat, round fee for all certification services (e.g., $100,000) and do not adjust it significantly or get into negotiations.

Instead, many cost drivers associated with being Islamic have to do with operational features: Islamic banks tend to be newer and smaller than their conventional counterparts and therefore (with some exceptions, like Al Rajhi in Saudi Arabia) may have weaker branch networks. Core banking software and accounting systems designed for Islamic financial institutions also lag behind the gold standard for conventional financial institutions,[15] causing problems with customer service, which is something Islamic banks often struggle with relative to conventional banks. Historically, another challenge has been the paucity of "high-quality shariah-compliant instruments by which Islamic financial institutions can manage their liquidity," as noted by Rifaat Ahmed Abdel Karim, then CEO of the International Islamic Liquidity Management Corporation,[16]though as Islamic banks grow, they can and do put more pressure on national governments to issue more Islamic paper.

On the other hand, particularly in the Middle East, being Islamic can bring special profitability advantages. Islamic banks often enjoy a significantly lower cost of funds than conventional banks because many pious depositors still refuse to take any return on their deposits, not even putting them in Islamic deposit accounts[17]—just like King Fahd in the preface of this book. So a range of factors balance one another out when Islamic banks compete against conventional ones, and consultants report that all told, a slight advantage can go unpredictably to one or the other depending on the macroeconomic climate each quarter.[18] Today, there is no regular disadvantage to being Islamic.

In environments where Islamic financial institutions are gaining substantial market share, the minimal additional costs associated with shariah-compliance certification contribute to what we might call the "kosher Coke effect." In the United States, only 1 percent of the population keeps kosher, but 100 percent of the Coca-Cola sold is certified kosher. Likewise, as Islamic finance scales up and the costs of being financially Islamic decline, shariah-compliant products can become nearly ubiquitous.

The Conversion Loop and the "Ante Effect"

The second loop is the "conversion loop" (figure 3.2). Shariah scholars approach Islamicity as a problem of legal compliance. This lets firms bureaucratize and compartmentalize shariah-compliance within their organizational structure and division of labor. They have shariah departments and shariah audits, just as industrial companies have departments and audits for health and safety. Religion becomes organizationally segregated within the firm from business strategy, operations, human resources, and other core functions. Since the business management of Islamic financial institutions differs little from that of conventional ones, employees ranging from CEOs to bank tellers can move easily from conventional institutions into Islamic ones. At the firm level, the segregation of religious functions and expertise allows conventional financial institutions to convert themselves into Islamic ones or launch Islamic branches and divisions. Indeed, much of the growth of Islamic finance worldwide has transpired this way. The segregation also allows fully conventional financial institutions, such as Goldman Sachs and Morgan Stanley, to underwrite Islamic securities, arrange Islamic loans, and structure Islamic derivatives by establishing their own shariah

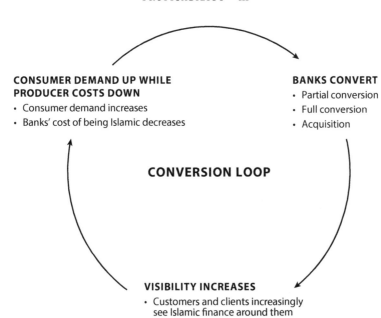

**CONSUMER DEMAND UP WHILE
PRODUCER COSTS DOWN**
- Consumer demand increases
- Banks' cost of being Islamic decreases

BANKS CONVERT
- Partial conversion
- Full conversion
- Acquisition

CONVERSION LOOP

VISIBILITY INCREASES
- Customers and clients increasingly
  see Islamic finance around them

FIGURE 3.2. The conversion loop.

boards or by retaining a shariah-advisory firm that has one. Non-Muslim employees can also participate in Islamic finance in most capacities other than being a shariah scholar, shariah auditor, or shariah-department member. Non-Muslims can and do participate extensively in engineering complex Islamic financial products, for example. As more employees and firms enter Islamic finance, the more ubiquitous it becomes, and the more consumers and investors come to consider it a trustworthy, mainstream option and take for granted that their bank offer Islamic services. Islamic finance shifts from a specialty offering into a must-have "ante to play": if you do not offer an Islamic option to your customers, you cannot remain competitive.

At the firm level, the conversion loop and ante effect have been even more powerful in some parts of the GCC than in Malaysia—especially in Saudi Arabia. It has altered the competitive landscapes of the GCC's national banking markets by increasing Islamic banking's market share without radically transforming the identities of the biggest market players. Between 1985 and 2002, Islamic banking's market share in the Gulf countries grew (figure 3.3).

But since the early 2000s, conventional incumbents in national banking fields have absorbed the challenge by "going Islamic" themselves, contributing to continued growth of Islamic banking's market share through the 2010s. At first, this meant opening Islamic "windows": counters in their bank branches selling only Islamic products. Conventional banks then began opening

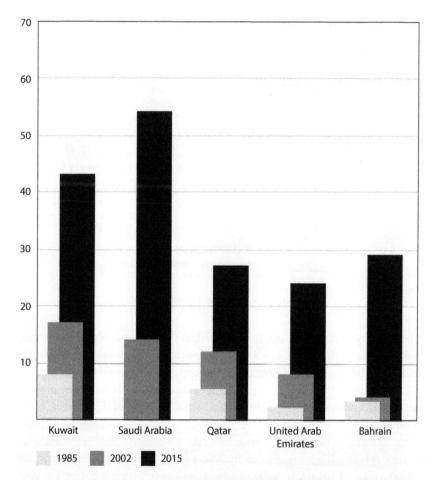

FIGURE 3.3. Islamic banking's percent market share in the Gulf Arab countries, 1985–2015. Note: In 1985, no Islamic banks had yet received banking licenses in Saudi Arabia. *Sources*: Ernst & Young 2017, 46–57; Habib 1989, 164–67; Paxton 1987; Presley 1988; von Pock 2007, 51.

dedicated Islamic branches. Some have acquired major stakes in Islamic banks. And some have converted themselves entirely into Islamic banks,[19] or are in the process of doing so, including the region's second-largest bank.[20]

The incumbents were able to go Islamic because the organizational innovations introduced by the pioneers of the 1970s, interest simulation and the shariah board, were by now standardized and portable. Any Gulf bank could establish a shariah board; it only had to find qualified scholars and offer them honoraria.

In the final analysis, the growth of Islamic finance has changed the rules of product structuring and marketing in the Gulf's national banking markets but has had limited effects on those markets' social order. The major incumbents in national banking markets have hardly changed since the early days of Islamic banking, as table 3.2 shows for the region's two largest banking markets.[21]

In the capital-markets arena, a more interconnected version of the ante effect can drive national financial systems toward full Islamization. Saudi Arabia is the best example. There, shariah scholars and academics have long maintained lists of shariah-compliant stocks. But since the 2010s, major initial public offerings (IPOs), like that of Aramco (discussed at the beginning of chapter 7), have stimulated great public attention to the shariah-compliance of equity markets. The privatization of large state-owned firms and the expansion of share ownership into the middle classes have furthered this interest. Meanwhile, Islamic banks, Islamic asset managers, Islamic investment and private-equity funds, government agencies such as ministries of religious affairs, charitable Islamic endowments, and family offices of ultra-high-net-worth pious investors all operate with mandates to invest only in shariah-compliant stocks, sukuk, and financings. "There's a reason why 85 to 88 percent of the Tadawul [the Saudi Stock Exchange] is now shariah-compliant," explained Sultan Al Nugali, a seasoned Riyadh-based investment analyst. "It's because most IPO participants prefer shariah-compliant companies."[22] There is now convincing quantitative evidence that not being shariah-compliant at one's IPO in Saudi Arabia hurts listing price and subscription multiples.

This cross-exposure effect in capital markets is not restricted to Saudi Arabia. Syarizal Rahim, partner at international consultancy EY's Kuala Lumpur office, notes that large Malaysian corporations seek out shariah-compliant financing so that when they issue shares, those shares can be certified as shariah-compliant. "One of the requirements for shariah certification . . . is the source of your financing," Syarizal explains. "If more than a certain percent is conventional financing, that will disqualify you from shariah certification [of your shares]."[23] Thus, demand for shariah-compliant equities begets demand for shariah-compliant financing and promotes corporate-sukuk issuance. Islamic finance in one form stimulates Islamic finance in another.

The Technocratic Loop and the "Depoliticization Effect"

From the 1970s through the 1990s, many national governments restricted Islamic finance formally or informally out of fear that its proponents might have associations with political Islam. Some suppressed Islamic finance, while others banned it outright, including Iraq, Syria, Libya, Morocco, and Oman. Ayatollah Muḥammad Bāqir al-Ṣadr, one of the pioneers of Islamic economics, was

TABLE 3.2 The Six Largest Banks in Saudi Arabia and the UAE, 1985–2015

Saudi Arabia	1985	2007	2015
#1	National Commercial Bank	National Commercial Bank	National Commercial Bank
#2	Riyad Bank	Saudi American Bank	Al Rajhi Bank
#3	Saudi American Bank	Al Rajhi Bank	Saudi American Bank
#4	Banque Saudi Fransi	Riyad Bank	Riyad Bank
#5	Arab National Bank	Banque Saudi Fransi	Saudi British Bank
#6	Saudi Hollandi Bank	Saudi British Bank	Banque Saudi Fransi

UAE	1985	2007	2015
#1	National Bank of Abu Dhabi	National Bank of Abu Dhabi	National Bank of Abu Dhabi
#2	National Bank of Dubai	Emirates Bank International	Emirates-NBD
#3	Bank of Oman	Abu Dhabi Commercial Bank	Abu Dhabi Commercial Bank
#4	BCCI	National Bank of Dubai	First Gulf Bank
#5	Abu Dhabi Commercial Bank	HSBC	Dubai Islamic Bank
#6	ARBIFT	First Gulf Bank	Abu Dhabi Islamic Bank

☐ Fully conventional
▨ Partly Islamic: Offers Islamic windows or branches and/or owns a major stake (25%+) in an Islamic bank
▨ Partly Islamic and has announced plans to convert into fully Islamic
▨ Fully Islamic

Sources: Bank annual reports; Habib 1989, 164–67; Al-Hassan, Khamis, and Oulidi 2010, 31–33.
Note: Domestic commercial banks only. Emirates Bank International and National Bank of Dubai merged in 2007 to form Emirates-NBD.

tortured and executed by Saddam Hussein in 1980. In most cases, these mostly authoritarian governments' concerns about Islamist power grabs using Islamic finance as a base proved unfounded, with a few exceptions, such as in Sudan, where the Muslim Brotherhood dominated national economic activity for a decade by using Islamic banks as distribution channels for capital.

Yet as the Gulf model spread, Islamic finance has become universally accepted from a political perspective, even by authoritarian regimes nervous about Islamism. Its resolutely technical, legalist nature reassures governments that permitting Islamic finance in their country will not usher in a revolutionary Islamic economic system. Today, not one government of a Muslim-majority country still bans Islamic finance. Even the governments of Uzbekistan and Syria, which have cracked down on Islamist insurgencies, have ventured into the industry. It has become an on-ramp for foreign capital, especially from the Gulf. And it usually does not pose a political challenge to the stability of ruling governments but rather technocratic ones: introducing favorable legislation, designing smart central-bank policy and securities regulation,[24] and providing liquidity and yield curves by issuing sovereign sukuk and Islamic interbank paper and cultivating a reliable secondary market.[25] As leaders look more kindly at Islamic finance, they come to view it as a source of jobs, foreign investment, affordable credit, and political currency with their pious middle classes and elites. They enter a "technocratic loop" (figure 3.4) that accelerates momentum for Islamic finance through favorable state policy.

My team's customer interviews in Pakistan and Saudi Arabia revealed no discernible link that proponents of Islamic finance drew between their support of Islamic finance and their vision for an "Islamic state" (however interpreted) or for a greater role for religion in politics. This is not to say there is no correlation at all but simply that in speaking with over 130 members of the general public between the two countries, we never heard people make these connections.

Perhaps more important than the political orientations of Islamic-finance customers are those of business leaders and state managers involved intimately with the Islamic-finance sector. Since the 1970s, the people who endorse and lead Islamic banks have shifted from envisioning an alternative to capitalism to being managers trained in the conventional banking system. It is not only unnecessary, but inexpedient, for such managers to align themselves with Islamist political forces. They are hired for their managerial skill, not their religious or political views. The involvement of central banks as key shepherds and supporters of Islamic finance since the 1990s and 2000s has also contributed to the sector's "depoliticization" (in the sense of religious politics) and its technocratization.

The partial exception is among elite shariah scholars, who may enjoy some autonomy in aligning themselves politically without losing their livelihoods. Some have been caught in the on-again, off-again rivalry between Qatar on one side and Saudi Arabia, the United Arab Emirates, and Bahrain on the other. Prominent shariah scholars such as Ali al-Qaradaghi and the international celebrity Yusuf al-Qaradawi have sat mostly on shariah boards in Qatar but not in the other three aforementioned GCC countries; likewise, prominent scholars based in Saudi Arabia, the UAE, and Bahrain tend to avoid overseeing Qatari financial institutions (though not completely). Regional politics

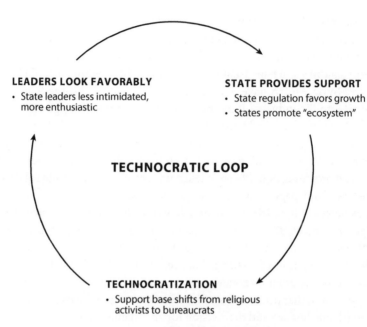

LEADERS LOOK FAVORABLY
• State leaders less intimidated, more enthusiastic

STATE PROVIDES SUPPORT
• State regulation favors growth
• States promote "ecosystem"

TECHNOCRATIC LOOP

TECHNOCRATIZATION
• Support base shifts from religious activists to bureaucrats

FIGURE 3.4. The technocratic loop.

also became something of a quiet controversy late in the life of Sheikh Hussein Hamid Hassan (1932–2020). Sheikh Hassan, who was Egyptian but lived in exile in Dubai for decades as chair of Dubai Islamic Bank's shariah board, became close to the Muslim Brotherhood government of Mohamed Morsi in Egypt (r. 2012–13) as a legal advisor, helping to write the Egyptian constitution promulgated by the Morsi government and developing a legal framework for sukuk issuance. Once the short-lived Muslim Brotherhood government fell, Sheikh Hussein quickly left Egypt but found himself a controversial figure back in his long-adopted home of the United Arab Emirates, and according to rumor was persona non grata at some GCC Islamic financial institutions for a few years thereafter. Yet such involvements are the exception, and reflect the tendencies of someone who was a leading figure of Islamic finance from the beginning rather than those of a typical shariah scholar, who works within the bureaucratic confines of a bank's shariah department.

Conclusion: Interest Simulation, Feedback Loops, and Ethical Progress the Scholars' Way

This chapter has explored how firms participating in Islamic finance, especially Islamic banks, manage to be profitable. Central to this process is interest simulation, which Islamic financial institutions execute using both the debt-based techniques described throughout this book—including ijara (leasing) in this chapter—and the modified equity-based techniques described in the previous chapter. Interest simulation does require adherence to certain shariah rules, such as the need for a lessor to take responsibility for maintaining the car she has leased. Yet Islamic banks remain profitable by displacing the liabilities associated with such responsibility, such as by requiring the lessor to buy Islamic auto insurance. The bottom line is that Islamic banks have become very good at staying within the letter of Islamic law while shifting to customers, investors, and third parties the financial risks associated with being a shariah-compliant financier.

The chapter has also shown how the social and organizational dynamics of markets have amplified the growth momentum of Islamic finance. Three feedback loops begin to operate when Islamic finance—especially Islamic banking—reaches a critical mass in a national market. First, there is a "cost loop": as Islamic finance grows, shariah scholars achieve consensus on what products are Islamically lawful. Firms can then develop the legal templates and technical systems to accommodate these products. Transaction costs thus go down, and the price premium on Islamic products relative to their conventional analogues declines—for many products in mature markets, sometimes to zero. Thus, Islamic finance becomes like kosher Coca-Cola in the United States: although only a small percentage of U.S. Coca-Cola consumers keep kosher, the costs for achieving kosher certification are so low that all Coca-Cola sold in the United States is now kosher-certified.

Second, there is a "conversion loop": with the growth in demand for Islamic finance, more and more conventional banks have opened Islamic teller windows, Islamic branches, and entire Islamic divisions. Some have converted completely into Islamic banks. In mature national markets—roughly, where Islamic bank deposits or Islamic banking assets have surpassed 15 to 20 percent—Islamic banking shifts from a specialty offering into a must-have "ante to play." You must offer an Islamic option to your customers if you want to survive.

Third, there is a "technocratic loop": as Islamic finance has grown worldwide, state leaders who once associated it with Islamist challengers to their political dominance now view it as a benign exercise in regulation—or even better, as a source of jobs, foreign investment, and political support from the pious bourgeoisie. These leaders are not wrong in their belief: the bankers, shariah scholars, lawyers, and regulators who work in Islamic finance are chosen for their technical skills and competence. My interviews offer no evidence that it is common for them to be chosen for having Islamist political sympathies (even though a portion do harbor such sympathies). This has helped shariah scholars in the most advanced markets for Islamic finance—the Gulf Arab economies and Malaysia—avoid the "crisis of expertise" that Gil Eyal has documented as affecting policy-relevant experts in much of the world.[26] Instead of presenting themselves as policy experts who mediate between politics and science, they actively disclaim policy relevance.

By investigating the practice of contemporary Islamic financial institutions, we start to form a picture of the unique ethical world of the Islamic-finance industry. To begin with, we have seen that Islamic financial instruments simulate the economic effects of interest. This truth leads many casual observers to dismiss Islamic finance as chicanery. In such a conception, ethical reasoning becomes either nonexistent or a minimalist, utterly rudimentary application of divine command, one completely subordinated to the profit motive: God said to avoid interest, but anything else goes so long as bankers make money and shariah scholars bless it. (In chapter 7, we hear from some members of the consuming public who take this cynical view.)

But this view is wrong, or at best quite narrow, for two reasons. First, today's practice of Islamic finance *is* embedded in an ethics, and a sophisticated ethics at that. It is, however, a juristic (and scholastic) ethics: that is, one in which *arguments must always be expressed in legal reasoning to be valid*. When debates about shariah-compliance arise among shariah scholars, they are legal debates. And like legal debates anywhere, they usually boil down to philosophical contests that turn on the appropriateness of analogies, the drawing of qualitative distinctions, and engagement with precedent. Does this contractual structure meet the typological conditions to qualify as a lease or a loan? As a valid or invalid partnership? As profit or usury? As any law-school student can attest, these sorts of definitional questions are foundational to the world's major secular legal systems too. (When I encounter academics new to Islamic finance, it is often law professors and moral philosophers who find its nuts and bolts most interesting.) Such questions rarely have unequivocally "right" answers. Instead, judges and jurists formulate different responses to them, and some of those responses—because of political leanings, economic expediency, and social convention—become entrenched in particular legal traditions. What becomes valid law varies across civil-law and common-law systems, across countries, and even across subnational jurisdictions like states and provinces. In this regard, the entrenchment of murabaha (markup-sale) financing in the Islamic-finance industry as an Islamically valid way of avoiding interest does not deviate from the way in which law, whether sacred or secular, has developed across space and time.

Second, many stakeholders in Islamic finance have a strong sense of *ethical progress*. As we saw, moral economists view some products such as tawarruq to be pernicious and hope to phase them out. They want to increase the weight of true profit-and-loss sharing in Islamic finance. Meanwhile, shariah scholars in the industry also want to improve Islamic finance, but by attending to what they consider failures of shariah-compliance. They want to be certain, for example, that when tawarruq is executed, reliable monitoring systems will ensure that assets being sold to simulate interest-bearing financings will always meet the Islamic legal conditions for valid possession and valid sale. To them, the *juristic* compliance of individual transactions is first and foremost before systemic factors can be considered. To have a notion of progress, you must have a sense of history and a vision for ethical improvement. These exist in Islamic finance in a way they do not in conventional finance.

This is not to say that we should accept full-throated defenses of today's Islamic-finance industry and its practitioners at face value. The embeddedness of Islamic finance in classical Islamic law imposes a high barrier to entry upon people without juristic training, arguments not expressed in legal terms, and extra-legal conceptions of Islamic economic virtue. In instantiating one ethical framework for looking at finance, today's Islamic-finance industry excludes other frameworks, particularly those less consonant with the interests of finance capital. While philosophers of law may find the shariah scholars' scholastic distinctions meaningful, economists are more likely to see Islamic financial practice as obfuscation and chicanery: as interest-based finance by another name. And as we have seen, the perspective of the "outsider" moral economists is deeply critical of current industry practice. The tension between the shariah scholars and the moral economists is more than a disagreement about finance. It represents disagreement about the very nature and content of shariah as an ethical framework.

Ultimately, this chapter shows how Islamic finance manages to be profitable within the competitive landscape of global capitalist finance while remaining deeply embedded in Islamic law and the strong authority of its experts, the shariah scholars. The fact that the interpretation of Islamic law in question is not universal, and that the shariah scholars themselves come in for criticism, does not prevent successful accommodation with neoliberal finance. The next three chapters address these topics.

4

Legitimation

I HAVE ARGUED that twenty-first-century fiqh-minded Islam and twenty-first-century capitalism are uniquely compatible. Shariah scholars are the matchmakers of the marriage between the two. To this end, they play three crucial roles: legitimation (described in this chapter), justification (chapter 5), and restriction (chapter 6).

Shariah scholars *legitimate* Islamic financial products and institutions. By this, I mean that scholars (a) have legitimacy and (b) deploy that legitimacy in the interests of individual firms by certifying products. This chapter explores the sources of the shariah scholars' legitimacy and finds that legitimation differs fundamentally in "low" and "high" Islamic finance. The growth of international high Islamic finance since the late 1990s has amplified the power of around a dozen scholars, cementing their status as "super-legitimators" who sit atop the scholarly pyramid. Many market participants complain that this top-heavy social structure of scholarly authority in Islamic finance—a structure not found in other scholar-certified sectors, such as halal foods or halal pharmaceuticals—impedes the codification and harmonization of shariah within and across jurisdictions.

Having Legitimacy

Shariah scholars have overwhelming legitimacy in the Islamic-finance industry. This does not mean that everyone involved with Islamic finance believes shariah scholars are infallible, that their interpretations of Islamic law are incontestable, or that their monopoly on certification is desirable. As Max Weber understood, the legitimacy of a social order or institutional arrangement is not upheld only by people who consider it morally right but by all who expect that most others will follow it:[1] in our case, by all those who expect other industry stakeholders to behave as if scholar-certified financial transactions are authentically "Islamic" or shariah-compliant. Those "imagined others" include people

expected to uphold the social order because they consider it righteous or ordained by God; people following tradition, mimicking others, or moved emotionally by others' appeals; and people adhering to the order out of self-
interest.[2] Even violators of a legitimate order, so long as they do not proliferate
too much or protest the order too convincingly, can bolster the order's legitimacy to some extent by trying to avoid its sanction: "a thief orients his action
to the validity of the criminal law in that he acts surreptitiously."[3] (We will see
such violators in the next chapter: bank sales reps and others who skirt shariah
regulations in order to fulfill their quarterly quotas.) The bottom line is that
legitimation entails a collective construction of social reality.[4]

Sources of Scholars' Collective Legitimacy: Fiqh-mindedness, Postcolonial Developmentalism, and National Political Consensus

What are the bases of shariah scholars' legitimacy? To answer this question,
one must explore the relationship of the scholars' profession to their social
capital (relationships), their pedigree, their relationships to other types of
elites, their recognition as "leading jurist[s]," and "symbolic capital such as
professional degrees," as Yves Dezalay and Bryant Garth propose.[5]

Shariah scholars in Islamic finance gain authority not only from their formal
designation as certification agents but from the influence and prestige that shariah scholars in general enjoy as a professional group. Although the world's population of fiqh-minded Muslims cannot be counted precisely—because fiqh-
mindedness is better understood as an orientation toward particular sources of
scriptural authority and exegetical expertise than a clear-cut membership
group—one estimate puts them at 15 to 20 percent of all Muslims,[6] or around
300 to 400 million people. Most fiqh-minded believers refer, at least occasionally,
to the views of shariah scholars for guidance. Shariah scholars participate in contemporary social and political debates,[7] and some have millions of social-media
followers. According to the *Muslim 500* list compiled by a Jordanian think tank,
six of the world's ten most influential Muslims, and eighteen of the top thirty, are
shariah scholars.[8] Most of the rest are heads of state.

Country-specific factors also affect shariah scholars' legitimacy as the
appropriate arbiters of financial "Islamicity." In the 1960s and 1970s, a postcolonial developmentalist ethos motivated many of the pioneers of Islamic
finance, such as Ahmed al-Najjar. So did the idea that existing interest-based
financial institutions imposed an un-Islamic, degenerate, and exploitative
"Western" form of finance onto Muslims, and that Muslims needed a financial system by themselves and for themselves. Today, such critiques still
bolster support for Islamic finance. Najeem, a fifty-eight-year-old textile

trader and Islamic-banking customer in Lahore, explained why he uses an Islamic bank:

> In America . . . everything is mortgaged: the house is mortgaged, the car is mortgaged, and nothing actually belongs to you. They don't have small shops [as in Pakistan]; they have giants like Walmart. And once [Walmart's] business goes down . . . [the employees] get fired and can't pay their mortgage. . . . That's why no economy should be based on interest.[9]

Scholars themselves give eloquent voice to such views. Sheikh Yusuf Talal DeLorenzo, who translates classical Arabic texts and writes historical novels when not busy monitoring nine-figure cross-border investments for shariah-compliance, links the long history of European financial exploitation to the present need for an indigenously Islamic form of finance:

> We had managed—we, as [in] our spiritual predecessors[10]—[to conduct] trade internationally, across borders, across oceans, across continents. Very effectively . . . for centuries. Did [we] need banks? . . . Was there a Bank of Rangoon in AH 505 [1111/1112 CE]? . . . No. We had . . . incredibly successful networks of trade for centuries, until along came the Europeans, and messed everything up. . . . Yes, they came with their swords, but far worse was that they brought their banks.[11]

Although historical arguments like DeLorenzo's resonate with many audiences, competing claims about what constitutes a truly Islamic financial system can also undermine the legitimacy of shariah scholars involved in Islamic finance, especially in certain countries. In chapter 7, which compares Pakistan and Saudi Arabia, I find that heavy contestation among alternative power centers of Islamic authority, such as Islamist parties of various stripes, as well as acrimonious interpretive debates about the nature of riba, can foment challenges to industry-affiliated scholars' claims to be endorsing a truly Islamic and truly alternative financial system. This has been the case for decades in Pakistan, where even fellow shariah scholars uninvolved in Islamic finance are not shy about questioning whether Islamic finance is particularly Islamic. And in Egypt, successive grand muftis have averred that Islamic banks are no more Islamic than conventional interest-bearing banks, or maybe even less so, undermining the Islamic-finance sector, which has remained small. Yet in Saudi Arabia, where scholarly authority to guide believers in living Islamically ethical daily lives is more widely accepted and the Islamic ban on interest far less of a politically charged issue, debates in Saudi newspapers and on Saudi airwaves mostly avoid the question of whether Islamic finance is legitimate tout court. Instead, they explore technical problems, such as whether a given company's IPO shares will be shariah-compliant.

Sources of Scholars' Individual Legitimacy: Pedigree

By one count, there are around one thousand shariah scholars serving on shariah boards today. Their legitimate authority is primarily intellectual, not traditional or charismatic. As academic experts in Islamic law, their successful claim to be the lone arbiters of the Islamic and the un-Islamic in the Islamic-finance industry depends partly on their educational pedigree and markers of academic distinction. The audience for such symbolic distinction includes the banks that appoint them to shariah boards, sophisticated clients—especially institutional ones—who want to minimize the risk that their Islamic investment decisions will be challenged, fellow scholars in the industry who must accept them as worthy peers, and, often, government regulators who impose minimum qualifications for shariah-board membership.

The pedigree of shariah-board members not only enhances their legitimacy but restricts access to the profession by establishing high barriers to entry. It also steeps them in the juristic perspective: they come to view fiqh as the appropriate lens through which Islam should govern markets. Like many "secular" academics, they see their work as a calling and have come to value deep knowledge—of Islamic law but increasingly also of finance—and the markers of this knowledge, such as publications and professorships.

Whether they work in Islamic finance or not, Islamic scholars have years of training in the classical Islamic sciences. For over a millennium, this education has defined entry into their social stratum. Without at least this minimum level of training, any claim to juristic authority will not resonate with most fiqh-minded believers. Historically, education in the Islamic sciences has begun in the pre-teen or teenage years—often once a child can read the Quran in Arabic—and has lasted for around seven to twelve years, at which point the graduate can claim scholarly competency and work as an imam. The course of study typically includes Arabic syntax, morphology, and literature; Quran, Quranic orthoepy, and Quranic exegesis; the hadith literature, the science of interpreting hadith, and hadith commentaries; shariah, fiqh, and the methodological principles for deriving Islamic legal rulings; creedal theology; the biography of the Prophet Muhammad and other key religious figures; Islamic history; logic and other philosophical disciplines; and other subjects. Given this broad background learning required, the fatwas produced in Islamic finance should be understood as part of a larger edifice of religious knowledge that, while having evolved greatly over the centuries, has significant continuity with the past.[12]

The shariah scholars who work in Islamic finance today have absorbed the Islamic sciences in various ways. Some studied a formal Islamic curriculum at a school or seminary. Many scholars from the Subcontinent, for example, have undertaken the Dars-e Nizami curriculum, which was born in eighteenth-century

India. Others were first exposed to the Islamic sciences in study circles led by religious scholars or imams at mosques or religious centers, or tutored by parents, relatives, or other local figures trained in these fields. Still others only began to study the Islamic sciences seriously as university undergraduates. Regardless, almost all studied shariah and other Islamic disciplines at university, whether an Islamic university or a conventional one. Many simultaneously took courses in "non-religious" fields such as the natural and social sciences, secular law, or engineering. Whatever the exact path, it is through rigorous university-level study in these Islamic sciences that one can present oneself as a scholar, and if one has focused in shariah or fiqh, as a mufti (*muftī*, one who can issue fatwas).

Today's shariah scholars in Islamic finance sit at the intersection of two educational trends. From one direction, higher education in business and finance has increased. The number of business schools and MBAs worldwide increased steadily throughout the twentieth century and has "exploded and gone global" since the 1980s.[13] Many of today's shariah scholars have had some form of business education, and on average they know far more about business and finance than did their predecessors in the 1970s. From the other direction, Islamic higher education has expanded. Malika Zeghal shows that throughout the Middle East, for example, even as states have "imported Western techniques of governance," "they have dramatically increased their per capita supply of public religious provisions, especially Islamic education."[14]

Some states have set minimum standards for shariah-board members. In Malaysia, shariah advisors must hold a degree in shariah from an institution recognized by the Malaysian government. They must also have prior work experience in Islamic finance and must never have been convicted of fraud, securities offenses, or financial malpractice.[15] Reflecting its hands-on role, the Malaysian state also encourages shariah advisors to attend continuing-education workshops. In Pakistan, shariah advisors must have at least five years' experience giving religious rulings, familiarity with the banking industry, and at minimum completed the eight-year Dars-e Nizami Islamic madrasah curriculum for youth. Higher Islamic studies are encouraged.[16]

States in the Gulf region (with the exception of Oman) lean toward a hands-off approach to shariah governance in Islamic finance, but that does not mean becoming a shariah scholar is easier. In Saudi Arabia, religious education is widespread and the community of religious scholars wields great influence. Requirements to become a shariah-board member in the kingdom are informal yet steep:

> In Saudi Arabia, official shariah qualifications [to sit on a shariah board in Islamic finance] are not a must, but unofficial shariah knowledge is a must. [Unofficial requirements include] very deep knowledge of shariah that can

take from twenty to fifty years of studying directly under one of the most talented and recognized [religious jurists], memorization of the Holy Qur-an and a few thousand of the Prophet Muhammad's hadith, mastery of the rules and tools for issuing fatwa, believing in and coming from the Ḥanbalī school of fiqh [the predominant school in Saudi Arabia], and the courage to use this knowledge in [issuing] fatwa, which is [effectively] equivalent to "signing on behalf of Allah."[17]

Given these daunting intellectual requirements, it cannot be emphasized enough that shariah scholars, especially elite ones—whether they work in Is-lamic finance or not—view themselves as academics, and with good reason. Most scholars who sit on shariah boards today hold postgraduate degrees, most commonly in shariah or fiqh. This establishes them not only as compe-tent to serve as imams or teachers of youth, which they could do without a postgraduate degree, but as academic experts qualified to engage in advanced scholarly debates. And just as in "secular" academia, the publication of journal articles and books is a valuable currency of their realm. Many have published on Islamic commercial jurisprudence and Islamic economics. Quite a few have also taught as university professors or lecturers in shariah or fiqh. A handful have served as judges in national shariah courts.

Expertise outside shariah and fiqh is increasingly important for shariah schol-ars in Islamic finance too. Many shariah-board members today hold undergradu-ate or graduate degrees in "secular" disciplines. Degrees in law and in economics are common, both from universities in Muslim-majority countries and from those in the United Kingdom, the United States, Canada, and (for Southeast Asian scholars) Australia. Among the younger generation of scholars—born in the 1970s, 1980s, and 1990s—it is also common to see degrees in Islamic eco-nomics or even in Islamic finance; Islamic finance was virtually unheard of as a degree-granting academic discipline until the 2000s. Finance expertise helps scholars bridge capitalist finance and fiqh. Figure 4.1 shows the institutions of higher education from which 320 shariah scholars around the world earned de-grees (including both undergraduate and graduate degrees).

Like other successful academics, elite scholars feel compelled to keep up with new academic literature and with current events relevant to their field. When I met with Mohamed Ali Elgari, for example, he had read five doctoral dissertations the week before. One examined Uber from an Islamic juristic perspective, and another venture capital. Elgari also reads the *Wall Street Jour-nal* daily.[18]

Just as in "secular" academic professions, it is increasingly important for shariah scholars in Islamic finance to know English. Islamic scholars around the world generally read and speak classical Arabic well, even though most do

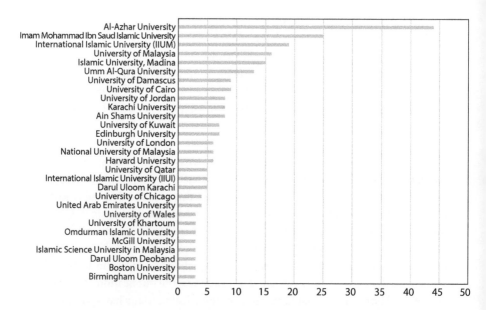

FIGURE 4.1. Institutions of higher education attended by 320 shariah scholars around the world. *Source*: Ünal 2010.

not come from the Arab world. (One-fifth of the world Muslim population is Arab.) But English is a different matter: its instruction is sometimes (though by no means always) deprioritized at Islamic schools and seminaries, and the scholarship that Islamic scholars reference and produce is mostly in Arabic or national languages (e.g., Urdu, Persian, Malay). Yet because the language of international business—and in many countries of domestic corporate business—is English, shariah scholars in Islamic finance differ from other ulama. To be a successful shariah-board member, speaking English "is a huge advantage, of course," notes Mohamed Ali Elgari:

> Everything now is in English, even at the local banks. And most of the literature in finance is in English. If you want to be updated on developments in finance, you have to know English.[19]

Zulkifli Hasan, a prominent Malaysian scholar, notes a generation gap:

> In Malaysia . . . the young generation of scholars speaks English and Arabic very well. But it is very rare to find both [among] senior scholars. If you do both in the senior generation, you can be a rock star.[20]

The overall picture, then, is of shariah-board membership—especially at the elite level—as a semi-academic vocation: one that requires specialized education to enter and in which a hefty academic pedigree, the ability to keep up with the latest academic publications, and English skills are important for rising to the top. Yet the scholarly elite in Islamic finance see themselves not as "ordinary" academics but as academics who follow a religious and moral calling. That calling is to help Muslims honor God's law. When I asked Sheikh Esam Ishaq, an internationally elite scholar from Bahrain, how he chose Islamic studies as a career, he gently corrected me: "I don't like to think of Islamic studies as a career."[21] I quickly realized my blunder: a career is a way to make a living, but the advanced study of shariah and its application to finance is a way to help Muslims follow God's path.

A Market Mentality

In these scholars' eyes, a divine calling to the study of Islamic law is not at odds with engagement with the capitalist economy. When I asked internationally elite shariah scholars about their personal backgrounds and the qualities that make a good shariah scholar in Islamic finance, they consistently cited experience with business. Mufti Muhammad Imran Usmani of Pakistan asserted that success requires "a commercial mindset." "You need to understand what's going on in business, and how it works," said Usmani, spinning his index finger to suggest a wheel turning at the fast pace of modern enterprise.[22] He noted that the great eighth-century CE jurist Muḥammad al-Shaybānī did not just sit in the ivory tower of the madrasah but went to the bazaar to observe transactions himself. "I notice that all of the people on shariah boards have been exposed in their life to commerce," reflected Sheikh Mohamed Ali Elgari of Saudi Arabia, "either by being directly involved in it or by having gone to business colleges, or something like this." As an example, Elgari mentioned that Sheikh Abdullah al-Manea, who after Elgari himself is the elite Saudi scholar most prolific internationally in Islamic finance, worked in his early years as a cashier for a major merchant in Saudi Arabia's Eastern Province.[23] Elgari holds a doctorate in economics from the University of California, Riverside; his dissertation touches on the changing role of the Hijazi merchant class in modern Saudi Arabia's economic development. Sheikh Nizam Yaquby, who hails from a merchant family in Bahrain, explained that when he returns home, he sits at a desk in one of the family's shops in Manama and answers questions about fiqh from anyone who wishes to come in.[24] Yaquby's countryman Sheikh Esam Ishaq is trained as a realtor; he thanks his father and brother for being "generous enough not to demand that [he] be there" to help out with the family realty business, allowing him to focus on shariah.[25]

Leading shariah scholars' "market mindset" not only helps them understand the businesses they certify but provides them with new business opportunities of their own. In addition to sitting on shariah boards, some well-known shariah scholars have founded or led their own shariah consultancies. Usmani & Company provides firms access to the expertise of president and CEO Muhammad Imran Usmani and his father, Taqi Usmani. Dar Al Sharia, the shariah-advisory division of Dubai Islamic Bank, was closely associated with Hussein Hamid Hassan until his death in 2020. And Amanah Advisors is the shariah consultancy of up-and-coming British shariah scholar Faraz Adam, who specializes in Islamic fintech and gives talks with titles such as "Zakat in the world of Web3."[26]

Dr. Mohammad Daud Bakar, the most prominent Malaysian shariah scholar in international Islamic finance, is the best example of a rock-star scholar who has converted his shariah expertise into a small empire of business advice. The shariah-advisory firm he founded, Amanie Advisors, serves institutions around the world looking to move into Islamic finance. Its client list includes several Gulf banks, PricewaterhouseCoopers, the trillion-dollar American asset managers Franklin Templeton and Prudential PGIM, and Malaysia's sovereign wealth fund. Daud is also a prolific author. In addition to books on shariah and Islamic finance, and his *COVID-25* series of pandemic novels, Daud has authored several books that combine theology and shariah with airport-bookstore business-guruism. They include *Mindset Is Everything*, which aims to "motivate . . . inquisitive young business minds"; *Corporate Matrimony: How to WOO Clients into Long-Term Relationships*, which promises that "if you have ever made a friend, dated somebody, [or] married or divorced your partner, you have a hidden talent for sales and marketing," and *I Have 25 Hours a Day: The Smart Way to Create More Time*.[27] The latter offers time-management wisdom gleaned from Daud's experience as a globe-trotting, start-up-launching scholar; its cover shows the scholar in a suit walking briskly through an airport, carry-on smartly in tow.[28]

Daud Bakar's interweaving of shariah and business into a highly public-facing, media-savvy appeal is particularly Malaysian, at least among Islamic-finance shariah scholars internationally. It exemplifies what Patricia Sloane-White calls "corporate Islam," which encompasses a corporate "shariah elite" of shariah scholars like Daud Bakar and Malay Muslim leaders of major Islamic enterprises, the ordinary Malaysian Muslims who work at such enterprises and "embrace their premises," and the "optimistic promise of profits and piety" that binds these groups.[29] Daud's promotion of Taylorist self-optimization likewise echoes the formal rationalization of Islamic authority being implemented through state organs such as JAKIM (Malaysia's Department of Islamic Development), which scrupulously regulates Malaysia's burgeoning market for halal-certified goods via a matrix of auditing regimes, ISO protocols,[30] and the "halal technoscience" investigated by Johan Fischer.[31]

At the same time, while Daud's appeal has specifically Malaysian aspects, his mass constituency has much in common with similar strata in other societies. As Vali Nasr observes, Muslim middle classes in much of the world, just like non-Muslim middle classes, aspire simultaneously to moral self-cultivation and economic self-help as they grapple with globalization, economic reform, and expanding markets for labor, consumer goods, and cultural products.[32] Moral entrepreneurs and institutions that combine neoliberal subjectivities with shariah-minded piety are also highlighted in the research of Mona Atia on Egypt; Maznah Mohamad, Johan Saravanamuttu, Daromir Rudnyckyj, Robert Hefner, and James Hoesterey on Indonesia; Sarah Tobin on Jordan; Daromir Rudnyckyj, Jessie Poon, Jane Pollard, and Yew Wah Chow on Malaysia; Cihan Tuğal and Emin Baki Adaş on Turkey; Michael Samers on the United Kingdom and United States; and Omer Awass at the global level in examining the intersection of fatwa issuance with neoliberalism.[33]

Deploying Legitimacy

Shariah scholars deploy their legitimacy by certifying financial products and transactions as shariah-compliant. However, the certification process and the audience for certification differ between what I call "low" Islamic finance and "high" Islamic finance. Drawing on the organizational literature on legitimacy, I distinguish between moral, pragmatic, and, in the book's conclusion, cognitive legitimacy.[34] In low Islamic finance, scholar certification provides *moral legitimacy*, assuaging customer anxieties about sin directly. In high Islamic finance, scholar certification generates *pragmatic legitimacy*, reducing transaction risk in capital markets and corporate finance.

"Low" Finance and "High" Finance

Financial services can be arrayed on a continuum along which the size, sophistication, and standardization of transactions vary according to customer segment. I use here the example of banking, but the same continuum applies to other financial sectors like asset management and insurance.

What we might call "low banking" comprises *retail banking*, which serves ordinary households, and *business banking*, which serves small and medium-sized enterprises (SMEs). In low banking, transactions are small in size and banks offer identical products to their millions of customers. Banks profit largely by providing the credit that keeps Main Street running: small asset financings, such as for autos or business equipment; credit cards; and non-asset financing, such as for medical bills, payroll, and rent. On the other side of the balance sheet, banks offer deposit products like savings accounts, checking accounts, and time deposits. They also provide rudimentary cash-management services. Low-banking products are of the "take-it-or-leave-it" variety:[35] customers can choose one of the bank's offerings or go elsewhere; the bank will not customize products just for them.

"High" banking comprises *corporate banking* and *investment banking*. Corporate banking is qualitatively like business banking in that it generates profit primarily by extending credit to firms. However, it functions at a larger, more sophisticated scale: that of the national supermarket chain or Fortune 100 auto manufacturer instead of the mom-and-pop convenience store or auto-body shop. Corporate-banking divisions regularly arrange financings in the hundreds of millions, or billions, of dollars. Just as in business banking, these may fund business operations and expansion: equipment purchases and leasing, inventory finance, trade finance, the rental and purchase of land, infrastructure, and mergers and acquisitions. At the high end, corporate banking has a significant transnational component, with global investment banks eager to participate. It can also involve derivatives and off-balance-sheet structures to manage risk.

Investment banking deals in the creation of, and investment in, financial capital on the capital markets. On the "sell side," investment banks structure, underwrite, and sell debt and equity securities. On the "buy side," they work with investment managers, pension funds, and hedge funds to purchase the same sorts of debt and equity securities. Securities issuances are typically in the hundreds of millions of dollars or above, and structured and underwritten by leading domestic investment banks or the major international ones. Often, multiple investment banks participate in a single deal so as to distribute the risks, capital requirements, and workload. Banks retain law firms to generate the thousands of pages of contractual material necessary to issue securities and derivatives. Despite their complexity, transactions must often be arranged in a few months. It may be uncertain until the end whether a securities issuance, merger, or structured-finance deal will go through, as these transactions are contingent on fluctuating conditions such as prevailing interest rates, exchange rates, and the availability of capital and interest from as many as six or more participating financial institutions and their clients. Hence, time is of the essence, and pressure is high.

Deploying Legitimacy in Low Islamic Finance: Assuaging Moral Anxieties

In low Islamic finance, shariah scholars deploy moral legitimacy: a positive normative evaluation that customers have of their probity and a belief in the rectitude of their decision-making procedures.[36]

From the beginning, the purpose of the shariah board has been to reassure clients and the general public that Islamic financial institutions are truly shariah-compliant. The first shariah board of an Islamic bank was established in 1977, at

Faisal Islamic Bank of Egypt. Many of the other early Islamic banks soon adopted it, including Jordan Islamic Bank, Kuwait Finance House, and the network of "Faisal banks" that Prince Mohammed bin Faisal Al Saud was setting up around the globe.[37] Prince Amr bin Mohammed Al Faisal Al Saud, son of Prince Mohammed bin Faisal and chairman of the Dar al-Maal al-Islami Trust (DMI), the umbrella Islamic-finance organization that founded and invests in the various Faisal banks, recalls that the idea was to set up an entity "not answerable to the management of the bank, nor to the board of directors, but to the general assembly [composed of] the shareholders." The goal of the earliest shariah boards, insists Prince Amr, was to convince the public—including many people suspicious about this new concept of Islamic banking—that the Islamic banks were really complying with shariah, "and not just lying and cheating you and telling you this is Islamic when it's not." The first boards were not established due to political pressure, he insisted. "None of the governments gave a damn," recalls the prince. "It was purely for the public."[38]

Today, shariah scholars who certify products as halal possess specialized knowledge about their production.[39] This is true not only in Islamic finance but in other segments of the global "Islamic economy." Sometimes the distinction between the religiously permissible and the sinful may seem obvious: to the fiqh-minded, pork is strictly off-limits. But twenty-first-century markets are home to a near-infinite, constantly changing array of products, and fiqh is a vast edifice of sophisticated legal reasoning and competing ethical imperatives. Advanced industrial capitalism raises new questions. Even if they may not eat pork, may believers buy shares of a hotel chain on whose premises pork is served? Or receive a vaccine created using porcine enzymes? Or eat chicken that might have nestled against pork in a shipping container while being imported? These are not simple questions. They require expert knowledge, just as determining acceptable levels of heavy metals in tuna requires that a safety inspector understand marine ecosystems and tuna processing.

Yet shariah scholars assuage anxieties not only by having specialized knowledge but by lifting responsibility for thorny ethical decisions off consumers' shoulders. Product certification requires philosophical reflection: the drawing of ethical red lines amid shades of gray. Just how much mercury poisoning is an acceptable level? This is not only a biological question but one that requires commensurating the value of life and health to the value of convenience and economic benefit.[40] Likewise, just how much must a garment worker be paid for trade in garments to be "fair"? And just how much of a hotel chain's revenues may come from pork or alcohol sales at the hotel restaurant before its shares are no longer halal? Ethical consumers have neither the time nor the inclination to work out the answers themselves. They look instead to the imprimatur of certification agents: an organics label, a Fairtrade® logo, a fatwa.

The desire to unburden oneself of ethical responsibility for consumption choices is visceral and powerful. Altaf, a wealthy forty-three-year-old poultry investor and Islamic-bank customer in Lahore, asserts that his Islamic bank has convinced him that it is interest-free by showing him fatwas of Mufti Taqi Usmani. He recently spoke with the bank's CEO, who assured him that returns on his deposits will vary because the bank has purchased a range of investments. But at the end of the day, the moral buck stops with the muftis.

> At the day of judgment in front of Allah, if a [customer] is found guilty [of having sinned through these investments], then we are not responsible; [the muftis who approved them] are responsible.[41]

Eskandar Shah is an associate professor of Islamic finance at Hamad bin Khalifa University in Qatar and was formerly deputy dean of INCEIF, Malaysia's Islamic-finance university. He holds a doctorate in finance and knows intimately how even the most complex Islamic financial products work. He also has quite a few criticisms of the Islamic-finance industry. "But even I go to Islamic banks," he explains. "It puts the responsibility on someone else—on the shariah boards. Because I want to feel like I'm not going to hell. At least that way I can sleep at night!"[42]

My interviews consistently showed that shariah-board certification matters to some small customers and many large customers, but in different ways. Most small (i.e., retail and SME)[43] customers do not know who sits on the shariah board of their bank or other financial institution. Their awareness is greater in countries and among groups with high levels of fiqh-mindedness (such as Saudi Arabia), but in general, most small customers are attracted to a bank by its pricing, customer service, branch location, and general proposition that the bank or its products are Islamic rather than by the specific names on its shariah board. Yet a majority do care that the Islamic bank *has* a shariah board composed of shariah experts who certify the bank's products, and that those experts are well-qualified. Thus the shariah board is to a bank somewhat like pilots to an airline: ordinary passengers may not know their pilots' names, but they feel at ease knowing those pilots are present and competent.

Deploying Legitimacy in High Islamic Finance: Reducing Transaction Risk in "High-Stakes Coordination Games"

In high Islamic finance, shariah scholars deploy pragmatic legitimacy, which appeals to the "self-interested calculations" of the organizational actors whose transactions they certify. These actors include large corporate and other institutional customers that issue shariah-compliant securities or borrow on the Islamic corporate-lending market (such as Islamic banks, Islamic insurance companies, Islamic funds, Islamic asset-management firms, and government or quasi-government entities); the investment banks that arrange, underwrite, and syndicate Islamic financings and issuances; potential Islamic investors in these issuances (which include the same sorts of private and public organizations, as well as private offices for ultra-high-net-worth Muslim households); and the shariah scholars who serve all of these entities. In such conditions, organizations' self-interest inheres in formal institutional mandates or informal institutional expectations from their constituents. For example, Islamic banks, insurance companies, funds, and asset managers have official mandates to invest Islamically. Some government agencies, such as ministries of religious affairs and Islamic endowments, have official mandates as well. Other government and quasi-government institutions may not have formal mandates but may invest or raise part or all of their funds Islamically so as to avoid embarrassing questions from journalists and religiously minded citizens. Finally, family offices are asked by their wealthy pious clients to place part or all of the family wealth in shariah-compliant investments. Ultimately, then, personal moral interests in shariah-compliance—on the part of citizens, shareholders, and wealthy families—do underpin the pragmatic interests of organizations in financing and investing Islamically. Yet the presence of an intervening bureaucratic layer of organizational actors, motivated by some combination of self-interest and public-mindedness[44] and operating in the fast-paced, high-stakes world of high finance, dramatically changes the mechanics of legitimation. Shariah scholars matter in a fundamentally different way in high finance than they do in low finance.

Scholarly legitimation in high finance is a crucial component of what I call a "high-stakes coordination game": a fast-paced process in which a large group of actors must settle on the details of a high-value shariah-compliant transaction. For example, when a sukuk, large Islamic-financing, or other large Islamic debt-type instrument is to be launched, multiple entities must affirm quickly that it is shariah-compliant: the originator, the investment banks serving it, the government regulator, and, upon launch, potential investors. There may be other parties concerned with shariah structure too, such as a credit enhancer and rating agencies. On a complex issuance or syndication, there are often four or more participating investment banks; all of their shariah boards must agree on the sukuk structure and sign off on its shariah-compliance. The government regulator too may have a shariah board or shariah unit of its own that vets all sukuk issued in its jurisdiction. Many institutional investors also have shariah-compliance mandates that require their shariah advisors to review issuances in which they invest. These investors include Islamic banks, Islamic funds, and Islamic charities, as well as some government agencies (such as ministries of endowments and religious affairs), quasi-government entities, and family offices. Even the Big Three international rating agencies of Standard & Poor's, Moody's, and Fitch, while not themselves in the business of adjudicating shariah-compliance, may consider downgrading a sukuk if a prominent shariah body questions its shariah-compliance.

During this high-stakes coordination game, speed is of the essence. Shariah certification by the banks often must happen in one to two months or less, as the entire process of a new sukuk issuance—from the moment a potential issuer approaches an investment bank through the canvassing of potential clients, initial pricing estimate, syndication, underwriting, regulatory work, a "roadshow" to pitch to more potential investors, final pricing, and sale— typically lasts a mere three to five months. Many fluctuating factors can alter the economics of a deal or doom it entirely, including prevailing interest rates and exchange rates, inflation, investors' appetite for risk and attitudes toward sukuk, unexpected credit ratings, and regulatory intervention. Issuances therefore become a frenzy of coordination within and among institutions, driven by bankers and lawyers working until the wee hours.

Shariah scholars can either lubricate the transaction or throw a wrench into it, imposing costly delays or blocking it entirely. In sum, establishing shariah-compliance in haute finance is a delicate, fast-paced, high-stakes coordination game: disapproval from just one shariah-board member can gum up the works, jeopardizing billions of dollars of financing for the issuer and millions of dollars of profit for each of the various market actors.

Elite Scholars Fill Structural Holes

This book's introduction opened with a scene of crowds clamoring around the globally elite shariah scholars at a conference. Why does this happen? Why does everyone in the industry act deferentially toward them? The answer lies with their pragmatic legitimacy: their power to connect powerful entities, each of whom has something (such as capital or an investment opportunity) that the other wants.

Arriving at this conclusion took years. At first, I suspected these scholars might be household names who could attract customers to banks simply by endorsing them. However, I quickly discovered that shariah scholars are not pitchmen. Despite their high profile, shariah-board members generally avoid explicitly endorsing the products or firms they certify. They do not appear in commercials or on billboards, and they do not laud the institutions they supervise as superior to competitors. Shariah scholars are loath to be seen as shills for the institutions they supervise, instead describing their mission as the impartial evaluation of shariah-compliance. Rare exceptions prove the rule. For example, in a two-minute video on the website of an app that screens stocks for shariah-compliance, the chair of the shariah board that approved the product describes it in very general terms as "useful" for Muslim investors. He speaks in a formal, emotionless tone and mentions no specific product features. The other two board members remain silent and do not even look at the camera, appearing uninterested. The video is not scripted or professionally produced, and seems to have been shot as an afterthought at the end of a shariah-board meeting.

I turned to a similar hypothesis: Could it be that shariah scholars attract customers simply by sitting on a bank's shariah board? That happens occasionally. Famous shariah scholars can serve as trusted brand names, offering customers peace of mind. This is particularly true in countries where the leading shariah scholars in Islamic finance also happen to be famous, well-respected public figures outside finance: Saudi Arabia is the best example, and Pakistan in the specific case of Sheikh Taqi Usmani, who is both the father of Pakistani Islamic finance and Pakistan's best-known Islamic legal scholar in general. Yet this hypothesis fails to hold water at the global level. Aside from Usmani, the shariah scholars in Pakistani Islamic finance are not household names. And in other major markets for Islamic finance, such as Malaysia, the United Arab Emirates, Qatar, Kuwait, and Indonesia, the most famous shariah scholars in Islamic finance are generally not among the most famous Islamic authorities in the country. Instead, the elite scholars of Islamic finance are celebrities *within the industry*—among employees at Islamic financial institutions.

The relative public anonymity of the shariah scholars of Islamic finance became even clearer when I interviewed people lower on the financial food chain. As I shifted from interviewing CEOs, middle managers, and shariah-department staff at Islamic banks—all people who engage with senior shariah scholars and implement their directives—to front-line staff like bank tellers and telephone sales reps, I found less and less convincing the idea that shariah scholars matter because the public cares who they are. Over and over, front-line staff estimated that only a small percentage of ordinary household and small-business customers—usually around 1 to 2 percent or less—asked about or mentioned their bank's shariah board. Even in Saudi Arabia, Salah, a bored-sounding telephone sales rep for an Islamic bank, quipped, "Nobody ever asks who's on the bank's shariah board. Ever." Salah himself could not name one member of the shariah board.[45]

So what do Islamic-bank customers care about, if not which scholars certify their bank? For the most part, it's pricing, not religion. First and foremost, "they want to know the profit rate on their financing, and how much their monthly installment will be," said Salah.[46] "I've been in Islamic banking for four years," said Muhammad Ehtisham, who sells auto financings and motorcycle financings for a Pakistani Islamic bank. "I've had three hundred to four hundred customers, and not one has asked me about the shariah board. Not one has asked to see a fatwa. They don't ask questions—they just assume [the products we sell are] Islamic."[47]

At this point, I faced a conundrum. On one hand, I had learned that the vast majority of customers at Islamic banks do not care which scholars sit on a bank's shariah board. Indeed, as noted by Dubai-based strategy consultant Mukund Bhatnagar of Kearney, "The bulk of customers [in mature markets for Islamic banking] don't have a strong preference" between Islamic and conventional banking.[48] On the other hand, evidence continued to mount that the shariah scholars were somehow important. It was not only strangers at conferences who addressed them deferentially; nearly everyone in the industry did. "I feel very privileged to have worked with scholars like Sheikh Nizam Yaquby, Dr. Mohamed Elgari, and Dr. Hussein Hamid Hassan," said Paul McViety, head of Islamic finance at the international law firm DLA Piper, naming three internationally elite shariah scholars.[49] The response from McViety, a non-Muslim lawyer with deep expertise in cross-border Islamic-finance transactions, was typical among professionals who work directly with elite scholars.

Studies of brokerage in networks point to an answer. Ronald Burt has famously argued that actors who serve as connectors or brokers between entities with complementary resources or information can accrue great benefits, in part because they can "see" and understand both sides in ways that others cannot. When they are among the first to fill such "structural holes," entrepreneurs can reap windfall profits and managers within firms can get promoted.[50]

We can think of the internationally elite shariah scholars as consummate brokers in the Burtian sense: they connect Islamic investors (that is, investors who want to follow Islamic law) with firms that want to raise capital from them. In "high" Islamic finance, the international scholarly elite provide what Mark Suchman has called "pragmatic legitimacy"[51] by reducing the risk of disagreements over shariah. In this sense, elite shariah scholars are not unlike other elite private regulators, certification agents, and mediators whose power arises from their professional reputations among peers and their skill at coordinating legal solutions that smooth transnational business: people like the international commercial arbitrators described by Yves Dezalay and Bryant Garth.[52] Elite shariah scholars receive very high remuneration relative to most of their scholarly peers because they have a good reputation among the law firms and investment banks that structure and arrange high-value transnational investments and securities issuances. These law firms and investment banks include many of the Global North's largest and most prestigious: the London-based "Magic Circle" law firms, their New York–based "white-shoe" peers, and the "bulge bracket" investment banks from across Western Europe, North America, and, since the 2010s, Japan. The same elite scholars enjoy the trust of the top law firms, investment banks, and wealthy pious families in local markets such as Saudi Arabia, the

United Arab Emirates, and Egypt. In the absence of binding transnational shariah standards, and against the backdrop of globalization and the expansion of cross-border high finance, the elite scholars play a vital coordinating role.

In an extension of the "structural holes" paradigm he introduced in 1992, Burt and his colleagues Ray Reagans and Hagay Volovsky have made a provocative finding: that people who attain monopolies on brokerage positions come to be regarded by network participants as leaders.[53] This may help explain the internationally elite shariah scholars' celebrity status within the Islamic-finance industry. Participants in the industry, such as Islamic bankers who attend conferences, notice the high remuneration that elite shariah scholars receive and know that those scholars vet high-value transnational deals. Perhaps these Islamic bankers are therefore more likely to view elite shariah scholars as leaders.

The Limits of Legitimation and Scholars' Relational Work

Nonetheless, the remuneration of shariah-board members has become a hot topic within the industry. For the most part, they are not bank employees but outside overseers. Hence, they do not receive salaries from the bank. Instead, they receive honoraria to recognize their commitment of time, just as corporate-board members (and academic speakers) do. The vast majority of shariah-board members sit on only one or two shariah boards; for them, shariah oversight may be a significant part-time commitment, but not one that makes them wealthy by the standards of global finance. Yet an international elite of around a dozen scholars sits on dozens of boards, with the most prolific sitting on as many as eighty-five boards around the world, according to one study.[54] The international elite command large honoraria: one interviewee set the figure at around US$300,000 per board per year as of 2021. Another interviewee, who manages one of the best-known international shariah consultancies and retains internationally elite scholars to review complex investment transactions for shariah-compliance, noted that a retainer of US$100,000 *per transaction* is typical. It is the consultancy staff, not the elite scholars, who draw up the contractual paperwork, which can reach hundreds of pages; the shariah-board members review it, suggest adding a clause here or there, and sign off. Since one elite scholar may review one such transaction in as long as it takes to read the documentation—perhaps a day or two—this type of ancillary shariah-advisory work generates significant returns.

In my experience, elite shariah scholars do not take kindly to being asked whether remuneration could cloud their decision making. The sober, disinterested mien they project comports with the idea that their religious obligations and professional responsibilities trump any possible material concerns. The logic goes thus: As religious authorities who issue fatwas, they answer to God, and as professional third-party monitors, they answer to Muslim consumers. Responding to the charge that scholars should not be paid large sums by the very firms they regulate, the internationally elite scholar Sheikh Hussein Hamid Hassan of Egypt invoked this double ethical obligation:

> What's wrong with getting paid for issuing a fatwa or reviewing the sharia compliancy of a financial instrument? . . . We're just like auditors, lawyers. Each one of us has years and years of experience in sharia law. We do our job and get paid for it. Nobody is allowed to question our honor, integrity and truthfulness.[55]

Hassan's comments speak to the way in which shariah scholars' legitimacy relies on both their religio-moral standing and their technical knowledge. On one hand, in comparing elite scholars' remuneration to that of auditors and lawyers, he invokes the logic of the market, which rewards elite providers of support services to international business. On the other hand, he implies that being a shariah scholar is a virtuous calling for which the reward cannot be measured in money. This conception extends much further back in time than modern Islamic finance; it reflects perceptions of shariah scholars as a status group. Their collective reputation for erudition, expertise, and integrity provides the legitimation that makes the other two functions of the scholars—justification and restriction—possible, thus allowing Islamic finance to survive alongside conventional finance and maintain a meaningful spiritual distinctiveness from the latter.

In defending their remuneration, elite shariah scholars are engaging in what economic sociologist Viviana Zelizer describes as "relational work."[56] Relational work entails people's efforts to manage economic exchanges so that they and others will consider the exchanges appropriate to the social relationships on which they operate. As a simplistic example, I would treat a "loan" of ten dollars to my daughter differently than ten dollars owed me by the phone company. Scholars of relational sociology trace different ways in which we humans manage, justify, account for, obfuscate, and transform our social relationships through our management of economic exchange, and vice versa.[57] It appears, for now, that shariah scholars' industry leadership—or perception of leadership, if the thesis of Burt, Reagans, and Volvovsky applies here—provides them some insulation from delegitimation over their remuneration.

Conclusion: The Bases of Scholarly Importance

In studying Latin American labor regulators, Andrew Schrank has explored the social, political, and economic conditions and the individual worldviews affecting governance authorities' integration into elite, powerful transnational circuits.[58] In this vein, this chapter has situated the foundations of the shariah scholars' professional legitimacy and entry into the international scholarly elite within their domestic and international prestige, their pedigrees, their language skills, and their views of themselves as "Weberian" technicians who dispassionately execute their duties. Scholars' prestige among the consuming masses matters directly in "low" Islamic finance: it offers moral legitimacy to everyday Islamic banking that serves ordinary households and small businesses. In contrast, the growth of international high Islamic finance since the late 1990s, in the form of big-ticket Islamic corporate banking and Islamic capital markets, has relied not only on internationally elite scholars' moral authority in the eyes of wealthy investors but even more so on their coordination authority, particularly in cross-border transactions where universal shariah standards are unenforced. The internationally elite scholars thus fill structural holes, and their ability to do so may indeed bolster their moral prestige. In other words, pragmatic legitimacy can increase moral legitimacy. These "super-legitimators" have pragmatic legitimacy: they reduce the likelihood of costly disagreements over shariah.

5

Justification

IN THE PREVIOUS CHAPTER, we saw that shariah scholars inhabit a fiqh-minded professional field: one that straddles Islamic academia, state Islamic courts, and state-sponsored juridical institutions such as fatwa-issuance agencies. They derive collective legitimacy from their long-standing reputation as custodians of Islamic ethical practice, and individual legitimacy from their schooling, professional appointments, publications on Islamic law, and increasingly from their fluency in finance and English too.

Now, we will see what shariah scholars do with that legitimacy. How do they practice Islamic law? What moral logics and styles of legal reasoning do they deploy, and with what effects? How do they conceive of what they do? This chapter reveals how scholars draw and defend borders between Islamic and conventional finance: between the shariah-compliant and the non-shariah-compliant. Shariah scholars *justify*, using the language of Islamic law, their own decisions to certify products, especially interest-simulating products. While the audience for legitimation is the universe of market participants, the audience for justification is narrower: fellow shariah scholars and other people with shariah expertise.

Shariah scholars do two things simultaneously on behalf of stakeholders in the Islamic-finance industry: they *minimize the otherworldly risk of sin* by embedding the practice of finance deeply in Islamic law, while they also *minimize market disruption* by authorizing what amounts, from an economic perspective, to the simulation of interest-based conventional finance.

Scholars minimize otherworldly risk by making constant reference in their fatwas and deliberations to classical Islamic legal precedents and by reasoning according to shariah principles. Their styles of legal reasoning reflect both their personal trajectories and their social setting. Reasoning in the analogical manner of Islamic commercial jurisprudence is ingrained in them; in Bourdieusian language, it is central to their habitus. They also follow, to some extent, the interpretive norms of the Islamic juristic school in which they were trained. Yet beyond these well-documented tendencies, I argue that shariah scholars in Islamic finance also seek to avoid being "called out" by fellow shariah scholars or by other shariah cognoscenti such as state regulators, product structurers, Islamic investors, and credit-rating agencies. Surprisingly, they also account for what "looks bad" or "looks good" in the eyes of laypersons who know little about shariah, noting that scrupulous adherence to the law will not suffice to maintain the reputation of a particular transaction or product if the average Aishah or Ahmad on the street considers it bogus. While they do come in some for criticism from some shariah experts who do not engage with Islamic finance, they maintain enough credibility in national and international fields of Islamic law, especially in key markets such as the Arab Gulf states and Malaysia, to sustain capitalist Islamic finance as a venture with broad (though not total) purchase in the eyes of the global scholarly community.

At the same time, shariah scholars involved in Islamic finance minimize disruption to capitalists by interpreting Islamic law in sometimes idiosyncratic ways, deploying a range of ethical logics. For example, when approving products that inhabit the gray zones of shariah, scholars have cited the Muslim ummah's need under modern economic conditions for easily accessible, sin-free financing. They have also argued that the Islamic-finance industry deserves legal concessions for the time being, while the state regulatory infrastructure and tax law supporting interest-free finance remain embryonic and government-issued Islamic debt remains paltry. Scholars have borrowed legal rulings and principles from across multiple schools of Islamic jurisprudence and patched them together too. They have even borrowed a key concept whole cloth from English common law. Such Islamic legal innovation is by no means restricted to finance, nor to the twenty-first century: as recent scholarship has shown, Islamic law has always been malleable, adapting deftly to economic conditions. And contrary to descriptions of Islamic financial engineering as obfuscatory,[1] shariah scholars innovate largely in the open: product structures generally become known quickly across the marketplace. In my conversations with them, scholars also reason reflexively and even ambivalently about what they and the industry are doing.[2] Nonetheless, their interpretive flexibility sometimes invites criticism, revealing limits to scholarly justification.

Ultimately, the shariah scholars of Islamic finance conceive of Islamic law not as a rigid cage but as a field of possibilities, adaptable to changing historical conditions and fundamentally pluralistic. They carefully negotiate between commitment to Islamic juridical tradition and the needs and wants of financial institutions, with an eye on government policy and public opinion too. In executing this balancing act, they serve as indispensable brokers between religion and capital, entrenching their centrality to capitalist Islamic finance.

The Adaptability of Islamic Law: Weber's Orientalist Conceit and Contemporary Rejoinders

The key characteristic of shariah enabling the development of Islamic finance is its adaptability, a quality which classical sociologists such as Max Weber considered absent. The stagnation of Islamic law was the dominant conceit among European scholars of the late nineteenth and early twentieth centuries. Nineteenth-century Orientalists such as Ignác Goldziher and Christiaan Snouck Hurgronje believed Islamic law had been capable of change only during an initial golden age of several centuries, after which all juristic development ceased and "the law became absolutely fixed."[3] This theory of the "closing of the gates of "ijtihad"[4] has been debunked.[5]

Weber concluded that Islamic law's failure to adapt to changing conditions made it inhospitable to modern rational capitalism.[6] Because of Islamic law's sacred roots, Weber asserted, commercial actors could not disregard the strictures it imposed on commerce and finance. Yet because it was unwieldy, Weber believed it could not truly be put into practice either. Instead, Islamic law became ad hoc law: a fatwa could be obtained in almost any case to say whatever was needed, citing past great jurists' opinions "like the opinions of oracles," without any statement of rational reasons.[7] In this picture, Islamic law does not adapt to changing circumstances according to any systematic reasoning developed in response to evolving social and economic conditions. Instead, each jurist shoots from the hip, driven merely by whim and acting differently on different occasions. In his comparative history of legal rationalization, Weber tended to portray legal change in Western societies as rational adaptation when it accommodated economic imperatives but as irrational and unsystematic in non-Western societies when it did the same.[8]

Since the late twentieth century, a good deal of scholarship has revealed how much Islamic law and Islamic jurists have adapted to changing economic circumstances. In modern times, jurists and legislators have mobilized Islamic law to suit a wide range of economic models, from agrarian to industrial, state-centric to market-centric. In eighteenth- and nineteenth-century Egypt and Palestine, for example, merchants, artisans, and a rising village bourgeoisie used the *salam* (forward sale) contract—also widely used in Islamic finance today—to fund incipient agrarian capitalism.[9] In eighteenth-century India, Islamic reformers promoted partial codification of Islamic jurisprudence in consonance with the interests of a rising capitalist class of merchants and bankers.[10] Subsequently in nineteenth- and early twentieth-century India, British administrators imposed Anglo-Muhammadan law, a "colonized," fully codified hybrid of Ḥanafī fiqh and English common law, to support the extractive capitalism of the Raj.[11] The 1876 *Mecelle*, or Ottoman civil code, represents a more comprehensive and authoritative codification of Islamic law in support of economic and social modernization.[12] And in Iran in the 1970s, prominent ayatollahs engaged in deep debates over Islamic law's position on private-property rights, wage labor, and banking in a modern industrial economy.[13] Their positions ranged from dirigiste to laissez-faire. These are just a smattering of examples that aim to show how modern Islamic finance is one more in an ongoing series of projects to construct and regulate modern social, economic, and political relations through the Islamic juristic idiom.

The Moral Logics of Justification

Normative Pluralism and the Flexibility of Islamic Law

Law, whether sacred or secular, is always an interpretive endeavor. Scholars of the law know that no two see the law in precisely the same way. But in Islamic law, the acknowledgment that differences of interpretation are legitimate—at least within certain bounds—rises to the level of a powerful norm within the global community of shariah scholars. Scholars must respect differences of opinion between individuals, regions, and juristic schools. If they do not, they face consternation from their peers.

Most shariah scholars around the world enshrine normative pluralism: the principle that fellow scholars may legitimately come to different legal rulings on the same matter, so long as those rulings do not manifestly contravene sacred sources or juristic consensus and are derived by knowledgeable Muslims using recognized methodologies. Normative pluralism hinges on the acknowledgment that human reasoning is contingent and fallible. Shariah scholars view fiqh as humans' imperfect effort to instantiate on earth the divine, perfect normative order (shariah). Ever since the separation of theology from jurisprudence and the formation of the major legal schools between the eighth and eleventh centuries CE, a strong norm has persisted among scholars that myriad legal doctrines and viewpoints can and should coexist peacefully and that dissent on legal details is not heresy.[14] Thus, while the Quran explicitly bans usury[15] and pork consumption,[16] scholars can disagree about what financial practices are usurious or how to cleanse a vessel that has touched pork—without deeming one another unvirtuous or irresponsible.

At the most general level, normative pluralism matters to our story because not all shariah scholars believe that shariah prohibits dealing in interest. A majority do, but there are important dissenting voices. Some of Egypt's highest-ranking ulama, including Grand Muftis Muhammad Abduh (r. 1899–1905), Muhammad Sayyid Tantawy (r. 1986–96), and Ali Gomaa (r. 2003–13), have argued that certain forms of interest are acceptable, and the latter two

have declared that Islamic banks are therefore unnecessary. Thanks to normative pluralism and the separation of juridical debates from theological ones,
disagreement on such a fundamental issue does not threaten a schism within
Sunni Islam.

Indeed, shariah scholars active in Islamic finance celebrate the fundamental
flexibility of Islamic law. "What was not important fourteen centuries ago has
become very important. . . . Shariah has the flexibility of responding to society," asserts Mohammad Daud Bakar, the best-known scholar in Malaysia's
Islamic finance community. He sees shariah's flexibility as central to its ongoing relevance. "We are blessed that shariah has not been expressed in detailed
principles but allows for flexibility. This is why shariah, God willing,[17] can last
forever."[18]

Sometimes, newcomers are surprised at just how flexible shariah can be in
the industry. Usman, a young scholar from India, had just joined the shariah
department of an Islamic bank in the Gulf a year before I interviewed him. Prior
to that, during his graduate studies in Malaysia, he had read much about the
higher objectives of shariah and had the impression that commitment to PLS
set Islamic finance apart from conventional finance. Yet when he joined the
bank and encountered Islamic finance as actually practiced, he saw very little
PLS. Instead, he found heavy reliance on tawarruq, ina (ʿīnah; sale-buyback),
and other interest-simulating structures that he considered dubious.

Initially, Usman was disappointed. However, over the course of his first year
at the Islamic bank, he came to see normative pluralism and the flexibility of
Islamic law as strengths:

> One of the things I've learned is to respect the opinions of others . . . I don't
> think that shariah-board members see something haram and call it halal.
> Rather, it's that in Islamic law, you have a lot of flexibility.
>
> Sale-buyback is blatantly a fictitious sale, yet the Shāfiʿī school says it's
> allowed. And if they have allowed it, others can't say it's completely prohib-
> ited. Fiqh has always been like that: some scholars agree, and others
> disagree.[19]

Accommodation as Ethical Worldview

In addition to thinking of Islamic law as pluralistic and flexible, shariah experts
in the industry stress that it is morally acceptable to find ways around restrictions that shariah may seem at first to impose. Zeeshan Ahmed, the dean of
one of Pakistan's leading business schools and a well-known Islamic-finance
educator, made this point to me by invoking Sufyān al-Thawrī, a noted jurist
of the eighth century CE.[20] Al-Thawrī quipped that any mediocre scholar can

give the strictest possible opinion but that true knowledge lies in "granting a proper concession upon a reliable basis."[21] In other words, finding ways to accommodate Muslims' goals by working skillfully within the formal scaffolding of Islamic law is not "cheating," assuming the scholar is not trying to justify manifestly harmful or unethical behavior. Rather, it is putting scholarly knowledge to good use. Skillful accommodations ease Muslims' hardship while allowing them to respect God's law. To underscore the point, Dean Ahmed cited a famous line from the Quran: "Allah intends ease for you, not hardship."[22]

Many of the elite shariah scholars I interviewed mentioned a personal connection to the world of business or markets—a connection that attuned them to the conviction that Islam values commerce and that Islamic law should accommodate the needs of Muslim businesspersons to the extent possible. The most colorful such testimonial came from Yusuf Talal DeLorenzo, the only American scholar among the international elite. (Everything about DeLorenzo's life is colorful.) In 1962, as a thirteen-year-old Massachusetts prepschool student, DeLorenzo first invested in the stock market, buying shares of the venerable U.S. automaker Studebaker. Although Studebaker promptly went bust, DeLorenzo became "very conscious from an early age of capital markets, and what they did, and why they were working." By the 1970s, DeLorenzo was studying the classical Islamic sciences with some of the most accomplished muftis in Pakistan. But he found his teachers to be dismissive of modern finance:

> I asked one of my teachers, the most respected among the muftis I studied with, what I should do with the stocks [that I had owned for years]. He gave the knee-jerk answer: haram, haram, haram.[23]

To DeLorenzo, the august mufti's reaction did not reflect any fundamental incompatibility between Islamic law and modern finance. Rather, it showed that recent generations of scholars had allowed the study of the relevant subfields of Islamic law to fall into senescence. Year after year, as DeLorenzo progressed through his advanced postdoctoral studies of fiqh in Pakistan, he studied with gusto denser and more complex books of classical law: the "yellow tomes,"[24] hand-copied and faded with age. But to his disappointment, his teachers neglected the sections on commercial law:

> Every year, the classes would start in the same place: the kitāb al-ṭahārah [the volume on ritual purity and hygiene]. And then you'd move on to kitāb al-ḥajj [the volume on pilgrimage], then marriage . . . and by the time you'd reached divorce,[25] the class had ended. You didn't get to commercial transactions,[26] and if you ever did, it was at the end of semester, and you raced through it.

That underscores that if something has fallen into disuse, it atrophies and dies. It becomes like a dead language.

DeLorenzo made it his mission to bring Islamic commercial law back to life and to uncover its compatibilities with modern capital markets. He aimed not so much to modernize Islamic law itself as to deepen contemporary scholars' understanding of classical Islamic law so they could use it creatively to meet modern needs.

Like DeLorenzo, many of the shariah scholars involved with Islamic finance today see their work as rejuvenating Islamic commercial jurisprudence and its historically sophisticated treatment of transactions. For the first millennium of Islam's history, Islamic jurists developed robust theories of contract that shaped, and were shaped by, the conduct of trade, investment, and lending in Islamicate societies (see chapter 1). But with European colonization, British, French, and Dutch administrators imported their own regimes of commercial law as part of their apparatuses of extraction and domination. Indigenous reformers, such as the Ottoman ministers of the late nineteenth century, likewise stripped commercial law of much of its classical fiqhī content. And after independence, postcolonial governments showed little inclination to bring shariah back into state regimes of commercial law, even as they incorporated Islamic legal principles into regimes of personal-status law governing marriage, divorce, and inheritance. So by the 1970s, when DeLorenzo was poring over the yellow tomes, Islamic commercial law was a moribund discipline for which few living Muslims had practical use. Islamic finance has changed all that. "Islamic commercial jurisprudence[27] used to be the area students didn't care about at al-Azhar and other Islamic universities," notes internationally elite Bahraini scholar Nizam Yaquby. But now, thanks to Islamic finance, "everyone wants to study Islamic commercial jurisprudence."[28] After all, working in Islamic finance is more lucrative and fast-paced than the traditional career options for graduates in Islamic sciences: becoming a madrasah teacher or an imam. And the number of such graduates has grown dramatically in recent decades, especially as Islamic higher education has expanded and admissions standards have relaxed.[29]

Why does it matter that leading shariah scholars in Islamic finance feel connected to the world of commerce and see themselves as revitalizers and modernizers of Islamic commercial jurisprudence? For one thing, real-world business experience makes them better at understanding the needs of the firms they supervise and advise. But I believe these inclinations also help explain how elite scholars view markets and shariah's appropriate relation to them.

In light of the reality that Islamic banks will fail in a competitive capitalist marketplace if they do not focus on profitability, adherents of the shariah

scholars' perspective feel that Islamic financial institutions cannot be forced—
or even expected—to go out of their way to advance collective socioeconomic
goals. "We have to know that Islamic banks are not charitable organizations,"
explains Aziz Ur Rehman, a Dubai-based mufti who heads the shariah department at Mawarid Finance in Dubai.[30] "Islam never says it is unacceptable for
a Muslim to maximize his profit across his investments, [so long as he] does
not violate [shariah] rules," insists Zeeshan Ahmed. Sometimes, he notes, it
can be un-Islamic to *forgo* profit opportunities:

> In fact, if you're an entrepreneur or investment manager[31] taking invest-
> ments from others with the mandate to earn a profit, it's your fiduciary
> duty—and your ethical duty in Islam—to make sure that you don't miss
> an opportunity to make a profit. And if the investor[32] drags you into an
> Islamic court and shows that you didn't act as a prudent businessman
> who did what he could to maximize profits, then the court will find you
> liable.[33]

In sum, people who believe Islamic financial institutions must be oriented
toward improving the socioeconomic condition of Muslims are "confused,"
says Yusuf DeLorenzo. Their confusion "starts with a fundamental misconcep-
tion: that religion equals charity." Just because Islamic finance has Islam in its
name does not mean it must bring about "goodness, godliness, justice, all of
those things," he continues. "Sure, that's a part of [Islam]—maybe the best part
of the religion—but finance is not religion."[34]

If the aim of Islamic financial institutions should not be to increase socioeconomic welfare, then what should it be? In the narrow sense, says Aziz Ur
Rehman, it should be to turn a profit. But how? "Allah *subḥānahū wa-taʿālā*
said, 'Don't make profit in illegal ways,'" he remarks. "'Do business with mutual consent.'"[35] The command not to profit in illegal ways is clear: Muslims
should avoid violating Islamic law in their exchanges. Yet the command about
mutual consent may be hard to grasp—is God telling Muslims to keep out of
extortion and kidnapping rackets?—until one recalls (see chapter 2) that the
classical Islamic jurists, just like the premodern Jewish and Christian jurists,
thought of usury as a violation of commutative justice, and hence as a form of
theft, which by definition cannot be consented to. In short, the mission of
Islamic financial institutions should be to make a profit by providing, in a
competitive modern marketplace, appealing financial products that avoid riba
and other transgressions of Islamic law.

From the perspective of shariah scholars, the pursuit of this mission is in
itself a moral venture, even if it is also a profit-oriented one. According to this
perspective, providing Muslims with a reasonably priced option for complying
with their religious duties is in itself an ethical act and a manifestation of piety.

After all, compliance matters before all else. Against the Islamic economists who claim that today's Islamic financial institutions fail to target the higher objectives of shariah, Zeeshan Ahmed replies:

> Do you know what the biggest *maqṣad* [higher objective] of all is? . . . Compliance! *Taqwá!*[36]

Ahmed's point is that fulfilling one's religious duties, and helping others do the same, is far more important in God's eyes than the improvement of social or economic welfare. He continues by pointing out that scripture commands Muslims to pay zakat first and foremost because it is their duty to God, and only secondarily because it helps the poor:

> Yes, we do see verses [in the Quran] that say that you should pay zakat in order to serve the poor. But that's only secondary. The very first [reason] is to purify the earnings of the person who is paying the zakat! Keeping the person paying zakat from spending eternity in hellfire is more important than giving one meal or two or three to some other guy.[37]

Ahmed is suggesting that Muslims be wary of imputing socioeconomic designs to God when He imposes rules. God may have such designs, or He may not; but in the absence of clear and convincing scriptural evidence, shariah scholars cannot force Muslims to behave *as if God did*, by imposing arbitrary restrictions on Islamic banks and their customers. Instead, what scholars must do is insist that Muslims follow the rules that are clear—such as, in Ahmed's eyes, the prohibition on borrowing and lending at interest. To demand supererogatory commitments infringes on the God-given liberties of Muslims to conduct commerce in the marketplace. This is the shariah scholars' staunch rebuttal of the moral economists.

Establishing the formal avoidance of sin as qualitatively more important than any other religious obligation has implications for the way shariah scholars understand the place of Islamic finance in a capitalist economy. Shariah scholars take the capitalist financial system as a given, not as a target of deep transformation and thoroughgoing Islamization. Most scholars I interviewed stipulated that in modern capitalist societies with competitive modern markets, firms have no choice but to respond to the forces of supply and demand. Within such constraints, they argue, Islamic financial institutions should focus on finding shariah-compliant ways to meet the practical needs of businesses and consumers. This means providing customers with shariah-compliant products that they want, not products that some theorist feels they should have—such as the profit-and-loss-sharing (PLS) instruments that many moral economists consider ethically superior to debt-based instruments such as murabaha. To those who criticize Islamic banks for simulating conventional financial products in substance while merely being Islamic in form, Mufti Irshad Ahmad Aijaz, chair of the shariah board at Bank Islami Pakistan, responds:

> [Among the critics,] there is a lack of understanding of financial need. If I need a car, and I go to a conventional bank, what do I want? I want a car. If I go to an Islamic bank, what do I want? A car. So if the needs are the same, the financial products are the same.
>
> If someone comes to me and says, "I need a car," and I say, "Here, take a glass of water instead," what good does that do? I don't say the mimicry criticism is absolutely invalid; there are some correct aspects. But people don't understand that when the need is the same, the products will be the same.[38]

In other words, Islamic banking will only survive if it provides people what they need; and what people need is reflected in the conventional products already on the market. So it is unreasonable to disparage Islamic banks for offering facsimiles of conventional products.

Public Interest: For the Industry's Survival

Along similar lines, shariah-board members sometimes adapt their rulings pragmatically to preserve the long-term viability of the industry, whose survival they consider to be in the public interest. Consider the interbank market for overnight funds. Every night, all banks keep a certain proportion of their liabilities (their customers' deposits, mostly) on hand to manage their needs for liquidity and avoid bank runs. In most countries, the exact proportion, known as the reserve requirement, is mandated by state law. But if by evening a bank has on hand more than it needs, it lends out the excess overnight, earning a small return. Conversely, a bank that falls below the reserve requirement at the end of the business day borrows to make up the shortfall. Funds on this interbank money market are exchanged using short-term instruments that are mostly interest-bearing, meaning the transactions are not shariah-compliant in the eyes of shariah scholars. The ideal solution for Islamic banks would be to lend short-term Islamic securities to one another. Unfortunately, governments and firms issue few of them in most countries, so the market for them is nascent, thin, and illiquid.[39] In trying to manage their liquidity and meet reserve requirements, Islamic banks therefore face a Cornelian dilemma. They can choose always to have excess reserves on hand in cash, putting themselves at a competitive disadvantage to conventional banks, which earn interest when lending out their reserves. Alternatively, they can place their overnight funds in the conventional interbank overnight market just as conventional banks do, dealing in non-shariah-compliant instruments and lending to conventional banks (which will in turn lend at interest). In short, Islamic banks can choose to be less competitive than their conventional peers or less shariah-compliant than their scholars would like.

Acknowledging this conundrum, shariah scholars in much of the Arab Gulf region have invoked the public interest as a religious justification for allowing an intermediate solution—for now. This is to engage in Islamic transactions with conventional banks using tawarruq (aka commodity murabaha). Because this solution requires Islamic banks to place funds with conventional banks that will in turn surely lend it out at interest, "it's frowned upon by most scholars," notes Ashruff Jamall, Global Islamic Finance Leader at PwC. "But until something more viable is found, it continues to be permitted."[40] Other similar situations exist. There are red lines scholars will not cross, but there are also numerous gray areas in which they explicitly balance religious rectitude against the survival of capitalist Islamic finance.

Once financial practices controversial to shariah scholars are justified in the name of the industry's survival and then become entrenched, they can prove difficult to dislodge. As soon as one Islamic bank adopts a controversial practice, others follow suit. Yet such practices do sometimes get phased out. Examples include Malaysian Islamic banks' use of the widely condemned ina technique of simulating unsecured loans and Pakistani Islamic banks' use of "special gifts"[41] to reward preferred customers with the economic equivalent of preferential returns on investments in common pools of assets.[42]

Incorporation of Secular Law

In order to make capitalist Islamic finance work under unhospitable market conditions, shariah scholars have even stepped outside the Islamic tradition and borrowed a concept that has no precedent in Islamic law.[43] The concept, beneficial ownership, originates in English common law and appears in many secular legal regimes. Beneficial ownership is a partial form of ownership. The beneficial owner of an asset may use the asset, obtain revenues from it, and enjoy most other privileges of ownership. However, it is separate from legal ownership, which refers to ownership of the title to the assets and hence the right to buy and sell them. Consider, for example, a wealthy family seeking to avoid taxes or unwanted attention. It could remain a beneficial owner of its stocks, bonds, and property so as to receive income from them but name a broker or trust as legal owner to hold title and thus be able to sell the asset quietly and conveniently.

To understand why beneficial ownership makes Islamic law more amenable to contemporary financial markets, consider sukuk ijara, a very common type of sukuk (figure 5.1). In an "ideal" sukuk ijara—that is, one considered

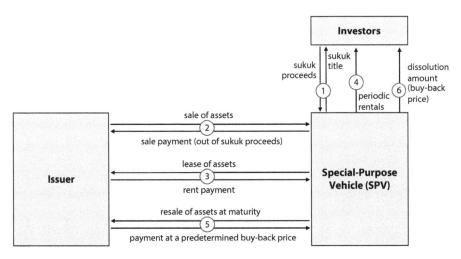

FIGURE 5.1. Sukuk ijara. *Source*: Adapted from Kusuma and Silva 2014.

unimpeachable by all shariah scholars involved with the industry, and in keeping with most classical Islamic law of property and sale—the investors become full owners of this land. The borrower then leases back the land from the special-purpose vehicle (SPV), which, acting as middleman, passes through lease payments to the investors (i.e., sukuk holder-landowners) as periodic distributions. When the term of the sukuk ends, the land is repurchased from the SPV, which then pays out the investors.

This "ideal" sukuk arrangement, described in the industry as "asset-backed," proved unattractive to both investors and issuers. From the investors' perspective, taking full ownership of a non-financial asset like land introduces undesirable risks, such as sudden ownership of illiquid assets and responsibility for liabilities related to those assets, like contaminated soil or ground water. For many issuers too, the "ideal" sukuk ijara poses problems. Government entities such as transport ministries and electric utilities often issue sukuk. Their highest-value assets include airports, seaports, and power plants. But selling these public assets to thousands of investors, some of whom may even be foreigners, can be prohibited under state law, not to mention politically contentious.

With the approval of shariah scholars, the Islamic-finance industry imported beneficial ownership from English common law to solve such problems. The sukuk holders become beneficial owners of the asset, able to receive lease payments from the issuer. Yet legal title remains with the SPV, which holds the asset in trust—or, in some cases, with the issuer itself, offering an extra layer of remoteness to protect both investor and issuer. The industry calls such sukuk "asset-*based*" (not asset-*backed*), meaning that the underlying asset or revenue-generating business arrangement put up by the issuer—such as a lease, markup sale, or silent partnership—functions only as a legal mechanism for justifying the channeling of funds from the issuer to the investors. In the event of default, investors do not enjoy access to the underlying asset or business arrangement, so their investment is effectively unsecured. Hence, potential sukuk investors focus on the creditworthiness of the issuer. Rating agencies such as Moody's, Standard & Poor's, and Fitch accordingly grade these sukuk based mostly on the creditworthiness of the issuer, and less so on the characteristics of the underlying asset. Agency ratings are tremendously important because they affect demand for the sukuk being rated. According to Hassan Jivraj, a finance journalist who has covered the sukuk market intensively for years, both the rating agencies and potential investors often see the asset as just a prop that exists to please the shariah board.[44]

From the moral economists' perspective, the trouble with asset-based sukuk is that they come very close to conventional unsecured lending. By turning the asset or business venture at the heart of the sukuk into something substantively irrelevant, they make it seem like a prop and undermine one of the alleged strengths of Islamic finance: its grounding in real (i.e., non-financial) economic activity.

Yet it is not only Islamic economists who criticize the use of beneficial ownership in sukuk. The Pakistani shariah scholar Mufti Irshad Ahmad Aijaz has witnessed resistance against the borrowing of secular law, particularly from scholars outside the industry whom he considers uncomfortable with change:

> If there are people who reject commingling law [from different juristic schools], do you think they'll accept commingling with English law, with Anglo-Saxon law? Of course not! So all these modern concepts, such as limited liability, stock exchanges, corporations, qualified ownership, beneficial ownership . . . scholars who stick to a very conservative classical position say, "Just reject them." But the modern[-style] shariah scholars say, "Ok, let's see. We may find a way to [draw on these concepts with] some changes, some amendments."[45]

The Craft of Justification

Shariah scholars active in the industry use a range of interpretive approaches to justify their approval of interest-simulating instruments. Shariah is not a unified, uniform set of rules but rather, as Anver Emon notes, a hermeneutic "claim-space"[46] in which various actors—including shariah scholars—put forward differing claims about what is and is not Islamically lawful and then defend those claims using many different methodologies and justifications. This section shows that shariah scholars in the Islamic-finance industry themselves stress the pluralistic, dynamic, and flexible nature of shariah. It then offers examples of the juridical arguments and techniques that scholars deploy to justify some common forms of interest simulation.

Developing New Law through Juristic Reasoning: Ijtihad

In Islamic finance today, just as in the aforementioned cases, Islamic law adapts to modern conditions thanks to ijtihad performed by Islamic jurists. Ijtihad is the formation of new law through independent juristic reasoning. According to classical juristic theory, it may only be performed by eminently qualified jurists, and only when the primary sources of law—the Quran and the Sunnah—and certain secondary sources (depending on the juristic school), such as juristic consensus and reasoning by analogy, fail to resolve legal questions. As mentioned above, Orientalists writing through the mid-twentieth century insisted that ijtihad died around seven hundred years ago,[47] being supplanted entirely by taqlid (*taqlīd*; literally "imitation"): conformity to legal rulings by prior jurists within one's tradition without full understanding of the bases of those rulings. But since then, some historians of Islamic law have rejected the "closure theory"[48] of taqlid as legal rationalization[49] and scaffold-building[50] rather than retrograde emulation, instead observing that after the so-called "Golden Age," "legal creativity simply had to be framed in a particular, disciplined fashion in order to be recognized as legitimate and authoritative."[51] Others have productively shifted the debate, noting the inherent openness of received texts to different interpretations by successive generations and focusing on the politics surrounding qualifications to ijtihad.[52]

Prominent members of the Islamic-finance community speak of ijtihad as a dynamic collective project essential to twenty-first-century Muslim piety. Examples of successful ijtihad performed by international organizations of eminent jurists include the obligation to pay zakat on shares of corporations, the use of geolocation to determine prayer timings, the legal status of margin trading, and the use of resuscitation devices. Islamic law's adaptation to modern finance thus forms part of a broader project of Islamic scholastic modernity, one that also spans bioethics and ritual piety in the context of digital technology and globalization. Coulson calls this adaptive trend "neo-ijtihad," which understands itself as reform in the name of progress. It has accelerated since the postcolonial legal reforms of the mid-twentieth century[53] and the worldwide expansion of Islamic juristic education since the oil shock of the 1970s.

Large international juristic organizations and conventions are the most influential and visible forums in which jurists engage in ijtihad, adapting classical

Islamic law to modern concerns and conditions. The oil bounty of the 1970s funded expansion of Islamic legal scholarship worldwide, giving rise to new transnational bodies of expert jurists including the Jeddah-based International Islamic Fiqh Academy of the Organization of Islamic Cooperation (founded 1981), the Mecca-based Islamic Fiqh Council of the Muslim World League (founded 1977), the Dublin-based European Council of Fatwa and Research (founded 1997), the Cairo-based International Union of Muslim Scholars (founded 2004), and other entities.[54] At the national level, and at major Islamic universities and research institutions, centers for fatwa issuance and research have also blossomed. Some of the shariah scholars most prominent in Islamic finance also sit on these transnational bodies. For example, Taqi Usmani is a permanent member of the International Islamic Fiqh Academy, and Ali al-Qaradaghi serves as secretary-general of the International Union of Muslim Scholars.

In the modern Islamic-finance industry, ijtihad has come to be used as a blanket favorable term encompassing all sorts of innovations, and the two competing ethical perspectives on Islamic finance that this book discusses—the moral economists' and the shariah scholars'—both use it to describe their own proposals in a positive light. The moral economists tend toward what Mohammad Hashim Kamali, one of the world's most frequently cited academics on the topic of contemporary ijtihad, calls *ijtihād maqāṣidī*: an effort to advance the higher objectives of shariah.[55] Moral economists associate these higher objectives largely with social welfare and economic development, and hence they understand ijtihad to subsume the development of Islamic financial instruments and institutions that advance welfare and development.[56] For example, moral economists have proposed countercyclical Islamic financial institutions such as risk-sharing sukuk linked to project earnings, commodity prices, inflation, and GDP.[57] Such instruments could ostensibly reduce systemic financial instability and national economies' susceptibility to commodity boom-bust cycles.

Shariah scholars, including most Islamic bankers and most of the elite shariah scholars active in the industry, welcome this type of ijtihad but spend much more of their time on what Kamali calls *ijtihād uṣūlī*. Here, *uṣūl* refers to the term "usul al-fiqh" (*uṣūl al-fiqh*), or the classical Islamic legal discipline that concerns correct principles and methodologies for deriving valid legal opinions. In practice, ijtihad uṣūlī entails the creative use of classical legal methodologies and classical opinions—including minority opinions—to develop instruments that allow Islamic financial institutions to be more profitable. The emphasis is on creative use of *legal* resources and *legal* reason. In short, moral economists tend to define and justify ijtihad in terms of social and macroeconomic goals of limited practical concern to capitalist actors in the Islamic-finance industry, while shariah scholars, while by no means rejecting that socioeconomically oriented form of ijtihad, focus on developing acceptable legal justifications for new solutions to market problems. The debate between these two perspectives mirrors larger debates over the purpose and evolution of Islamic law in the modern world. It is "a debate over neo-ijtihad," explains Kamali.[58]

Below, I focus on ijtihād uṣūlī—the more legalistic type of ijtihad—because it is the central way that shariah scholars accommodate capital in the industry. To put some meat on this abstract discussion, I discuss the techniques of ijtihad that shariah scholars use and permit and the justifications they present for these techniques. We begin with the invocation of dire necessity: the idea that Islamic financial innovation is justified, even if it contradicts the opinions of a majority of classical jurists, because it resolves a pressing need facing Muslims.

Necessity and Need

Islamic finance faces many headwinds. The most obvious include stiff competition from conventional finance and a lack of familiarity and trust among customers. But Islamic financial institutions also face structural disadvantages, such as regulatory regimes established with conventional finance in mind, tax codes that penalize the asset trades and leases used in Islamic finance, and a dearth of Islamic liquidity-management facilities (i.e., a lack of shariah-compliant short-term instruments into which they can park their temporary excess funds to earn a return greater than zero). Absent vigorous state efforts to accommodate Islamic finance, which in turn require political will and government bureaucratic capacity, Islamic finance remains a square peg trying to fit in a round hole. Shariah scholars in Islamic finance often point to these challenging circumstances when they extend Islamic law in creative directions to accommodate capital.

At the same time, scholars face the expectation, from their peers inside and outside Islamic finance, to justify such concessions using logics of extenuation that carry weight in the Islamic legal tradition. One is the logic of dire necessity (ḍarūrah). Although jurists have offered various definitions,[59] most have roughly concurred with the great Andalusian scholar al-Shāṭibī (1320–1388 C.E.) that necessities are those things without which life in this world would become impossible or deeply corrupted.[60] A well-known Islamic legal maxim says "Necessities relax prohibitions."[61] To illustrate this maxim, the Saudi jurist Ibn Bāz notes that shariah permits anyone to uncover her or his genitals before a doctor for medical reasons, or even to consume a corpse if the alternative is starving to death. These examples suggest that jurists have historically invoked the necessity exemption to allow Muslims to violate their legal obligations—especially obligations manifestly established by the Quran and Sunnah—under conditions of considerable danger or duress. Jurists have also invoked a lesser category of exigency than necessity, roughly translated as "need" (*ḥājah*), to justify actions that might otherwise be considered violations of shariah. According to al-Shāṭibī, needs are things humans require for ease and comfort and for the elimination of distress and hardship.[62]

The general logic here is that fulfilling one's duties as a Muslim should not bring undue privation. A refrain I heard often from scholars and Islamic bankers is that God wants ease for Muslims, not hardship.[63] This comports with an understanding of shariah not as a straitjacket but as an inspired framework for living a good, healthy, and moral life. To elucidate, Zeeshan Ahmed, the business-school dean in Pakistan, explained to me that shariah prohibits Muslims from drinking milk from a vessel if animals have already sipped from it—but makes an exception for cats, which are common household animals and therefore harder to avoid. In fact, Ahmed argued, God's tendency to alleviate undue hardship is especially pronounced when it comes to economic transactions. He mentioned that when God's prohibition of usury was revealed, the early community of Muslims in Medina asked Muhammad what alternative they might have to the interest-bearing loans they had been taking. The Prophet told them they could use the salam contract to sell their commodities in advance instead.[64] The implication is that God is benevolent; He does not want Muslims—including Muslims doing business—to suffer unnecessarily in order to follow His path. And today, Islamic financial engineers use salam to structure shariah-compliant derivatives.

Some shariah scholars have extended this viewpoint to assert that shariah is fundamentally compatible with all requirements of actors in a modern capitalist economy. "Sharia has unlimited products to suit every customer and every project under any circumstances," averred the late rock-star scholar Sheikh Hussein Hamid Hassan (1932–2020).[65] An Islamic bank, he explained, can finance an aircraft, a ship, or a plant. It can offer fixed or floating rates, tied to any benchmark or index. It can securitize receivables. And as Hassan showed in his work with Deutsche Bank, it can offer derivatives. Hassan's longtime collaborator, the Islamic financial engineer Humayon Dar, recalled the sheikh often saying, "There is nothing impossible in Islamic jurisprudence [beyond explicitly impermissible things and actions]. . . . If Islam shuts one door, it opens a hundred more." Yet Dar insisted that the sheikh was not "a liberal jurist," and did not feel rules could be bent and broken. Unlike many of his fellow rock stars, for example, Hassan prohibited organized tawarruq, a controversial but widespread practice described in chapter 6. Rather, Dar considered the sheikh someone whose knowledge of fiqh was so deep that he could find ways of achieving nearly any goal desired by financial-sector actors while remaining "within the mainstream domain of Islamic juristic thought."[66]

Shariah scholars have invoked need, dire necessity, and the avoidance of undue hardship to justify transactional arrangements that make Islamic finance competitive and profitable. One of the most consequential arises in murabaha financings, which are the "bread and butter" of Islamic banks' balance sheets worldwide. Recall how murabaha works: instead of lending the customer Amount X as a conventional bank would do, the Islamic bank buys a good from a supplier for Amount X, paying for it on the spot, and then sells it on to the customer at a markup, for Amount $(X + m)$, to be paid later. One controversial matter is that in industry practice today, the Islamic bank virtually always appoints its customer (the party seeking financing) as its agent to purchase the good on its behalf before it sells the good on to the customer at a markup. Islamic banks thus avoid expending time and manpower to acquire and physically take delivery of goods that they will immediately sell on to the customer anyway. Yet this creates an odd situation called "dual agency" in which the customer (as agent) is selling the good to herself (as buyer).

Choosing and Borrowing Law Pragmatically

So from a shariah perspective, can the Islamic bank appoint the customer as its agent? Historically, many classical Sunni jurists argued that a transaction in which a person sells something to herself is not a true sale. Most also prohibited dual agency.[67] They worried about conflict of interest, for presumably, the principal would want to sell at the highest possible price while the agent would want to sell (to herself) at the lowest possible price.[68] Yet a minority of classical jurists did allow dual agency when the agent agrees to certain restrictions imposed by the principal, such as a minimum sale price. Others in the minority considered dual agency acceptable if the principal was present at the sale session to make sure nothing dodgy transpired.[69] Such restrictions were meant to mitigate the principal-agent problem.

One key point here is that in permitting dual agency, today's shariah boards are pragmatically choosing a classical interpretation that suits the needs of Islamic banks, even if that interpretation was historically a minority position. This pragmatic choosing of a classical opinion, known variously through history as *talfīq* ("patching together"), *takhayyur* (also *takhyīr*; "selection"), or *tattabuʿ al-rukhaṣ al-madhāhib* ("following the licenses of the juristic schools"), is itself a practice with a long history in Islamic law. Premodern and modern jurists have written copiously about when and how it may be done, with various political and social objectives in mind.[70] So if we take the classical corpus as providing methodological precedent and guidelines, then today's shariah scholars are not "cheating" by picking and choosing favorable opinions but carrying on a long-standing practice.

Talfiq has become more common in the late colonial and postcolonial periods.[71] For example, classical Ḥanafī law held that women could only remarry without a divorce if their husbands had been missing for ninety years. Because no major classical Ḥanafī ulama had ruled differently, strict adherence to Ḥanafī law effectively barred the wives of missing husbands from ever remarrying. In practice, precolonial Islamic judges did not adhere to the ninety-year ban. In India, a Ḥanafī region, they enjoyed a fair amount of leeway and regularly used their discretion to allow remarriage much earlier. Yet when the British insisted on importing classical Ḥanafī judgments into a universal "Anglo-Muhammadan law" that was to govern all of British India's Muslim subjects, this leeway disappeared, and Indian jurists sought a new solution.[72] In 1939, they engaged in *talfiq*, adopting in the Dissolution of Muslim Marriages Act the Mālikī convention that set the duration at four years.[73]

To see *talfiq* at work in Islamic finance, we can look again to murabaha. In chapter 1, we heard Yusuf Talal DeLorenzo explain that in the industry's infancy, a subset of scholars allowed Islamic banks to bind their customers legally with a promise to buy the financed goods from the bank. Because this judicial decision made murabaha much less risky for Islamic banks, these scholars stayed in the industry, while dissenting scholars were shuffled out.

The business-friendly scholars arrived at their favorable ruling by using *talfiq*. Most classical jurists did *not* consider a promise to be irrevocably binding. However, an early Iraqi jurist of some (but not tremendous) renown from the Mālikī school of jurisprudence named Ibn Shubrumah (d. 761) did. In Dubai in 1979, just as modern Islamic banking was getting off the ground, the scholars attending the First Conference on Islamic Banks quoted him to justify binding customers to their promise to buy the goods traded in a murabaha.[74] This alone was controversial in some scholars' eyes. But to make matters more complicated, the Mālikī school does not consider murabaha a valid contract, although the other three major Sunni schools do.[75] Hence, the Dubai conference scholars had to patch together different rulings from different schools to meet the Islamic banks' needs. Subsequently, influential bodies of scholars have affirmed the Dubai conference's position on murabaha, including the International Islamic Fiqh Academy of the Organization of Islamic Cooperation.[76] In this way, accommodations initiated by a few scholars in the earliest years of modern Islamic finance have received further legitimation.

Other cases of selecting favorable opinions and patching together opinions from different schools abound in modern Islamic finance. Arriving at the "right" decisions on these issues makes a huge difference: otherwise, loopholes arise that canny customers can exploit, and Islamic banking in its current form becomes too risky for the banks to find profitable. Returning to our earlier example of a murabaha financing, we find several key examples of takhayyur and talfīq. Can the Islamic bank demand a down payment from the customer for the shipment of cars, and keep that down payment if the customer refuses to buy the cars? Although the other three major Sunni schools say no, the Ḥanbalī school says yes, so the industry relies on the Ḥanbalī opinion.[77] If the customer buys the cars but finds some to be defective, is the bank liable? The Mālikī, Shāfiʿī, and Ḥanbalī schools insist that it is, but the Ḥanafī school allows the bank and the customer to contract in advance that the bank not be liable, so the industry adopts the Ḥanafī adopts the Ḥanafī ruling.[78] And what if the customer falls behind on payments? Shariah scholars in the industry agree unanimously that Islamic banks may not benefit from the delinquency of debtors, but may banks impose late payment penalties that go to charity? Here too, industry shariah scholars say yes so that banks can incentivize delinquent debtors to pay. Yet the scholars rely here on the opinion of an individual Mālikī jurist, Muḥammad ibn Ibrāhīm Ibn Dīnār; most scholars from all four major Sunni schools do not allow charity to be made compulsory.[79] These examples show that fundamental aspects of the Islamic-finance industry's most common financing mechanism, murabaha, rely heavily on takhayyur and talfīq. The scholars who have aimed to make Islamic finance commercially viable have done so agentically and creatively, pulling minority opinions from the vast classical corpus and sewing them together into a new legal tapestry that hangs comfortably on the wall of modern capitalist finance.

Some scholars defend the robust use of talfīq by presenting it as a form of cosmopolitanism. This makes sense given that Islam's juristic schools not only represent different approaches to legal reasoning but coincide with geography too. In such a narrative, talfīq becomes a vehicle of global consensus-building for the sake of bringing fiqh up-to-date with contemporary needs. Mufti Irshad Ahmad Aijaz, a prominent scholar in Pakistan's Islamic-finance sector, asserts that among well-known shariah scholars inside and outside Islamic finance, "the prevailing opinion . . . is that for modern development, we need cosmopolitan fiqh."[80] Others contend that talfīq recaptures an intellectually catholic spirit that has long existed in Islam. "In reality, other than in the area of pure rituals,[81] all of our scholars have always been unrestricted to a specific juristic school,"[82] argues Sheikh Esam Ishaq, an internationally elite scholar from Bahrain who sits on many shariah boards around the world.[83] Ishaq notes that some of the colossi of Islamic law have issued opinions "not in line with their *madhhab*" on commercial and financial issues, including al-Nawawī (1233–77 CE) of the Shāfiʿī school, Ibn Qudāmah (1147–1223 CE) of the Ḥanbalī school, Shihāb al-Dīn al-Qarāfī (1228–85 CE) of the Mālikī school, and al-Sarakhsī (d. 1090 CE) of the Ḥanafī school.

This pragmatic choosing of opinions can nonetheless invite criticism. For example, shariah scholars outside Islamic finance sometimes criticize scholars involved with the industry for drawing on opinions from juridical schools other than their own. Aijaz constantly has to defend Pakistani Islamic banking against this charge. "We take the concept of [contractually mandating] charity from Mālikī fiqh, not Ḥanafī [the dominant school in Pakistan], and they say we're doing it just for the money," he laments. (When I ask who "they" are, Aijaz says there are too many such critics to count: they are as ubiquitous in Pakistan as "supporters of capitalism are in America.") Aijaz considers these critics to be uninformed and parochial, bound by blind adherence to local custom. "But the next generation are more in support of commingling fiqh," he says hopefully.[84] Yet internationally renowned experts in Islamic law have also accused the Islamic-finance community of playing fast and loose with its pragmatic patchworking.

When jurists justify the choice of one classical interpretation over another, they usually invoke a pressing need, and that is exactly what contemporary shariah scholars do in Islamic finance. In its widely referenced shariah standards, the Accounting and Auditing Organization for Islamic Financial Institutions (AAOIFI)—the most influential international standard-setting body for the industry, with elite scholars sitting on its shariah board—states that "the customer *should not* be appointed to act as an agent *except in case of a dire need*."[85] Yet the AAOIFI standard does not say what constitutes a dire need. In the absence of such guidance, the question ostensibly devolves to individual shariah boards at Islamic banks around the world. The exception has become the rule: in practice, every major Islamic bank in the world appoints the customer as its agent in murabaha financings. So one could infer that the dire need is simply the need for Islamic banks to stay in business by offering competitive and convenient products. In this way, the market, operating via business-friendly shariah scholars, has come to shape and entrench Islamic law.

Naturally, the same question arises over and over when employing these various justifications for renovating and reimagining the law: What constitutes a dire need? In what scenarios is the hardship is so great, and are the alternatives so limited, that the justifications are justified? Islamic jurists and historians of Islamic law have penned many volumes on this question, but to simplify grossly, the answer in practice has been that it depends—on social, political, and, yes, economic context. As Talal Asad writes, orthodoxy is a power relation; and as Muhammad Khalid Masud writes, Islamic jurisprudence is a social construction.[86]

Internationally elite scholar Sheikh Yusuf DeLorenzo also invokes need in a more abstract sense to justify engaging with conventional banks at all when they participate in Islamic finance. He has no illusions that the world's

conventional-banking behemoths, many of which he and his fellow elite scholars have worked with, are benevolent institutions. After all, he notes, each has
been fined hundreds of millions of dollars for its misdeeds. "It's just incredi-
ble," he sighs. Instead of sticking his head in the sand, DeLorenzo says, he has
condemned them publicly for their sins. Yet "even if their intentions are not
so good, we [in the Islamic-finance community] should work with them," he
opines, "because it helps us develop ways and means of pushing our own project forward."[87] DeLorenzo cites a hadith in which the Prophet Muhammad
predicts that there will come a time when riba is so prevalent "that it's like
smoke from a fire, and you won't be able to breathe without getting some of it
in your nose." "No matter how far you get from the fire, the smell of smoke will
stick to you." If Muslims hope to build a refuge in which to breathe riba-free
air, DeLorenzo insists, they must work alongside the "Wall Street types."[88]

Bracketing Social Concerns

The shariah scholars' market-friendly shariah relies heavily on two concepts
drawn from classical Islamic jurisprudence. The first is the Aristotelian belief
that interest violates commutative justice. According to this view, interest is
transactionally unjust, like theft (see chapter 2). Islamic scholastics, being legally minded like their Jewish and Christian counterparts,[89] therefore analyze
the transactions and contracts Islamic banks use: the sales, leases, partnerships, and so on that serve as building blocks of Islamic banks' product offerings. Shariah scholars ferret out usury much the way tax auditors reviewing a
company's books ferret out tax evasion: carefully and impersonally. Being
focused on contractual detail, the shariah scholars do not have to worry as
much about distributive justice. They can generally avoid the thornier and
more politically charged problem of what downstream impact financial transactions might have on social equity and welfare. Likewise, tax auditors do not
spend their time worrying about whether a company's operations make society better, or how existing tax laws affect the working class.

The second juristic underpinning of neoliberal shariah is the doctrine of
permissibility, which justifies a laissez-faire style of religious regulation. An
oft-cited juristic maxim states that in transactions, "the fundamental principle
is permissibility."[90] This means commercial and financial dealings enjoy the
presumption of being Islamically lawful unless they are conclusively proved
otherwise. Whether in London, Dubai, Karachi, or Kuala Lumpur, shariah
scholars invoke this doctrine regularly to argue that Islam does not simply
deem things unlawful because they could have negative effects. Many critics
accuse the Islamic-finance industry of failing to advance what they consider
the "higher goals of shariah," which usually include relatively abstract goods

such as faith, life, lineage, intellect, and property.[91] I asked the aforementioned Sheikh Nizam Yaquby of Bahrain, one of the industry's most prominent shariah scholars, to respond to such critiques. He replied:

> Everyone agrees that these *maqāṣid* are good. Of course. But can anyone actually apply them scientifically? You know, we have the maxim *al-aṣl fī al-ashyā' al-ibāḥah* for *mu'āmalāt* [transactions]. So unless we can prove scientifically that something violates shariah, we have to allow it.[92]

One young British scholar put it simply: "A Big Mac isn't haram just because it's unhealthy."[93]

Together, the focus on contracts and the doctrine of permissibility allow shariah scholars in actual practice to bracket the Islamic regulation of capitalist finance, leaving "big-picture" questions about social welfare largely outside the bailiwick of shariah even as they subscribe to the idea that an Islamic financial system will advance the moral and socioeconomic condition of all Muslims. I asked shariah-board members around the world whether they consider it their responsibility to evaluate the downstream social and environmental consequences of the financial products and deals they certify. Every scholar gave a strikingly similar answer. Mufti Irshad Ahmad Aijaz, chairman of Bank Islami Pakistan's shariah board, put it thus:

> RC: Should shariah boards evaluate the effects of financial products on social and environmental welfare?
>
> MUFTI IRSHAD: There are two categories [of situations]. One is clear, like if someone says, "I want financing for terrorism or drugs." No one would allow this—not government regulators, not shariah scholars, no one. But the other [category] is philosophical and debatable. Take emissions, for example. Someone comes to an Islamic bank and says, "I want financing for a big 450-horsepower Audi." Some people say Islamic banks shouldn't allow this for ecological reasons. . . . Or financing to sell soft drinks. A doctor could say that's harmful. So what do we do?
>
> But take tobacco. . . . Tobacco is not haram. Millions of people in Pakistan smoke. [Nevertheless,] a majority of shariah scholars have included tobacco in the category of [things screened out of Islamic funds]—not because it's haram but because it's harmful to society. And I think that's a good decision.
>
> RC: So why go one way on Coca-Cola and the other way on tobacco?
>
> MUFTI IRSHAD: Tobacco is something that almost all statistical studies have shown to be bad. The government even puts a warning on packs. So because the regulatory authorities have clearly said it's dangerous,

we screen it out [of Islamic investment funds] even though it's not haram. But you can't make this decision about Coca-Cola, because then [we would have to screen out] all soft drinks. And all genetically enhanced foods. Look at the laptop you're using here; some people say the battery is dangerous for the ecosystem. We can't enter into never-ending debates . . . we could end up financing nothing![94]

Mufti Irshad is suggesting that shariah-board members should seek to avoid harm but that they must restrict their harm assessment to conclusive formal evidence from relevant outside experts and secular regulatory authorities. Shariah-board members thus rely on the formal division of labor and expertise in bureaucratically governed modern societies to determine where Islamic authority over the economy begins and ends. As experts in the science of law, they feel compelled to avoid broad, substantively rational social-welfare concerns, for these turn quickly into slippery legal slopes.

Other scholars highlight how the bureaucratic division of authority and information access within firms restricts Islam's ability to regulate capitalism. Regal in flowing robes and round, thin-rimmed glasses, Sheikh Esam Ishaq sits with me at a Kuala Lumpur conference. Despite having just been thronged by Malaysian, Indonesian, and Pakistani businessmen for an hour, he answers my questions with cerebral calm.

> RC: Should shariah boards take environmental impact into account when evaluating the shariah-compliance of projects that Islamic banks and investors finance?
> SHEIKH ESAM: Yes, absolutely! But there's always the question of how well the investment team actually knows the environmental spillovers and effects caused by the project they are presenting to the shariah board [for shariah certification]. And if they do know, how much are they required to disclose to the shariah board? And who ensures that they do disclose? But yes, if the shariah board have any inkling of environmental spillover detrimental to society, it is their responsibility to ask the right questions.
> RC: Does this hold for social impact too?
> SHEIKH ESAM: Yes. But of course the thing is, the more macro the questions are, there's only so much you can do to address them.[95]

At a Q&A in England, I pose the same questions to Hussein Hamid Hassan, then one of the industry's most prominent shariah scholars and chairman of Dubai Islamic Bank's shariah board. Sheikh Hussein gave a blunter answer:

> Environmentalism and social responsibility are good things that Muslims should support. But that is not our job as shariah-board members. That's

the job of the corporate board. Our responsibility is to ensure that the bank adheres to shariah.[96]

Here it is worth recalling Max Weber's quote about the specialized bureaucratic systems of control that prevail in modern rational capitalism: "Most of the time this domination appears in such an indirect form that one cannot identify any concrete master and hence cannot make any ethical demands upon him."[97]

Mufti Irshad, Sheikh Esam, and Sheikh Hussein all feel responsibility for social and environmental welfare. But they also conceive of the shariah board as one locus of scientific expertise and bureaucratic authority among others. They acknowledge that the formally rational division of labor and authority in modern societies necessarily restricts Islam's scope for regulating market activity.

The upshot, then, is that Islamic law has proved quite capacious in the hands of shariah scholars involved with Islamic finance. Scholars skilled at grounding their justifications in the methodologies and logics carried through the centuries from classical law have afforded the Islamic-finance industry considerable latitude to structure financial products that are functionally very similar to those found in conventional finance. This is not to say that these contemporary shariah scholars' justifications would have passed muster with all or even most of the great classical jurists.[98] Rather, it is to say that classical law provides both red lines that may not be crossed and flexible tools for argumentation about everything else.

The Limits of Justification:
Mohammed Khnifer Takes on Goldman Sachs

We have seen that shariah scholars in the Islamic-finance industry draw creatively on various juristic norms and principles to justify interest simulation. They rely on normative pluralism. They invoke necessity and the public interest. They borrow and patch together opinions from across schools of Islamic jurisprudence. They bracket social and environmental concerns as being outside their bailiwick. They even incorporate English law. In so doing, they massage and reconceptualize Islamic law to accommodate the needs and habits of actors in contemporary markets and economic activities: something Islamic jurists have always done, and especially since the nineteenth century.[99] They do not do it in secret or through obfuscation. Rather, they view themselves unabashedly as rejuvenators of Islamic commercial jurisprudence, a discipline made moribund by colonial rule. They see themselves as reviving sacred law to serve the needs of twenty-first-century Muslims, adapting to a world

dominated by interest-based financial markets and their regulatory infrastructure and hoping gradually to carve out a pious space in that world.

But how far can scholars go in justifying interest simulation? In the next
chapter we will see how shariah scholars in the industry not only justify interest
simulation but restrict it. While contemporary Islamic finance is grounded in
a shariah-compliance-oriented formal approach, it is not entirely immune to
welfarist critics outside the tight community of Islamic finance scholars. Addressing criticism from both the Muslim street and the *fiqhī* ivory tower, the
industry may face pressure to move beyond its preoccupation with formal
shariah-compliance and broaden industry norms governing what it means for
finance to be Islamic. "We stakeholders in [Islamic finance] have a tendency to
live in the past," reflected Rushdi Siddiqui, an entrepreneur and venture capitalist who led the team at Dow Jones that launched the first Islamic equity index
in 1999. "We're still against pork and interest, you know? Pork and interest, pork
and interest. People want to see how Islamic finance is humane and ethical."
Siddiqui proposes that the industry move from asset-based to truly asset-backed
sukuk and that Islamic banks commit to being more tolerant of homebuyers
who default on their Islamic mortgages when their families encounter serious
health problems.[100] Dato' Mohammad Faiz Azmi, executive chairman of PwC
Malaysia and former head of the firm's global Islamic-finance practice, observes
a similar trend in the emerging intersection of Islamic finance with "green" or
"ESG" finance. "Up to now, the scholars have resisted putting any obligations
[on Islamic investing and lending] beyond shariah[-compliance]," he noted. Yet
he was encouraged that two weeks earlier, a sustainable Islamic equity fund had
been launched by the asset-management division of Maybank, Malaysia's largest
bank. "[The scholars have] relented, and that's been a huge shift," he asserts. "It's
the next evolution of Islamic finance, going from halal to *toyyib* [wholesome]."[101]
In Malaysia, the "toyyib" concept—shorthand for the idea that Islam promotes
not just shariah-compliance but healthy, wholesome, sustainable consumption
and production—is spreading fast in sectors such as halal foods, halal pharmaceuticals, and halal logistics. Its adoption in finance is no surprise.

Occasionally, there are even non-scholars within the industry who openly
challenge on shariah grounds the interest-simulating structures approved by
elite scholars. This is rare, for within the industry, elite scholars usually get the
last word on shariah-compliance. But in one highly visible case, a relatively
unknown practitioner rattled the industry, pushed around a titan of global finance, and embarrassed senior scholars.

In 2011, Goldman Sachs announced it would issue a US$2 billion sukuk
murabaha. Given the bank's renown and its large issuance, this was to be one
of the year's splashiest sukuk flotations. However, a thirty-one-year-old freelance sukuk expert and former journalist named Mohammed Khnifer pored

over the sukuk prospectus and cried foul, arguing on his blog that the Goldman sukuk was not shariah-compliant. His posts went viral,[102] and in an article titled "Goldman Sucks?" he offered three compelling critiques. First, he said, the sukuk was not actually based on murabaha as Goldman claimed but on an organized reverse tawarruq structure. Major international juristic bodies have declared organized tawarruq—and its mirror image, organized reverse tawarruq—to be "deception" that seeks to disguise usury. Second, Khnifer predicted that Goldman, being a conventional bank, would inevitably use the sukuk proceeds to fund its interest-based activities. Third, Goldman planned to list the sukuk on the Irish Stock Exchange. Because tawarruq is a debt-based structure, trading would send the yield up or down, meaning secondary buyers would be trading in debt at a value other than par—something most industry scholars prohibit.[103]

A war of words ensued. Goldman Sachs said it was "entirely confident" that its sukuk was shariah-compliant.[104] Khnifer received angry e-mails and LinkedIn messages from bankers; he was called an "ignorant industry outsider" with "crackpot ideas" on online forums.[105] Critics said he would never find work in the industry, and as a freelance consultant, Khnifer worried for his future.[106] Meanwhile, a journalist who asked a Goldman Sachs employee in New York technical questions about how Goldman managed to secure shariah certification for the sukuk and how it would use the sukuk's proceeds found herself angering the Wall Street banker. "Look, I don't care about that, honey. I don't give a shit about the little guy," she recalled him saying. "I just want to make sure you get the facts straight."[107] Yet Khnifer and this journalist were not the only ones to question Goldman Sachs's approach. When planning the sukuk structure, Goldman Sachs had approached Harris Irfan, who for the previous decade had led the Islamic-finance units of Deutsche Bank and Barclays, for advice. Irfan found Goldman's plan to be audacious for the same reasons Khnifer did and wanted no part of it.[108] Later, once Khnifer had stood up to Goldman publicly, a leaked memo from Abu Dhabi Islamic Bank's shariah board declared the Goldman sukuk noncompliant.

In bringing his allegations of non-shariah-compliant structuring, Khnifer was challenging not only Goldman Sachs but some of the most august members of the fraternity of internationally elite scholars. Goldman Sachs had hired Dubai-based shariah consultancy Dar Al Istithmar to structure the bonds. The chairman of Dar Al Istithmar's shariah board was Sheikh Dr. Hussein Hamid Hassan. Hassan not only defended the Goldman Sachs sukuk but claimed that he had sent a copy of the structure to the other very senior scholars on Goldman Sachs's shariah board and that they had never responded.

Matters got worse for Goldman Sachs a few weeks later when three top-tier scholars whom Goldman Sachs had listed in the sukuk's documentation as having approved the sukuk issuance claimed that they had never done so. The scholars were Mohamed Ali Elgari, Abdullah al-Manea of Saudi Arabia, and Mohammad Daud Bakar of Malaysia. "I have neither seen nor signed nor given any approval to the American sukuk in question," said al-Manea to a Saudi newspaper. "[Goldman Sachs's] claim that I was one of the scholars responsible for approving [its sukuk] is illogical," said Elgari.[109] Goldman Sachs now stood accused of both having played fast and loose with sukuk structuring and having attested the approval of leading scholars on false pretenses.

In the end, Goldman Sachs closed down its involvement in the sukuk market, the Dar Al Istithmar shariah consultancy closed down, and some elite scholars were temporarily embroiled in controversy. The power of young Mohammed Khnifer to rattle Goldman Sachs demonstrated that technical expertise in fiqh, even from a little-known non-scholar, could stymie questionable interest simulation by one of the world's preeminent bearers of financial capital.

Conclusion: The Legal Work of Minimizing Otherworldly Risk

We have seen in this chapter that shariah scholars embed the practice of contemporary finance deeply in classical Islamic law. In the eyes of many customers (and investors and clients and so on), this work by the scholars—which generally takes place beyond the consumers' eyes and outside their sphere of interest and expertise—minimizes the risk of otherworldly sin. To justify certifying interest-simulating instruments, the scholars invoke various moral logics, including normative pluralism (the idea that differences of opinion among qualified scholars are legitimate), action in the public interest and in the face of threats to the survival of Islamic finance, and the furtherance of financial opportunity for pious Muslims who want to avoid usury. They also craft their fatwas justifying interest-simulating contracts by patching together legal decisions from multiple schools of Islamic jurisprudence, borrowing legal concepts and principles from secular legal traditions, and bracketing out some potential downstream consequences of Islamic financings to focus instead on the shariah-compliance of the transaction at hand. It is through this kind of legal work that shariah scholars align sacred law with the interests of investors, financial institutions, and ordinary customers.

As we saw in the previous chapter, industry shariah scholars have become specialists in financial matters, strengthening their ability to monopolize certification authority. Few finance specialists would claim to know classical shariah as deeply as the industry scholars do, and few shariah scholars outside the industry would claim to know finance as deeply. Thus, the shariah scholars have considerable autonomy as monopolists of a new hybrid expertise.

Yet as freelance sukuk expert Mohammed Khnifer's takedown of the Goldman Sachs sukuk demonstrated, that autonomy is not total. As university curricula and training institutes increasingly offer this hybrid science that Jonathan Ercanbrack calls "Islamic finance law,"[110] and as elite scholars continue to be in tremendous demand and keep overseeing a high number of big-ticket transactions, more situations like this may arise. Thus, the social structure of authority not only supports the market growth of Islamic finance but can be destabilized by it too.

6

Restriction

BANKS GET FINED all the time. In the decade after the 2008 financial crisis, eleven of the world's largest banks paid almost a quarter of a trillion dollars in fines—for offenses such as misleading investors and failing to follow anti-money-laundering regulations.[1]

But Meezan Bank, Pakistan's largest Islamic bank, does something different: it fines itself. The offense? Engaging in a transaction that does not meet the shariah board's standards. Meezan's internal shariah department hunts for transactions barred by the bank's shariah board that employees have nonetheless executed and can force the bank to "purify" such transactions by donating to charity any profits the bank earns from them. "[Our bankers have] to get the process flow exactly right, or [the Product Development and Shariah Compliance department] will come down hard on them," insists Muhammad Waseem Bari, one of Meezan's area managers in Karachi. "We've literally had them give away one million [rupees] in profit to charity because there was a problem with the process flow."[2] Shariah departments employ a combination of shariah scholars and finance types with some shariah training; all look to the senior scholars of the shariah board for ultimate guidance. While not all Islamic banks around the world have shariah departments this zealous, nearly all are required by state law to have shariah departments that police transactions systematically. As the shariah scholars' bureaucratized deputies, these shariah departments stand as a barrier against capital's seemingly ineluctable tendency to drown religious principles in "naked self-interest" and "the icy water of egotistical calculation."[3]

Although Bari spoke with pride about his bank's stringent shariah restrictions, not everyone appreciates stringency. Shariah scholars can demand time-consuming process checks and sheaves of extra paperwork that conventional banks do not. Potential customers balk at enduring delays, so some sales reps grumble about the shariah rules and quietly skirt them. Shariah stringency can also gum up big-ticket corporate transactions, especially if they involve new contractual structures. One Riyadh-based investment banker at a top-ten multinational bank vented to me about the head of the shariah department at one of the Gulf's largest Islamic banks. This well-known shariah scholar had jeopardized an innovative sukuk issuance—worth hundreds of millions of dollars and syndicated among several banks—by asking too many questions about its structure at the last minute. "We were doing a roadshow, and we only had four or five days to pitch the sukuk," noted the investment banker. The price of the sukuk had been fixed, so time was of the essence: any drop in demand could cost all participating banks dearly. "What this guy does is raise shariah objections, even when the shariah boards of all the banks have already signed off, and when we don't have time to restructure the whole thing!" exclaimed the investment banker, exasperated.[4]

In the previous three chapters, we have seen how shariah scholars facilitate an interest-simulating form of Islamic finance profitable to capitalists. Yet if all they did were accommodate capitalists' interests, there would cease to be anything distinctive at all about Islamic finance. How does Islamic finance persist, and why do millions of Muslims continue to take it seriously, when it clearly simulates the economic effects of interest-based finance? I argue in this chapter that Islamic finance persists in part because shariah scholars and their deputies apply restrictions that cost capitalists real time and money. They intervene in billion- and centimillion-dollar transactions, occasionally even at the last minute, with complex structuring conditions that capitalists must meet. "Shariah scholars are . . . perceived by many market participants . . . to be more influential than the CEO," says Murat Ünal, author of a highly publicized 2010 study of shariah scholars around the world.[5] Scholars on the shariah board also oversee a bureaucratic apparatus of shariah-compliance officers and shariah auditors who serve as the long arm of their law, monitoring products, transactions, customers, and even sales staff for shariah-compliance. This restriction is what keeps Islamic finance Islamic: without it, capitalists could push the shariah envelope as far as they wanted, and Islamic finance would go the way of scholastic Catholic finance and scholastic Jewish finance, effectively accommodating any profitable transaction at all and ceasing to have a distinctive religious identity (see chapter 2).

Yet we will see that there is a twist. Since the early 2000s, the Islamic-finance ecosystem has grown large enough that when shariah scholars reject certain arrangements as noncompliant, entrepreneurial product engineers stand ready to design and sell platforms and services that address the scholars' concerns. They deploy technical and technological innovations that rationalize the ever-more-scrupulous application of shariah to finance. Thus the scholars' imprimatur does restrict capital, but ultimately, it also creates new opportunities for profit and new, more-efficient strategies for interest simulation. The logic of shariah-compliance and the logic of capital's relentless creation of new market possibilities reinforce each other.

Individual Scholars against Capital

This section explores two cases in which scholars have pushed back against capital. In the first case, one elite scholar rebutted another elite scholar whom he felt had "pushed the envelope" of shariah-compliance so far that it might cease to mean anything at all. In another case, an elite scholar took on the entire global sukuk market. In both cases, scholars defended the border between conventional and Islamic finance and forced capitalists to conform to demands for intensified shariah-compliance that proved costly.

Sheikh Yusuf DeLorenzo versus the Doomsday Derivative

Decommodification is the process of detaching or protecting goods from self-regulating markets.[6] As Bruce Carruthers observes in the context of "fair value" accounting rules, contests over how to value and categorize financial assets can affect the prospects for decommodification.[7] Islamic finance, even in its most market-friendly interpretations, seeks to decommodify finance by requiring that real non-financial assets or services mediate debt-based financing relationships. Yet because these decommodification requirements constrain what capitalists can do in Islamic finance and impose extra burdens on them, capitalists constantly "push the envelope." The story of the Islamic total-return swap (TRS) is a story of Islamic financial engineers, endorsed by one of the world's most famous scholars, who went a bridge too far, testing the outer limits of shariah-compliance and finding their path blocked by another famous scholar.

Launched in 2004, the Deutsche Bank–Dar Al Istithmar (DI) venture developed complex Islamic financial structures on behalf of sophisticated clients, mostly in the Gulf. Geert Bossuyt, a brainy Belgian derivatives specialist, was leader of the Deutsche Bank side of the mash-up. Bossuyt put some of Deutsche's brightest financial engineers in front of the same whiteboard as shariah experts from DI, a shariah consultancy. Bossuyt and his bosses at Deutsche Bank believed that shariah-compliant investors could and should have access to the full panoply of conventional risk-management and investment tools available to shariah-compliant investors. Innovation, they felt, would drag Islamic finance into the twenty-first century—and earn them a healthy profit along the way.[8]

In a 2007 white paper that would become notorious, the Deutsche Bank team outlined a structure for an Islamic TRS, which Deutsche Bank had brought to market with approval from DI's shariah board. A conventional TRS allows sophisticated investors—hedge funds are typical users—the ability to benefit from exposure to assets, such as stocks or bonds, without needing to put down the cash to invest in them. In other words, a TRS replicates the economic effect of investing in assets without actually investing in them. Deutsche Bank's Islamic TRS would do the same but in the process would cross what many industry stakeholders considered a religious red line. The Islamic TRS would allow shariah-compliant investors to swap the returns from a halal asset they owned for the returns from a non-halal asset owned by someone else. It effectively let Muslims "invest" indirectly in underlying un-Islamic assets—in theory, even interest-bearing bonds, brewery shares, or pork bellies—by "wrapping" the returns in a shariah-compliant structure.

The Islamic TRS stirred heated debate. Not surprisingly, moral economists staunchly opposed it, as it falls far beyond the pale of what they consider Islamic and has no evident social or economic benefits to boot. Of much greater commercial import was what occurred among shariah scholars, where views were more divided. Something rare happened: one world-famous shariah scholar publicly and stridently criticized a product approved by other world-famous scholars. The most famous scholar backing the product was the Egyptian-born Sheikh Hussein Hamid Hassan. Hassan chaired the DI shariah board as well as many others around the world, including that of Dubai Islamic Bank. The most vocal public critic was Sheikh Yusuf Talal DeLorenzo, the best-known American shariah scholar in international Islamic-finance circuits. DeLorenzo called the consenting scholars' approval of the Deutsche Bank product a "doomsday fatwa" that, if widely accepted, "could spell the end of the need for authentic Islamic products, services, and methodologies."[9] If Islamic investors could use this stratagem to invest in noncompliant products, he reasoned, what use would there be for Islamic financial instruments at all?

Ironically, Sheikh DeLorenzo and Sheikh Hassan were personally close. They had known each other well since the 1980s, when Hassan was president of the International Islamic University, Islamabad, and DeLorenzo was on the faculty. DeLorenzo called Hassan by phone before publicly announcing his opposition to the Islamic TRS. "I gave him the courtesy of talking to him first," DeLorenzo recalls. Yet the two did not reconcile their clashing views. "Basically, we agreed to disagree, and there it was." Also opposed to the Islamic TRS was Sheikh Dr. Mohamed Ali Elgari of Saudi Arabia, a huge name among Islamic-finance shariah scholars worldwide. According to DeLorenzo, it was Elgari who first referred to Hassan's ruling as a "doomsday fatwa."[10] This was a rare clash of Islamic-finance titans.

At a conference in Dubai in November 2007, DeLorenzo appeared on stage next to Hussein Hassan of Deutsche Bank, a structuring expert who had helped design the Islamic TRS. (This Hussein Hassan is unrelated to the late sheikh who shared his name.) In DeLorenzo's words, the two had "an open debate" on stage at the conference.[11] At the heart of their differences lay some fascinating questions about the nature of money and prices. Hassan explained to the audience that Deutsche Bank consulted its shariah board during the structuring process and got the board's approval. He also stressed that Deutsche Bank carefully segregates Islamic investors' assets from haram assets.[12] By this logic, the Islamic TRS is shariah-compliant because tainted money does not flow directly from an un-Islamic source or structure to the Islamic investor. Instead, Deutsche Bank argued, the Islamic TRS merely relied on interest-rate benchmarks such as LIBOR to set a price for the funds that would flow to the Islamic investor. Deutsche Bank noted that the use of interest-rate benchmarks to price Islamic products is a common practice (used often in sukuk, for example). Indeed, most shariah scholars active in Islamic finance have accepted it for years. Their logic is simple: if I sell grape juice at the same price as you sell wine, my grape juice does not suddenly become haram.

DeLorenzo retorted that there is a difference between using LIBOR simply as a benchmark and what the Islamic TRS does. "While LIBOR is a benchmark used to set a price by marking value," he later wrote, the agreement underlying the Islamic TRS "is used to actually deliver that price, even if it does so synthetically."[13] In an age in which the vast majority of money exists and moves digitally, Deutsche Bank's argument seemed disingenuous—a clever way of pouring wine into grape-juice bottles. In the face of such opprobrium, Deutsche Bank eventually withdrew its product from the market, but not before trying to lure Sheikh DeLorenzo over to its side. Six months after DeLorenzo's "debate" appearance, Geert Bossuyt approached him at a conference in London. "Geert . . . basically wanted to co-opt me," DeLorenzo remembered. "He invited me to join their shariah board, thinking that if I became a member . . . I don't know what he was thinking!"[14]

The lesson is that shariah scholars do defend the boundaries of Islamic finance, protecting it from being "secularized away" by capitalists who take liberties that scholars consider excessive. Market forces have their limits.

Mufti Taqi Usmani versus the Sukuk Sector

Mufti Taqi Usmani has unquestionably been one of the biggest-name shariah scholars in Islamic finance for decades. He chairs the most influential shariah board in the industry: that of the Accounting and Auditing Organization for Islamic Financial Institutions (AAOIFI), the transnational body whose shariah standards serve as non-binding but widely followed guidelines in many countries and cross-border transactions. He also chairs, among others, the shariah boards of Pakistan's first and largest Islamic bank (Meezan Bank), the UAE's second-largest (Abu Dhabi Islamic Bank), and Bahrain-based Arcapita, one of the best-known Islamic private-equity houses, which has owned name-brand American chains such as Church's Chicken and Caribou Coffee. He has been intimately involved in the development of international Islamic capital markets, having chaired the shariah boards of Dow Jones Islamic, HSBC, and Citi Islamic Investment Bank as well as an early Luxembourg-based Islamic equity fund targeting high-net-worth Gulf investors. So if any scholar might be expected to avoid "rocking the boat" by disrupting the smooth flow of capital into Islamic financial instruments, it would be someone in Usmani's structural position.

And yet in November 2007, Usmani issued the most notorious fatwa in the history of modern Islamic finance, shaking the nascent sukuk sector just as it was gaining momentum. Usmani's fatwa asserted that two very common types of sukuk were un-Islamic:[15] the sukuk musharaka, which was then the most common type in the world, and the structurally similar sukuk mudaraba, which was also very common. According to media sources, this meant Usmani was effectively declaring 85 percent of the world sukuk market to be haram.

The fallout was rapid and intense. After Usmani's pronouncement, sukuk yields rose, and global sukuk issuance dropped from $48 billion in 2007 to $18 billion in 2008 (figure 6.1). While much of the drop was due to the global credit crunch, sukuk also likely lost popularity relative to conventional bonds. Usmani had created uncertainty and shaken markets like an Islamic chair of the Fed. Mohamed Damak, global head of Islamic finance at S&P Global Ratings, said Usmani's pronouncement probably pushed up sukuk yields for "a few days or a few weeks" because "people didn't understand what would happen."[16] The furor was amplified "because of [Usmani's] prominence," for "generally shariah scholars like to be in consensus when it comes to these structures; they don't like to take opposing views to each other," noted Atif Hanif, head of the European Islamic finance practice at the law firm Allen & Overy.[17]

Many observers felt Usmani rattled the reputation of Islamic finance itself by showing that individual scholars could and would destabilize the investing environment on a whim. "It is clear that clerics can paralyze entire markets with a fatwa," opined *Der Spiegel*.[18] Usmani's fatwa got so much attention because sukuk were, and still are, the flagship product type signaling the maturation of Islamic finance. At the time, Islamic and conventional investors alike were still getting to know sukuk, which only began making serious inroads into international debt markets in the early 2000s. "Sukuk issuances are high-profile because of their public nature," remarked Paul McViety, head of Islamic finance at the law firm DLA Piper. "You typically have an offering circular, marketing materials, and announcements; people know when a sukuk issuer is going to market."[19] In light of its impact on the industry, veteran Islamic-finance journalist Mushtak Parker called Usmani's declaration "ill-timed."[20]

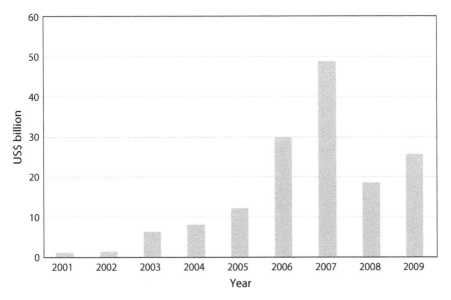

FIGURE 6.1. Worldwide issuance of sukuk, 2001–9. Sheikh Taqi Usmani's declaration that 85 percent of sukuk worldwide are un-Islamic came in November 2007. *Source*: Alvi et al. 2011.

Usmani's fundamental criticism of sukuk musharaka and sukuk mudaraba was that instead of acting as they theoretically should, they were being perverted to mimic conventional bonds. In sukuk musharaka and sukuk mudaraba, the investors (i.e., sukuk holders) buy into a pool of assets, projects, or business ventures. The pool is then managed by the sukuk issuer, who—in theory—pays a return that varies based on the performance of the pool (figure 6.2). Crucially, mudaraba and musharaka are equity-type profit-and-loss-sharing (PLS) partnership contracts, meaning that the return investors earn cannot be established in advance and that investors' principal is not guaranteed to be returned in full. (After all, if you take an equity stake in my pizza business, we cannot establish in advance what percent return your investment will generate—it must be linked to my future profitability selling pizzas—and we cannot guarantee that your investment be returned in full. If your investment did both, it would effectively be a loan, not an equity stake.) Yet as Usmani[21] noted, virtually all sukuk mudaraba and sukuk musharaka in existence did both. Usually, they guaranteed sukuk holders a return, such as LIBOR plus 3.0 percent, linked to a benchmark interest rate. They achieved this using a clever mechanism called "profit smoothing" described in chapter 2. If the underlying partnership generated more than the guaranteed return (e.g., LIBOR plus 3.7 percent), then the partnership manager (i.e., the sukuk issuer)

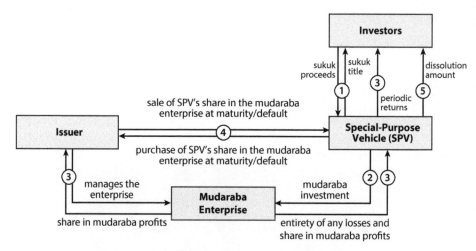

FIGURE 6.2. Sukuk mudaraba. *Source*: Kusuma and Silva 2014.

could keep the excess (0.7 percent), ostensibly as an incentive for good performance. If the partnership generated less than the guaranteed return (e.g., LIBOR plus 2.6 percent), then the manager could choose to pay the shortfall (0.4 percent) to the investors as an interest-free loan. This loan would then be paid back out of excess returns during future periods or by lowering the cost of repurchasing the assets possessed by the partnership. This "collar" mechanism assured a return no higher than, and no lower than, the guaranteed return (e.g., LIBOR plus 3.0 percent). Moreover, in the event that the partnership lost money, the investors were guaranteed to get their principal back. This was achieved via a binding promise by the issuer or the manager to repurchase the pooled assets, projects, or ventures at face value (i.e., the same price at which they were initially sold to investors).

Usmani's fatwa challenged on shariah grounds these various elements that made industry-standard sukuk musharaka and sukuk mudaraba act like bonds.[22] He argued that it was bogus to allow the sukuk issuer to keep any excess beyond the established return as an "incentive," for an incentive is something that "may logically be ascribed to good management." In truth, the "incentives" being offered were merely linked "to the costs of financing or to the prevalent rates of interest in the market [e.g., LIBOR]; rates that vary . . . every hour of the day."[23] Thus, he reasoned, the "incentives" bore no relation to managerial skill. Usmani also argued against allowing the issuer to provide a loan covering any shortfall below the established return because the Prophet Muhammad is said to have prohibited linking a sale to a loan. Since issuers sell sukuk certificates to investors, linking such sales to loans to those same investors was unacceptable in Usmani's eyes. He stressed that "the entire com-munity of scholars" past and present had agreed on this prohibition.[24]

As for the issuer's promise to repurchase assets at face value, and hence to guarantee the investors' principal, Usmani also cried foul. "The legal presump-tion with regard to Sukuk is that there can be no guarantee that capital will be returned to investors," he averred.[25] Rather, investors have the right to the "true value"—that is, the market value—of the sukuk assets. If those assets decline in value, so be it; to Usmani, being a sukuk holder meant having taken owner-ship of those assets, and ownership comes with market risk. "In shariah compli-ant dealings, reward always follows after risk,"[26] he declared, alluding to a juris-tic maxim that scholars and Islamic economists cite as a fundamental principle of Islamic finance. Failure to guarantee the return of principal was to Usmani a desirable feature of sukuk, not a bug that should or could be engineered away.

In the bigger picture, Usmani's fatwa was not just a critique of particular aspects of particular sukuk but a clarion call to drag the wayward practice of Islamic finance back to bedrock religious logics. Usmani clearly distinguished two such logics. The first was juristic. It suffused most of the fatwa, which was written in the style and mode of reasoning common to classically trained sha-riah scholars past and present. At each plank in his argument, Usmani cata-logued how renowned classical jurists ruled on the legal question at hand, drawing the reader to the conclusion that existing industry practice flew in the face of premodern juristic consensus. Moreover, he showed concern for what one internationally elite scholar, the Syrian-born Sheikh Osaid Kailani, de-scribed to me as "the higher objectives of the contracts."[27] By this, Kailani meant a respect for the functions and essential aspects of nominate Islamic contracts such as sales, leases, and partnerships as they had long been estab-lished by the consensus of jurists. In this view, equity partnerships like mush-araka and mudaraba should actually function as equity partnerships, not be contorted into taking on the features of debt. Ownership should be true ownership, with the attendant risks that shariah has always demanded an owner bear. An incentive should actually incentivize. In short, if a product walked, swam, and quacked like a duck, no one should get away with calling it a chocolate bar. Usmani, like Kailani, was effectively calling for respect for shariah as a tradition of legal thought, and specifically for the edifice of Islamic commercial law, built on hallowed categories that jurists had used for centu-ries. In recent years, the bankers and lawyers, and quite a few of the scholars, had been reimagining and stretching these categories. Now, Usmani was draw-ing the line. He was calling for renewed fealty to fiqh-mindedness.

Quite unusually for a fatwa, Usmani's fourteen-page declaration went even further and shifted explicitly in its last two pages from the perspective of Islamic jurisprudence to a second religious logic: that of fealty to "the higher purposes of Islamic economics." Usmani adopted the perspective of the moral economists, arguing that "the mechanisms used in Sukuk today . . . strike at the foundations" of the "higher purposes of Islamic law" and "the objectives of Islamic economics" insofar as they "render the Sukuk exactly the same as conventional bonds in terms of their economic results." The purpose of Islamic banks, he said, was not to mimic conventional finance but to open "new horizons for business, commerce, and banking that would be guided by social justice." Usmani acknowledged that shariah boards and academic councils had initially allowed "operations that more closely resemble stratagems than actual operations" so as to help the nascent industry survive when Islamic banks were few and lacked capital and human resources. These boards and councils, he said, had expected that Islamic financial institutions would gradually distance themselves from what resembled interest. Instead, however, they were "march[ing] backwards," competing on the basis of their ability to simulate conventional interest-based finance, "using ploys that sound minds reject and [that] bring laughter to enemies."[28]

Some defenders of the status quo complain that international ratings agencies would not issue investor-grade ratings to sukuk unless they promised to return investors' principal and paid specified rates of return. Nonetheless, Taqi Usmani skewered this justification in his 2007 fatwa. The ratings agencies, he said, were myopic: they could only acknowledge the quality of investments with such characteristics and failed to see quality from an Islamic perspective, which valued "the sharing of risk and the equitable distribution of profits between investors."[29] Islamic financial institutions had grown in number to the point where they could circulate sukuk among themselves so as to move beyond riba; an Islamic ratings agency had even recently been established. So the time had come—with the encouragement of shariah boards worldwide—for Islamic finance to cast off its training wheels and hew more seriously to shariah. If shariah boards continued with their permissive policies, Islamic banks would stumble, and there was a danger "that this virtuous movement [would] fail."[30]

Navigating the Usmani Edict

After an initial period of confusion and uncertainty that coincided with the 2008–9 financial crisis, capital adapted to the Usmani edict. The investment bankers, lawyers, and shariah consultants who structured sukuk turned away from using musharaka and mudaraba as the underlying contracts and toward ijara (which had long been popular), murabaha, and wakala (*wakālah*, agency contract).[31] Each of these structures has its advantages and disadvantages but on balance, they were able to fill the gap in the ecosystem created by the rapid decline of musharaka and mudaraba.

The unusual inclusion of the moral economists' arguments in Usmani's fatwa (otherwise driven by an industry-standard formal-legalist critique) makes the response of the Islamic-finance sector particularly illustrative: after the shock had worn off and it became clear that sukuk musharaka and sukuk mudaraba could not be quickly rehabilitated, major players in the industry adjusted through classic formalist techniques. They deployed existing instruments to cover new sukuk issuances in the short term; in the medium term, as shariah scholars and industry lawyers digested the fatwa, they designed new instruments to conform to Usmani's requirements. Having made the formal adjustments, the industry continued largely as before. The substantive critique raised by moral economists, with its implicit challenge to the raison d'être of the industry, was ignored by capital.

Policing: The Long Arm of the Scholars' Law

Policing is the nitty-gritty work of monitoring financial institutions for shariah-compliance. (State regulators do some of this work too, but I focus here on private monitoring.) Policing provides credible assurance—to upper management, shariah boards, government regulators, and ultimately customers and clients—that products and services sold as shariah-compliant are indeed so. The shariah "police" defend the Islamic-finance industry from being "de-Islamized" by market pressure on firms to neglect shariah-compliance as they pursue profit. Shariah policing is simultaneously a unique feature of Islamic finance and a manifestation of global audit culture[32] in the late twentieth and early twenty-first centuries.

Internal and External Policing

Policing is done by two types of organizations: internal shariah departments and external shariah auditors. Internal shariah departments are units within Islamic financial institutions. Their mission is to ensure that all products and transactions meet the requirements of shariah and that the directives of the bank's shariah board are faithfully executed on a daily basis. A typical shariah board has three to eight members. Most are not dedicated full-time to the bank's affairs, and some may live thousands of miles away. Shariah-board members therefore rely on a bank's internal shariah department for day-to-day oversight of bank operations.

Internal shariah policing is not glamorous work. Shariah-department members monitor accounting records and product documentation for transgressions. They also ascertain compliance in physical, material ways, such as by visiting clients' warehouses to make sure inventory is present, halal, and bought or sold as promised. Internal shariah departments may also conduct periodic internal shariah audits, which scrutinize the bank's products, operations, and zakat payments comprehensively.

When bank employees or customers are found to have broken rules, the shariah department reprimands them and counsels them on getting their act straight. It records violations in a log that will be visible to the shariah board and upper management, and it may even levy a financial penalty on the bank itself, typically by insisting that any noncompliant earnings be donated to charity. Most importantly, the internal shariah department tries to catch violations before government regulators do. Thus, the shariah department operates under the shadow of both the shariah board and the state.

Unlike the internal shariah department, external shariah certifiers and auditors arrive from outside. Like conventional auditors, they are contracted and paid by the institution to come and scrutinize its books and operations. They do many of the same things that internal shariah departments do during internal audits but on a temporary or intermittent basis. They may provide quarterly, semi-annual, or annual reviews of the same firm, or they may be retained on a one-off basis to certify a particular deal or product issuance. Because the firm being audited often does not have its own shariah board, external auditors hold their clients accountable to whatever shariah standards are recommended or required by the regulatory authority governing Islamic finance in the client's country: typically the central bank or the national securities commission. If the audited institution passes shariah muster, the external auditor grants an audit fatwa or audit certificate saying so. If it fails, the auditor presents a list of necessary fixes.

The Transgressions

What kind of violations do the police discover? I put this question to employees at Islamic banks in Pakistan, the UAE, Saudi Arabia, Malaysia, and Oman. In retail and commercial banking, violations stem most often from failures to possess or transfer assets at the right time relative to when money is being exchanged or contracts are being signed. In conventional banking, a client who needs financing receives a loan from the bank, uses it to buy something— machinery, for example—and then pays the bank principal plus interest. Whether the client pays the machinery vendor before or after taking physical possession of the machinery does not matter much. But in Islamic banking, as we will see, this timing matters greatly because the Islamic bank or the client may effectively be selling or leasing out an asset that it does not yet possess. This turns a shariah-compliant financing into a prohibited one, as Islamic jurists prohibit selling something you do not own.

Below, I give three examples of violations discovered by internal shariah departments. All were considered typical by my informants, and all concern murabaha financing, which is, with its sibling tawarruq, the most widespread transaction in the industry. Internal shariah departments find violations associated with many instruments; for simplicity's sake, I focus here on murabaha.

PROBLEMATIC MURABAHA, SCENARIO 1:
FINANCING PEPSI WHEN IT'S TOO LATE

Bilal (not his real name), a member of the shariah department at an Islamic bank in Pakistan, described the following scenario.[33] Ahmad, a hypothetical grocery-store owner, orders a shipment of Pepsi from a beverage distributor on the first of every month. Usually, Ahmad does not finance his purchase: he pays cash in full. The supplier does not demand payment until the eighth of the month, when the supplier's truck arrives at Ahmad's warehouse. One summer, however, Ahmad checks his bank account on June 3, finds his cash balance lower than usual, and—after already having ordered the Pepsi on June 1—decides that he wants to finance the order because he will not have sufficient funds on June 8. He calls an Islamic bank and asks for a 100,000-dinar murabaha financing on the Pepsi.

This poses an ethical quandary for the sales rep at the Islamic bank. In a murabaha financing, the bank buys the asset first and then resells it to the customer. Yet Ahmad has already placed the order for the Pepsi himself. Therefore, the Islamic bank's sales rep cannot agree to finance Ahmad without violating shariah. Yet if the paperwork is not scrutinized closely, or if the sales rep can fudge the dates on the paperwork, no one will notice.

Bilal tells me with disgust that Islamic banks in this situation often provide financing even if they know the order of operations is wrong. "What happens at [my Islamic bank] is that we allow [the murabaha financing] even after the customer has placed the [purchase] order [on his own behalf]. Even if [the asset] is in transit. Even if it's about to reach the warehouse, [we] allow it then as well!" It angers Bilal that Islamic banks flout the basic logic of the murabaha contract, which is that the bank buys the goods first and sells them to the customer.

PROBLEMATIC MURABAHA, SCENARIO 2:
FUDGING THE DATES ON AN AUTO FINANCING

Shoaib (also not his real name), a middle manager at an Islamic bank in the United Arab Emirates, likewise observed that Islamic banks often execute the components of a murabaha financing in the wrong order. (My conversations with Shoaib always took place in his car or home, for he worried about being viewed inside his Islamic bank as a turncoat.) Shoaib had witnessed shortcuts on murabaha not just as a banker but as a customer:

> My wife was buying a car and getting financing from an Islamic bank. The guy [i.e., the bank employee] just gave me the set of documents and said, "Take them to your wife and have her sign them, and then when she's signed them all, make sure you put these particular times and dates on the contracts so they [appear to be] in the right order. And once that's done, I'll do the whole murabaha on the back end, in the platform."[34]

What happened to Shoaib's wife was problematic because in a murabaha auto financing, failure to sign and execute promises and contracts in the right order means that the bank is technically selling the car before owning it. To cover up the malfeasance, the banker had Shoaib fictionalize the times and dates on his wife's paperwork and would do the same thing with the back-end paperwork (i.e., the bank's log of the transaction). After this experience, Shoaib ruminated: "Is it just window dressing, or is a murabaha really taking place?" Shoaib felt that Islamic banks operate this way because their managers care mostly about profit margins and their customers care mostly about pricing. "At the end of the day, [Islamic bankers] are just like conventional bankers: they're always talking [within the Islamic bank] about net [profit] margins and [to customers] about rates, rates, rates."

PROBLEMATIC MURABAHA, SCENARIO 3: AN IMPOSSIBLE OIL TRANSFER

While shariah violations may result from bank employees' negligence or malfeasance, or customers' ignorance of the rules, they can also occur when customers obfuscate or lie. Indeed, shariah-department employees complain that many bank customers are willing to secure financing by hook or by crook, shariah be damned. "They only want money!" lamented a mufti who works in the shariah department of a Pakistani bank.[35]

Because customers may doctor their paperwork, the police must draw on their experience and common sense to judge whether a transaction smells fishy. An internal shariah auditor at Pakistan's Faysal Bank described a trick that unscrupulous clients pull: falsification of invoices. To prove that goods are moving at the right moments relative to the exchange of funds, murabaha clients must produce an invoice showing that they have purchased the goods from the supplier on behalf of the bank. "A client once submitted an invoice saying 4,000 metric tons of oil had been shipped to him in one day," said the Faysal Bank auditor. "But I used to work at a bank in the GCC, and I knew that no more than 2,500 metric tons of oil could have moved through that pipeline in one day." What would have happened, I asked, if he had not possessed this background knowledge? "[The violation] wouldn't have been caught!" he replied. "A transaction may *look* shariah-compliant, but we have to review both how it looks and how it's being used." In some cases, a shariah-department member may even visit the client's warehouse to inspect the goods and verify their presence.[36]

The three aforementioned violations occurred at commercial Islamic banks and were relatively simple. But in the sophisticated world of haute finance, the violations become more complicated. Yasser Dahlawi is CEO of Shariyah Review Bureau (SRB), a leading external shariah-audit provider in Saudi Arabia and elsewhere in the Gulf region. Dahlawi's clients include investment funds and investment banks, insurance companies, and other financial-services firms. One of the most common violations Dahlawi sees in his audits is the failure of shariah-compliant equity funds to properly screen non-shariah-compliant companies out of their funds. Other common violations involve failing to follow a shariah board's instructions carefully.

However, Dahlawi feels most transgressions he sees are unintentional:

> With the tight government regulation, it's rare to find intentional [violations among shariah-compliant investment funds] . . . and if your shariah-compliant fund intentionally [invests in noncompliant companies], sooner or later you'll be found out, and then you'll have to purify your earnings [i.e., donate ill-gotten portions to charity]. This will be reflected in the ROI [return on investment], so people will pull out of the fund, or at least know you're not doing a good job managing it.[37]

Thus a combination of private auditing, government regulation, shariah-board guidance, and scrutiny by clients creates powerful incentives for shariah-compliant funds to follow the rules.

Nonetheless, Dahlawi does encounter sophisticated financial actors who push the envelope of shariah-compliance. They are not intentionally breaking the rules so much as exploring gray areas and experimenting with what industry observers pejoratively call tahayul (*taḥāyul*): clever tricks that circumvent the substance of shariah while staying within its letter. For example, an Islamic investment fund might try to raise capital by setting up a special-purpose vehicle (SPV), having a lender make a conventional loan to the SPV, and then having the SPV provide an Islamic financing to the fund in the same amount. The SPV functions merely to pass through and "launder" the noncompliant nature of a conventional loan. "In our view, this is not right," Dahlawi avers. "You're trying to put a shariah label on a conventional loan."[38] Sometimes, clients will have Dahlawi sign a nondisclosure agreement so they can get his opinion on an iffy technique before launching it. But "when we see companies that really want to do tahayul," he says, "we say no to the [entire] project." Such cases show how the police patrol the very borders of Islamic finance: the boundaries of what can legitimately be called shariah-compliant. And as explained by the exasperated investment banker in the opening of this chapter, shariah policing can impose real constraints on transactions valued in the hundreds of millions of U.S. dollars.

The Moral Universe of the Police

The bureaucratic ethos is strong among the police: they see themselves as executors of the shariah board's interpretations of Islamic law, not as free agents allowed to imprint Islamic finance with their personal views. "Our point of reference is the shariah board, and not personal opinion," remarked a shariah scholar working in the internal shariah department at an Islamic bank in the UAE. The scholar explained that all meetings of the shariah board were recorded and transcribed; he and his colleagues in the shariah department carefully reviewed the meeting minutes for marching orders. "You might disagree, but inside the bank you have to abide by the board," he noted.[39]

The same ethos of impersonal commitment to directives from above obtains among external shariah auditors too. Yasser Dahlawi described to me how he vets his potential employees:

> They go through a series of interviews, and the last one is with me. And I ask them—because I know they're students of shariah, with their own different approaches to different questions of shariah—"What happens if the shariah decision [you have to implement] for a product goes against what you believe in, or against your *madhhab* [juristic school]?" ... I look in their eyes to see how they react.[40]

By saying he "look[s] in their eyes to see how they react," Dahlawi means he will only hire candidates who appear inclined to execute the directives of the shariah board faithfully, regardless of their own views. Dahlawi's ideal shariah auditor is Max Weber's ideal-typical bureaucrat: one who "proceeds *sine ira et studio*, not allowing personal motive or temper to influence conduct, free of arbitrariness and unpredictability . . . following rational rules with strict formality."[41]

Yet even if shariah police espouse an impartial bureaucratic ethos, they need a favorable incentive structure if they are to avoid being swayed by their organization's profitability concerns. Ideally, the police should be free to evaluate a firm's activities without fear of retribution from management. For external shariah auditors, this is feasible. But for an Islamic bank's internal shariah department, conflicts of interest may arise. How aggressively can internal police chase violations when finding too many of them could damage the bank's bottom line?

On one hand, the shariah-department members I interviewed in Pakistan, the United Arab Emirates, and Malaysia said they felt they could candidly report violations to their bosses—typically, the head of the shariah department. Indeed, they regarded themselves as reputational armor for the bank: if they didn't catch violations, then the government regulator might do so, or outsiders might start criticizing the bank for questionable practices. Both of these outcomes would be far worse for the bank.

On the other hand, over weeks of chatting and socializing inside and outside their workplaces, I found that all of the shariah-department employees I befriended were relatively critical of common industry practices. All believed their work was important and that Islamic banking as a whole is ethically superior to conventional banking. Yet many were jaded or disillusioned; some were outright angry. Some even sought me out furtively to share their critiques, after I had given a talk or interviewed their superiors.

Crucially, however, few presented the standard critique made by moral economists: that today's Islamic-finance industry fails to advance Muslims' socioeconomic conditions. Most did not fault Islamic banks for being profit-maximizing businesses and for therefore relying heavily on interest simulation. Along these lines, Bilal and Shoaib—whose critiques of murabaha transactions at Islamic banks were discussed above—did not criticize murabaha financing *as a general practice* on the grounds that it simulates interest. Rather, they accepted the scholarly consensus within the industry that murabaha financing is Islamically lawful. Their ethical concerns were different: they worried that their Islamic banks were not *executing* murabaha responsibly and were cutting corners in order to retain customers. Many shariah-department members complained to me similarly about other banking products too. These respondents accepted the worldview of shariah scholars but faulted banks for cutting corners on shariah-compliance, usually behind their shariah boards' backs. They all believed uncaught shariah violations were widespread in Islamic banking—sometimes at their own institutions, and certainly at competing institutions.

Moreover, prominent industry figures have worried publicly that some internal shariah departments face pressure from executive management to let questionable practices slide. "We must develop a system where the administration cannot pressure the internal shariah auditors and their team," insisted Sheikh Nizam Yaquby, an internationally prominent shariah scholar. "They must not feel like they could be fired based on what they find. Otherwise, [management] will sack anybody [from an internal shariah audit department] that they don't like!"[42] Sheikh Esam Ishaq, another elite shariah-board member, argued that Islamic financial institutions should structure their lines of command accordingly. "Ideally, the internal shariah audit department should report directly to the shariah board," he argued.[43] In practice, however, internal shariah departments tend to report to both executive management and the shariah board. Since they form a unit within the financial institution and are hired and fired by firm management (unlike the shariah board, which serves at the pleasure of the corporate board), it may be difficult to insulate them completely from management's profitability concerns.

Informants say the shariah department's autonomy from profitability pressures varies from bank to bank and that it depends considerably on the respect commanded in the organization by the leader of the shariah department. Some shariah-department leaders are known as uncompromising on shariah-compliance, yet deeply knowledgeable and successful in devising shariah-compliant solutions to business problems at the same time. Such shariah-department leaders have made names for themselves within national Islamic-banking markets and sometimes globally. They simultaneously protect their bank's reputation as truly shariah-compliant while allowing for innovative product development. This kind of reputation matters from a commercial perspective because some clients think of certain Islamic financial institutions are more Islamic than others.

Scholarly Restriction Closes Some Doors
for Capital but Opens Others

So far, this chapter has argued that shariah scholars place real, meaningful restrictions on capitalists. Although scholars' restrictions do not prohibit interest simulation, they place exacting conditions on how firms must execute it. In closing, I show that the two countervailing forces generate a third that resolves their tension. After big banks push the envelope outward and shariah scholars cry foul and restrict them, innovators emerge who design platforms to achieve the bankers' goals efficiently and cheaply while enforcing the scholars' exacting processual conditions more scrupulously than others have been doing. As an example, I consider "organized tawarruq": the most controversial instrument in Islamic finance, yet perhaps the most widespread (or at minimum the second-most widespread). This instrument simulates a cash loan through three sales of an asset. While some prominent shariah scholars involved in the industry prohibit organized tawarruq, some consider it acceptable, and many large Islamic banks use it. Yet even those scholars who permit it worry that banks and brokers fail to execute it properly, with real assets failing to change hands as they should. In response, innovators have partnered with prominent scholars to build technically sophisticated solutions to the problem of shariah-compliance.

Capitalist Expansion: The Debate over Organized Tawarruq

As mentioned earlier in this book, tawarruq is one of the most common and important structures in Islamic finance today thanks to its flexibility and low transaction costs. It is said to represent around half of all Islamic banking transactions in Malaysia, and half at Saudi Arabia's largest Islamic bank. At the level of high finance, tawarruq is incorporated into sukuk structures, project finance, Islamic derivatives, and instruments for liquidity management and debt restructuring.[44] At the level of corporate banking, it is often used to provide revolving credit, working capital, cash lines, and term finance. And in retail finance, it appears in personal financing, savings accounts, time deposits, student financing, and credit cards. Despite its near-ubiquity, however, tawarruq remains deeply controversial in the Islamic-finance industry, and reformers have called for it to be phased out. Oman's central bank banned it entirely.[45]

Shariah scholars distinguish between two types of tawarruq: "classical" and "organized." Classical tawarruq (figure 6.3) is a simple transaction that some Islamic jurists approved in medieval scholarship. Imagine that a customer (C) desperately needs cash right away. She buys some asset—a gemstone, for example—on credit from B, say for $210. She then sells the gemstone immediately on spot terms in the open market to someone else (D) for $200. So C gets $200 now and will owe B $210 later. In this case, C does all the legwork herself: for example, she herself finds the initial gem supplier (B) as well as the final gem buyer (D). Classical tawarruq is accepted by some shariah scholars, but not by others. However, it does not actually exist as an institutionalized practice in the financial sector because people seeking quick financing from a bank typically do not want to spend their time seeking out sellers and buyers of commodities.

Organized tawarruq, however, is widely practiced in the Islamic-finance industry today. It differs from classical tawarruq in that all details are arranged in advance to streamline the process of getting cash to the customer, reduce transaction costs, and effectively eliminate the risks of price fluctuation and noncompletion of the transaction by any party. Today, organized tawarruq depends on digital trading technologies. It typically proceeds as depicted in figure 6.4. The outcome is that Customer C has effectively taken a cash loan from Islamic Bank B. The copper was traded electronically three times but never moved physically. All of these steps take place quickly—in an hour[46] or even less. The Islamic bank may own the commodity for a matter of minutes

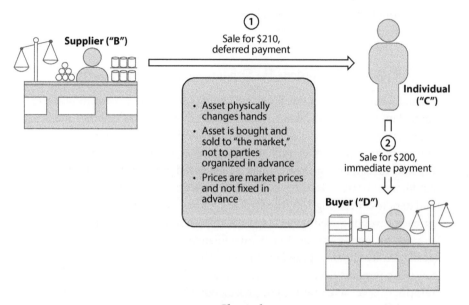

FIGURE 6.3. Classical tawarruq.

or even seconds, and yet this ownership of a real asset for some non-zero period of time is what shariah scholars say grants the bank the right to charge a markup on it, following the Islamic legal maxim "Entitlement to profit depends on bearing liability for losses."[47]

Tawarruq is perhaps the most hotly debated structure in Islamic finance. Moral economists staunchly oppose it. They feel it vitiates the advantages of Islamic finance and reproduces the ills of interest-based finance. For example, the influential Islamic economist Mohammad Nejatullah Siddiqi (1931–2022) noted that easy credit in conventional finance has led to "mountains of credit card debts and other consumer debts," "skyrocket[ing]" government borrowing, and Third World indebtedness. In his eyes,

> The Islamic prohibition of interest serves as an effective check on the above trend. . . . Tawarruq sabotages this unique feature of Islamic finance by introducing lending as a means of doing business. It makes it easy to borrow. It puts Islamic financial institutions on par with conventional financial institutions, [with] both [of them] under competitive compulsion to lend in order to make use of surplus liquidity.[48]

"[Tawarruq] hijacks Islamic finance and entrenches [debt]," laments economist Obiyathulla Ismath Bacha.[49] Some also feel it replicates an interest-bearing cash loan so overtly that Muslims would be better off taking

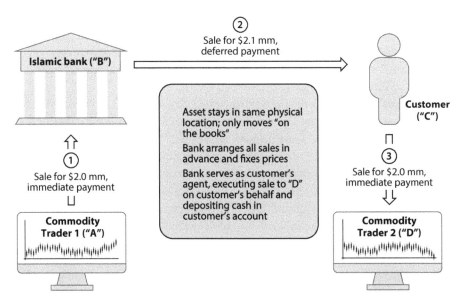

Islamic bank ("B")

②
Sale for $2.1 mm,
deferred payment

Customer
("C")

①
Sale for $2.0 mm,
immediate payment

Asset stays in same physical
location; only moves "on
the books"

Bank arranges all sales in
advance and fixes prices

Bank serves as customer's
agent, executing sale to "D"
on customer's behalf and
depositing cash in
customer's account

③
Sale for $2.0 mm,
immediate payment

Commodity
Trader 1 ("A")

Commodity
Trader 2 ("D")

FIGURE 6.4. Organized tawarruq.

interest-bearing loans. "All you're doing with tawarruq is charging more" by
creating transaction costs that would not exist in a conventional loan, insists
economist Mahmoud El-Gamal,[50] author of an influential law-and-economics
critique of the Islamic-finance industry.[51] El-Gamal borrows a colorful
metaphor from ibn Qayyim al-Jawzīyah (1292–1350 CE), who deemed tawarruq unlawful and asserted that riba "on the ground" (i.e., done in plain view
as interest) is less harmful than riba "atop a tall ladder" (i.e., performed via
elaborate ruses).[52] Because they consider the asset being traded to be a mere
prop, moral economists also feel tawarruq pulls Islamic finance away from its
grounding in "real" economic activity and its connection to "real" assets. They
complain that tawarruq, which is debt-based, crowds out ethically superior
equity-type forms of Islamic financing based on profit-and-loss sharing. They
also worry that tawarruq makes Islamic finance look farcical in the public's
eyes.[53]

Among industry shariah scholars, opinions are more ambivalent. Some find
tawarruq perfectly acceptable, referring to premodern jurists who permitted
the practice. Others consider it technically shariah-compliant but imperfect
because the asset being traded functions merely as a prop: "From the Islamic
law perspective, [tawarruq] is allowed but that is not the ideal," asserts prominent Malaysian shariah scholar Mohamad Akram Laldin. "It does not really
help in creating real economic activities. Basically you are giving cash."[54] For

the same reason, Malaysian shariah scholar Zulkifli Hasan approves tawarruq only for liquidity purposes, and "only for the last resort."[55] Meanwhile, the two most influential international bodies of shariah scholars both permit classical tawarruq but ban organized tawarruq. Nonetheless, Islamic financial institutions continue to use organized tawarruq widely.

When tawarruq takes the straightforward "classical" form, many industry shariah scholars consider it perfectly acceptable, some consider it detestable but not prohibited, and some prohibit it outright.[56] The general logic for approving tawarruq conforms to a quintessential Islamic merchant ethics, which values the freedom to trade as one wishes while conforming to God's law and preserving the social harmony of the marketplace (see chapter 2). Jurists who accept tawarruq argue that each leg of the transaction, a credit sale on markup and then a spot sale, is permissible. Say someone has bought silk on credit. She may keep the silk in a warehouse, sell it at whatever price she can get, use it to make clothes, or otherwise dispose of it as she wishes. According to this logic, no outsider has the right to decide for her. Merchant ethics affirm such freedom of exchange so long as money is not traded for money (for that is usury), transactions are transparent, contracts are clearly written, and other shariah rules that keep the marketplace operating smoothly are observed.

Indeed, jurists have defended tawarruq by saying it meets people's need for cash—a need present in any marketplace—without forcing them to borrow at interest.[57] Shamsul Akmal Ahmad, now CEO of the Bursa Suq al-Sila' commodities-trading platform for tawarruq, invoked this spirit:

> Being a good Muslim isn't just prayers and fasting; every aspect of life must be shariah-compliant. In China, [some Muslims] approached us for assistance in enabling shariah-compliant financial transactions by adopting our tawarruq platform. And we want to give this facility to them, so that all the transactions they do are in compliance with shariah. Although they are in a non-Muslim, communist country, we must help our brothers as an *ummah*. . . . That's part of the missionary work[58] that we're doing. And when we go to suppliers [of commodities for the platform], we send the same message: You're part of the community that's providing an avenue for the Muslim community to do something they really need.[59]

For these various reasons, contemporary scholars who accept tawarruq feel they have firm ground on which to stand. Accordingly, leading international juristic organizations, including general bodies (the Organisation of Islamic Cooperation's International Islamic Fiqh Academy, the Muslim World League's Islamic Fiqh Council) and bodies specific to Islamic finance (the shariah board of the Accounting and Auditing Organization for Islamic Financial Institutions) have ruled it permissible.

If so many jurists and august international juristic organizations approve tawarruq, then one might think it would face limited resistance from shariah boards. However, there is a huge caveat: these juristic organizations permit the classical form of tawarruq. That form is also known as "individual tawarruq" because it is executed entirely by an individual.

Scholars' Ambivalence about Organized Tawarruq

Prominent shariah scholars are much more divided about organized tawarruq, which is the form of tawarruq actually practiced in the Islamic-finance industry. Positions on organized tawarruq range from asserting that it is perfectly shariah-compliant so long as it is executed properly to asserting that it is completely noncompliant, with many scholars falling in between and saying it is problematic or even detestable from a shariah perspective but not unlawful. Speaking off the record, one internationally known shariah scholar described two "cartels" of shariah scholars in the Gulf region, one headed by Sheikh Nizam Yaquby that permitted organized tawarruq and one by Sheikh Hussein Hamid Hassan that was much more restrictive about it.[60] Indeed, Dubai Islamic Bank, the institution whose shariah board Hassan chaired for decades and with which he is most closely associated, did not allow the use of tawarruq for financing while he was chair.[61] Nor did Emirates Islamic Bank, whose shariah board Hassan also chaired. Instead, it publicized the restriction as a sign of piety, boasting in its 2006 annual report that its growth had "not been based on products of ill repute" such as "personal loans based on tawarruq."[62]

Being more likely to prohibit a controversial product than to permit it, the same international juristic organizations that have approved individual tawarruq have banned organized tawarruq: the OIC International Islamic Fiqh Academy, the Muslim World League's Islamic Fiqh Council, and AAOIFI. Likewise, many individual scholars and shariah boards have either refused to allow organized tawarruq or restricted the circumstances under which it may be used. Yet scholars who are more comfortable with organized tawarruq point out that the international juristic organizations banned the practice late in the game, well after it had become entrenched throughout the industry. This has put Islamic banks in a difficult spot, victims of the fact that norms in their infant industry are still evolving. "You can't tie the hands of the Islamic banks, throw them in the sea, and say, 'Make sure you don't get wet!'" lamented elite scholar Sheikh Esam Ishaq of Bahrain.[63]

Today's shariah scholars voice various concerns about organized tawarruq,[64] especially as it is implemented at the London Metal Exchange. While these concerns may sound arcane, they reveal how the infrastructure of twenty-first-century commodity markets both facilitates and frustrates efforts to comply with Islamic commercial law and Islamic merchant ethics. First, scholars insist that the broker who sells the commodity actually own it, for they unanimously prohibit selling something you do not own.[65] They are right to worry: in 2019, the Dubai Financial Services Authority sanctioned two Dubai-based brokers, David Barnett and Christopher Steer, at the commodity murabaha broking desk of a major international inter-dealer brokerage for reusing old, invalid titles to metal commodities to execute tawarruq instead of buying new titles that reflected actual ownership.[66] Second, at all stages of the tawarruq transaction, the commodity owner must also possess it—actually or constructively—and be able to specify it precisely, indicating its location, type, and characteristics so there is no confusion as to what is being bought and sold. And third, the commodity must not travel in a loop and end up where it started. In other words, the initial merchant who sells the commodity to the financing institution—which then sells it on to the customer needing financing—must not be the same merchant that buys the commodity from that customer at the end.

Stella Cox CBE, managing director of DDCAP Group—the largest of several UK-based brokers that dominate the facilitation of organized tawarruq via London Metal Exchange (LME) commodity trades—stresses that LME trades meet shariah scholars' criteria in these regards:

> The London Metal Exchange is quite unique. I think it has the largest physical OTC [over-the-counter] environment of any market worldwide. And it has this system of having metals on LME warrants itself. This means that the metals have been deemed eligible, meeting certain standards and criteria set by the LME. So from a shariah perspective, that ticks the box, you know—it's certain, and you can be sure of the quality as well.
>
> Also, the warrant gives proof of existence. That warrant tells you that the metal is *allocated*. Say you're trading in aluminum, and it's supported with warrants, and each warrant represents 25 metric tons of aluminum; then each warrant you're buying represents *those* 25 metric tons of aluminum. It's there; it's tangible.
>
> Shariah scholars also like very much the fact as well that they are able to access the LME's warehousing environment. The LME now has over seven hundred warehouses worldwide.... The LME goes out and does due diligence and audit on them ... [ensuring that] the metal that's on warrant is in those warehouses. Validation visits [by shariah scholars] have been possible. So this whole [question of] "Do the commodities exist? Do they not exist?" [isn't an issue].[67]

Cox is a widely respected industry veteran. Shariah scholars and Islamic bankers consistently spoke highly of her and described her as deeply knowledgeable—something I confirmed in a two-hour conversation at DDCAP headquarters in central London. Nonetheless, industry participants occasionally express concerns about shariah-compliance problems that they feel arise when trading through the LME. "Many of the transactions are done [only] on paper," while the goods themselves could "be on the high seas," asserted Mohammad Ali Qayyum, director-general of the Institute of Islamic Banking and Insurance, a London-based nonprofit that has been training people since 1994.[68] A shariah scholar who works in the shariah department of a large GCC bank and requested anonymity expressed the same idea in more specific language:

> SCHOLAR: They—DDCAP and Condor—have been in this business for a long time. Do they really have this commodity with them? Because they have never refused our request [to buy a commodity from them]. We have this MOU [memorandum of understanding] that says we're going to buy from Condor and sell to DDCAP. So anytime we need a commodity, we buy from where we've already agreed [to buy]. . . .
>
> RC: What makes you uncomfortable about this?
>
> SCHOLAR: How is it possible to sell hundreds of millions [of dollars] worth [of commodities] on the basis of a one-page document? And how have they never refused [a sale because they don't] have the commodity? No one has ever audited them. So how do we know they're actually owning this commodity, and that it's located where it's supposed to be?[69]

Sheikh Esam Ishaq of Bahrain got into even further detail. He complained in 2016 that a major LME broker would not provide the warrant numbers for specific ingots of metal. Without these numbers, Ishaq worried that the broker could be selling the same ingots of metal to different buyers at the same time. Even if the ingots of metal being traded in tawarruq sit in the same warehouse and never move physically, scholars insist that constructive possession move from buyer to seller. But if the broker will not provide ingot numbers, who can say which ingots were constructively possessed by whom? The concern arises that brokers are literally just selling Islamic banks "a bill of goods," as the idiom goes.

> We asked the broker to tell us in writing that they would not sell the product during the period when they were also selling it to someone else. And they refused! They refused to give it to us in writing![70]

Such problems arise because the Islamic-finance industry is piggybacking on an international commodity-trading architecture that was not designed to accommodate the demands of Islamic law. Although LME commodity trades make up a big portion of Islamic financial institutions' activities, the reverse is not true: Islamic finance represents merely a niche client segment.

The oversight of shariah scholars takes contemporary finance and overlays a binding moral and legal order derived out of Islamic merchant ethics, where considerations of ownership, possession, specification, transfer, and so forth are not mere technicalities to be abstracted away but dispositive conditions. Through shariah considerations, Islamic finance reintroduces philosophical questions—What is ownership? What is possession?—to an economic order optimized for profitability and not much else. This yoking together of ethical considerations with accommodation of market necessities for Muslims explains how the scholars' interventions can be simultaneously scrupulous and yet not disrupt the basic structure and action of market forces: *because they are not intended to.*

Restrictions on organized tawarruq have real effects on firms, which must abide by their shariah boards' orders. For example, many shariah boards allow the use of organized tawarruq for liquidity management, which they see as a life raft for Islamic banks struggling to survive in banking markets and regulatory environments in which shariah-compliant liquidity-management options are few, while heavily restricting tawarruq-based consumer-finance products such as credit cards and personal financings, which they consider inessential even if they are profitable.

Even proposing a tawarruq-based product that goes beyond the shariah board's comfort zone can get employees in hot water. "Only 13 percent of the Pakistani population is banked," noted Hasan Faraz, senior vice president of product development at Meezan Bank. Serving unbanked Pakistanis by opening new bank branches and expanding credit might require "com[ing] up with products that are borderline Islamic, such as tawarruq." But when Faraz proposed a tawarruq-based personal-finance product, he "was kicked out of the room" by the shariah scholars, as he recalls with a grin.[71]

Restricting Capitalists, Facilitating Capital

Shariah boards impose real restrictions to which individual capitalist firms must adhere. Adherence can mean failing to offer certain products that competitors offer, such as tawarruq-based financings. In the short run, individual scholars' decisions can affect firms' bottom line.

One might therefore expect that "natural selection" would operate again as it did when weeding out anti-murabaha scholars in the 1970s and early 1980s, this time with Islamic banks refusing to retain anti-tawarruq scholars on their shariah boards. Yet this is not the case. Hussein Hamid Hassan, for example, was constantly being offered board invitations until his death in 2020. And

Pakistan's Mufti Taqi Usmani, who considers organized tawarruq detestable, finds it to be "vulnerable to many violations" when carried out on international exchanges, and allows it only if strict conditions are met,[72] is Pakistan's most sought-after shariah-board member domestically and internationally.

So why aren't banks selecting against anti-tawarruq scholars today the way they selected against anti-murabaha scholars in the 1970s and 1980s? First, dropping an elite scholar from a shariah board could jeopardize a bank's reputation. Elite scholars' names are worth more now than they were then. Shariah-board members received hundreds or thousands of dollars per board annually in the industry's early days, but internationally elite scholars now earn hundreds of thousands of dollars per board. These high honoraria reflect the premium that domestic and international financial institutions place on securing reliable, knowledgeable experts trusted by multiple constituencies: ordinary consumers, corporate clients, financial markets, and even state regulators. Today's elite scholars have built this trust over decades in the industry, whereas at the industry's dawn in the late 1970s, everyone was new to the field. Relatedly, scholars on shariah boards have developed personal relationships and networks that connect them with the banks they oversee. All of this means famous scholars are almost never asked to leave shariah boards.

Second, firms do not aggressively "select against" scholars who oppose organized tawarruq because they can find alternatives to it. Product structuring is far more sophisticated today than it was in the 1970s and 1980s. Laws and regulations have adapted to accommodate the special asset sales and leases that Islamic finance demands, such as by setting them on an equal tax footing with conventional interest-based transactions. Technical infrastructures such as commodity brokerages and securities exchanges have also improved in their ability to accommodate Islamic transactions. This means not only that most mainstream conventional financial instruments can be simulated Islamically at much lower cost than decades ago but also that they can be simulated in two or three different ways. For example, an alternative to tawarruq's use in liquidity management that started becoming common in the 2010s is wakala (*wakālah*; agency). The party with cash (the principal) deposits it with an agent, who invests the funds in a pool of assets and then returns the profits to the principal, less a fee taken by the agent. In liquidity-management structures, the expected profit is often set relative to a benchmark interest rate such as Euribor, and in practice, the return ends up being at or extremely close to that expected profit, with the agent permitted to keep any excess returns.

Thus in the long run and big picture, individual scholars' restrictions on what firms may do have not prevented Islamic finance from flourishing. This is partly because scholars designate certain accommodations, such as tawarruq-based liquidity-management products, as temporarily necessary for the survival of Islamic finance even if these scholars deem the underlying contractual structures problematic. It is also because Islamic banks can find alternatives to controversial products. Sheikh Hussein Hamid Hassan prohibited tawarruq-based financing, so Dubai Islamic Bank could not offer tawarruq-based credit cards. However, it adapted a different contract, salam, to offer credit cards with similar functionalities. When in 2020 Dubai Islamic Bank acquired Noor Bank, a rival UAE Islamic bank that did offer tawarruq-based credit cards, Dubai Islamic converted all of Noor's tawarruq-based cards into salam-based cards with relative ease.

Not only does capital find ways to profit from Islamic finance despite scholarly stringency, but in the long run, scholarly stringency can create new profit opportunities. The saga of tawarruq demonstrates this. As Islamic finance grows, more scholars are alleging problems with organized tawarruq as it is typically executed through the London Metal Exchange or other commodity brokers. And since the late 2000s, new vendors competing with the London Metal Exchange have emerged, trying to address the scholars' concerns using technology.

Building a Better Mousetrap: Technical Innovation in Response to Scholarly Restriction

Some innovators have responded to the never-ending tawarruq controversy not by seeking to avoid organized tawarruq but by building new systems that ever more scrupulously address the concerns of scholars who approve it in theory but fear it could be executed incorrectly in practice. In the cases I discuss below, innovators have constructed high-tech platforms to execute the commodity trades that underlie tawarruq.

PALM OIL IN MALAYSIA

Bursa Malaysia, the main Malaysian stock exchange, sits in a huge neoclassical edifice in Kuala Lumpur with nine-story-high columns. The building gives a sense of solidity and rigidity, as stock-exchange buildings should. But inside, as I listened to Bursa Malaysia staff explain their new computerized platform for trading crude palm oil (CPO) to facilitate tawarruq transactions, my head was spinning.

The introduction in August 2009 of Bursa Malaysia's web-based, multicurrency tawarruq platform, called Bursa Suq al-Sila' (BSAS; *sūq al-sila'* is Arabic for "commodities market"), coincided well with multiple trends: growing questions about how tawarruq was being carried out, the global financial crisis and consequent attention toward Islamic finance as an alternative paradigm, the phasing out of ina in Malaysia and shift toward tawarruq instead, and the globalization of Islamic finance.

Raja Teh Maimunah, then global head of Islamic markets at Bursa Malaysia, explained the rationale for introducing BSAS:

> The industry had suffered some reputational issues regarding rogue trades whereby commodities purchased for this purpose were either encumbered, i.e., they cannot be freely dealt with, the same commodities were being sold to several parties simultaneously, or, in some cases, simply didn't exist.[73]

Figure 6.5 shows the BSAS system. Tawarruq using BSAS is similar to tawarruq transactions conducted using the London Metal Exchange, except for the crucial difference that the BSAS computerized trading and settlement engine intercedes between commodities providers (producers and suppliers of crude palm oil), Islamic financial institutions, and their customers. The BSAS engine accepts offers for CPO trades each morning and systematically matches the bids placed by the IFIs with the offers and inventories accumulated in the BSAS system. The system tracks the ownership of CPO from suppliers' tanks to the Islamic financial institutions and their customers. Bursa Malaysia Islamic Services (BMIS), the entity that owns and operates the BSAS platform, acts as a counterparty to mitigate counterparty risk (the risk of not being able to sell the commodities once client institutions have acquired it) and market risk (by fixing the commodity price on BSAS for the entire trading day). Settlement risk is mitigated by netting the obligations of each party to a trade. Randomization (figure 6.5, step 4) reduces almost to zero the chance that the initial seller of CPO will be the buyer of the same CPO within the same cycle, a crucial shariah requirement in the eyes of some scholars.

BSAS represents a curious nexus between the financial economy and the real economy. The larger the volume of (financial) tawarruq transactions taking place, the larger the amount of (real) CPO that suppliers must store in tanks connected to the system. In order to fend off accusations that the same CPO is being "recycled" over and over very quickly for tawarruq transactions, or that the CPO being traded is not actually there, Bursa Malaysia must therefore convince major producers of palm oil to participate in the system and to store substantial volumes of their product each morning in the requisite warehouse tanks.[74] "The more CPO suppliers we have, the lower the probability that the CPO will go back to the initial seller," explained shariah scholar Ustaz Muhammad Hasanan Yunus, then head of shariah governance at Bursa Malaysia's wing for Islamic capital markets.[75] BSAS therefore seeks to attract as many CPO suppliers as possible into the trading system—even though all the metric tons of CPO they provide will be sitting idle in tanks, going nowhere physically as they whir around the world virtually. BSAS also conducts

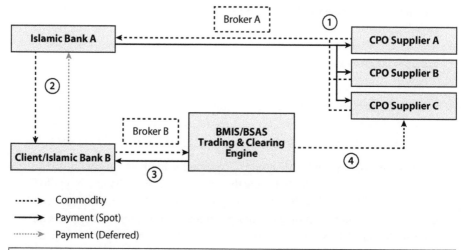

------▶   Commodity

⸻▶   Payment (Spot)

·········▷   Payment (Deferred)

Step 1
- Before 9:00 a.m.: Suppliers of crude palm oil (CPO) can place offers to sell. Islamic Bank A can place bids to buy.
- 9:00 a.m.: Market opens. Engine begins matching buyers and sellers.
- Via Broker A, suppliers sell CPO to Islamic Bank A for immediate cash payment. Ownership of CPO transfers to Islamic Bank A.
- If Islamic Bank A requests physical delivery of the CPO, BSAS ensures delivery. (In practice, this request is almost never made.)
- System generates e-certificate that verifies transaction details.

Step 2
- Islamic Bank A sells CPO to its client or to Islamic Bank B at a marked-up price on deferred-payment basis (i.e., Client / Islamic Bank B must pay sometime in the future).
- Ownership transfers from Islamic Bank A to Client / Islamic Bank B.

Step 3
- Via Broker B, Client / Islamic Bank B sells CPO to Bursa Malaysia Islamic Services (BMIS) for immediate cash payment. Ownership transfers to BMIS.
- System generates e-certificate that verifies transaction details.

Step 4
- BMIS places offers to sell CPO. Suppliers place bids to buy.
- Engine matches BMIS to a supplier on random basis. Ownership transfers from BMIS to supplier.

Note: Commodities besides CPO that can be offered on BSAS include aluminum, coal, cocoa, coffee, copper, cotton, crude oil, crude palm kernel oil, diesel, fuel oil, gasoline, iron ore, methanol, nickel, palladium, plastic resin, RBD palm olein, rubber, timber, tin, and zinc.

FIGURE 6.5. Bursa Malaysia's Suq al-Sila' system for trading palm oil electronically to facilitate tawarruq financing transactions. *Source*: Adapted from "BURSA Suq Al-Sila'" (marketing brochure), available online at https://www.bursamalaysia.com/.

random shariah verification audits to ensure that the palm-oil suppliers actually possess the real physical commodity that they sell to the banks and are not
short selling (i.e., selling palm oil they do not own) and that the CPO is free
of any encumbrances.[76] All of this attention is paid to the material supply of
CPO into the BSAS system even though no one involved will actually be taking physical delivery of any CPO. Indeed, Bursa Malaysia chose to use CPO
because it is one of Malaysia's major commodity exports: Indonesia and Malaysia are by far the world's largest producers, and Bursa Malaysia itself has
been the world's largest hub for trading CPO futures since 1980. Thus, Malaysia's strength in the production and export of CPO has contributed to BSAS's
success as a financial-services platform.

When new platforms emerge to address prominent scholars' concerns, the
scholars' shariah boards—and even the prominent scholars themselves—may
travel to inspect the platforms personally. Shamsul Akmal Ahmad, now CEO
of BSAS, has hosted such delegations from most of the Gulf's major Islamic
banks, as well as from many other countries, including Brunei, Hong Kong,
Mauritania, Pakistan, Singapore, and Tanzania. Most of the delegations have
approved BSAS as shariah-compliant, but some scholars have proved especially challenging. Sheikh Ali al-Qaradaghi, an internationally elite scholar,
flew from Qatar to Malaysia on a Qatari bank's behalf. He grilled the platform's
designers for two days, then inspected a rural palm-oil plantation on the third,
climbing up a three-story storage tank to verify its contents. "After all that, did
he end up approving the platform?" I asked Shamsul. "Not on that visit,"
Shamsul replied with a grin.[77] Al-Qaradaghi raised an exacting technical objec-
tion: that the randomization engine could not yet guarantee, with total certainty, that the provider of CPO might not also be its buyer. In response, BSAS
got to work redesigning its supply system, which took years. By 2018, after
acting on Sheikh al-Qaradaghi's feedback, it had eliminated the small possibility of sin that had bothered him, and the elite scholar granted his approval.

DIAMONDS IN DUBAI

"We're sitting on at least $1 billion worth of diamonds," said Paul Boots matter-
of-factly.[78] We were on the fiftieth floor of Almas Tower in Dubai's Jumeirah
Lakes Towers district, a shimmering new complex of commercial and residential high-rises among man-made lakes and manicured lawns. Almās means
"diamond" in Arabic, and Almas Tower is the center of Dubai's burgeoning
diamond trade. Armed guards patrol the building's lobby, and its thick floors
support dozens of stories of safes and strong rooms with reinforced steel walls.
Inside those rooms, specialists grade and sort the bags of diamonds that merchants buy from mining companies like De Beers and Rio Tinto.

Because of a happy symbiosis between the commodities trade and Islamic finance, Almas Tower is also home to a new effort to make tawarruq more shariah-compliant. I was there to meet with Boots, an energetic, polished Dutchman in his thirties who is the architect of the Dubai Multi Commodities Centre's Tradeflow system. Tradeflow is a web-based platform that allows the electronic trading of warehouse warrants for commodities.

Although originally developed to help companies in the commodities industry secure financing, Tradeflow turned out to be ideal for Islamic financial institutions executing tawarruq. When commodities traders put their commodities—such as diamonds, steel, or tea—in a warehouse in Dubai, Tradeflow issues them an electronic warrant. A warrant is basically a tradable receipt. The traders can then approach a bank and use this warrant as collateral to get a loan. Alternatively, they can trade the warrant to anyone who wants the commodities. The warrant includes specific information about the commodities: their amount, type, quality, and exact warehouse location.

Conveniently, it is exactly this kind of specific information about an asset's physical location and characteristics that shariah scholars demand when Islamic financial institutions arrange tawarruq trades. One of the shariah scholars' biggest criticisms of existing tawarruq solutions—such as those executed through the London Metal Exchange—is that it is difficult to track the exact location and type of the underlying assets being traded, or even to verify that they still exist. Shariah scholars worry that Islamic banks are trading ghost-like electronic apparitions of commodities, and not real commodities themselves. They also worry that the same commodities are being used for different transactions, making a mockery of the idea that trade underlies tawarruq. Tradeflow aims to solve that problem. So like Bursa Malaysia's Suq al-Sila', though with different mechanics, Tradeflow is competing to be the infrastructure that Islamic financial institutions use to make their tawarruq trades more reliably shariah-compliant—and thus to keep their shariah scholars happy.

Like many Western expats in Dubai, Paul Boots has an adventuresome, entrepreneurial streak. While studying finance and business at Babson College in Boston in the early 2000s, he founded a laundry start-up on campus. He then used his connections to land a job in Brussels with Euroclear, a securities clearinghouse that is also part of the infrastructure of global capital markets. Two years later he was in the diamond business, setting up the Dubai Multi Commodities Centre's Antwerp office and promoting Dubai as an up-and-coming global diamond hub. The Dubai Multi Commodities Centre (DMCC) is a Dubai government agency whose mission is to increase Dubai's GDP by attracting foreign investment in the commodities business: in short, to spur Dubai's economic growth by making it a global hub for as many kinds of commodities as possible. In 2002, Dubai's imports and exports of diamonds totaled around $5 million. "This is now up to around $40 *billion*," said Boots.[79] Dubai is now one of the world's top three diamond hubs: rough diamonds are traded in Antwerp and Dubai, then go to India to be polished.

The story of Tradeflow shows how the world's tawarruq infrastructure is expanding on the back of the growth, globalization, and financialization of the global commodities trade—and state efforts to promote it. When Paul Boots was first designing the precursor to Tradeflow in the mid-2000s, Islamic finance was not on his mind. But in Dubai, commodities and Islamic finance were both hot, and by 2010, Boots found himself talking to the Islamic-finance sector:

> We had no idea [that Islamic banks would be interested]! They said, "At the moment, we call our brokers in London, or we go to Malaysia. But if you guys can offer us something here, with commodities that are in Dubai or the UAE, and that our shariah scholars can actually go to the warehouse and inspect, and on a platform that's locally hosted, with a government entity . . ." They were like, "This would be perfect! This would be like bringing it home!"[80]

Boots and his team approached Dubai Islamic Bank and its spin-off shariah consultancy Dar Al Sharia. They worked for a year and a half to design a way to make Tradeflow support tawarruq that would satisfy Hussein Hamid Hassan, the senior shariah scholar at Dubai Islamic Bank and Dar Al Sharia. Today, a growing number of firms in the Gulf and beyond are using Tradeflow to facilitate tawarruq.

Conclusion: More Capital, More Shariah

This chapter has shown how shariah boards, internal shariah departments, and shariah auditors place meaningful restrictions on what capitalists can do. These organs apply the bureaucratic ethos of audit culture in implementing the directives of leading shariah scholars. Since the 1970s, bureaucratic control of shariah-compliance has become progressively more institutionalized inside and outside the firm, including at government banking and securities regulators.

Shariah boards and their agents have grown increasingly scrupulous about shariah-compliance as the market for Islamic finance has grown. This finding is striking in that it militates against what we might call the "secularization thesis of modern markets": the expectation that the influx of capital into Islamic finance, including capital from large financial institutions owned mostly by non-Muslim investors and controlled by non-Muslim managers, will enfeeble shariah regulation of finance. Instead, more capital has translated into more shariah supervision, and more intensive shariah supervision, not less.

More capital has translated into "more shariah" because of the social characteristics of the global field of shariah scholars. As members of the professional field of ulama, shariah scholars everywhere—whether they work in Islamic finance or not—are expected by their peers to remain loyal to an academic ethos. We saw this in chapter 4, when we learned that shariah scholars accrue symbolic capital through publications, doctorates, professorships, and judgeships, and in chapter 5, when we observed how shariah scholars must reference the classical Islamic legal tradition and adhere to established methodological conventions even when deviating from majority juristic viewpoints.

When capitalists attempt to introduce a new product, security issuance, or deal that "pushes the envelope" of existing consensus among leading scholars, they must get approval from at least one or two highly respected scholars. Elite scholars regularly encounter attempts to push the envelope. As explained by the finance lawyer Nathaniel Armstrong, managing partner of Dentons's Abu Dhabi office, all parties to a major transaction other than the shariah scholars—including the banks, investors, and securities issuers—are trying to "mimic a conventional [transaction]" to make it attractive "not only to people who want it to be Islamic but to people who just care about risk allocation and pricing." To the extent possible, they want products "congruent with conventional financings" that "essentially operate like conventional ones on financial metrics." Armstrong has seen junior shariah scholars at less-stringent banks turn a blind eye to "indemnities thrown in left, right, and center" by product structurers attempting to skirt shariah requirements they think could create new risks or costs. In contrast, he finds that banks where "the scholars kind of run the show" are less amenable to such sleights of hand.[81] Indeed, the longtime head of Abu Dhabi Islamic Bank's shariah department, Sheikh Osaid Kailani, is a member of the international scholarly elite—and one of the few shariah-department chiefs in the elite category—precisely *because* he has a global reputation for being "very conservative," as finance journalist and sukuk expert Hassan Jivraj puts it and as others corroborate.[82] Armstrong's account underscores that scholarly resistance to capital, especially from elite scholars and institutions where shariah scholars enjoy power and respect, is real.

Any senior scholar who signs a fatwa approving an envelope-pushing product or transaction is putting her or his (usually his) academic reputation on the line. And as this chapter has shown, elite scholars such as Sheikh Yusuf DeLorenzo have called out other elite scholars for pushing the envelope. Even a young practitioner, Mohammed Khnifer (see chapter 5), triggered widespread market suspicion about a Goldman Sachs sukuk that had been authorized by internationally elite scholars. In the age of social media, shariah scholars thus have an incentive not to be overly permissive and instead to demonstrate their bona fides.

Fortunately for elite scholars, the industry has grown rapidly, and with it demand for their seal of approval. Growth has been especially rapid in the complex and often transnational domain of high Islamic finance, where the approval of rock-star scholars is especially important in attracting investors and smoothing deals (see chapter 4). Thus, being scrupulous does not really seem to cost elite scholars the opportunity to sit on shariah boards. Instead, the most prominent scholars turn down supervisory work "left and right" because they are offered more opportunities for it than they can handle.[83] (In the event that the industry reverses course and starts shrinking, it will be interesting to see if shariah scholars continue to hold the line as closely.)

Yet this chapter also offers a caveat: scholarly stringency does not usually end up pushing Islamic finance closer to the moral economists' vision of a welfare-oriented, systemically distinctive form of finance. This is because of a dialectical pattern: finance capitalists push the envelope, shariah scholars demand scrupulous compliance, but then innovators develop technical solutions that help the finance capitalists achieve their aims while meeting the scholars' shariah demands. This chapter has presented the Dubai Multi Commodities Centre and Kuala Lumpur's Bursa Suq al-Sila' as two attempts out of many to "build a better mousetrap" that executes tawarruq in compliance with prominent shariah scholars' wishes.

Ultimately, scholarly restrictions can give rise to new business opportunities: chances for innovators to build trading platforms and infrastructures that deploy technology cleverly to simulate interest in more scrupulously shariah-compliant ways. Hence, more shariah and more scholarly scrutiny can mean *more* opportunities for capital, not fewer. Wedded by the scholars, fiqh and capitalist finance prove compatible yet again.

7

State and Society

TWO THOUSAND NINETEEN, like so many years before and after, was one of anti-government protest in Pakistan. In May, Prime Minister Imran Khan negotiated a $6 billion bailout from the IMF in exchange for eliminating energy subsidies, tightening tax collection, and depreciating the rupee. Demonstrations ensued. One, led by the Islamist party Jamaat-e-Islami in June, decried high unemployment and the rising cost of petrol, sugar, cement, pens, and books. Though the prime minister himself had promised to implement an Islamic welfare state, his opponents branded him an enemy of the Islamic economy and a stooge of international finance. Jamaat-e-Islami party chief Siraj ul Haq stressed that the government budget was mired in the interest-based system, with Pakistan paying billions of rupees to the IMF in interest alone.[1] This burden of interest, he continued, was "eating" Pakistan; outsiders were deliberately depriving Pakistanis of their freedom by entangling them in usurious loans. "It has become hard for the common man to breathe," he fumed. Demonstrations crescendoed through the summer and fall. By October, hundreds of thousands of religious conservatives marched on the nation's capital. Leading the march was Pakistan's largest political party of religious scholars, Jamiat Ulema-e-Islam. Its leaders branded the prime minister a Zionist and demanded his resignation.

In Saudi Arabia around the same time, public discussions about the nature of an Islamic economy were of a different sort. There were no overt challenges to the Saudi government's economic stewardship, and no public vituperation against the interest-based international financial system—even though the Saudi state is deeply enmeshed in that system, not least as one of the world's largest holders of U.S. Treasuries. Instead, Saudis debated whether particular investments are shariah-compliant, with eminent shariah scholars opining on technical details. One hot topic was the shariah-compliance of the 2019 initial public offering (IPO) of Aramco, the Saudi national oil company and the world's largest corporation by market value. On social media, homemade videos warned that Aramco shares were sinful because the company had billions of riyals in interest-bearing debt. In response, Sheikh Abdullah al-Mutlaq, a member the Council of Senior Scholars—Saudi Arabia's very influential state-sponsored fatwa-issuance authority—and a member of the shariah boards of many of the kingdom's largest banks, went on the radio to defend Aramco shares as halal.[2]

Meanwhile, the Bitcoin bug had bitten the kingdom, and as the cryptocurrency's price bounded up and down, the country's leading religious scholars discussed in the news and on popular religious TV programs whether it was shariah-compliant. The two Saudi shariah scholars most active in Islamic finance, al-Mutlaq and Sheikh Abdullah al-Manea, appeared in major media outlets to declare Bitcoin trading haram.[3] Although other scholars opined too, these two enjoyed regular coverage in the business news not only because they were members of the Council of Senior Scholars but because they were finance specialists. Al-Mutlaq averred in 2018 that trading in Bitcoin, a very volatile asset, was tantamount to gambling[4] and tinged with gharar. And in 2021, al-Manea appeared on a popular ask-a-mufti television show and pointed out, echoing both classical Islamic law and classical Western European monetary theory, that money must be a medium of exchange, a unit of account, and a store of value. Without a state or other powerful entity guaranteeing its value, the sheikh asked, how could it function effectively, or Islamically, as money? In sum, the Saudi religious authorities opining most visibly on what counts as legitimately Islamic financial activity were confirming the capitalist status quo. Their concern was helping individual investors earn a profit while avoiding the anxiety of breaking God's law. They did so while affirming the Saudi state's authority to manage currency, and they did not criticize capitalist finance as a domestic or international system.

These examples illustrate stark differences in popular understandings of usury and in the way these understandings are activated in public life. In Pakistan, a poor debtor nation with a political culture forged in resistance to imperialism and neo-imperialism, and where shariah scholars are one group among many competing for religious authority, the problem of usury makes its appearance as a political football, invoked by opposition Islamists to rattle the government and direct the masses' ire at international finance capital. In Saudi Arabia, a middle-income nation with widely institutionalized roles for shariah scholars in public life, long-standing alliances with Western capitalist powers, and a tightly controlled public sphere nearly devoid of contentious politics, the problem of usury arises in mass discourse when influential scholars, aligned with capital and the state, speak out to assuage individual investors' anxieties about sin.

What shapes country differences in the development and character of Islamic finance? A lot of serious research has investigated the growth drivers of Islamic finance in national or regional contexts. One major stream, authored mostly by political scientists, stresses the state and elite politics.[5] Other accounts focus on hydrocarbon rents,[6] the Islamic revival,[7] the neoliberal globalization of financial and legal services,[8] the ascent of middle-class[9] and ultra-rich[10] Muslim bourgeoisies, identitarian movements,[11] the U.S. state's financial Islamophobia after September 11,[12] "corporate Islam,"[13] and the individual pioneers who launched the first Islamic banks.[14] Still others assert that the historical "Islamic economy" has always been capitalist[15] and consider the Islamic-finance industry's present success a reprise. Indeed, any effort to explain the success of Islamic finance at a comparative level will necessarily tell a complex story, and the account presented here builds on the aforementioned advances in scholarship.

This book shows that shariah scholars too have been an essential part of the formula for the growth of Islamic finance. This chapter in particular illustrates how shariah scholars mediate the impact of crucial variables on the prospects for capitalist Islamic finance in a country. These factors include a country's position in the world-system; the relative weight of juristic (i.e., fiqh-minded) versus social-welfarist interpretations of shariah among the population and within school curricula; and the political contentiousness or quiescence of public conversations about shariah's place in state, society, and economy. If these factors favor the stable dominance of shariah scholars who pragmatically accept interest simulation and are willing to "play ball" with capital, as in Saudi Arabia, then shariah scholars, firms, and the state develop a consensus in favor of capitalist Islamic finance. But if these factors undermine the popular legitimacy and certification authority of the pragmatic faction of shariah scholars, then capitalist Islamic finance faces headwinds, as in Pakistan (until around the 2010s, following the country's "reset" of Islamic finance in the early 2000s).

Terminological Note: Riba and Sood

In interviews, my research assistants and I asked respondents to discuss usury: sood (sūd) in Urdu, riba (ribā) in Arabic. A terminological challenge arises. The Arabic word "riba" translates well as "usury" given that it always refers to an unethical and Islamically unlawful increase on a loan. Regardless of debates over its definition, it always has a pejorative connotation, just as the word "usury" and its cognates have always had in English and other Western European languages. The word "riba" also has an indelibly religious character owing to its explicit prohibition in the Quran and the hadith literature. This contrasts with the Arabic word "faida" (fā'idah), which simply means "interest" and has the same straightforward, neutral connotation as that English word.

In contrast, the term "sood" in Urdu does double duty as both "interest" and "usury." It is used in neutral technical language, such as "the State Bank

FIGURE 7.1. A bus in Lahore bears the slogan "Interest is a curse." Author photo, 2016.

raises the interest rate,"[16] but also to mean an unethical or religiously prohibited increase. *Sūd-khor*, literally "interest-eater," means "usurer" and can function as a somewhat vulgar epithet; one might not utter it around one's mother.

Schoolchildren in Saudi Arabia are taught that riba is sinful, and in Pakistan that sood is sinful, as we will see. To complicate matters further, Pakistanis who have pursued Islamic studies in Arabic in religious seminaries sometimes know the term "riba." But most do not, and think of sood as what Islam prohibits.

Public Views on Usury, Islamic Banking, and Shariah Scholars

"Interest Is a Curse": A Fear and Loathing through Which People Interpret Their Life Histories

Buses and trucks in Pakistan are riotously colorful, ornamented, and covered in calligraphy. They bear poetic messages of love ("A mother's prayer is a breeze from heaven"), life on the road ("Wherever I lay down my bags, that is home"), and cheeky romance ("My heart is for sale. The price: One smile").[17] Moral apothegms are common too. One afternoon, I found myself stuck in a Lahore traffic jam behind a bus that announced, "Interest is a curse"[18] (figure 7.1).

The simple idea that interest is a curse encompasses a wide range of negative emotions, associations, and moral logics that many Muslims attach to interest. I will argue shortly that some of these ways of thinking about interest are more common in Saudi Arabia and others in Pakistan. But before focusing on national differences, I share a few stories from my interviewees to illustrate the fear and loathing that interest can arouse. If one did not grow up Muslim, or if one grew up in a Muslim family without such concerns, it may be hard to appreciate how viscerally uncomfortable a good chunk of humanity—hundreds of millions of people, perhaps over a billion—feels about interest. Interest is deeply repugnant to them.

My interviewees often described interest-bearing debt the way many people describe drugs or gambling: as both an affliction and a depredation, an individual trouble and a social ill. Some have studiously avoided interest their whole lives, worrying that a single bank loan would taint them with sin or lead them down the debtor's lonely path to perdition. Sumayyah, a university graduate in her late twenties, lives in Riyadh. She was strapped for cash two years ago but absolutely did not want to take an interest-bearing loan. She liquidated her savings and sold her gold instead. "My knowledge of religion is pretty simple," she concedes, but God's command is clear: "Usury is explicitly prohibited in the Quran." She had first heard about usury around third or fourth grade, just when she was starting to read, and then learned more about it in university. Today, she defers to knowledgeable shariah scholars on the details of shariah-compliance and says she would never bank at a usurious bank but feels comfortable dealing with Al Rajhi, the kingdom's largest Islamic bank.[19]

Others have learned the hard way, having struggled to climb out of debt or watched friends and family do the same. Tabish is a forty-something upper-middle-class executive at a medium-sized business in Karachi. Wearing a smart blue suit, chunky watch, and his hair slicked back, he is the picture of affluence. Yet ten years ago, he found himself spending a lot on credit cards, in thrall to their purchasing power. Then the banks started calling him, demanding their money. He and his wife had to sell off her jewelry to repay their debts. "Never again," they decided. They have not touched interest since.[20]

Wealthy people tell cautionary tales too. Shafqat is a premium customer at an Islamic bank in Pakistan. In 1973, as part of the wave of South Asian labor that flowed into the Arab Gulf economies with the oil boom, he arrived in Oman to work as an accountant at a bank. The pay was good, but he felt nagging malaise working at an institution tainted by the sin of interest. When Shafqat's three-year contract expired, the bank offered him a promotion that came with a hefty raise and a car, but he turned it down despite having no other job offers in hand. He describes this as a turning point in his life. Within a week, he got an even better offer as financial controller at an airline. Shortly thereafter, he met and married his wife. They lived happily in Oman for thirty-five years as he climbed the corporate ranks at the airline. Shafqat's adult children have heeded his admonition to avoid interest and the financial sector; all of them, he proudly explains, hold graduate degrees and are very successful nonetheless.[21]

Some of Shafqat's old friends, Pakistanis who stayed in the banking sector, have been less fortunate. One friend became district manager of a bank in Pakistan. He opened a new branch, but within fifteen days it was robbed. He was devastated, but Shafqat was less than sympathetic. "Who told you to open a bank?" he asked his friend. "You're back at zero. Leave this life [of a banker] behind!" Shafqat boils down his stories to a simple lesson: "Interest is haram, and a haram thing can never bear blessings."[22]

Some people even compare banks to loan sharks. Shakir is a mustached twenty-three-year-old restaurant employee and aspiring mechanic from Lyari, an area of Karachi known for gang violence. He wears a string bracelet to ward off the evil eye. Although he appreciates banks for paying his salary on time, he considers them, whether conventional or Islamic, no better than loan sharks. "They'll give you ten and charge you twenty [in interest]," he complains, "so how can they be halal?" After all, he explains, there is a hadith that says taking interest is like committing adultery with your mother.

Between wiping down tables, Shakir shares a wrenching story that shows what an odious curse he considers interest to be. His wife had complications during pregnancy, so he needed money for surgery to save her and the baby. He asked his friend, a mufti, whether it was acceptable to take an interest-bearing loan. The mufti said no, so Shakir didn't take the loan. (For the record, most Islamic jurists worldwide would likely have said yes under these circumstances.) Fortunately, his restaurant's management helped pay for the surgery. "We lost the baby, but my wife survived," Shakir recalls. "And I'm really glad I didn't take the bank loan, because I know things would have turned out worse."[23] As Akos Rona-Tas and Alya Guseva note, "context matters in whether debt is perceived as stressful or not."[24]

Usury: Public Conceptions

Many Muslims around the world worry about usury and its consequences. However, there are different ways of worrying. Saudi respondents in our study were more likely to take a juristic perspective and Pakistani respondents the moral economists' perspective.

To be sure, when asked how they would define riba or sood, the most common answer in both countries was the same: any increase on a loan or, phrased differently, money charged for the use of money ("money on money")—in short, interest. Muhannad, a thirty-two-year-old Saudi hospital employee, gave a typical version of this answer, describing riba as "the increase when borrowing": for example, "when you borrow ten riyals from the bank and must return twelve, or when you deposit ten and they give you back twelve." He considered riba and faida to be the same thing.[25] Raha, a twenty-five-year-old Saudi living in a Riyadh suburb who holds a business degree but is not employed, said she defines riba as "taking money for money with increase."[26] Pervez, a neatly coiffed forty-five-year-old recruiter at a Karachi-based trucking company, similarly defined sood simply as "money on money."[27] Rasheed, a seventy-year-old retired Pakistani welder, had heard of riba when learning about Islam from his family as a child. He equated riba to sood and defined both as "money on money."[28] As discussed in chapter 2, this basic conception of usury as any increase on a loan—money on money, or what we today call interest—prevailed throughout the premodern world. It was also foundational to religious jurists' financial ethics for most of the history of Judaism, Christianity, and Islam.

SAUDI ARABIA: THE JURISTIC UNDERSTANDING OF USURY AND ITS ELABORATION IN SCHOOL CURRICULA

Although the money-on-money definition of usury is widespread in both countries, a closer look reveals national differences. When Saudis elaborated further about usury beyond the money-on-money conception, they often introduced concepts and examples that suggested juristic ways of thinking. For example, some mentioned substances besides money that can be the subject of a usurious loan. Premodern religious jurists in the three Abrahamic traditions discussed this topic too (see chapter 2). Usury can arise not only in monetary dealings but "in dealings with gold and silver," explained Abdulaziz, a thirty-one-year-old university lecturer in international affairs from Jeddah.[29] Amru, a thirty-eight-year-old small-business owner and day trader from Mecca, initially described usury as simply an increase on a loan but added that "a more comprehensive definition" would note that the usurious increase could come in the form of services, not just monetary or material consideration.[30] Amru's remark reminded me of rabbinical debates among the Amoraim (ca. 200–500 CE) as to whether Jewish law permits a lender to stay in the home of a borrower free of charge. And Muneer, a thirty-eight-year-old civil servant from Dammam with a master's in engineering, offered the humble caveat "I'm no religious scholar," but then correctly noted that increase on a loan constitutes only one of the two major forms of usury that Islamic jurists designate; in addition to this "usury of delay" (ribā al-nasīʾah), he mentioned a type less familiar to most Muslims called "usury of excess" (ribā al-faḍl) that can arise in sale and barter when the same commodity is exchanged in unequal amounts or in exchanges not made on the spot.[31] Classical jurists wrote at length about this second type of usury, but in contemporary financial life, it arises much less often than the first type—yet Muneer knew about it. Such nuanced juristic familiarity with usury arose very rarely during our interviews with Pakistanis.

Our Saudi interviewees' sophisticated juristic understandings of usury made more sense to me after I examined the Saudi public-school curriculum. My Saudi research assistant and I reviewed every mention of usury in the high-school textbooks used throughout the kingdom. Saudi schoolchildren begin studying fiqh in first grade (age seven). By the time they graduate high school, they have been exposed to all the juristic distinctions respondents mentioned in the previous paragraph. For example, the tenth-grade fiqh textbook discusses the distinctions between the different types of usury. It also explains that usury of excess arises not only when money is exchanged for money but also gold for gold, silver for silver, dates for dates, wheat for wheat, salt for salt, and barley for barley.[32] And the eleventh-grade fiqh textbook points out that if someone borrows 100,000 riyals at zero interest but pledges his car to the lender as security, the lender may not use the car, for that would be usury[33]— in other words, that usurious increase can come in the form of services.

In fact, Saudi high-school education on usury and the fiqh of financial transactions goes well beyond such relatively simple examples to strikingly complex levels. By twelfth grade, Saudi students learn how usury can arise in transactions that involve collateral, mortgaging/pawning, late payment fees on loans, debt settlement and write-down, and sales of agricultural commodities.[34] They also learn practical accommodations that jurists have permitted to facilitate commerce in spite of these restrictions. Consider the following passage:

> Example: A car costs 80,000 riyals cash. Someone buys it for 100,000 riyals, to be paid in installments over four years. After two years, the buyer agrees with the installment company to pay off all remaining installments, with the company reducing the price to 90,000 riyals.
> Ruling: This compromise is permissible provided that it is not stipulated in the original contract. It is not permissible for the two parties to agree in the contract on the percentage of discount that the creditor is obliged to offer in the event of early repayment. Instead, they may only agree on this once the buyer [expresses] a desire to repay early.[35]

This passage caught my attention for two reasons. The first is simply its level of technical sophistication. Saudi high-school students arguably study Islamic financial jurisprudence at a level comparable to that at which first-year law students in the United States study contract law, and in a similar manner. Presented with scenarios, the Saudi students must decide the appropriate ruling and state the legal rationale behind it. They cite the Quran and hadith literature on their exams the way U.S. law students cite the Constitution and federal code, and refer to fatwas of renowned classical Islamic jurists the way U.S. law students refer to decisions by justices of the Supreme Court and federal bench. But second, in contradistinction to contemporary secular legal traditions, this ruling reveals a quintessentially scholastic mode of reasoning. Because usury is a sin, the question of intent—and hence of timing—arises. If a discount is "premeditated" by the buyer and seller of the car at the initial moment of sale, it is usurious, because Islamic jurists argue that usury is baked into the difference between discounted and original price (here 90,000 riyals and 100,000 riyals). However, if it is decided later between buyer and seller, it is acceptable. Again, this reasoning is similar to that of premodern jurists in the three Abrahamic traditions. It flies in the face of economic thinking, for the economic outcome is identical in the two cases.

Saudi high-school students also learn how to meet ritual obligations while engaging in accommodations to modern capitalist financial practice. For example, they learn how to purify ill-gotten gains, a major concern for equity investors.[36] And they learn that a customer may take a credit card from the bank and put down collateral against it, so long as the customer continues to pay zakat on the value of the collateral.[37]

The moral economists' perspective on usury appears in just one Saudi textbook. The tenth-grade fiqh textbook devotes exactly one page to the harm usury causes individuals, society, and economy.[38] This page's discourse is certainly anti-capitalist. Not only does usury imprint the heart of the usurer with selfishness, greed, miserliness, and servitude to money, but it divides society into two classes, the rich and the poor. Capitalist society is usurious society: the rich in capitalist societies grow richer through usury "without toil," while the poor labor and sell off their possessions just to make their interest payments; and when the poor default, the usurers mercilessly sell off their collateral. As the debt of the impoverished multiplies, "the inevitable result is that the rich get richer while the poor get poorer." Meanwhile, usury deprives society of productive investment, which gets diverted instead to lending. Economic development suffers. Moreover, as money is shunted from productive to unproductive purposes, the purchasing power of the national currency declines; and because productive entrepreneurs must borrow to finance their projects, they raise the price of the goods and services they produce for the community. In sum, usury corrupts morals, increases inequality, stunts economic development, and causes inflation.

This is the standard-issue moral economist critique of interest-based finance made since the 1920s, and most vociferously between the 1950s and 1980s, by Islamic economists and the neorevivalist Islamist activists who shared the Islamic economists' views on finance, such as the Muslim Brotherhood and Jamaat-e-Islami (see chapter 2). This critique has become canonical in textbooks and seminars on Islamic finance around the world, even when introducing contemporary forms of Islamic finance thoroughly integrated into the global capitalist financial system, such as sukuk and Islamic derivatives. (It can be jarring to see references to the depredations of capitalist finance and to Islam's call for social justice followed by instructions for structuring shariah-compliant wealth-management vehicles in "tax-efficient" jurisdictions like Luxembourg and the Cayman Islands.)[39]

Even in the Saudi curriculum, the anti-capitalist social and economic critique feels incongruous and shoehorned. Of the many pages focused on usury in high-school textbooks, this critique occupies just one. It is written entirely in the abstract, not mentioning the term "Saudi Arabia" or any other proper nouns. It does not designate actually existing contemporary persons or institutions that rely on usury or seek to eliminate it. The rest of the curriculum takes for granted that Saudis will be operating in a capitalist financial system and guides them in meeting their religious obligations within it. On the margins, there are some economically substantive distinctions that shariah, as understood by the Saudi textbooks, demands that Saudis respect—such as restrictions on the way debts may be collected. But in actual practice, firms offering Islamic financial services find ways to accommodate these distinctions within a standard capitalist business model (see chapter 3).

This disconnect in Saudi textbooks—between the anti-capitalist motivations attributed to Islamic finance and its practical prescriptions for pious living in a capitalist financial system—has historical roots. Saudi Arabia was a haven for Muslim Brothers from around the Arab world in the 1970s and 1980s, when the House of Saud welcomed them as a counterweight to Arab socialism. Schoolteachers were among the Brotherhood's core constituencies in the kingdom, and the left-leaning Islamic economics the Brotherhood espoused back then made its way into the curriculum. Moreover, many of the pioneers of modern Islamic finance adopted a broadly neorevivalist social orientation; they expected Islamic finance to be a real cure for social ills (see chapter 1). At the time, anti-capitalist discourse was synonymous with the very idea of Islamic finance. Yet the juristic conception of what makes transactions Islamic has stronger, longer institutional roots in Saudi Arabia. It is Islamic jurists, not Islamic economists, who write the content of Saudi textbooks on fiqh. And aside from the anti-capitalist credo that appears on one page, the linchpin contracts of the Islamic economists' profit-and-loss-sharing (PLS) conception of Islamic finance, musharaka and mudaraba, do not appear in Saudi textbooks of fiqh or other Islamic sciences. Meanwhile, economics, including Islamic economics, is not part of the standard high-school curriculum.

As adults, Saudis are also exposed to discussions about riba that lead many of them to think of it in juristic terms. We asked respondents whether their understanding of riba had changed since they first heard the term. Many expressed that they had become aware of technical nuances they had not known about in their youth. Muhammad, a retiree in Dammam with a secondary-school education, had known for as long as he could remember that riba is prohibited according to shariah, but as an adult he found that sheikhs (i.e., shariah scholars) "explain questions and cases in detail and give you advice about riba."[40] Similarly, Abdul Muhsin, a forty-four-year-old security guard in Medina, first learned about riba at age ten or eleven but has since gained a broader view. "Now I know that riba has a million shapes and forms," he explained. Without prompting, he also cited a relevant hadith: "The Messenger of Allah cursed the one who consumed riba, and the one who charged it, those who witnessed it, and the one who recorded it."[41] Sumayyah, the university graduate from Riyadh in her late twenties, experienced a usury-related situation at work that prompted her to dig for jurisprudential detail. Upon taking a job, her new employer deposited a token sum on her behalf in the company's interest-bearing savings account. Suspicious, she consulted a sheikh, who told her not only that the token transaction was Islamically unlawful but that the whole company's business model was unlawful too. She eventually quit the job.[42]

PAKISTAN: THE MORAL ECONOMISTS' UNDERSTANDING OF USURY AND ITS ELABORATION IN SCHOOL CURRICULA

Pakistani interviewees tended to define and discuss usury or interest from the perspective of a moral economist. Themes from Islamic economics appeared often in their explanations.

As mentioned earlier, both Saudi and Pakistani respondents defined usury most often as "money on money." Yet Pakistani respondents did so less often. Tellingly, the other definitions Pakistanis gave reflected moral economist financial ethics.

For example, fourteen of the sixty-nine Pakistanis we interviewed described usury as a fixed return on an investment. (In contrast, only one Saudi interviewee mentioned fixed returns.) They felt that a variable return—that is, one not specified in advance—was evidence of usury's absence. The respondents described this in a number of ways: "What we have been told and taught since childhood is that a fixed amount other than your principal is called riba," said Sarfraz, a thirty-eight-year-old middle manager at an IT company in Lahore.[43] Tabish, the forty-something executive, noted, "If there's fluctuation—profit and loss—then this is not riba. It's purely profit. It's 100 percent from our Prophet."[44] Ramiz, a twenty-eight-year-old MBA from Okara and dispatch manager for an American transportation company, explained, "Islamic law is very straightforward. If the profit rate is flexible, if it's not fixed, it's ok."[45] And Sanam, a well-to-do thirty-four-year-old abaya-wearing Karachi housewife, said, "Riba is sood; it's when the rate on a loan is fixed, so it's haram."[46] (Concern about usury did not stop Sanam from proudly flashing a wallet full of premium credit cards. She and her husband, a stockbroker, always paid them off before they accrued interest.)

Closely related to the idea of fixed returns being usurious is the idea that usury constitutes profit without risk-taking. Such views have suffused Pakistani society. Shozab is a thirty-two-year-old small-business owner investing in poultry and liquified petroleum gas. He explained that Islam allows people to go into business together on the condition that they share the profit and loss: "But [if] only I [earn] profit, and the loss is all yours, that's where Islam draws the line."[47] Saqib, a sixty-year-old partner in a Lahore car dealership, says that when you deposit money in a conventional savings account, "there is 100 percent chance of profit . . . and no chances of loss." To Saqib, this is "the definition of usury."[48] This stance was quite common among Pakistanis but hardly arose in our conversations with Saudis.

In Pakistan, shariah scholars and Islamic banks propound the idea that Islamic banks avoid fixed returns and invest in businesses on a profit-and-loss-sharing (PLS) basis instead. Indeed, Islamic economists and neorevivalists have for decades asserted that PLS is what makes Islamic finance Islamic (see chapter 1). Pakistani interviewees' conceptions of Islamic banking reflected this view. "The muftis say that banking works on the sood system. So they ask people to go for Islamic banking instead. Because if there's a fixed percentage, it's called riba," Tabish said. He assumed that Islamic banking is PLS-based. When I asked how Islamic banks avoid sood, he said they take customer deposits, invest in businesses, and give the profits back to depositors.[49] I asked the same question of Nawaz, a twenty-four-year-old university student majoring in commerce and working at an ice-cream shop: "They invest in businesses; the return isn't fixed."[50] Islamic banks also educate customers directly by suggesting that Islamic banks avoid fixed returns. Ashfaq, an eighty-year-old retired civil servant sporting a karakul hat and white shalwar kameez, was told by a branch manager at Meezan Bank that the bank invests in companies and then distributes back to its customers the profits it earns. "So sometimes we get maybe 3 percent, 4 percent, 8 percent; but it is not fixed, unlike other banks," Ashfaq explains.[51] Amina, a thirty-one-year-old Karachiite housewife, was told the same when she opened her Meezan account. "[The bank] told me they invest in halal businesses on a profit-and-loss basis. There is up-and-down fluctuation. If it were fixed, it would be sood," she recalls.[52] Syed Muhammad, a fifty-nine-year-old former army officer who now trades textiles and property, trusts the savings accounts at Dubai Islamic Bank because "every month they calculate how much profit to pay you, and every month it varies."[53] He says he would avoid any fixed-rate savings account. (In practice, the rates on Islamic savings accounts in Pakistan do vary within an expected range, but this range is smaller than some quoted customers think.)

Some Pakistanis understood usury to constitute profit without work. This perspective reflects a virtue ethics, widely attested in premodern and modern critiques of moneylending, in which only human labor legitimizes earnings and usury constitutes lazy, parasitical rentierism.[54] This viewpoint was much more common among working-class and petit bourgeois Pakistanis; it never arose among well-to-do banking clients. Ali Amir, a twenty-five-year-old unemployed Karachiite, said he considered sood to be wrong because money should be made by working hard, not by lending.[55] I asked Chiragh, a twenty-five-year-old accounts officer in the navy, if he would put his savings in a bank account that paid interest. "No, I'd rather do work and earn the money myself,"[56] he replied. Chiragh incorporated this view into a disdain for banks of all kinds, conventional or Islamic. He criticized banks for taking interest, charging high rates, and hounding you to repay loans. "Banks are just a way for the elite to move their money around. They don't do anything for the poor," he quipped.[57] Faiza, a fifty-nine-year-old manager at a Karachi grocery, said, "Sood is taking money without contributing any work. That's why Islam bans it." She broke into an impassioned lilt. "I work twelve, fourteen hours a day. How long do those bankers on I. I. Chundrigar [Road] work?" she asked, referencing the "Wall Street of Pakistan."[58]

Once again, textbooks tell us a lot. With the help of three Pakistani researchers, I reviewed all discussions of usury, interest, and the Islamic economy in the textbooks used in all grades (1–12) of the major national curriculum tracks. The Pakistani textbooks interpret usury through the lens of a moral economist more than a juristic one. They also depict usury's elimination as part of a concrete Pakistani state project to build an Islamic economic system.

Most Pakistani students' education in fiqh is far less comprehensive than most Saudi students' and offers less background to naturalize a juristic approach to finance. Pakistani schoolchildren absorb less of all the classical Islamic sciences in general: when my Saudi research assistant reviewed the O-level *Islāmiyāt* syllabus used in the ninth to eleventh grade in the most challenging Pakistani curriculum (used in elite private schools), he observed, "We had already learned all of this by fourth grade."[59] According to two Pakistani secondary-school educators, most Pakistani schoolchildren start learning the basics of Islamic law in fifth grade;[60] this compares to first grade in Saudi Arabia. There is virtually no exposure to classical Islamic law of transactions as a complex intellectual subject matter in the Pakistani national curriculum:

unlike Saudi schoolchildren, Pakistani students do not study the Islamic law of property, ownership, contract, sales, leasing, mortgage, or partnership in a sophisticated way. Yet these are the intellectual building blocks for a juristic understanding of capitalist Islamic finance.

A partial exception to this rule is the nearly one-tenth[61] of Pakistani children who attend *madrasahs*, or traditional Islamic schools and seminaries. School-age madrasah education, which is mostly unregulated, focuses on reading and memorizing the Quran, learning Quranic Arabic, and learning the classical Islamic sciences. However, madrasahs in Pakistan overwhelmingly serve poor, rural students, largely because they are often free of charge or nearly so and provide meals and sometimes housing. Many serve areas and communities, including refugees, where government schools do not exist and literacy is low. In such settings, advancement to late secondary school and tertiary education, where training in fiqh becomes more advanced, is limited to a minority of students. To be sure, it is from this minority of advanced madrasah graduates that many of Pakistan's growing contingent of shariah scholars involved in Islamic finance arise.

Returning to the standard Pakistani curricula, we find that whereas deep juristic background on usury avoidance is lacking, the idea of an interest-free real-world Islamic economic system is constantly reinforced. In the state of Punjab's standard curriculum, the term "Islamic economic system" appears in five textbooks over four years (fifth, ninth, tenth, twelfth). If we include discussions about the impoverishing effect of interest in premodern Islamicate societies and in modern capitalist ones, then Pakistani students get this "socioeconomic" critique of interest nearly every year from fifth grade onward. Strikingly, this message appears in similar form over and over in three very different topics of instruction: Islamic studies (including History of Islam[62] and Islāmiyāt courses), economics, and Pakistan studies.

The critique of usurious capitalism that appears in the Pakistani curriculum is the same neorevivalist critique that appears in the Saudi curriculum; the Pakistani curriculum just contains more of it. A ninth-grade Islāmiyāt textbook explains in simple terms that in the capitalist system, interest is "a means of earning a living," but in the eyes of Islam, it is "the root of oppression and corruption."[63] An eleventh-grade Islāmiyāt textbook goes further, offering a rudimentary class analysis nearly identical to the Saudi tenth-grade fiqh textbook's:

In an interest-based economy, capital is more valuable than labor. Therefore, the working class constantly gets poorer and poorer, and the capitalist class seizes the wealth of the working class in various ways. Thus, the economic system becomes paralyzed.

The Quran expresses this fact in these words: "Allah abolishes interest and increases charity."[64]

As in the Saudi curriculum, we also find an Islamic virtue ethics. An economics textbook notes that Islam despises usurers as "those who take advantage of the compulsions of others facing difficult situations" in contravention of Islam's emphasis on justice and brotherhood.[65] An Islāmiyāt textbook likewise describes interest as a degenerate and destructive source of income comparable to injustice, dishonesty, bribery, theft, robbery, hoarding, fraud, and gambling.[66] Such language could have come verbatim from anti-usury tracts in medieval and early modern Western Christendom.

However, the Pakistani curriculum makes the socioeconomic problem of usury come alive in a way that the Saudi curriculum does not: by emphasizing interest's role in the misfortune of present-day Pakistanis, particularly as denizens of the Global South in an age of neoliberal globalization. In twelfth grade, economics students learn that Pakistani farmers face a credit shortage: the country has too few agricultural lending institutions, and those that exist lend to influential landlords instead of directly to farmers. Hence, farmers turn to moneylenders and middlemen who charge very high interest rates and trap them in debt their entire lives.[67] In the same textbook, students read that under capitalism, interest-based business concentrates wealth in the hands of a few, leading to monopolistic multinational companies. Interest helps these multinationals ensnare people worldwide in an exploitative net.[68] Students also learn that the government of Pakistan has extensive external debt and spends heavily on the associated interest payments. In a country where agriculture accounts for half the employed labor force,[69] the plight of indebted peasants is widely known, multinational corporations and their brands have proliferated in recent decades, suspicion of Bretton Woods institutions is high, and awareness of global inequality is keen, these passages contribute to the case for abolishing interest and financing development in a more solidaristic, more Islamic way.

The Pakistani curriculum also breaks from the Saudi curriculum in offering a public-policy solution to the moral, social, and economic problem of usury: PLS-based interest-free banking. In fifth-grade Pakistan Studies, pupils learn that Islam is "a base of Pakistan's economic system."[70] What follows is effectively a précis of Abu al-Aʿla Mawdudi's neorevivalist economic thought.[71] God owns everything in the universe but has granted man the trusteeship and productive use of all earthly goods. Hence, the fifth graders learn, "the Islamic economic system teaches us to increase national production"—a statement that, in the Mawdudist vein, makes religious imperatives synonymous with reasons of state—by making full use of the forests, animals, mountains, and seas. The textbook then presents twin policy pillars of an Islamic economic system. The first is zakat, which advances the Islamic economic system's concern to circulate wealth and distribute it fairly. The second is an "interest free system of banking," which addresses the Islamic economic system's prohibition on receiving or giving interest. In tenth-grade Economics, students also learn that in Islamic society, people can invest using mudaraba, a structure in which an investor and manager of capital share profits. Through this mode of investment, the Islamic economic system promotes "an untainted and exploitation-free society."[72]

While the textbooks stress the pressing need for an Islamic economic system today, they also present it as having governed the perfect society that existed during the Prophet Muhammad's lifetime. Ninth graders learn that "the Islamic economic system was . . . put into practice by the Prophet Muhammad," with interest, gambling, and trade in haram things forbidden.[73] The Prophet's abolition of usury redressed the widespread business of usury, which prior to Islam's arrival was "carried out by Jews who used to rob poor farmers by giving them loans on strict terms." Once a farmer took interest from these Jewish usurers, "he could not easily escape their clutches."[74]

The Pakistani government has implemented interest-free PLS-based banking and other fundaments of the Islamic economic system. Tenth graders are taught in Pakistan Studies about the country's constitution, which declares Islam the state religion, encourages citizens to practice an "Islamic mode of life," and insists that "steps will be taken to abolish interest, prostitution, gambling, and alcohol."[75] On the next page, students learn about Zia-ul-Haq's 1977–88 Islamization program, including the introduction of PLS-based bank accounts in 1981 and the conversion of all savings accounts to PLS accounts in 1984. Yet the Pakistani curriculum does not mention the incomplete and haphazard nature of the state-imposed conversion to interest-free banking under Zia, nor the eventual rollback of this measure under Pervez Musharraf in the early 2000s.

The Pakistani textbooks' incorporation of a neorevivalist, welfarist perspective on usury and Islamic banking opens the door to politicization of these issues in a way that does not happen in Saudi Arabia. The astute Pakistani high-school student might wonder why it is still possible to get an interest-based savings account in Pakistan—indeed, why most savings accounts in Pakistan are interest-based—if the state outlawed interest-based banking in the 1980s and replaced it with PLS-based banking. She might wonder why the government allows interest at all if it impoverishes her country's farmers and subjugates the national treasury to the IMF. She might be confused by the contradiction between two understandings of usury presented in the same twelfth-grade economics textbook: the neoclassical conception, in which "interest is . . . compensation for the use of capital," and on the next page the Islamic conception, in which interest is never legitimate because it is founded on oppression.[76] The Saudi curriculum, by contrast, does not include economics and avoids any mention of state policy vis-à-vis usury or Islamic banking.

MINORITY VIEWS

While Saudi interviewees tended toward juristic understandings of usury and Islamic banking and Pakistani interviewees toward welfarist understandings, sizable minorities in both countries lay outside this framework. They tended to lie at high and low levels of education in, or engagement with, religious and economic ideas.

In both countries, there were respondents who thought a great deal about the religion-economy nexus and argued passionately that a certain level of interest may be Islamically acceptable—that is, non-usurious. Referring to scripture, many considered the essence of riba to be exploitation or oppression but argued that interest-bearing loans from a modern bank are not inherently exploitative or oppressive. For centuries, some Muslim intellectuals, including some leading religious scholars in Egypt, have taken this position too (see chapters 3 and 4). Muhammad, the retiree from Dammam, put exploitation at the center of his definition. He had clearly thought a lot about the ethics of usury. In his view, if someone lends 10,000 riyals to someone else and gets back 11,000 riyals, so long as the transaction is consensual and clearly established in advance, there is no usury. But if someone lends 20,000 and demands 30,000 back, this is usury. "You have to take into consideration the [borrower's] circumstances, and whether he can afford to pay you the interest [you're charging]," he explained.[77] Abdulaziz, the university lecturer from Jeddah, associates usury with humiliation. He could imagine usury being a problem if taking a loan involved debasing oneself before the lender.[78] But in his view, a modern free market in financial services changes the ethical calculus. If a bank offers him a loan at 2 percent, and he can show it an offer of 1.5 percent from another bank, it is the banks that are groveling for his business, not the other way around. He came to this view after studying economics and working in investment; he describes himself as "a liberal with purely capitalist ideas."[79]

Like Abdulaziz, some interviewees who challenged the usury-interest equivalency were highly educated; quite a few had studied overseas. Imtiaz Ul Haq was a young economics professor at Pakistan's top-ranked university, the Lahore University of Management Sciences (LUMS). (He has since been a visiting fellow at Harvard and now works at the World Bank Group.) Imtiaz grew up in a conservative Punjabi family, launched a fintech start-up in Chile, then earned a doctorate in finance and accounting at the University of

Manchester. We attended a seminar on Islamic finance led by Saad Azmat, a finance professor at LUMS who invoked Keynes, Tobin, Samuelson, and Piketty and used theories of asymmetric information to illustrate the economic wisdom of act-based prohibitions such as a total ban on interest (as opposed to harm-based prohibitions that rely on a consequentialist logic of managing outcomes).[80] As we listened, Imtiaz wrestled with the question of riba, sounding respectfully skeptical. "My main question was why Islam prescribes a zero interest rate, and I still don't have an answer for that," he sighed. "I have trouble believing God wouldn't account for inflation and the time value of money."[81]

Imtiaz's thoughts on riba formed part of a larger set of reflections that arose in the process of becoming a cosmopolitan academic. While studying abroad, he wondered constantly about how to reconcile his faith with what he was learning and experiencing. In Santiago, a city of six million, there had been only one place to get halal food: a mosque forty-five minutes away that sold halal chicken every Friday. And at the University of Manchester, where his friends' social life centered on drinking, he faced a choice: guard his religious habits, principles, and identity or set them aside to assimilate into British academic custom. He spent over a year reading a translation and interpretation of the Quran—"really reading it, searching for answers." Sometimes he found them, sometimes he didn't. Eventually, through this process, he made the decision to retain his religious principles. However, avoiding interest was not one of them. In light of his advanced economics training, Imtiaz felt it simply did not make sense. Our seminar leader Saad Azmat, like other prominent Islamic economists, pursued research that sought to uncover the economic logic behind the interest ban and other Islamic rules governing markets. "I've seen the wisdom in the rules of [Islamic] law," Azmat told the audience. But Imtiaz wondered if there was a danger in this approach. "What if [economists] do this research, find nothing, and lose their faith?"

On the other end of the spectrum, there were respondents who simply did not think much about usury. Many had relatively low financial literacy. Typically, they had heard of riba or sood but struggled to define it. Sadia, a thirty-two-year-old middle-class housewife from Karachi wearing a dupatta and shalwar qameez, lived directly above a branch of an Islamic bank. I asked if she would open a conventional savings account that offered 10 percent interest. "Yes, because that's profit, not sood. We've investing money and getting a return." I then asked her to define sood. She said she couldn't, though she remembered hearing about it in school. "All I know about banks is that I go to the ATM and withdraw money," she laughed. She had no concern for muftis' opinions, about finance or anything else: "I don't listen to them. I just do whatever I want."[82] Others understood religious conventions but couldn't be bothered to worry about them. Kainat was a twenty-four-year-old Pakistani

MBA student wearing a colorful dupatta and no veil. Riba and sood, she said, were money on money—she had just learned this in a course on Islamic finance. She had also learned that Islamic banks avoided riba by using partnerships and felt that while they might not be perfect, they were certainly better than conventional banks, which were unquestionably sinful. So, I asked, would she put her money in an interest-bearing conventional savings account if offered a 10 percent return, or accept a 2 percent return from an Islamic bank instead? "The 10 percent," she insisted without hesitation. "We're already committing a lot of sins! Yeah, sood is a sin, but it's just another one."[83]

Public Attitudes toward Islamic Banks and Shariah Scholars

In addition to probing respondents' views on usury, my research assistants and I asked them about their attitudes toward Islamic banks and the shariah scholars who supervise them. I discuss below how socioeconomic status, country, and sect seemed to inflect responses.

EDUCATION AND SOCIOECONOMIC STATUS: CONFUSION AMONG LOWER SEGMENTS ABOUT ISLAMIC BANKING

In both countries, respondents of low and lower-middle educational and socioeconomic status tended to be confused about what Islamic banking was and how it differed from conventional banking. This group included manual workers, low-end service workers, and unemployed people who had not graduated university. Many felt that usury was bad, but often, they could not name an Islamic bank correctly. In Pakistan, people in this segment had typically heard of Islamic banking but were not sure what it was. Roshana, a conservatively dressed middle-aged worker at a Karachi big-box store, had no idea how Islamic banks avoid interest. When asked if Islamic banks differ from conventional banks, she said she wasn't sure and "would have to look into it."[84] The lack of knowledge may stem from lack of exposure: Islamic banks only had 8–11 percent market share in Pakistan at the time of the interviews. In Saudi Arabia, respondents of low and lower-middle education and SES often believed that all banks in the kingdom were Islamic because they assumed the Saudi state would not permit un-Islamic institutions. Bandar, a lower-middle-class soldier in his early thirties who grew up in Riyadh, was asked if all banks in Saudi Arabia should become Islamic. "They *are* Islamic. It's God's law," he explained over his McDonald's meal.[85]

Part of the confusion among respondents of lower socioeconomic status in both countries arose from their having shallower, simpler business relationships with banks in general than middle-class respondents do. Some admitted that they do not deal with banks at all, often because someone else in the family handles household finances. More common among low-SES respondents in both countries was to have only a free current account from which the respondent withdrew cash at an ATM. For this constituency, the issue of usury was largely moot because current accounts in Saudi Arabia and Pakistan, as in most countries, pay no interest anyway. Yet even rudimentary banking relationships can lead to confusion. Adnan, a lower-middle-class fast-food worker, aspiring auto mechanic, and boxer from one of Karachi's poorest neighborhoods, claimed the main difference between conventional and Islamic banks was that conventional banks' debit cards offer discounts at retailers like KFC, McDonald's, and Puma, whereas Islamic banks' debit cards do not. To get more retailer discounts, he had opened five current accounts—including two at Islamic banks that he apparently did not know were Islamic banks.[86]

PAKISTAN: FREQUENT SUSPICION OF SHARIAH SCHOLARS AND WELFARIST, SYSTEMIC EXPECTATIONS OF ISLAMIC BANKING

In Pakistan, the call for Islamic finance manifested in the 1970s as a popular social movement led by neorevivalists. They considered interest not only an individual sin but a socioeconomic cancer too. Imposing Islamic law on the financial system and stamping out interest, they said, would alleviate poverty and promote growth. They demanded that the state reengineer Pakistan's financial system, replacing interest-bearing loans with profit-and-loss-sharing (PLS) equity partnerships and investments.

However, Pakistan's neorevivalists have not had a monopoly on public debate about the place of religion in national financial affairs. Public attitudes toward the involvement of shariah and shariah experts in finance vary greatly, as our interviews showed. Some customers at Pakistan's largest Islamic bank, for example, expressed strong confidence that the elite shariah scholars Mufti Taqi Usmani (chair of the shariah board and Pakistan's most famous shariah scholar) and his son Mufti Muhammad Imran Usmani (head of the shariah division), by virtue of their expertise and probity, ensure the bank's shariah-compliance. "Mr. Taqi Usmani is a very renowned and respected person," said Agha, an Islamic-bank customer in Lahore, in a typical statement. Agha had left a job at a conventional bank because he became convinced working there was sinful. He now patronizes an Islamic bank overseen by Usmani.[87] "I salute Mufti Taqi Usmani and the other scholars of Dars-e Nizami,"[88] said Shaheen, an eighty-year-old former civil servant in Karachi with a long white beard who goes to the same Islamic bank as Agha. It is a stand-alone Islamic bank: one independent from any conventional bank. However, Shaheen expressed suspicion of Islamic banking divisions of conventional banks, which are common in Pakistan and many other countries: "It's like cooking halal food in the same pot someone used to cook haram food, or eating halal and haram food with the same spoon. It can't be proper."[89]

Not surprisingly, Pakistanis who do not patronize Islamic banks were more often ambivalent or downright cynical toward shariah scholars and their views on usury. Some consider the country's scholars sanctimonious charlatans or atavistic purveyors of mumbo-jumbo irrelevant to twenty-first-century life. Arshad, a thirty-seven-year-old office clerk in Lahore, considered Pakistani scholars particularly backward. (He patronized an Islamic bank but only because it was near his house.) Arshad pointed out that the polio vaccine had been around for over sixty years and had saved millions of children, and had been approved by most Islamic scholars around the world, but that some Pakistani religious scholars were still not convinced it was halal:

> They say, "No, it's haram, because it's made from monkeys." And then the children of that village or community refuse to get the vaccine. Total nonsense! So anyway, I don't have much faith in Islamic jurists.[90]

Nasreen, a thirty-year-old in orange dupatta shopping at a big-box store in a middle-class Karachi neighborhood, echoes a common view in Pakistan that muftis can be more hypocritical than virtuous. She sometimes watches the celebrity Deobandi scholar Tariq Jamil preach on television. But when asked if she would conform to Jamil's views on usury (sood), she replied: "Not necessarily. I'd make up my own mind. After all, the guy who took a selfie with Qandeel Baloch was a mufti."[91] Nasreen was referring to Abdul Qavi, a Pakistani mufti who took selfies with Instagram personality Qandeel Baloch—"Pakistan's Kim Kardashian," known for her risqué outfits[92]—and was later shown on video with Baloch sitting on his lap. Baloch claimed the mufti was smoking cigarettes and drinking soft drinks with her during the Ramadan fast. And recall Mahira, the fashion designer mentioned in this book's introduction who sneered that she would do the opposite of whatever scholars said to do.

When they questioned the religious legitimacy of Islamic banking, educated Pakistanis often posed a question that none of our Saudi respondents did: How can Islamic banking be truly different from conventional banking when both are regulated by government agencies? "Islamic banks and conventional banks are all the same," insisted Nasreen, the thirty-year-old who referenced the selfie-taking mufti. "The SBP [Pakistan's central bank] is running it all—same dad, different sons."[93] "There's no difference [between Islamic and conventional banks]," agreed Khurram, a twenty-seven-year-old engineer in the army, "because the regulatory bodies are the same: the SBP and the SECP [Pakistan's securities commission]."[94]

Educated Pakistanis' suspicion of shared regulatory authority reflects the view of the moral economists, who have deeper intellectual roots and stronger policy influence in South Asia than in the Gulf, that genuinely Islamic finance must be a segregated economic *system* in which capital circulates in fundamentally different ways. In contrast, in the contemporary scholastic view that is more influential among industry shariah scholars worldwide and among the educated public in the Gulf, the central features making Islamic finance Islamic are the contracts and organizational procedures that guarantee avoidance of riba and transaction-level shariah-compliance. In brief, a welfarist-systemic view prevails among the Pakistan public and a scholastic-transactional view among the Saudi public.

Some of the difference between Pakistan and Saudi Arabia in attitudes toward Islamic finance has to do with position in the world-system. Pakistan is a poor, largely agrarian debtor nation with a history of anticolonial and postcolonial resistance against Western financial hegemony—resistance often presented by activists and intellectuals in Islamic terms. When I met Shahid Iqbal, a finance reporter for the Pakistani newspaper *Dawn* who covers Islamic banking regularly, I expected him to have the cool, detached air I associate with business journalists. Instead, he gave a heartfelt critique of Islamic finance for failing to improve social welfare. Iqbal recalled interviewing peasants in rural Punjab and Khyber Pakhtunkhwa who, deeply indebted to their landlords, had to make gut-wrenching, inhumane decisions:

> A small peasant can borrow from someone and pay 100 percent, 150 percent, 200 percent interest. The same practice has been going on for centuries in rural Pakistan. And nobody asks whether it's Islamic or not.
>
> I met a security guard from Sultanpur village in Sargodha Division in Punjab. He said, "I sold a kidney for 1 lakh rupees."[95] He had to give the entire amount to the landlord[96] [from whom] he'd borrowed. He had to pay that money just to leave the village to go to Faisalabad and get a job as a security guard. In Khyber Pakhtunkhwa, it's worse: if you can't pay, they take your child.
>
> Generation after generation, [these small peasants] are simply slaves. They get no money for their work. Now how do you relate the Islamic-finance system and this system? For centuries, this [has been] happening. What are these Islamic scholars doing for them? Islamic finance is only a game for people who have money.[97]

If shariah scholars are so concerned about eliminating usury, Iqbal asked, "Why aren't they fighting to get these peasants out of slavery?" In suggesting that the formal rationality of market-driven halal certification substantively neglects Islamic values, critics like Iqbal seem to bear out Max Weber's prediction that the calculative rationality of modern markets will clash with the caritative ethos of salvation religions.[98]

Autonomy of Islamic-Finance Scholars: High in Saudi Arabia, Low in Pakistan

In Saudi Arabia, shariah scholars uninvolved with Islamic finance tend to treat their peers who are involved with it as colleagues who happen to have deep subject-matter expertise in finance—just as they themselves may possess subject-matter expertise in a different field, like bioethics or inheritance. Although divisive fault lines do exist in the field of Saudi shariah scholarship, they do not concern Islamic finance but rather scholars' attitudes toward the Saudi state. The majority of shariah scholars in Saudi Arabia declare the rule of the pro-Western House of Saud legitimate. While some occasionally nudge the monarchy on issues such as cultural mores and school curricula, they refrain from overt criticism, especially of the Al Saud's right to rule. However, a minority of Saudi scholars have vocally challenged the Al Saud's legitimacy. They include some Sunni scholars aligned with the Muslim Brotherhood or with other, more militant Sunni organizations, as well as Twelver Shia scholars who decry persecution of the Twelver Shia community concentrated in the kingdom's east. These critical scholars do not get involved with Islamic finance. Some have been imprisoned, while others have been temporarily or permanently excluded from the informal circle of pro-establishment scholars who serve on the major shariah boards at Islamic financial institutions in the kingdom.

In contrast, Islamic finance comes in for significant criticism in Pakistan from some prominent ulama. (This is also true in some other countries, such as Egypt.)[99] Mufti Muhammad Naeem (1958–2020) was the founder and chancellor of Jamia Binoria Aalamia, a large and well-known Deobandi seminary in Karachi. Naeem was on good terms with prominent scholars involved in Islamic finance—Taqi Usmani led his funeral prayers—and never criticized scholars involved in the industry in the fiery terms that the *Dawn* journalist Iqbal did. Yet as we sat cross-legged on his office floor, Naeem questioned just how Islamic the Islamic-finance industry was.

He asserted that Islamic banking reproduces conventional banking's main problems. "My own personal opinion—and I'm not criticizing anyone—is that Islamic banking doesn't really serve the poor," he averred. Echoing a critique of usury common in early modern England,[100] he asserted that Islamic banking instead encourages profligacy and immoderation, which he saw as ills of Western capitalist societies. "In America, even a low-wage worker can lease a Ferrari and then be stuck paying it off for twenty years," he explained. (Naeem has visited the United States.) Islamic banking, he claimed, was leading Muslims down the same path. He referenced a *du'ā'* (supplication): "O Allah, make me content upon whatever You have granted me."[101] Instead of "stretching according to his blanket"—that is, spending within his means—and living a stable life, the businessman who leverages himself tenfold, whether through a conventional bank or an Islamic one, multiplies his risk of bankruptcy. To make matters worse, Naeem insisted, Islamic banking, just like conventional banking, sucks capital out of the productive circuit. "An Islamic bank opened, so a guy closed his factory and put his money there. He put two hundred people out of work, [then] . . . sat at home all day earning a profit." And ultimately, Naeem noted, Islamic banks all rely on Pakistan's central bank, which is interest-based and tied to American banks and the World Bank. In a way, "it's all the same thing," he concluded. "Why take a Muslim who is burning in hellfire [due to usury] and drown him in water? Better to get him out of banking altogether."[102]

Mufti Naeem's criticism of Islamic finance illustrates that the domestic subfield of shariah scholars active in Islamic finance is not as autonomous from the domestic field of all shariah scholars as it is in Saudi Arabia. Mufti Naeem is not the only Pakistani shariah scholar to have criticized Islamic finance and interest simulation. A group of Pakistani shariah scholars outside the industry issued a fatwa questioning Taqi Usmani's extensive participation in the industry on the grounds that his justification of interest simulation was incorrect.[103] The fatwa even deployed Usmani's own erstwhile criticisms of the Islamic-finance industry to question his deep involvement in it. The fatwa's authors were based mostly at Jamia Uloom-ul-Islamia in Karachi's Banuri Town,[104] a Deobandi seminary almost as famous as Usmani's Darul Uloom Karachi, but included also Mawlana Saleemullah Khan, then one of Usmani's few living teachers, lending it the air of an instructor castigating his famous but wayward student.[105] The fatwa challenging Usmani created a brouhaha in the academic world of Pakistani shariah scholarship and highlighted its deep tensions over capitalist Islamic finance.

In contrast, shariah scholars in Saudi Arabia who are involved in Islamic finance rarely get criticized publicly by other scholars. They are treated by fellow "establishment" scholars (i.e., those not critical of the House of Saud) as subject-matter experts in finance. Meanwhile, the central bank is happy to focus on prudential regulation and leave shariah questions to scholars. Unlike regulators in countries such as Malaysia, the United Arab Emirates, and Pakistan, the Saudi central bank and securities regulator have not appointed their own shariah boards.

Another important difference concerns religious diversity in the public sphere. In Saudi Arabia, religious diversity certainly exists—we interviewed Sunnis, Twelver Shia, and Ismaili Shia in the kingdom—but among ulama with much influence on state policy, Salafism and Ḥanbalī fiqh preponderate almost completely. They also pervade the copious religious programming on

domestic airwaves. Meanwhile, in Pakistan, different religious traditions—
Barelvi, Deobandi, Ahl-e Hadith, Twelver Shia, Ismaili Shia, Ahmadi, Hindu,
Christian—have been widely visible since the country's birth in 1947. The
government reflects this diversity in its official governance of Islamic finance:
as of 2024, the shariah board of Pakistan's central bank is chaired by a Deobandi shariah scholar, with its other two shariah scholars being Barelvi and
Twelver Shia.

There is also a more vibrant sphere for public debate in Pakistan, including
over large-scale questions about the organization of economy and society. Islamists who have advocated a thoroughgoing Islamization of state and society
have long had a voice—ever since the late 1970s—in newspapers, on the airwaves, and now in social media. Debates are strident and highly political, often
being tied to political party and parliamentary factions. In Saudi Arabia, the
permissible sphere of public debate about the structure of the economy and
the financial system is more limited, and there is no aboveground party politics
to speak of. There certainly are debates about finance as it relates to Islam, but
they mostly concern technical issues of shariah-compliance, as discussed
above. Not debated is the question of whether the entire economic system
needs to be overhauled.

Political Economy

Saudi Arabia: Shariah Scholars Are Insulated
from Contentious Politics

Although Western news media covering Islam in the Middle East tend to highlight militant discourses, "establishment Islam"[106] has in fact dominated national religious fields in Saudi Arabia and the other Gulf Arab states since the
1970s. This term refers to a matrix of state-sponsored Islamic institutions and
Islamic scholars aligned with, and broadly supervised by, national states. Establishment Islam emerged in the nineteenth and twentieth centuries as modernizing states sought to absorb some of the scholarly elite's legitimacy while
controlling and bureaucratizing Islamic institutions.[107]

Since the 1970s, the Saudi monarchy has maintained a grand bargain with
the establishment ulama. The establishment ulama oversee endowments and
charities, mosque administration, shariah courts, religious curricula, and institutions for fatwa issuance.[108] Meanwhile, they support—or at least avoid
challenging—the pro-Western foreign policies and market-oriented, elite-
friendly rentier economic policies of the authoritarian dynasts.[109]

The establishment ulama are also embedded deeply in the society of
Saudi Arabia and its Gulf neighbors. In the 1970s—as today, if to a lesser

extent—ordinary citizens could approach famous religious scholars for advice on everyday matters, sometimes visiting their homes and personal offices.[110] In the 1970s and 1980s, the boom in religious programming on state-controlled radio and television channels also expanded the establishment ulama's mass audience.[111] Religious education also grew in the 1980s—and in some Gulf countries well into the 1990s—increasing the ulama's influence. This was most dramatic in Saudi Arabia, where more than half of doctorates granted in the late 1990s were in religious sciences.[112]

Saudi Arabia: Interest as a Problem of Individual Sin, Not Social Structure

Saudi Arabia's state-aligned ulama have never seriously questioned the centrality of the hydrocarbon economy. After all, they have had little incentive to challenge the rentier model. Their interests are not served by impugning a system that deployed hydrocarbon revenues to enhance their influence. Furthermore, economic conditions for nearly all citizens were objectively improving in the 1970s and 1980s. The oil windfall brought free health care, free education, subsidized housing and food, and new roads to Saudi Arabia and its Gulf neighbors. This contrasted with the days of subsistence agriculture, camel herding, date-palm harvesting, pearling, and British suzerainty before World War II.[113]

Unlike in Pakistan, the most prominent Saudi ulama in the 1970s and 1980s did not assert strenuously that the Quranic usury ban provided a blueprint for an anti-capitalist, emancipatory, welfare-oriented Islamic financial *system*. They specialized in classical Islamic sciences; few had studied modern economics. In broad strokes, they insisted that Islam enshrines free enterprise, private property, and the wage-labor relation while proscribing immorality, corruption, and exploitation. Their fatwas reflect this view. For example, Ibn Bāz, the most influential figure in Saudi establishment Islam in the late twentieth century, wrote:

> Islam protects private property and its acquisition in lawful ways that avoid injustice, deceit, usury, oppression, and infringement upon others. It also respects personal and collective ownership.[114] . . . Islam permits and encourages the acquisition of money, but only in judicious ways[115] that do not stand in the way of being obedient to God and his Messenger or of performing one's duties to God.[116]

The following excerpt from a 1978 fatwa endorsed by powerful establishment ulama from the Jeddah-based Muslim World League is also typical, expressing the belief that shariah enshrines free enterprise and limits state interference in the economy:

The concept of Islamic economy . . . allows individuals to carry out [their] various economic projects. The state's role should be only as a complementary element to what individuals could be able to do and as a guide and monitor to ensure the success of these projects.[117]

Still, the establishment ulama regularly stressed that usury is a grave sin *at the individual level*. Saudi Arabia's establishment ulama categorize usury with adultery, alcohol consumption, filial impiety, banditry, and sodomy.[118] They do not extrapolate nearly as often as Pakistani ulama to a larger economic system of which the usury ban might be a pillar.

Saudi Arabia is probably the most fiqh-minded society in the world. Not only are religious scholars highly visible household names, but the idea of religious scholarship as a legitimating framework for morality is ubiquitous in Saudi Arabia. Not only do Saudi schoolchildren receive detailed education in fiqh, but aspiring scholars from around the world also come to study fiqh and shariah in Saudi universities. Public policy, personal and family morality, and commercial and financial affairs are regularly discussed in the language of Islamic jurisprudence, from both "liberal" and "conservative" directions, making for a public sphere of religio-ethical discourse in which debate, while circumscribed by tacit prohibitions against criticizing the state and the royal family, can be quite lively. All this means Saudis are less likely than Pakistanis to disparage religious scholars *as an entire group* as corrupt, clueless, or irrelevant in a modern age, even if they may disagree with individual scholars or find some to be behind the times (as when senior ulama banned Pokémon GO in 2016, causing many Saudi youth to roll their eyes). This is not to say that all Saudis live their lives with guidance from religious scholars, or there are not alternative modes of piety, such as Islamic mysticism (Sufism), that sit alongside fiqh-minded ones in Saudi Arabia. But it does suggest that the portion of Saudis who take fiqh and its scholars seriously is high relative to most other Muslim-majority countries.

Pakistan: Shariah Scholars Embroiled in Contentious Politics

Since the mid-twentieth century, the problem of interest has been more politically charged in Pakistan than anywhere else—for at least two reasons. First, the state of Pakistan was founded in the name of Islam, yet Pakistanis have never agreed on the appropriate relationship between Islam and their state.[119] Disputes over the place of Islam and shariah in the legal system and in the regulation of public morality have persisted more or less continuously since independence in 1947, pitting generals, modernizing bureaucrats, and cosmopolitan elites against Islamic groups.[120] Interest has been embroiled in these disputes. Second, intellectual debate about the acceptability of interest in Islam has deep roots. As discussed in chapter 2, South Asia—first British India, then Pakistan—was one of the main intellectual centers for such debate since the early twentieth century, with socially conservative Islamic factions overwhelmingly considering interest un-Islamic.

Throughout Pakistan's independent history, two groups have consistently demanded that the state ban interest. The first is the ulama: most prominently Deobandi scholars but also Barelvis and the less numerous Ahl-e-Hadith. In Pakistan as elsewhere, the ulama have historically reproduced their authority through seminaries and Islamic schools that teach traditional Islamic sciences such as Quran studies, hadith, jurisprudence, theology, and Arabic language. But in Pakistan, unlike in Saudi Arabia and many other Muslim-majority countries, the ulama have not usually enjoyed "establishment" status.[121] Instead, some have formed political parties independent of the state, such as the Deobandi Jamī'at Ulema-e-Islam (JUI) and the Barelvi Jamī'at Ulema-e-Pakistan (JUP). The second group that has demanded an interest ban is the neorevivalist Islamists, who had contentious relations with the Pakistani state until 1977. (Many of Pakistan's neorevivalists are also Islamists, meaning they seek an Islamic *state* that will build a truly Islamic society.) Pakistan's Jamaat-e-Islami (JI), founded in 1941, has been Pakistan's dominant neorevivalist Islamist organization, and one of the world's two most influential since the mid-twentieth century, alongside the Muslim Brotherhood. Its founder and longtime leader, Sayyid Abu al-A'la Mawdudi (1903–79), theorized "Islamic democracy" and "the economic system of Islam."[122]

Pakistan: Islamic Banks Face Unpredictable, PLS-Supporting State Intervention

Between 1977 and 1988, the popular movement for Islamic finance fortuitously gained state support and policymaking influence. In 1977, General Muhammad Zia-ul-Haq toppled Prime Minister Zulfikar Ali Bhutto in a coup. Zia owed his success partly to the neorevivalists: from 1975 to 1977, Mawdudi had spearheaded a right-wing populist Islamic opposition coalition that criticized Bhutto's left-wing populism. The coalition combined religious conservatives, industrialists, shopkeepers, landed gentry, and the urban middle classes.[123] It united behind a platform called Nizam-i-Mustafa (Order of the Prophet), which included demands for the elimination of interest. After the army ousted Bhutto, General Zia drew the JI toward him. "For the first time in its history, the [JI] had become part of the ruling establishment."[124] From 1979, Zia drew some of the ulama into his fold as well,[125] though their main parties, the JUI and JUP, had fallen out with him by the early 1980s.

Zia and the JI formulated a top-down plan to Islamize Pakistan's economy and society. Following Mawdudi's vision, Zia proposed to abolish interest, establish Islamic banks, institute PLS schemes, impose the Islamic land tax, mandate zakat for Sunni Muslims, and create institutions to study Islamic economics.[126] Pakistan was to become the first modern interest-free country. On the legal front, Zia established shariah courts; criminalized adultery, fornication, and blasphemy (though these were hardly ever prosecuted); and instituted Islamic punishments (also rarely imposed). In the schools, Zia's government revised curricula to incorporate Islamic studies and ordered female students to cover their heads.

Pakistan's neorevivalists also disseminated Islamic economics. Some of the world's leading Islamic economists in the 1970s and 1980s were connected to the JI: Khurshid Ahmad, for example, served as the organization's deputy leader. Islamic economists spread through Pakistani academia and advised the state on eliminating interest.[127] They gained greater influence on state policy in Pakistan in the 1980s than they have had anywhere in the world before or since and propagated the idea that a PLS-driven economy is feasible.

Zia's rule gave supporters of financial Islamization powerful organizational resources through which to drive forward their vision. Through the late 1970s and early 1980s, Zia had the Council of Islamic Ideology (CII) submit reports on elimination of interest and the advancement of PLS.[128] JI members received cabinet posts and senior ministry positions.[129] Zia also created powerful new Islamic judicial institutions, such as the Federal Shariat Court and the Shariat Appellate Bench of the Supreme Court. Renowned ulama and specialists in Islamic law, most of whom opposed interest, were appointed to the new courts.

By the late 1970s and early 1980s, conditions for implementing an Islamic financial system in Pakistan looked more favorable than ever. In its 1980 report, the CII declared that interest could and should be eliminated by 1984.[130] Zia went to work, converting all interest-bearing savings accounts in state-owned banks into PLS accounts and mandating Islamic windows at their branches, and directing government agencies to finance through PLS.[131] The state also issued PLS-based corporate-finance certificates[132] and let PLS-based investment funds trade on the Karachi bourse.[133]

In practice, however, state-led financial Islamization disappointed the Islamists for several reasons. First, it was actually much less PLS-based than promised. Proper infrastructure for PLS-based finance did not yet exist. Fearing that PLS could generate moral hazard and perturb the financial system too quickly, the state gave banks the option of offering interest-simulating instruments as a temporary stopgap.[134] Just as in the Gulf, Islamic-banking operations therefore tilted heavily toward interest simulation: in 1984, only

3.1 percent of financing by Pakistani banks was PLS-based,[135] while banks invested 86.7 percent of their portfolios in markup-style interest simulation.[136] Second, Pakistan's banks in the 1980s were widely suspected of merely engaging in Islamic financing "on paper," and credibility suffered.[137]

Third, the Pakistani state was itself deeply embedded in interest-based debt markets at the national and international level. Even banks accepting deposits on a PLS basis had to invest them in interest-based government securities. The government also allowed interest on foreign-currency deposits[138] and continued to pay interest on its sovereign debt. These conditions frustrated financial Islamization domestically.

Ultimately, an alliance between religious authorities, capital, and the state failed to materialize in Pakistan around the issue of financial Islamization because each group held different ideas of financial piety and sent unclear signals to the public. The neorevivalists still considered interest simulation "a disguised form of interest payment," and many of the ulama agreed.[139] The CII, which advised the state, claimed to support PLS but offered ways to sidestep it. Zia himself issued murky statements, saying markup-based interest simulation is not immoral but "markup on the markup" is.[140] Customers were confused and disillusioned: the state had promised that their financial returns would increase with PLS, but they had not.[141] Many thought Islamic banking meant zero-percent financing and were disappointed to learn otherwise.[142] Banks generally opposed Islamic finance, for it added costs, time, and hassle—without competitive advantage, since all banks were required to offer it. As one Pakistani economist lamented in 1986, Islamic finance in Pakistan was "a muddle."[143]

From the late 1980s through the 1990s, financial Islamization foundered in an increasingly inhospitable domestic and international context. In 1988, Zia died in a mysterious plane crash, so the project lost its powerful patron. From 1988 to 1999, the prime ministership flipped back and forth between Benazir Bhutto and her rival Nawaz Sharif, with caretaker governments in between. Bhutto opposed Zia's Islamization program but did not eliminate it.[144] Sharif, a social conservative, had supported Islamization. However, in the neoliberal 1990s, as IMF and foreign creditors pressured Pakistan to privatize and liberalize its financial sector,[145] Sharif could hardly advocate for a PLS-based financial system. Ultimately, the Pakistani movement for Islamic finance could not buck the neoliberal financial order and its dominant institutions. It could not impose its own rules of the game, even at home.

Even though the Islamist anti-usury coalition has failed to create a viable financial model based on welfarist values, it has proved capable of interfering with the rollout of the Gulf model. In 1991, Pakistan's Federal Shariat Court ruled not only that shariah prohibited all interest but also that "if the banking system is to be Islamised, 'mark-up' [i.e., interest simulation] is no solution."[146]

The Pakistani state's fitful support of PLS-based models and opposition to interest-simulating Islamic finance have created an environment of uncertainty, where even developments conducive to the Gulf model risk reversal.

Saudi Arabia: From moneychangers to Islamic banks

Interelite struggles among branches of the House of Saud may help explain why Prince Mohammed bin Faisal and Sheikh Saleh Kamel were not granted licenses to open Islamic banks in Saudi Arabia. Modern Saudi Arabia was founded by King Abdulaziz Al Saud (r. 1932–53), and since his death, the sons of Abdulaziz have ruled the country and developed factions of their own. Jean-François Seznec, a political scientist who worked as a banker in the Gulf in the 1970s and 1980s, argues that the sons of King Faisal bin Abdulaziz (r. 1964–75) were widely respected inside and outside the royal family but that after King Faisal's death they held enough powerful positions—such as leadership of the secret service and the Ministry of Foreign Affairs—that partisans of other royal factions would not have wanted to grant significant power in the Saudi financial sector to one of their number, such as Prince Mohammed bin Faisal.[147] "[King] Fahd's group worried that the money [from Islamic banking] could be used for political purposes, especially Islamist [purposes]," adds Seznec, who knew Prince Mohammed personally.[148] The factionalism of the Al Saud affected banking regulation because the Saudi central bank,[149] after having been relatively independent from political interference under chairman Anwar Ali (who died in 1974) and King Faisal (who died in 1975), reverted toward dependence under Fahd (first as crown prince and then as king).[150] As for Saleh Kamel, Seznec notes that he was the main business agent for Prince Sultan bin Abdulaziz and that the bureaucrats at the central bank would have balked at letting Kamel and the Sultan clan into the Saudi banking sector.[151] (People with connections to the Saleh Kamel business empire dispute this, arguing that Kamel stayed out of Saudi Arabia because he considered it his mission to spread the blessings of Islamic banking to other, less wealthy nations.)

Yet despite the Saudi central bank's apparent antipathy toward Islamic banking, one Islamic bank did manage to get a banking license in 1987: Al Rajhi Bank, which has grown into the world's largest Islamic bank. The Al Rajhis were no strangers to finance, having been among Saudi Arabia's business elite for decades. Before the oil boom and their rise at the helm of diversified family conglomerates, the Al Rajhi brothers were best known as moneychangers. Other renowned Saudi businesspersons who would go on to found Islamic banks, such as the Al Rajhis' friend and competitor Mohammed Ibrahim Alsubeaei, began as moneychangers too.

Moneychangers had been crucial financial intermediaries in the Arabian Peninsula for over a thousand years, serving pilgrims to Mecca and Medina.[152] The early Saudi state's endemic monetary instability kept them in business in the mid-twentieth century. From 1928 to the early 1950s, the House of Saud pegged the silver Saudi riyal to gold. This misguided bimetallism caused bullion to flow in and out of the country, benefiting the moneychangers. There was no state monetary authority for some years, so Indian rupees, British sterling, and even Ottoman riyals and Maria Theresa thalers circulated alongside the Saudi riyal. Moneychangers also provided liquidity to the Saudi government, which until the 1950s was frequently bankrupt, its fiscal capacity depleted by military spending, uneven pilgrimage revenues, patronage payments to princes and tribal leaders, and prestige purchases.[153]

As the oil economy grew, moneychangers started to function more like modern banks—but without dealing in interest, and without being regulated much. In the 1940s, the prominent moneychanger Mohammed Alsubeaei bought pilgrims' currencies in exchange for gold that they could use while in Saudi Arabia. He buried the foreign currencies in the sand by an airstrip, guarded it overnight, and flew it out the next morning.[154] Then, as foreign workers streamed into the kingdom from the 1960s onward, moneychangers came to dominate the lucrative remittance business. Their family-run shops in the souq were open far later than the banks, and their informal nature, limited documentation, and low fees drew long lines of foreign laborers.[155] Moneychangers also provided financial services for Saudi Arabia's fast-growing businesses. Nasser Alsubeaei began work for his father, Mohammed, in the mid-1960s as a child of seven or eight years old, just as pilgrims were becoming less important as customers than Saudi businesses suddenly flush with funds. "The clients in the 1970s, they would bring cash in big bags, and I had to count it," he recalled. By then, the Alsubeaei business was trading currency by telex, issuing checks, transferring funds, and offering current accounts. Yet their father avoided dealing with banks and resisted intermingling with the interest-based financial system. "Every time we talked with our father, from an early age, he would warn us about riba," remembered Abdulaziz Alsubeaei, Nasser's brother.[156]

Despite being virtually unregulated by the state, the moneychangers held accounts at large Western banks such as the Bank of New York, through which they deployed funds quickly and cheaply to correspondent banks in labor-sending countries such as India, Pakistan, Yemen, and Egypt.[157] As late as 1981, when in most of the world banks controlled the flow of money within and across borders, moneychangers still handled one-quarter of the turnover of all money circulating in Saudi Arabia and one-third of all remittances.[158]

The Al Rajhis began seeking a banking license around 1983 and finally received one from the central bank in 1988. Several factors may explain why the central bank granted the license to Al Rajhi, the first being regional connections to political and religious elites. The Al Rajhis hail from Najd, the region of central Arabia that includes Riyadh and that is home to the royal family.[159] By contrast, most other families who were major Saudi moneychangers or elite bankers were based in Jeddah (long the country's commercial hub) and were originally from Ḥaḍramawt, a region of Yemen famed for producing merchants who traveled the world. Specifically, the Al Rajhis come from al-Qassim, which is just one of Saudi Arabia's thirteen administrative regions but by one measure produces around 80 percent of the country's elite Sunni religious scholars. The Al Rajhi family has long been intertwined with Saudi Arabia's preeminent family of religious scholars, the Āl al-Shaykh, whom Nabil Mouline has called "the Levites of Hanbali-Wahhabism."[160]

Other factors also made the Al Rajhis good candidates for the central bank's blessing. The Al Rajhis enjoyed elite business connections and were already regarded as a large and reliable force in the national economy, especially in Riyadh. By the early 1980s, Saleh Al Rajhi was allegedly Riyadh's largest landowner.[161] At the same time, he had a sterling reputation for probity among the city's masses, serving informally as their universal banker, as Jean-François Seznec recalls:

> Saleh Al Rajhi was viewed as being one of [the people]. If you had a little money and didn't want to keep it in your house, you brought it to Saleh. People would say, "I have my money with Saleh; he keeps it for me." And then, say you want to buy a car. You go to the car dealer and say, "Here's a letter; Saleh Al Rajhi will pay you 10,000 Saudi riyals." Well, that's a check. This was even earlier than the 1970s. He was the trusted financial dealer for people in Riyadh.
>
> I knew a Palestinian guy who . . . went to Saleh and said, "I want to start a company selling water heaters." Saleh Al Rajhi said, "Nice idea," and began supplying the guy with water heaters. [Saleh] became his largest shareholder, too. [Saleh] even gave him short-term loans to pay his workers.[162]

The Al Rajhis had not only capital but a banking infrastructure. Their moneychanging operation was effectively already one of the country's largest banks, with a larger branch network than any commercial bank. Unlike the major commercial banks, which tended to finance large corporations, the state, and elite families' businesses, the Al Rajhi operation enjoyed a particularly strong base among the middle classes, the petty bourgeoisie, and religious conservatives who sought to avoid interest.

By the 1980s, the decision to allow Saudi Arabia's largest moneychanger to convert into a bank also served the central bank's goal of modernizing and rationalizing the kingdom's financial system. As much as the central bank was suspicious of Islamic banking, it was perhaps even more frustrated with the moneychangers, who operated as a parallel unregulated banking system.

In Saudi Arabia, Islamic finance blossomed even though the state avoided acknowledging its Islamic character until the early 2000s. It did not want Saudis to ask why their government would allow any un-Islamic finance. Although not allowed to call itself an Islamic bank, Al Rajhi Bank flourished thanks to its vast branch network, reputation for shariah-compliance, and support from prominent ulama. Al Rajhi's success prompted two other Islamic banks to launch—Bank Albilad in 2004 and Alinma Bank in 2006—and led Bank AlJazira to convert into an Islamic bank in 2007. Islamic branches and windows of conventional banks (see chapter 3) have flourished too. Today, many educated Saudis know which prominent shariah scholars are involved in Islamic finance, and business media cover their debates about the shariah-compliance of IPOs and new financial products. While these debates have negligible structural consequences for the Saudi economy, their visibility entrenches the scholars' fiqh-minded financial ethics.

Pakistan: The 2002 "Reset" and Adoption of the Gulf Model

It took a military ruler to quash the crisis over interest. In a 1999 coup, General Pervez Musharraf ousted Nawaz Sharif. In 2001, Musharraf's government challenged the Shariat Appellate Bench's ruling.[163] The court confirmed its initial ruling, but in 2002, Musharraf sacked Justice Taqi Usmani—a fervent opponent of interest—from the court and packed it with judges of his choosing. He also gave the remaining justices a 30 percent raise.[164] The court proceeded to vitiate its own 1999 ruling, and Pakistan's economic elites breathed a sigh of relief.

In the end, the Pakistani movement for revolutionary financial Islamization failed both because it clashed with powerful interests and norms in the international financial system and because it allied with a state whose support proved fickle. In Malaysia, the UMNO–Barisan Nasional machine remained in power from independence until 2018. Even in Saudi Arabia, the same royal family has ruled since the country's birth. Pakistan, however, has had eighteen prime ministers since independence and frequent shifts from military to civilian rule. Leaders' positions on Islam's role in the economy have fluctuated. Linked to such an unstable state, the movement for financial Islamization foundered.

Musharraf's government did not kill off Islamic finance; instead, in 2002, it pressed "reset."[165] The state liberalized Islamic finance and aligned it with the interests of domestic and international capital. By then, the Gulf model of Islamic finance had become the global model, and the Pakistani state adopted it. Instead of forcibly converting all banks into Islamic banks, the government would now license and regulate Islamic banks alongside conventional banks. Customers would choose freely between the two. Conventional banks would also be allowed to open Islamic branches and subsidiaries. Shariah boards would certify Islamic products. And while the central bank pledged to support a gradual long-term shift toward PLS, interest-simulation practices such as murabaha financing would remain the norm in Islamic banking practice.[166]

The neoliberal model of Islamic finance has not only migrated to Pakistan but brought foreign capital with it. All of Pakistan's full-fledged Islamic banks except one were founded primarily by Gulf investors. This is in line with historically strong ties of investment, trade, and labor migration between Pakistan and the Gulf states, especially since the oil boom.[167] Yet Gulf investment in Islamic finance is also a phenomenon of the neoliberal era. Pakistan's major banks were nationalized between 1974 and 1994. With the convergence of Pakistani banking liberalization and high oil prices in the 2000s, Islamic banking has opened a new channel through which Gulf liquidity has found an outlet in Pakistan.

Ironically, Pakistan's Islamic banks have stabilized the post-2002 field of neoliberal Islamic finance by integrating famous ulama into their shariah governance system. Of the five justices on the Shariat Appellate Bench who ruled in *Khaki v. Hashim* (2000)[168] that the state must eliminate interest immediately and institute PLS, three went on to chair major shariah boards. Justice M. Taqi Usmani in particular has become the face of Islamic finance in Pakistan and one of its most sought-after shariah-board members worldwide. His "brand" as a religious scholar has earned many millions of dollars for Pakistan's largest Islamic bank, whose shariah board he chairs.[169]

Conclusion: How National Differences, Mediated by the Scholars, Shape the Fortunes of Capitalist Islamic Finance

This chapter has shown how domestic and international political, economic, and social factors permit or prevent shariah scholars from overseeing and certifying a stable market for Islamic financial services. The crucial "independent variables" include the breadth and depth of fiqh-mindedness among the populace (shaped in part by school curricula), the presence or absence of a political culture amenable to scholastic, capital-friendly interpretations of usury, and whether state and corporate institutions reinforce those capital-friendly interpretations or challenge them.

In Saudi Arabia, the factors in question are favorable. Usury is widely understood by the populace and by leading shariah scholars first and foremost as a problem of individual piety. The state too treats it as such, taking a laissez-faire approach that allows the banker-scholar alliance to proceed smoothly with interest simulation. "Saudi is an example of a market where Islamic finance is flourishing purely because of demand," not state support, according to veteran Islamic-finance journalist Mushtak Parker.[170]

Ahmed Abdulkarim Alkholifey, then governor of the Saudi Central Bank, acknowledged this when I interviewed him in 2019. Over the past twenty years, "Islamic finance [in Saudi Arabia] has been driven by the market, not the regulator," Alkholifey remarked. The central bank "did not issue, for example, instructions about how governance should work in Islamic finance."[171] Indeed, Alkholifey made clear that he would let shariah scholars decide about shariah issues while the central bank focused on prudential regulation, liquidity provision, and macroeconomic stability. If interest simulation furthered those goals, shariah scholars accepted it, and if it operated in ways similar to conventional interest-based banking, then Alkholifey had no designs to ban it.[172] This is not to say the Saudi Central Bank was completely hands-off: it was injecting Islamic liquidity instruments into the market, and Alkholifey was busy beefing up its expertise in Islamic finance. Rather, Alkholifey's comment underscores how the Saudi state's intervention in Islamic finance has been far lighter than that of the Pakistani state—or of the Malaysian state, which is renowned for its comprehensive, interventionist shepherding of Islamic finance.[173] That Islamic banking's share of total banking assets in Saudi Arabia, at 75 percent in 2023, far exceeded that in Malaysia (31 percent) and Pakistan (20 percent) speaks to the market-boosting power of widespread fiqh-mindedness and a stable scholar-banker-state consensus about interest simulation.

By contrast, in Pakistan, fiqh-mindedness is less widespread among the masses: it is certainly present but among a minority who have received a specialized Islamic education. Usury is widely perceived to underpin inequality and subjugation, from the village to the capitalist world-system. The authority of shariah scholars as a group is regularly challenged or even disparaged, and the political culture situates the moral economists' understandings of usury within contentious Islamist politics. Judicial elites and prominent politicians also sometimes intervene to prod capital away from interest simulation. For all these reasons, the dominance of capital-aligned shariah scholars who accept interest simulation as uncontroversial is not assured, and capitalist Islamic finance faces headwinds.

Conclusion

Recapitulation

This book has confronted two paradoxes. First, many Muslims who abhor interest patronize Islamic finance—even though it openly simulates interest. Second, there exists today a multi-trillion-dollar Islamic-finance industry, yet no other religious-finance industry of comparable size and scope.

In response, I have argued that shariah scholars resolve for industry participants the tensions inherent in interest simulation. Furthermore, they deploy their religious imprimatur, legal and financial knowledge, and business habitus to legitimate and justify a form of Islamic finance compatible with contemporary capitalism. Shariah scholars are therefore decisively important to the commercial success of Islamic finance. They insist that back-office processes conform to their legal interpretations, but allow business strategy, branch operations, and labor relations to function much as they do in conventional finance. As a result, conventional banks and their employees—from tellers to CEOs—can transition easily into Islamic finance, accelerating its growth. Yet industry shariah scholars and their deputies also restrict profit-seeking capitalists from pushing the envelope of interest simulation too far and "secularizing Islamic finance away."

In short, the scholars play a "Goldilocks" role: they keep religious finance from drifting too far toward permissiveness on one hand and restrictiveness on the other. They staunchly defend the usury ban and other ethical principles that have disappeared almost entirely from conventional finance, drawing red-line borders around Islamic financial products and imposing costs on capitalists who transgress those borders. Yet the shariah scholars also accommodate capitalists' interests enough to make Islamic finance profitable and efficient. Today's shariah scholars thus bring sacred law and business interests into alignment. So did the premodern scholastic religious jurists in Islam, Christianity, and Judaism.

Where today's shariah scholars differ from their premodern predecessors is that they must make scholastic conceptions of money and usury workable and meaningful in twenty-first-century financial markets. This is a big task. Today's financial markets are hyper-competitive and fast-moving, dominated by powerful multinational firms and mediated by advanced technologies that ferry commodities and securities across the globe in fractions of a second. They are bureaucratically complex, given to coding capital in reams of documentation written by armies of lawyers in (secular) legal language and regulated by powerful state bureaucracies chasing financial stability. They are also diverse, encompassing a wide range of products and investments separated into a "low" realm of finance serving minnows (ordinary households and small businesses) and a "high" realm for big-fish institutions and complex billion-dollar transactions. One of the lessons of this book is that today's shariah scholars not only manage to govern Islamic finance *despite* these modern constraints but in fact marshal these characteristics of modern markets to expand their terrain of regulation and to monitor and apply their interpretations of Islamic law in ever more precise ways. Thanks to the shariah scholars, intensified capitalism means more shariah, not less. More capital, more shariah.

This book has demonstrated various ways shariah scholars align religion and finance in the era of financialization, allowing religious finance to be profitable yet religiously distinctive. The two most important are in serving as *certification* authorities and in permitting various modes of *interest simulation*. These two features, plus a *liberal model of state involvement* in which customers and investors may choose freely between conventional and Islamic finance, constitute what I call the "Gulf model" of Islamic finance because of its origins in the unique circumstances of the Arab Gulf states during the oil boom of the 1970s.

By sitting on shariah boards whose fatwas certify Islamic products and transactions as shariah-compliant, shariah scholars legitimize Islamic financial products to customers and investors, to finance professionals, and to state regulators. The wealthy pioneers of Islamic finance established the first shariah boards in 1976, just one year after the first for-profit Islamic bank appeared. The establishment and spread of the shariah board was tremendously important, for it entrenched shariah scholars as the powerful professional experts who determine the meaning of "Islamic" in the term "Islamic finance." In low finance, scholarly certification lets customers sleep at night. In high finance, certification lubricates big-ticket transactions in which time and coordination across shariah boards and across borders are of the essence. The fact that the certification agents are scholars of religious *law* whose professional training focuses on the deep analysis of Islamic nominate contracts allows secular lawyers to learn Islamic-finance law[1] and work extensively alongside the scholars, especially in the realm of high finance, where secular lawyers do the essential work of making large transactions such as securities flotations and syndicated financings come alive as executable, risk-minimized thickets of contracts.

The fact that industry scholars authorize various flexible modes of interest simulation allows firms to create and sell financial products and services that are distinctively Islamic in their contractual structure and back-office processes, yet that function almost identically to conventional products and services in their economic characteristics. Common modes of interest simulation include markup financing (based on the murabaha contract), lease-based financing (based on ijara), tawarruq (based on the tawarruq contract, authorized by some industry scholars), and asset-based sukuk (based on a range of contracts). Interest simulation makes it easier for firms to design, market, and sell financial instruments, for customers to shop for them, for investors to evaluate their risk-return profiles, for rating agencies to rate them, and for government regulators to assess their contributions to prudential reserves and systemic risk.

In the late 1970s and early 1980s, the shariah scholars who authorized certain legal interpretations that facilitated interest simulation were adopted by the fledgling first-wave Islamic banks as certification agents. Together, these bankers and scholars developed a hybrid institutional logic in which interest simulation was morally acceptable and a way to help the industry survive. Those scholars whose rulings confounded interest simulation were sorted out. The latter group threatened the very possibility of establishing commercially viable Islamic finance in markets where it would compete against conventional finance and in regulatory environments and tax regimes built with conventional finance in mind.

Aside from authorizing interest simulation, shariah scholars who participate in the industry have adopted various other legal interpretations and normative orientations that align with IFIs' interests. For example, when assessing shariah-compliance, industry scholars bracket out most social, environmental, and economic assessments of financial transactions' possible consequences (unless those consequences appear imminent and nearly inevitable). They focus instead on contractual mechanics. Industry scholars also justify adopting minority viewpoints from classical Islamic law, drawing on and suturing together rulings from across various juristic schools, and even importing concepts from secular legal traditions. Often, they justify using these legal techniques to accommodate capitalist interests by invoking the Islamic legal doctrine of necessity. Unless they authorize such techniques, they say, Islamic finance will fail to survive in competitive marketplaces whose regulatory and tax architectures were built with conventional finance in mind. They also argue that few outcomes would be worse than the collapse of Islamic finance, for even if today's IFIs are not perfect from a shariah perspective, their shortcomings pale in comparison to the grievous sin that Muslims commit when dealing in interest with conventional financial institutions. Some also argue that in deploying interpretive techniques that step outside the tendencies of most classical Islamic legal reasoning, they are renovating Islamic law and making it relevant to twenty-first-century circumstances.

Together, certification and interest simulation facilitate the bureaucratic rationalization of shariah governance in firms. Since shariah boards comprise mostly or entirely shariah scholars, and since industry scholars adopt a bracketed and predominantly *legal* conception of financial shariah-compliance, IFIs can segregate the religious-compliance function within their organizations relatively cleanly from major business functions such as strategy, operations, marketing, and human resources. Islamic financial institutions can therefore establish shariah departments and shariah audits that monitor compliance with their shariah boards' rulings without getting into thorny, abstract ethical questions about the potential downstream consequences of financial activities for social welfare. For business functions outside the shariah function, financial institutions can therefore easily hire staff—from CEOs to bank tellers— with backgrounds in conventional finance. This radically expands the availability of labor for IFIs and imbues them with the pragmatic profit orientation of capitalist finance: executives at Islamic banks are just as focused as their counterparts at conventional banks on stock price and shareholder value. The organizational segregation of shariah also makes it possible for conventional financial institutions to convert into Islamic ones, for conventional institutions to merge with and acquire Islamic ones, and for conventional institutions to open Islamic branches or entire Islamic divisions. These pathways have amplified industry growth greatly.

Despite accommodating capital through these various means, shariah scholars working in Islamic finance also restrict it. They insist that firms structuring new products, transactions, and service platforms meet conditions that can take months and even years to comply with. In rare cases, they even threaten at the last minute to blow up financings and sukuk issuances worth hundreds of millions or billions of dollars. Rarely but very consequentially, scholars even publicly criticize new Islamic financial products and services already certified by other scholars. Public dissent of this kind shook the global market for sukuk in 2008 and has undermined confidence in other newly issued, highly complex Islamic financial products as well. While industry scholars usually resolve differences quietly, work with firms in advance to avoid last-minute crises, and keep their advice to firms "in-house," the knowledge that they *can* go public or blow up a transaction at the last minute provides a deterrent credible enough to have its own name among investment analysts: "shariah risk."

Even restriction can create new opportunities for capital, however. When enough shariah scholars consistently find fault with a particular way of structuring Islamic financial transactions, entrepreneurs seize the opportunity and develop new commodity-trading platforms, shariah-compliance investing apps, and other solutions that purport to obviate some of the scholars' concerns. Shariah scholars then inspect the new solution and, if they feel it passes muster, may recommend it to the financial institutions on whose shariah boards they sit. Hence, scholarly restriction of capital spawns entrepreneurialism and inventions that apply shariah to finance in ever more technically complex, bureaucratically rational, cost-efficient, and shariah-scrupulous ways. Even when shariah scholars restrict capital, the industry expands and advances.

Shariah scholars' ability to align Islam and capitalist finance also depends on national economic, political, and social specificities. Comparing the development of Islamic finance in Saudi Arabia and Pakistan, we see that when and where conditions empower business-minded shariah scholars and stabilize their social prestige and their ability to govern finance privately (as opposed to publicly, as agents of the state), capitalist Islamic finance tends to flourish. Thus, conditions favoring the growth of Islamic finance including widespread fiqh-mindedness among the populace, a political culture amenable to business-friendly interpretations of Islamic law, and state and corporate institutions that stabilize and reinforce shariah scholars' views and social prestige pave the way for capitalist Islamic finance to blossom. These conditions obtained in Saudi Arabia but not Pakistan.

Islamic Finance as Form of Life

It appears to me as though a religious belief could only be [something like] passionately committing oneself to a system of reference. Hence although it's belief, it is really a way of living, or a way of judging life. Passionately taking up this interpretation. And so instructing in a religious belief would have to be portraying, describing that system of reference and at the same time appealing to the conscience.

—LUDWIG WITTGENSTEIN, *CULTURE AND VALUE*[2]

In the end, what is Islamic finance? For one thing, it is a multitrillion-dollar industry. Yet it also encompasses not-for-profit institutions, such as charities that engage in nonprofit Islamic microfinance; I spent a day each at two such charities, observed daily operations, and interviewed staff, but have decided to leave them out of the book for the sake of focusing on for-profit finance. More broadly, Islamic finance is a religio-economic project with deep intellectual roots, not only in the Arab Gulf states—from which emerged the institutional characteristics of today's capitalist Islamic-finance industry—but in the Islamic economic theorizing throughout the twentieth century of anti-imperialist intellectuals and political activists from South Asia, Egypt and other Arab countries, Iran, Southeast Asia, and elsewhere, and further back, the economic thought of Islamic scholastics.[3]

Yet I believe Islamic finance is also something else: a "form of life."[4] This aspect became clear only gradually over my years of fieldwork, especially as I got to know members of the Islamic-finance community on a personal basis, including some who remain dear friends. It bubbled up as I followed these friends around at work over weeks and months, met their families, drove for hours with them on the ring roads and flyovers of Abu Dhabi, Dubai, Karachi, Kuala Lumpur, London, and Riyadh en route to meetings, and shared countless conversations over late-night biryani, satay, or knafeh. I will explain briefly what I mean, and then illustrate with examples.

A form of life is the social and cultural background—including tacit and symbolic knowledge, dispositions, and moral orientations—necessary for a particular usage of language, or a "language game," to make sense. While Wittgenstein's own applications of the term leave room for ambiguity, most redeployments of "form of life" stress that language is always social, that it manifests in real institutions, and that it cannot be reduced to its systemic elements (morphology, syntax, and so on).[5] It is not enough to know the formal rules of language to comprehend a usage of language; we are only able to take language in its particular uses as "given" because we share judgments and ways of judging. The notion of form of life has a fair amount in common with Pierre Bourdieu's concept of habitus.[6] However, unlike Bourdieu's habitus, it is rarely affixed to one individual. This is because it emphasizes and derives from the use of language—not only as a means of performing distinction or signaling class position but as something that serves to define a human community (even one not formally defined as such) as those people who share what is required for mutual intelligibility. Language-games nest within one another and overlap with one another, just like forms of life and the communities they correspond to.

Fiqh-Mindedness as Form of Life

Classical Islamic law, its unique vocabulary, and the norms of speaking through and about it comprise the language-game through which one takes up a fiqh-minded form of life. To the fiqh-minded, rulings by shariah scholars and knowledge of Islamic law provide guidance for "reading" everyday situations through a juridico-ethical lens and making decisions about how to act. Yet the ability to engage fluidly in fiqh-minded piety does not come easily or immediately, say to people who have newly converted to Islam and hope to follow a fiqh-minded path. Nor does it come from simply reading enough rulings by scholars. To become socially "fluent" in the fiqh-minded form of life, one must absorb the symbolic vocabulary and ethical grammar of fiqh, learn how others distinguish among shariah scholars and their reputations, learn when others turn to fiqh and when they do not in their everyday decisions, learn terms of respect accorded to famous scholars past and present, learn about tendencies of the main juristic schools, learn how distinctions of dress and grooming (such as of facial hair) may or may not convey symbolic meaning in different social settings, and even learn how to make jokes about living a fiqh-minded lifestyle that are funny yet unlikely to offend.

Contrary to stereotypes, fiqh-minded Muslims do not live as automatons beholden at all times to a draconian, authoritarian version of Islamic law.[7] Neither are they obsessive nor plagued by constant anxiety (at least not more, on average, than the typical twenty-first-century subject) about God's punishment in the event that they, deliberately or not, transgress God's law. After all, God is merciful and forgiving. Nor is adherence to Islamic law their sole criterion for judging piety or ethical probity (a view that contradicts "legal-supremacist" conceptions of Islam).[8] Fiqh is instead for many believers an ethical endeavor in which one does one's reasonable best when one reasonably can. Moreover, as Rumee Ahmed[9] notes, fiqh-minded Muslims often show less interest in establishing definitive, universal answers to moral questions (e.g., Is using narcotics wrong?) than in reasoning about how to do things ethically (e.g., When is narcotics use justifiable?). This reflects awareness of the context-specific nature of morality.

The following example may help shed light on the fiqh-minded form of life.

Faris Almaari is a twenty-four-year-old Saudi international student at Johns Hopkins University. He is a typical Johns Hopkins undergrad: he wears JHU Blue Jays sweatshirts to class, volunteers as a tutor, re-tweets cat videos, and gets a remarkable percentage of his caloric intake from Chipotle. (He also happens to be my research assistant.) At the same time, he embraces a fiqh-minded approach to Islamic piety; he could be described as a fiqh-minded Muslim. He takes Islamic law seriously as a system of guidelines for behaving piously in daily life, and he turns for guidance to shariah scholars whose intellectual reputation he respects.

Faris finds himself Googling for scholarly opinions several times a month or more. Shortly after arriving in the United States to study, for example, he was wondering how he should pray. Islamic jurists have long agreed that believers may shorten and combine the obligatory five daily prayer cycles while traveling. But is an international student traveling? After all, home to Faris is Jeddah, not Baltimore; he has neither the intention nor the right under state law to make the United States his permanent residence. He searched the internet and found fatwas by ʿAbd al-ʿAzīz ibn Bāz (1910–99) and Muḥammad ibn al-ʿUthaymīn (1925–2001), often called the two greatest Saudi jurists of modern times, asserting that he could only perform the compressed version of his prayers for the first three days after arriving in the country where he would study; thereafter, he was no longer a traveler. Many other jurists whom Faris considered reputable said the same, so he treated the matter as settled. In Baltimore, he would pray five separate times a day.

A few weeks later, Faris visited Washington, D.C. He was about to pray at the National Mall when he wondered if he could compress his prayers now that he was away from Baltimore. Googling from his iPhone, he found that the majority of jurists of the Ḥanbalī, Mālikī, and Shāfiʿī schools set a minimum distance from home of around eighty-nine kilometers—a span they deemed equal to two average days' travel by heavily loaded camels—before one could be considered a traveler. But Google Maps said Faris was only sixty-eight kilometers from his Baltimore dorm. He completed the full prayer cycle, again feeling good about having checked.

That Faris is fiqh-minded does not mean legal thinking *dominates* his way of being Muslim in the world: there are myriad other dimensions to his religiosity. For example, God provides solace during difficult times and intervenes in unexpected ways. Faris took a job right out of high school and was proud to be supporting himself fully, but the daily grind felt meaningless. Then, when he began university in Saudi Arabia, he found his professors uninspiring and the coursework dull. He was depressed but continued to believe God had more in store for him—and then got accepted to Johns Hopkins, with a full scholarship from the Saudi government. "This is what God intended for you," Faris thought. The sudden change in his life couldn't be understood through the lens of shariah-compliance and *taqwá* (moral responsibility to God; reverential and obedient virtue): he did not think of his new educational opportunity as a reward for following God's law, for he would never impute a logic of quid pro quo to the Almighty. Rather, going to Johns Hopkins was his *rizq*, the beneficence God bestows upon each individual. "I just felt the presence of God when that happened," Faris explains. We start talking about free will and predestination in Islam. This kind of reflection elides legalistic reasoning.

Yet even when thinking in theological terms, Faris turns to a scriptural mode of discourse consonant with fiqh-mindedness. He makes apposite references to the hadith literature—the vast, meticulously curated corpus of records of statements and deeds attributed to the Prophet Muhammad—in an easy and knowledgeable manner, reflecting years of tutelage in the religious sciences in the Saudi public-school system and a childhood spent among people who know this literature well. "There is a *ḥadīth qudsī*[10] in which God says *Anā ʿinda ẓanna ʿabdī bī* [I am to my servant as he thinks of Me]," Faris explains. In other words, God will do things for those who believe He can. Abstractions like faith, conviction, and hope crystallize in scriptural references that the learned believer can insert into everyday conversation. Fiqh-mindedness, then, entails not only *belief* in the relevance of Islamic law and its scholarly experts but a subjectivity: an internalized comfort with a system of meaningful references among sacred texts and the long tradition of scholarly commentary on them. It is a form of religious intellectualism.

Fiqh-Mindedness in Financial Dealings

Many contemporary Muslims had never engaged in Islamic interest simulation until they became customers of Islamic banks. Yet in some locales and communities, Islamic interest simulation was already common before Islamic banks bureaucratized it and marketed it widely. In Saudi Arabia, for example, "classical tawarruq"—that is, tawarruq not arranged and bureaucratically streamlined by a large firm the way "organized tawarruq" is—was often practiced by individuals. Sometimes, it still is. Here, I describe someone who engaged in classical tawarruq in the 1980s, when Islamic banking was in its infancy. This case demonstrates how some pious Muslims engaged in interest simulation as a practical way of managing financial needs while adhering to juristic interpretations that permit tawarruq and prevail in some areas, such as Saudi Arabia. It thus conveys what financial fiqh-mindedness looks like as a general tendency.

In 2009, Abdulkarim needed money to build the family a home. He had already taken a shariah-compliant financing from the bank for this purpose, but it had not covered all the construction costs. The bank refused to give him more. Abdulkarim could have approached a private moneylender who would have charged interest, but he wanted to avoid dealing in interest, so he executed a tawarruq transaction (figure 6.3), which most Saudi shariah scholars deem permissible. He bought a new GMC Acadia sport-utility vehicle from a car dealer for 120,000 riyals, agreeing to pay for it in installments over the next 60 months, and then immediately resold the car to another buyer for 110,000 riyals cash, paid on the spot. Abdulkarim now had 110,000 riyals in his pocket that he could use to finish building his home, and he owed 120,000 to the car dealer, which he would pay off over the coming 60 months. (I have rounded the numbers for clarity's sake.)

The way Abdulkarim handled his need for cash was a quintessentially fiqh-minded approach. From the perspective of his wallet—that is, according to a purely substantive economic rationality—he had effectively taken a 110,000-riyal loan and was paying 10,000 riyals of interest on it. Some quick math shows that he was paying an effective annual interest rate of 3.48 percent. However, Abdulkarim felt comfortable knowing that Islamic law, as interpreted by prominent Saudi shariah scholars, permitted what he was doing as something fundamentally different from taking an interest-bearing loan. Today, Islamic financial institutions have rationalized the same process, executing it electronically in quantities of billions of dollars a day (figure 6.4; see chapters 1 and 6). Finding a car to buy from one dealer and then finding another guy who wanted the same car was not exactly convenient, and it took up a day of Abdulkarim's life, but he considered it worthwhile. It addressed his financial need while avoiding the remorse from taking an interest-bearing loan.

Learning to Be Financially Virtuous

The more people see Islamic finance around them, the more they come to take it for granted that what Islamic financial institutions sell is genuinely Islamic. Scholar-certified finance takes on what Mark Suchman describes as "cognitive legitimacy": coming to accept an institution as "*necessary* or *inevitable* based on some taken-for-granted cultural account."[11] Customers, investors, finance practitioners, regulators, and the general public come to take for granted that shariah scholars are the necessary and inevitable arbiters of financial Islamicity. They come to equate Islamic finance with scholar-certified finance.

This cognitive legitimation works partly through "shallow" exposure: constantly seeing billboards, storefronts, and television commercials for banks, for example. It also operates through the circulation of online videos via social media, particularly videos of shariah scholars discussing Islamic finance. (Many of our interviewees in Pakistan and Saudi Arabia reported receiving such videos constantly from friends and relatives, even if they themselves had little interest in Islamic finance.)

Yet the exposure loop has deep effects too: effects that can construct a familiarity with financial piety where none existed before. Consuming Islamic financial products usually involves little rumination or sacrifice. As we saw in chapter 3, the "halal price premium" is low or nonexistent in mature consumer markets for Islamic finance (see table 3.1). In some situations, however, consumers must "learn the ropes" of Islamic finance and expend money, time, and effort not required of conventional consumers.

At first, Waqas, a forty-six-year-old owner of five general stores in a middle-class Karachi neighborhood, was keen to try Islamic banking. Previously, he had taken interest-bearing bank loans to buy inventory, albeit grudgingly:

> It was partly for religious reasons [that I tried to avoid bank loans]. I would hear *maulvis* say on the radio that [interest] is prohibited. I didn't really think about it a lot, but yes, I tried to avoid [taking loans]. They made me a little uncomfortable. . . . But sometimes, loans were just necessary.

In 2012, a sales rep from an Islamic bank dropped by Waqas's shop and explained how shariah-compliant inventory financing worked. It seemed simple: the bank would buy the inventory from Waqas's supplier at Price X, and then sell it to him at Price $(X + i)$ on credit. "'Sure, I'm Muslim, so why not try [Islamic banking]?'" Waqas recalls thinking. The Islamic bank's pricing was slightly higher than its conventional competitors', but this seemed like a reasonable cost to sleep well at night.

However, Waqas discovered that being an Islamic-banking customer demanded more of him: "They wouldn't just give me the money like a conventional bank would." Instead, someone from the Islamic bank pored over his accounts and demanded to see physical inventory at his warehouse. This was for religious reasons, not business reasons. Shariah scholars insist that specific assets be present on a client's books, and often physically present in the client's warehouse, to be available for the trades and leases that replicate the financial effect of an interest-bearing loan.

The Islamic bank's demands irked Waqas. Previously, he had only tracked his inventory once a week. "As long as I knew when my shipments came and went, I was fine. But now these guys wanted me to track my inventory every day! And they charged more!" Fed up, Waqas called the Islamic bank to say he wanted to switch back to a conventional bank. However, an account manager convinced him to stay:

> [The account manager] explained why . . . I have to keep the accounts every day and . . . track the inventory. Because shariah says that we can't sell what we don't own. And he explained how riba works. In school they say God prohibits riba; but they don't really explain what it means.

Waqas began devouring everything he could find about Islamic banking. He watched lectures on YouTube by famous scholars and preachers and read Taqi Usmani's book on Islamic finance. He became a believer in Islamic banking:

> I used to think Islamic banks were the same as conventional banks. People say conventional banking is like this [grabs his right ear with his right hand] and Islamic banking like this [reaches over his head and grabs his right ear with his left hand, implying a contorted way of achieving the same result]. But when I read Mufti Taqi Usmani's book, I realized that it really is different. I understand now what riba is, and why it's a problem, not just for the person who takes a loan but for the whole world.

I heard similar accounts from three other small-business owners in Karachi and Islamic-bank customers in other countries.

Waqas and these other customers not only embraced Islamic banking; they discovered a new avenue through which to live according to shariah. They engaged in what Daromir Rudnyckyj[12] calls "economy in practice": reflecting and acting on economic rationality from an ethical perspective. Put differently, through the consumption of Islamic finance, they had to learn a new language-game (fiqhi reasoning about finance) and soon became absorbed in the associated form of life (financial fiqh-mindedness).[13]

Waqas was unusual in that he was a customer who took it upon himself to "learn" Islamic finance as a form of life. I found this type of effort to be far more common among Islamic bankers and other industry professionals, though by no means universal. It was particularly common among middle-level employees: knowledge workers constantly confronted with shariah as a set of scholar-promulgated rules that they had to put into practice, often in sophisticated settings, such as in a shariah department. By contrast, on the low end, tellers and telephone salespersons were too busy with simple, repetitive tasks and rarely confronted shariah-related questions. On the high end, C-level executives had to answer to shareholders: they paid lip service to their personal and corporate commitment to shariah, but they typically did not *embrace* financial shariah the way I saw many middle managers do.

To these fiqh-minded managers, Islamic finance became more than a career: it became an intellectually stimulating path to pious self-actualization. As they studied the logic of the scholars' rulings and spelled out to customers why Islamic finance is truly different from conventional finance, they felt themselves becoming better, more knowledgeable Muslims.[14]

"Knowledge gives you faith," explained Muhammad Aftab Athar, branch manager at an Islamic bank in Karachi.[15] Aftab spent two to three hours every day educating customers about Islamic finance and answering their questions. These customers, he remarked, were more educated than the average Pakistani, or even the average bank customer. Many worked in business or had studied economics, and they were also pious; they wondered seriously about what made Islamic finance Islamic. They tended to think philosophically too, demanding evidence and sound reasoning. Their most common question for Aftab was: How can Islamic banks be Islamic if they, just like conventional banks, benchmarked their profit rates to KIBOR,[16] Pakistan's benchmark interest rate? Aftab would respond by describing an interest rate as just a number, and very different from the substance of interest himself. Just as shariah scholars do, he used metaphors, explaining that if you sell your grape juice at the same price as your neighbor's wine, your grape juice doesn't turn into wine. Customers also asked: If your Islamic bank is regulated by Pakistan's central bank[17] just like conventional banks are, then how can it be Islamic, since the central bank engages in monetary policy by lending to banks at interest? Here, Aftab had to get technical, explaining that the central bank has a separate stockpile of overnight shariah-compliant liquidity-management paper for the

Islamic-finance sector and demonstrating how it worked. Sometimes the customers were convinced; sometimes they weren't. But Aftab was. He felt his own attraction to Islamic finance growing: not just his belief that it avoided sin but a sense of fascination with its principles and the possibility of putting them into action as much as possible.

I met many Islamic bankers like Aftab who took Islamic finance seriously. They often sought to build their base of knowledge of classical Islamic commercial law through reading and watching lectures, not only for work-sponsored trainings but even on their own time and their own dime. In Pakistan, I met two who in night school or on weekends had even become inspired while working at an Islamic bank to pursue the Dars-e Nizami, a curriculum in the classical Islamic sciences specific to the Ḥanafī school of jurisprudence that takes years to complete and is a mark of great distinction.

What struck me most about these Islamic bankers I met around the world was that when I asked them to narrate how they came to be so interested in Islamic finance, not one of them mentioned anxiety about sin or a fear of hellfire. Instead, they described a gradual process of falling in love with Islamic finance through a dialectical combination of learning and practice, in which exposure begat curiosity and vice versa. Often, the process began accidentally. The story of Ni Putu Desinthya, an Indonesian former Islamic banker who now works in a presidential commission to promote the Islamic economy, encapsulates these common elements. To finish off her accounting major in college, she took a course on Islamic accounting on a lark. She had no exposure at all to Islamic finance before then except hearing about it in passing. An Islamic bank hired her for an internship, which turned out to be more stimulating than she expected: while her friends interning elsewhere made tea and twiddled their smartphones, she shadowed Islamic bankers and Islamic accountants through various divisions: financial analysis, reporting, and even customer service. "I learned the difference between Islamic and conventional banking," she explained, "and that it's in line with my values."[18] She went on to study Islamic finance at INCEIF, the Islamic finance university in Kuala Lumpur, and to do a master's in Islamic finance at the University of Durham, working with some of the world's leading Islamic economists. Now, between reflections on the technical details of central-bank policies to provide Islamic liquidity, she talks excitedly about promoting the Islamic economy across Indonesia, and shows me with pride a children's book she wrote on how to live a halal lifestyle. She has also become an authority to her friends, who increasingly hear about Islamic finance on WhatsApp message groups and ask her questions: What do the fatwas say that justifies murabaha transactions? What is a wakala-based mortgage?

For people who inhabit Islamic finance as a form of life, intellectualization is possible because debate and differences of opinion are acceptable. Taking scholar certification for granted in Islamic finance does not mean accepting whole cloth what every industry shariah scholar says. "Taken-for-grantedness is distinct from evaluation":[19] one can take for granted that shariah scholars are the right group of people to inspect financial products for Islamic legality yet disagree with the rulings of a given scholar or shariah board. As chapter 5 notes, most shariah scholars worldwide enshrine the doctrine of normative pluralism: the principle that well-qualified scholars may legitimately come to different legal rulings on the same matter. For example, as we have seen, industry shariah scholars disagree about the lawfulness of tawarruq ("cashification"), one of the most common transactions in Islamic finance. Occasionally, non-scholars go public in questioning the Islamic legality of a shariah board's ruling, as Mohammed Khnifer did with Goldman Sachs's sukuk (chapter 5). And very occasionally, elite scholars even question one another's interpretations and authorizations publicly, as when Yusuf DeLorenzo questioned the Deutsche Bank shariah board's "doomsday fatwa" (chapter 6). Nonetheless, these people inhabit capitalist Islamic finance as a form of life together, and interpretive disagreement is rarely acrimonious. The capacity to acknowledge legitimate differences of interpretation civilly—"you've got your interpretation of shariah, and I've got mine"—helps to intellectualize Islamic finance for those who delve into it. Islamic finance becomes a stimulating field of scholastic debate and reasoning. The cognitive legitimacy of scholar certification and the embeddedness of Islamic finance in Islamic law are not weakened by disputes, but strengthened.

In sum, learning Islamic finance allows some people who come into contact with it to find new sources of meaning in life. Research on what makes life meaningful to Americans has highlighted three bundles of "meaningful practices": one focused on relationships (e.g., family, friends), one on ideals and lifestyle (e.g., social and political causes, learning new skills), and one often oriented toward religious commitments.[20] The simple act of buying an Islamically certified product might tap into the bundle oriented toward religion, but devoting time and effort to *learning* Islamic finance, and coming to inhabit it as a form of life, granted Waqas, Aftab, and Ni Putu access to the "ideas and lifestyle" bundle. It reveals, in Daniel Winchester's words, "how particular actors in specific social contexts construct moral lives and selves."[21]

Whither Islamic Finance?
The Possibility of Ethical Progress

Islamic-finance law is a language-game largely nested within the language-game of classical Islamic law, although with many neologisms and novel practices adapted to twenty-first-century finance. Its corresponding community of "speakers" includes people who not only know, in a formal sense, the meaning of words like *murabaha* and *sukuk ijara* but also make ethical judgments for contractual structures based on them, offer reasons for those judgments, and debate those of others. In other words, people who inhabit Islamic finance as a form of life come to see it as a terrain for fine ethical distinctions.

While to most customers the ethical distinction between conventional finance and Islamic finance appears as a straightforward split between the sinful and the sin-free, the internal ethical universe of Islamic finance is complex and contentious to those who inhabit Islamic finance as a form of life. Not all Islamic financial products are equally virtuous in the eyes of stakeholders in the broader project of Islamic finance, which extends beyond the industry to include academics, government officials, and external religious authorities. Among shariah scholars, bankers, and even customers and investors who inhabit Islamic finance as form of life, opinions differ about the ethical valence of common industry practices and contractual structures. Some even implicitly rank-order them. Sheikh Osaid Kailani, head of the shariah department at Abu Dhabi Islamic Bank, explains:

> At the end of the day, whatever we use has to be shariah-compliant. But . . . if we look at [Islamic-finance] products, and we have a barometer for the halal, we see that some of the products are at the bottom: they are halal, can be used, but the difference between them and the conventional products are very thin. Others on the barometer are in the middle; others are on the top.[22]

We have seen, for example, how some scholars consider organized tawarruq to be ethically problematic or sinful, while others see it as acceptable so long as it is executed scrupulously.

Thus, Islamic finance is not just an industry but a shared meaning-making project in which stakeholders invest great hope, and about which they have strong feelings. Where there are such rank-orderings of virtue, ethical progress becomes possible. The industry can, at least in theory, move away from less-virtuous products and toward more-virtuous ones. Indeed, these gradients of virtue that form part of the Islamic-finance form of life generate moral responsibility: if moving up the gradient is possible, it would seem incumbent on industry leaders to drag industry practices upward.

When state intervention is absent or leans laissez-faire, innovation tends to move in directions that serve the needs of capital. Consider the BSAS palm-oil trading engine in Malaysia and the DMCC diamond-trading platform in Dubai, both of which facilitate cheaper, more exacting executions of tawarruq. Other examples abound. In the frothy years leading up to the 2008–9 global financial crisis, unbridled Islamic financial innovation seemed to grant capital an ever-greener light each year. And then, during and after the crisis, some members of the Islamic-finance community sounded a triumphant note, observing that Islamic financial institutions, prevented by shariah from buying mortgage-backed securities (MBS), collateralized debt obligations (CDO), and credit default swaps (CDS), were maintaining better capital ratios[23] and not experiencing financial contagion to the degree their conventional competitors were.[24] They asserted that Islamic finance might be the antidote to future financial crises.[25] But in November 2008, as the financial sky was falling, I asked Harvard Business School emeritus professor of investment banking Samuel Hayes how he felt about this claim. "Sure, there's something to it," replied Hayes. Hayes, with Frank Vogel, coauthored a book on Islamic law's financial applications[26] that became essential reading for Islamic financial engineers in the late 1990s and 2000s. "But it's only because the Islamic financial engineers got a late start." Hayes meant that Islamic financial engineers had already been *trying* to structure shariah-compliant versions of MBS, CDO, and CDS, but when the crisis hit hadn't yet gotten their products to market. "Had the crisis come five years later, Islamic banks would have been hit just as hard [as conventional banks]," Hayes averred.[27]

Yet Islamic finance also retreats back from go-go innovation sometimes. After my conversation with Hayes, I dug up a prominent Islamic financial engineer's 2007 paper explaining how to engineer an Islamic CDO. In 2010, I turned up at a talk the financial engineer was giving and asked during Q&A whether he still endorsed building an Islamic CDO. "No," he said with an air of humility. "We learned some lessons from the crisis." And indeed, the Islamic simulation of complex structured-finance products and financial derivatives has never returned to the heights it attained before 2008.

Moreover, public conversations in the global Islamic-finance community have recently turned toward pressing social and environmental concerns, such as the use of "green sukuk" to fight the Covid-19 pandemic and mobilize funds to combat global warming. There are many reasons to be skeptical: green finance, whether conventional or Islamic, has yet to prove itself convincingly as a vehicle for addressing environmental and social concerns effectively; and investors in the Gulf region especially have been slower than those in North America, Western Europe, and East Asia to express enthusiasm about green finance.[28]

So where is Islamic finance headed? It could very easily continue along its capital-friendly path and accommodate only a veneer of social and environmental commitment. Large capitalist firms can reliably be expected to advance socioeconomic and environmental welfare only if it suits their bottom line, or if laws and regulatory authorities force them to. Could shariah scholars, as private regulatory authorities and legal experts, drive Islamic-finance firms and their clients in such a direction? Given industry scholars' present tendency to bracket out socioeconomic and environmental concerns from their assessments of shariah-compliance, the answer, for now, seems to be no.

But what would happen if a transformative socioeconomic or environmental crisis shook the Arab Gulf countries or other areas where Islamic finance is most commercially advanced? Economic crisis could occur in the Middle East if global energy use shifts faster than expected from hydrocarbons to renewable energies. The high standard of living to which most GCC citizens are accustomed would become unsustainable if the world stopped buying oil, and social dislocation and political upheaval could ensue. Consumer credit has already expanded dramatically since the 1990s in much of the Middle East, including Saudi Arabia,[29] raising the stakes. Currently unknown shortcomings in the state and private regulation of Islamic financial instruments could be laid bare in a downturn, just as the failure of U.S. regulators and the major credit-rating agencies to comprehend new forms of securitization were exposed after the 2008–9 financial crisis.[30] Any of these potential crises could portend a fracturing of the presently stable alliance of prominent shariah scholars and Islamic bankers that has so far maintained consensus to preserve overall industry growth. Such a process might prove comparable to the fragmentation of the U.S. corporate elite since the 1970s, as chronicled by Mark Mizruchi.[31]

Moreover, socioeconomic and ecological crisis could undermine the legitimacy of the shariah scholars, who have largely bracketed socioeconomic and ecological concerns out of their decisions about financial shariah-compliance. States and firms that depend on the scholars for legitimacy might then seek to "rescue" the scholars' ability to regulate—a process Gil Eyal has theorized.[32] States and firms could pursue *inclusive* strategies to rescue the scholars, such as integrating more non-scholar experts into shariah boards and increasing transparency about shariah boards' decision-making processes (two processes already underway in Malaysia), or they could pursue *exclusive* strategies that would seek to keep the scholars firmly in charge, such as doubling down on gatekeeping, credentialing, and technocracy. Either way, would the scholars push Islamic finance toward new sets of concerns? Would other parties seek to change the industry's ethical calculus? Perhaps.

So What?

At the beginning of this book, I asserted that the Islamic-finance boom can tell us something about the relationship between religion and the economy at the present moment, as we enter the middle of the twenty-first century. So what does it tell us that should interest social scientists, or anyone else? What's going on here?

From Thinking Territorially to Thinking Chemically

Let us begin by situating Islamic finance briefly in relation to the once-dominant secularization paradigm and responses to it. From the nineteenth century through the late twentieth, ascendant streams in social theory and the sociology of religion asserted that religious authority cannot regulate the modern economy. According to this view, religious authority governed much premodern economic activity but abdicated this role as industrial capitalism spread. This perspective forms part of the broader macro-level secularization paradigm, which posits that religion separates from other functional spheres as societies modernize. It asserts that religion has been "progressively forced to withdraw from . . . the modern capitalist economy and to find refuge in the newly found private sphere." Sociologist Peter Berger went so far as to situate "the original 'locale' of secularization . . . in the economic area, specifically, in those sectors of the economy being formed by the capitalistic and industrial processes."[33]

Some observers of Islamic finance have concluded that the industry's growth entails such a capitulation: that in intertwining itself with capitalist motives and organizations, anything meaningfully Islamic has been secularized away.[34] Indeed, some readers of this book may arrive at that conclusion. As the book's preface said, Islamic finance is a mirror in which we all see different things, and get a view of ourselves. When an economist colleague and I proposed to give a talk on Islamic finance at a university economics department in the United States, one of the economists who would have hosted us quipped: "Just tell me one thing. Do they find some way to charge interest without calling it interest? Because if they do, I'm not interested."

In the 1970s and 1980s, Peter Berger reversed himself completely and advanced the desecularization thesis: the idea that people and institutions are becoming more religious, not less so. The desecularization thesis dovetailed with the growing literature on fundamentalisms. Both argued that counter-secular movements are on the rise, characterized by scripturalist, literalist, ritualistic, anti-scientific, and millenarian orientations. These movements tend to be presented as defensive and reactive, turning to religion's hallowed, unfalsifiable sureties as havens from encroaching liberalism, pluralism, globalization, Westernization, neocolonialism, Darwinism, and secularization. While scholars adopting the desecularization framing focus most on politics (e.g., political Islam, Hindu nationalism, Christian conservatism), some have examined efforts to reassert religious authority over the economy: the Buddhist-inspired "sufficiency economy" and "gross national happiness" movements, for example, or liberation theology's radical advocacy on behalf of the poor. Just as we could describe the ascent of Islamic finance as a secularization, we could also describe it as a desecularization: a Polanyian reembedding of the economy in extra-economic principles in response to the social dislocations of spreading capitalism.[35] Like Berger, José Casanova has raised the possibility that such trends have the power to tame the market.[36] So has Amy Reynolds, who shows how evangelicals in the United States, Canada, and Costa Rica seek to bring market forces to heel.[37]

Yet calling the rise of Islamic finance a case of either secularization or desecularization creates conundrums. If we dub it secularization, how do we account for the fact that religious authorities are becoming more powerful than they were before and are making increasingly scrupulous demands of capitalists who want to participate in Islamic finance (the "more capital, more shariah" trend)? Contrarily, if we call the rise of Islamic finance an instance of defensive desecularization and Polanyian reembedding, how do we explain that capitalists are making a lot of money in Islamic finance, and that the moral economists' welfare-centric ethical vision of Islamic finance has been relegated mostly to academia, with little impact on industry practice?

The difficulty with both models stems from their shared conceptualization of religion and the modern market as distinct, antagonistic domains. "The Market" and "Religion" are flattened into rival value-spheres waging a zero-sum war over territory. In the secularization paradigm, the Market drives Religion to retreat; in the desecularization paradigm, the Market provokes Religion to strike back. To illuminate Islamic finance, it is necessary to develop a theoretical perspective that moves beyond this bipartite division.

Much research has already challenged this division. Economic sociologists, historians, and anthropologists have revealed modern markets to be inescapably moral institutions that evolve through moral reconfiguration. For instance, as Viviana Zelizer has shown, life insurance succeeded commercially because religious activists recast it as fulfilling sacred familial duties.[38] Some analysts of religion, meanwhile, have started retreating from defining religion as a distinct analytic category, instead treating it as yet another site, like medicine or education, in which to make empirical and theoretical observations about social life.[39] Many have explored how religiously motivated actors treat economic life and capitalist markets as sites for pious action in the modern world, and conversely how economically motivated actors pursue commercial success using religious institutions, discourses, and worldviews. They have shown how Indonesian Muslims link piety and entrepreneurship,[40] Mexican evangelicals foster self-discipline in business,[41] Hollywood creative workers find consolation at church from insecure jobs,[42] and "prosperity gospel" preachers wrap late-capitalist consumerism in an ethos of self-help and divine favor.[43] Such research confirms that religion has hardly disappeared from modern economies. We should heed Robert Hefner's reminder that neoliberal capitalism is "neither singular in its ethics nor unitary in its social organization" and that it is far more consumerist than it was in Max Weber's day.[44] Contemporary capitalism presents the consumer with "a slew of taste-making and identity-destabilizing enterprises." When diverse Islamic subjectivities and forms of piety intersect with it, the outcome is unpredictable and manifold.[45]

To make sense of the Islamic-finance boom, I have therefore avoided framing it as an encroachment by "religion" in the abstract into the "economy," or conversely as an irruption of the economic ethos into the pristine religious domain. Yet this does not necessarily mean we should jettison the entire conceptual apparatus that secularization research has developed. As Philip Gorski and Ateş Altınordu[46] assert, there is pressing need to study secularizing and desecularizing processes further, especially in non-Western cases and in non-congregational milieux.

Using metaphors from chemistry, we could ask: What initial conditions allow a "reaction" to occur or "solution" to form between some religious phenomenon or ethos on one hand and some arrangement of markets on the other? What institutional-level ("molecular") affinities and dynamics bind the two? And how does the chemical reaction transform existing modes of piety and market arrangements and produce new hybrids? In the case of Islamic finance, the initial conditions included the oil boom of the 1970s, which brought great wealth to a region where fiqh-mindedness was widespread, and the expansion and globalization of finance, which created new appetites for complex financial products. The religious phenomenon is an interpretation of fiqh and an attendant form of fiqh-mindedness that "dissolves" readily into liberal markets. The outcome has been the growth of a certification-oriented, capitalist form of Islamic finance.

The "chemical" approach is compatible with the type of scholarship on Islam and Islamic scholars that has shaped this book. First, by asserting that particular religio-economic hybrids emerge under particular conditions, it makes room for *contingency*—for individual-to-individual differences in the interpretation of Islamic law and the diverse institutional, social, and political conditions that facilitate and constrain this interpretation—while also accepting the *continuity* of fiqh as "a discursive tradition that connects variously with the formation of moral selves, the manipulation of populations . . . , and the production of appropriate knowledges."[47] It is at this intersection of continuity and contingency that Muhammad Qasim Zaman, Malika Zeghal, and others have situated the evolution of Islamic juridical authority, and debates over that authority, in the era of the modern state and modern markets.[48] Second, the chemical approach to the study of religion does not have to be bound by national borders as its unit of analysis; it can be *global*. It can situate micro-level piety and market practice within the historical evolution of the world-system and within a "sociology of transculturality" that, as advanced by Armando Salvatore, highlights the circulation and cosmopolitanism of twenty-first-century globalization.[49] Finally, the chemistry metaphor is apt for tracing the *formation and transformation of pious selves* and the effects of these changes. It addresses Bryan Turner's call for a "cultural sociology of piety" that investigates the emergence of different types of pious selves, Muslim and otherwise, as part of a larger cultural sociology of capitalism.[50]

Absorption into Global Neoliberalism

The rise of capitalist Islamic finance into an international industry larger than the entire financial sector of Eastern Europe, South America, or India[51] has been one of the major developments in finance over the past half century. How should sociologists study the global economic transformations of the neoliberal age?

Sarah Babb and Alexander Kentikelenis propose a three-pronged research agenda. The first prong consists of an organizational sociology that examines not only the diffusion of norms and a shared global culture (such as the audit culture enshrined by the "police" in chapter 6) but also "knowledge of the diverse logics that drive [international] organizations that depend on financing mechanisms, decision-making structures, and strategies of transnational rulemaking." This book has explored the organizationally embedded logics that shape Islamic finance: the competing Islamic logics of the moral economists and the shariah scholars and their interplay with the ever-present logic of profit-seeking. The second prong is a postcolonial perspective, including world-systems theory, that stresses how actors in the Global South drive change in international economic practices and norms, even in the face of colonial legacies and the United States' "informal empire." Islamic finance first appeared as a postcolonial project, and although it has integrated thoroughly with the U.S.-led global financial infrastructure, it has flourished thanks to the agency and entrepreneurship of actors in the Global South. The third prong is emphasis on the social foundations of global change: on the way "individual, class, or organizational interests . . . are embedded in a variety of social structures and identities."[52] Accordingly, this book has examined how the industry's novel hybrid of classical Islamic law and capitalist finance depends on respect for the pedigree and expertise of shariah scholars, their interpretations of Islamic law, and an orientation toward fiqh-mindedness among populations (as in Saudi Arabia more than Pakistan, for example).

But what are we to call this new hybrid religio-economic formation of which the Islamic-finance industry is an example? Vali Nasr has described the Islamic-finance boom and the rise of other halal sectors such as Islamic entertainment, shariah housing, and modest fashion as the rise of "*Islamic capitalism.*" Nasr conceptualizes Islamic capitalism in terms of consumerism: as the thirst of an upwardly mobile global Muslim middle class for the same "life-enhancing goods and services" that all other middle-class people want but in a form that comports with the present "resurgence of traditional Islamic belief."[53] Additionally, we might describe the Islamic-finance boom as an instance of "post-Islamism": Asef Bayat's term for the condition after which Islamism has exhausted itself even among its once-ardent supporters and reinvents itself under the pressure of its own contradictions.[54] While Bayat first applied the concept to Iran in the mid-2000s, we could extend it here, depicting capitalist Islamic finance as what a "maximal"[55] conception of Islamic piety can look like when it is not enacted principally by Islamists wielding state fiat but rather introduced as a neoliberal policy prescription designed to keep the pious middle and upper classes consuming, employed, and happy. Indeed, in Iran as in Pakistan, post-Islamist states have backed off from state imposition of Islamic finance by fiat. Even the Iranian state, still left out in the international financial cold by U.S. sanctions, is adopting aspects of global capitalist Islamic finance, such as efforts to penetrate the international sukuk market.[56]

Relatedly, we could conceptualize Islamic finance—particularly in the case of Pakistan, as described in chapter 7, but in a global sense too—as what Cihan Tuğal depicted in the Turkish case as the *absorption of the Islamic challenge into global neoliberalism*. In Turkey, this process constituted a Gramscian passive revolution organized by the neoliberal Islamists of the Justice and Development Party (AKP), bringing in disparate social and economic forces under the AKP umbrella.[57] While this type of passive revolution organized by a single political party across civil society, political society, and the market does not apply to a given national case of the rise of Islamic finance (except perhaps Sudan's in the 1980s and 1990s under the Muslim Brotherhood), Tuğal emphasizes elements of neoliberal Islamism that have likewise been vital to the rise of Islamic finance, including its positioning from the 1970s onward as part of an Islamization of everyday life, an individualist conception of religion popular with merchant classes and businesspersons, and a deradicalization that saps the revolutionary potential of the Islamic revival. A form of piety manifested partly through individual consumption, like the financial fiqh-mindedness of Islamic finance, shares this individualist orientation with what Grace Davie has described as "believing without belonging": a noncongregational approach to religious commitment.[58] Consumerist individualization saps the possibility of revolutionary solidarism.

Indeed, Islamic finance seemed to have revolutionary potential in the 1960s and 1970s, when it was still a utopian experiment. So how did it, like Turkish Islamism but in a very different way, get absorbed into global neoliberalism?

First, there was an accident of timing and geography: the vast oil wealth that has accrued to the Arab Gulf, a region particularly fiqh-minded relative to others, from the 1970s onward. Originally conceived as a South-South project by liberation-minded Islamic ideologues, Islamic finance—especially "high" Islamic finance—quickly took on elements of a North-South partnership in which bankers, lawyers, and commodities brokers from Europe and North America migrated to the Gulf to provide newly rich families and institutions with an Islamic solution to the task of investing their wealth. From the 1970s onward, oil wealth coincided with American and British maintenance of a stable post-independence alliance with the Arab Gulf states, held together by military protection and sales of hydrocarbon and arms. As financial liberalization, financial engineering, and the global relaxation of capital controls proceeded under the U.S. security umbrella and the global extension of English law in offshore jurisdictions, "high" Islamic finance merged smoothly into international networks of capital and financial expertise.

Second came the bureaucratization of religious authority over finance, beginning with the establishment of the first shariah board in 1976 by Faisal Islamic Bank of Egypt. The model of voluntary private certification by religious scholars proved consequential in various ways. Not only did it establish a certification system that would convince customers Islamic finance was legitimate, but it entrenched the shariah scholars as its totally dominant certification authorities. The literature on certification stresses how public conflict among certifiers can quickly undermine trust in the certification badge.[59] If the moral economists had been able to challenge the shariah scholars' dominance in the Gulf early on as they did in Pakistan, or if scholars with differences of opinion about interest simulation had bickered publicly and extensively, capitalist Islamic finance could have been doomed from the start. Instead, the shariah-board model of bureaucratization proved essential because it allowed shariah authority over capitalist finance to become "modular." For example, the shariah board's authority could be extended by internal "shariah police" and external "shariah auditors" who served as the long arm of the board's law; alternatively, an investment bank based in New York or Tokyo could retain a shariah board on a one-off basis to certify a sukuk issuance.

There is something special about a legal conception of piety that has been bureaucratized: it is uniquely consonant with economic modernity. This is true for two simple reasons. First, modern economies are already governed by a thicket of secular laws, so religious laws can be layered on top of them without too much trouble, and without reinventing the way things are done. Rule by rules is a defining feature of modernity, after all.[60] Second, capitalists have reason to seek out rules, even if they also have reason to bend and break them. As Bruce Carruthers points out, "private financial actors engage law selectively to create a more certain environment for themselves and their profit-seeking activities."[61] Regulation, whether secular or Islamic, can provide predictability, and capitalists like predictability.

Yet the twenty-first-century context for applying Islamic law to financial matters differs dramatically from premodern contexts, as Wael Hallaq has noted.[62] Unlike premodern states, modern states already regulate nearly everything. They impose health regulations that limit heavy metals in tuna, safety regulations that set the maximum height of ladders, and financial regulations defining what banks can do with their clients' money. And unlike premodern businesses, modern firms impose countless rules upon themselves. They determine who in the firm may hire and fire whom, and what paperwork an auto-loan customer must fill out in what order. So when a shariah board issues a fatwa saying that an Islamic bank must structure its financial instruments a certain way, bureaucrats within the firm already know how to develop process flows that translate the shariah scholars' religio-legal demands into rules about what paperwork an Islamic auto financing requires, and in what order. Legions of bankers, lawyers, accountants, regulators, and legislators do the work of making Islamic contracts and instruments work in the existing context of conventional finance. It is hard work but nowhere near as hard as building a completely separate Islamic economic system from scratch that operates outside the capitalist marketplace according to fundamentally different economic principles.

Is Islamic Finance Secular?

In this sense, it is worth thinking about Islamic finance as growing not only in the soil of a certain "religious" set of social conditions, such as widespread fiqh-mindedness and respect for shariah scholars, but also in the presence of certain forms of secularity. As Jeffrey Alexander, Talal Asad, and Robert Bellah have noted in their own ways, nominally "non-religious" institutions and states are shot through with their own sacreds: the sanctity of national symbols like flags and holidays, crises placed beyond time and human conception like the Holocaust, and restraints on free speech militantly protected by "liberal secular" states, such as blasphemy laws and copyright laws.[63] And as Asad, Elizabeth Shakman Hurd, and Saba Mahmood have shown, the definitions of religion adopted by liberal secular states produce new exclusions, inequalities, and injustices within and across borders.[64]

The scholars' legal conception of piety, combined with the modularity of the shariah board, effectively opened Islamic finance to Muslims and non-Muslims alike who embrace a form of secularity that Charles Taylor calls "Secularity 3." To Taylor, Secularity 1 is religion's retreat from public spheres like politics, science, and the arts, and Secularity 2 is the decline of individual religious belief. But Secularity 3, which interests Taylor most, involves not so much the decline of religion as the reorientation of the psychological and social conditions for being religious: "a move from a society where belief in God is unchallenged and indeed, unproblematic, to one in which it is understood to be one option among others."[65]

As a voluntary regulatory system, fiqh can sit inoffensively atop binding state laws and regulations. Customers, not governments, decide whether to apply religious law when they consume. Moreover, when fiqh becomes a formal system of voluntary regulation, a wide range of firms and entrepreneurs can deploy it creatively to new kinds of products. The legalism of the shariah scholars and its bureaucratization has also contributed to a curious form of internally secularized differentiation at the organizational level: it has effectively split Islamic banks and other Islamic-finance firms into two parts, "Islamic" and "secular." The shariah board sits at the top of the Islamic part. The rest of the Islamic part comprises corporate units tasked with ensuring shariah-compliance by executing the shariah board's requirements, such as the internal shariah department—that is, the aforementioned "shariah police" who vet transactions for shariah-compliance—as well as the back-office operations that engage in the asset sales and leases that facilitate Islamic instruments. As a result, even non-Muslims can play major roles in Islamic finance: while they may not work as shariah scholars, they may do almost everything else involved with running an Islamic financial institution. One American non-Muslim from Texas even served as the CEO of the world's largest Islamic bank for four years.[66]

Yet capitalist Islamic finance does not simply represent the dominance of bureaucracy, certification, individualization, and depoliticization—the triumph of the "cool passions" of calculative rationality (whether Islamic-legalist or profit-maximizing) over the "hot passions" of religious fervor. Recall Waqas, the Karachiite shopkeeper who effortlessly taught himself the rules of Islamic finance, or Aftab in Lahore and Ni Putu in Jakarta, who came to love and evangelize Islamic finance for its intellectual nuance by practicing it, studying it, and teaching about it. Islamic finance is for these people and thousands like them a form of life, or if you prefer, a habitus, that gives meaning to everyday financial tasks. At the same time, for those like Shakir and his wife in chapter 7, who lost their unborn baby rather than deal in interest, and to all others for whom dealing in interest is viscerally unsettling and powerfully unnatural, Islamic finance is a very human matter indeed.

ACKNOWLEDGMENTS

LABĪD, ONE OF the seven virtuosi whose verses hung in the Kaʿbah before the age of Islam, describes how rain brought the parched torrent-beds of al-Rayyān to life:

> The star-borne showers of Spring have fed them, the outpouring
> of thundercloud, great deluge and gentle following rain . . .
> Then the branches of aihakan [*ayhuqān* (wild rocket)] shot up, and
>   the ostriches
> and antelopes brought forth their young on both valley-slopes.

> —"MUʿALLAQA OF LABĪD" (TRANSL. ARBERRY)

These acknowledgments are long because many people have watered this project with their support over many years. Unfortunately, I could not quote many people I wanted to, even when their input fascinated me. Others remain anonymous. Yet in every case, the people who shared their time made this project come to life. I appreciate their contributions deeply.

Beyond granting interviews, some people provided valuable contacts, access, data, and teaching. I mention some here by country; please forgive the lack of titles and honorifics. In Australia, I thank Bernardo Vizcaino; in Bahrain, Muzammil Kasbati, Nizam Yaquby, Esham Ishaq, and Lujain AlSaibai; in Canada, the ever-hospitable Joanna, Piotr, and Teresa Wrzesniewski and Summer Tan; in Indonesia, Tushar Agarwal and Edwin Utama; in Kuwait, Issam Altawari; in Luxembourg, Eleanor de Rosmorduc; in the Philippines, Anne-Sophie Gintzburger; in Qatar, Anouar Adham and the Euromoney Qatar organizers.

In Malaysia, I thank Mohamad Akram Laldin and ISRA; Zulkifli bin Hasan; Engku Rabiah Adawiah Engku Ali; Mohammad Hashim Kamali; Obiyathulla Ismath Bacha; Eskandar Shah; Wan Muhammad Najahuddin bin Wan Fuad; Izzat Ilham Adnan; Ahmad Zaki Salleh and Mohamad Zaharuddin Zakaria; Syarizal Rahim; and Mohammad Faiz Azmi, Nik Shahrizal, and Mohamed Zharif Agil. In Oman (or linked to it), I thank Saeed al-Muharrami, Suleman Muhammad, Emily Voight, the Critical Language Scholarship program, and especially Khalfan Barwani, who graciously arranged high-level meetings.

In Pakistan, Ahmed Ali Siddiqui opened countless doors that facilitated my research. I also thank Sarwat Ahson, Irum Saba, Azam Ali, Marium Zehra, and especially Shazia Farooq, who spent many hours organizing and leading interviews. Irfan Siddiqui authorized research access throughout Meezan Bank, where Waqas Yasin, Irsa Ahmad, Muhammad Azeem, Muhammad Saleem, Muhammad Aftab Athar, Abdullah Rizwan, my friend Hasan Faraz, and many others helped me. My gratitude extends to all Meezan branch staff who made customer interviews possible. Imran Usmani kindly let me tour Darul Uloom Karachi and the Hira Foundation School. I gratefully acknowledge Irshad Ahmad Aijaz, Muhammad Mohib ul Haq Siddiqui, Khawaja Noor ul Hassan, Hasan Junaid Nasir, Faysal Bank's Shariah Audit section, and Muhammad Akhlaq. Waseem Akhtar kindly brought me to COMSATS. I thank Imtiaz Ul Haq, who found research assistants and arranged my survey; Anam Fatima; and my hard-working research assistants Fatima Qamar, Ayesha Umar, and Rumassah Chohar. Zaid Ansari, Misbah Aamir, and Kashif Shafiq pored through Pakistani textbooks. Tariq Raza and Yasir Tariq generously organized a full-day visit to Wasil Foundation's Islamic-microfinance operations in Sharaqpur. Finally, I acknowledge the late Muhammad Naeem and the Jamia Binoria Alimiya staff for organizing a daylong visit.

In Saudi Arabia, I thank the King Faisal Center for Research and Islamic Studies for arranging visas and high-level research access, and Faisal Abualhassan and Shahad Turkistani for the crucial connections. Suad AlBibi was a remarkable research assistant who secured crucial interviews and data in two countries. Abdul Azim Islahi, Masum Billah, and Abdullah Turkistani graciously welcomed me at King Abdulaziz University. I am also very grateful to Mohamed Ali Elgari, Ahmed Abdulkarim Alkholifey, Fahad Ibrahim Alshathri, Ayman Mohammed Alsayari, HRH Amr bin Mohammed Al Faisal Al Saud; Azmi Omar; Rajiv Shukla and Faisal Qadri; Abdulla Alaqil, Hani AlGhuraibi, and Othman Al-Abdulkarim; Sultal Al Nugali; Karim Ghandour; and Dina Almaari. Salman Syed Ali and Mohammed Obaidullah kindly hosted me at the Islamic Development Bank. Samir Abid Shaikh unsparingly provided many crucial pages of responses to my questions. Nasser and Abdulaziz Alsubeaei warmly welcomed me and shared memories of their father, a tour of his museum, and the best dates I have ever tasted.

In the United Arab Emirates, I am indebted to Iman Ali, Talal Malik, Fawad Siddiqui, Noman Tahir (twice!), Sayd Farook, Kamran Sherwani, Cassim Docrat, Abdurrahman Habil, Ajmal Bhatty, Mohammed Paracha, Shehab Marzban, Mukund Bhatnagar, and Jorge Camarate. Salman Khan and I shared long, enriching conversations. My Al Ain Centre friends always encouraged me, especially Claire, Ebrahim, Hissan, Maria, Meera, Mr. Anonymous, Ronald, Samantha, and Shahid.

In the United Kingdom, I am grateful to Abdul Kadir Barkatulla, Sultan Choudhury, Stella Cox, Humayon Dar, Richard de Belder, William Glaister, Emran Mian, Mushtak Parker, Mohammed Ali Qayyum, and Azeemeh Zaheer. In the United States, I thank Baber Johansen, Sam Hayes, Michael McMillen, Abdulkader Thomas, Yahia Abdul-Rahman, Joshua Brockwell, Kal Elsayed, Salman Ali, and Riffat Lakhani. I appreciate Rushdi Siddiqui for many reflections and contacts, Mohamed Abdelaziz for investigative help, the ever-generous Blake Goud for industry insights; Jean-François Seznec for historical data, contacts, and a day at his Annapolis farm; and Yusuf Talal DeLorenzo for sharing his remarkable life story and writing. The late M. Nejatullah Siddiqi kindly provided incisive comments on my writing by phone and e-mail.

At Harvard, Wheeler Thackston, John Schoeberlein, James Russell, Ayesha Jalal, and Ali Asani fostered my love for studying Islam. I also thank my colleagues at the consultancy where I worked for three years thereafter. They taught me about business and introduced me to Islamic finance.

At Berkeley, three exceptional people invested the most in me. John Lie, whose intellect is as deep and wide as the ocean, drove me to explore what exactly makes Islamic finance Islamic. The dazzling Marion Fourcade pushed me to investigate the moral dimensions of Islamic markets while always giving wise counsel. Neil Fligstein, to the world a pathbreaking theorist of markets and fields, is to his students a font of encouragement too. Jim Wilcox too served on my dissertation committee and taught me about banking and its regulation. And I thank other faculty who went beyond their teaching duties: Irene Bloemraad, Vicki Bonnell, Michael Burawoy, Beshara Doumani, Peter Evans, You-Tien Hsing, Dylan Riley, and Cihan Tuğal. The CCOP and GEMS forums provided crucial feedback. The Javits, Al-Falah, and Center for British Studies fellowships generously funded my research.

Many comrades at Berkeley read and commented on my work. They include Abigail Andrews, Dan Buch, Cyrus Dioun, Barry Eidlin, Fidan Elcioğlu, Sam England, Eli Friedman, Sarah Garrett, Eric Giannella, Adam Goldstein, Jacob Habinek, Pat Hastings, Paul Hathazy, Gabe Hetland, Graham Hill, Kimberly Hoang, Katherine Hood, Daniel Immerwahr, Daniel Kluttz, Daniel Laurison, Zach Levenson, Roi Livne, Louisa Lombard, Sarah MacDonald, Laura Mangels, Damon Mayrl, Freeden Oeur, Marcel Paret, Alina Polyakova, Sarah Quinn, Nicholas Hoover Wilson, and Graeme Wood. Sam England has remained unstintingly helpful in solving Arabic conundrums. Graeme Wood has provided vital input on writing.

I have benefited greatly from interactions with the growing community of social scientists studying Islamic finance. Ibrahim Warde advised me extensively in this project's early years. My intellectual debt to Ibrahim will be clear to those who read his work, as everyone interested in Islamic finance should.

Aaron Pitluck and Lena Rethel organized a seminal panel at SASE Milan. Their research has illuminated my own, as has that of Rumee Ahmed, Fulya Apaydın, Mehmet Asutay, Obiyathulla Ismath Bacha, Aisalkyn Botoeva, Anver Emon, Bridget Kustin, Jikon Lai, Daromir Rudnyckyj, Sarah Tobin, and Imtiaz Ul Haq. Mehmet Asutay is a linchpin of the global Islamic-finance community.

Kevan Harris has supported my research in crucial ways, including by hosting me at UCLA, where he, Omar Lizardo, Assaf Bondy, Andrew Chalfoun, Sima Ghaddar, Bowei Hu, Nanum Jeon, Isaac Jilbert, Zep Kalb, and Shiva Rouhani gave essential feedback on chapter 1. Mark Gould unstintingly provided rich, nuanced comments on multiple chapters. Jeff Guhin has been an enlightening interlocutor for years. Nina Bandelj, Tim Bartley, Fred Block, Ruthie Braunstein, Alya Guseva, Dan Hirschman, Charles Kurzman, Gerardo Martí, Matthew Norton, Fareen Parvez, Akos Rona-Tas, and Gabriel Rossman have provided valuable input.

Several people have performed astounding kindnesses. In Kuala Lumpur, Aida Othman arranged my research attachment at Zaid Ibrahim & Company's shariah consultancy, where I learned from the inside how Islamic finance works, often directly from Aida. In Dubai, Maria Arnau let me stay in her apartment for weeks, refusing to accept recompense. In Lahore, Hissan Ur Rehman and Laila Bushra spent days acquainting me with their beautiful city.

I could not imagine a better place to write about Islam and global capitalism than Johns Hopkins University. The JHU Catalyst Award and the Berman Institute of Bioethics (special thanks to Maria Merritt) generously funded my research. Erin Chung gave thoughtful feedback and sage advice. Librarians Stephen Stich and Joshua Everett unearthed hard-to-find sources. My RAs Nitin Nainani, Evan Harary, and Eliana Drescher provided great support, as did Mira Haqqani. Andrew Halladay and Gianni de Nicolò answered tricky questions. The Krieger School leadership, especially Chris Celenza, Chris Cannon, and Mary Favret, facilitated medical leave and were supportive as I recovered from an injury, as was Cherina Cunningham. And in Islamic Studies, I thank Ali Khan, Naveeda Khan, Homayra Ziad, our International Studies supporter Sydney Van Morgan, and especially Niloofar Haeri, who has been inspirational and encouraging since I arrived on campus.

In Sociology, Beverly Silver and Joel Andreas have supported me at every turn and pored over the manuscript, helping me tackle big questions. They have also organized the fruitful Arrighi and PGSC seminars. Andy Perrin, Ho-fung Hung, and Andy Cherlin have been unfailing champions and mentors as chairs. Discussing the exorbitant privilege from a southern perspective with Ho-fung has helped me rethink the book. Jessie Albee, Rick Sanchez, and Terri Thomas are world-beating staff. Finally, I appreciate the feedback and comradeship while writing from Rina Agarwala, Emily Agree, Rishi Awatramani, Ilil Benjamin, Julia

Burdick-Will, Stefanie DeLuca, Yige Dong, Kathy Edin, Zophia Edwards, Meredith Greif, Şahan Savaş Karataşlı, Manasi Karthik, Şefika Kumral, Huei-ying Kuo, Conrad Jacober, Sebastian Link, Tian Liu, Luo Qiangqiang, Katrina Bell McDonald, Steve Morgan, Tim Nelson, Daniel Pascuti, Christy Thornton, Nima Tootkaboni, Smriti Upadhyay, Vesla Weaver, and Alexandre White.

Finally, I thank a few people who made signal contributions. At Princeton University Press, Meagan Levinson and Erik Beranek were superb editors who moved mountains to take this book from prospectus to print. (Sometimes I was the mountain.) The two anonymous reviewers gave thorough, tremendously insightful feedback that made the book far better. Jenn Backer's fastidious yet style-sensitive editing has improved the manuscript markedly, as has Jenny Wolkowicki's oversight. And I am grateful to Eric Crahan, Rachael Levay, Katie Osborne, Lauren Reese, William Pagdatoon, Sydney Bartlett, Emma Walden, Virginia Ling, and all PUP staff who are behind this project.

On the home front, Steph Tepkasetkul was a constant supporter over two years. The inimitable Koyuki Wilson is my daughter's Japanese-language tutor and has helped raise Kuri since she was six months old. *Taihen osewa ni narimashita.* Matthew Peters is a doctor as empathic and charismatic as he is smart. He has made it possible for me to finish this book and to flourish. While I am unable to put his face on the cover as we discussed, he deserves it. Hassan Jivraj—finance-journalist extraordinaire and the "Sultan of Sukuk"—has provided expertise, scores of industry contacts, and friendship. Someday, we will drive a Cadillac Escalade golf cart together again.

Fulya Apaydın, Damon Mayrl, and Sarah Quinn read my entire manuscript and spent a day workshopping every chapter with me. Having three brilliant, cutting-edge scholars digest my work and reconceptualize it made this the most rewarding day of my academic life. Emma Andersson and William Kao are superstars to whom the title "research assistant" does not do justice. They generated data, figures, references, and sparkling memos. They formatted the manuscript and performed countless other vital tasks. Emma's superhuman leadership skills and efficiency and William's technical adroitness made this book possible.

Nicole Eaton has deployed her analytical sophistication and historian's eye for prose and evidence to review my work many times over. She has kept me focused year after year. Her husband, novelist Srdjan Smajić, carefully and comprehensively edited several chapters. Writer Nina Aron spent long hours editing my work, cleverly slicing through knots. Kuba Wrzesniewski has pored over too many versions of this book to count. He has brought to bear prolific historical knowledge, spare rooms in four countries, and awareness of my personality to push and pull this book to completion. He is a true friend. Mike Levien has read, re-read, and helped me think through nearly every chapter.

His rigorous feedback has been so insightful that I find myself returning to it over and over, sometimes years later. His camaraderie, hospitality, and culinary skill, and those of Suchi Pande, know no bounds.

My parents Toshiko and Kent Calder have supported me in every way possible, believing in my work even when I did not. They also raised me to work hard, be curious about the world, and see as much of it as I can. They are model academics and educators, and it is an honor to follow in their footsteps. My sister and brother-in-law, Mari and John Montague, have been unfailingly encouraging too. My parents-in-law Debra and Richard Herrala have moved snow and earth—literally—so I could finish this book. As I worked every year through what were supposed to be family vacations, they showered me with support and set up a trailer at their farm in Michigan's Upper Peninsula so I could write. Deb brought me food every day.

Nasir Razak deserves thanks that extend beyond what I could put on a page. He opened Islamic finance in Pakistan to me, generously serving as research coordinator, translator, fixer, and expert informant for weeks—on a volunteer basis, and while working a demanding full-time job in Islamic banking. The hours we spent discussing Islamic finance, and life, while driving around Karachi made him a lifelong friend. I thank Nasir's brother Ahsan too. And Faris Almaari was not an ordinary research assistant; he was a hero. When family commitments prevented me from going to Saudi Arabia a third time, Faris went instead. He flew, drove, and walked all over the kingdom. From morning to midnight, he approached strangers, conducted interviews, and wrote notes before collapsing into bed. Over three years, he also hunted down data and experts, coordinated Zoom interviews and transcriptions, and vetted my Arabic. Faris too is a friend for life.

Finally, I thank the two people dearest to me. My daughter, Kuri-chan (Cleo), came into this world as I was writing and researching this book, and at every stage—from chunky one-year-old to cheeky five-year-old—has awed me and melted my heart. I thank her for the drawings, sumo matches, fashion advice, and hugs. She is the light of my life. And being married to Elise Herrala, one of my favorite sociologists, is an unceasing joy, even if she once resolved never to marry a fellow sociologist. Her contributions have spanned this book's research, conceptualization, structuring, editing, and production. The immense debt of social reproduction I owe her will take years to repay, though she never treats it as debt. And whenever she muses about the quirks of capitalist society, stands with me when the chips are down, and makes me burst out laughing, I fall in love with her anew. This book is dedicated to her.

Methodological Appendix

Expert Interviews

SIXTY PERCENT OF the interviews conducted for this book were expert interviews: semi-structured conversations with people I targeted for their knowledge of Islamic finance. (Table A.1 summarizes the interviews and interviewees by country and type.) Most of the time, I conducted expert interviews in person and by myself[1] but when necessary relied on video call or phone call. The vast majority of expert interviewees were based in—but sometimes not citizens of—the five countries where I spent the most time: Pakistan, Saudi Arabia, the United Arab Emirates, Malaysia, and the United Kingdom. Other interviewees were based in Australia, Bahrain, Canada, Curaçao, Indonesia, Iran, Japan, Jersey, Kuwait, Luxembourg, Oman, Qatar, Turkey, the United States, and Yemen. This global orientation proved invaluable because it revealed national and regional differences in the competitive landscape, shariah governance, and state regulation of Islamic finance, and especially in what I call "low" Islamic finance, which serves mass-market households and small and medium-sized businesses. The global scope also let me map out and gain a feel for transnational "high" (*haute*) Islamic finance: the markets for large-corporate banking and capital markets, including sovereign and large-corporate sukuk (Islamic "bonds"), Islamic IPOs, cross-border shariah-compliant equity funds and syndicated financings, and shariah-compliant wealth management for the ultra-rich. Because English is the lingua franca of international business, the expert interviews were overwhelmingly in English. Of the remainder, I conducted five in Arabic, which I speak, and—with simultaneous translation by a research assistant—six in Urdu, which I do not speak. Most expert interviews lasted between 45 and 90 minutes, with some running as long as three hours.

The experts I interviewed fell into four categories. The most numerous were "practitioners," as they call themselves in the industry: private-sector participants in Islamic finance who include commercial bankers, investment bankers,

Table A.1. Number of Persons Interviewed and Number of Interviews

Country	Persons Interviewed			Interviews		
	Expert	Consumer/ Member of Public	Total	Expert	Consumer/ Member of Public	Total
Pakistan	45	69	114	43	69	112
Saudi Arabia	29	47	76	21	47	68
Malaysia	36	1	37	29	1	30
United Arab Emirates	26	0	26	26	0	26
United Kingdom	18	0	18	19	0	19
Oman	12	0	12	10	0	10
United States	7	0	7	7	0	7
Canada	3	0	3	3	0	3
Qatar	3	0	3	3	0	3
Jersey	2	0	2	2	0	2
Yemen	2	0	2	2	0	2
Indonesia	2	0	2	1	0	1
Turkey	2	0	2	1	0	1
Australia	1	0	1	1	0	1
Bahrain	1	0	1	1	0	1
Curaçao	1	0	1	1	0	1
Iran	1	0	1	1	0	1
Japan	1	0	1	1	0	1
Kuwait	1	0	1	1	0	1
Luxembourg	1	0	1	1	0	1
Total	194	117	311	174	117	291

Note: "Interviews" differs from "Persons Interviewed" because I occasionally interviewed two or three people at once, and because I occasionally interviewed the same person twice or, in two cases, three times.

lawyers, management consultants, shariah consultants, shariah auditors, accountants, fund managers, commodities brokers, fintech entrepreneurs, and representatives of credit-rating agencies. I add to this group representatives of nonprofit Islamic microfinance organizations I visited in rural Pakistan. Key interview topics included differences between managing or working at Islamic financial institutions versus "conventional" (i.e., non-Islamic) ones; differences among national markets for Islamic finance; the structuring, marketing, sale, shariah-compliance monitoring, and credit rating of Islamic financial instruments; the early history of Islamic finance and its evolution over time; the practitioners' views of their clients and customers; the interviewees' experiences working with shariah scholars; and the interviewees' trajectories into and through the industry. Some practitioners became my friends—in a few cases, close friends—who confided their anxieties and frustrations about the industry and revealed what they considered to be laxities and failings in true shariah-compliance. Along the way, I came to appreciate the ethical dispositions that working in Islamic finance can cultivate in practitioners (see the book's conclusion).

The second most numerous interviewees were shariah scholars,[2] including some who sit on shariah boards (the panels overseeing Islamic financial institutions) and some who work in the internal shariah departments of Islamic financial institutions or as independent shariah advisors. Because shariah scholars have deep academic training in Islamic law, speaking with them both required and strengthened my technical knowledge of Islamic contracts and the way Islamic financial institutions use them. I also encouraged shariah scholars to share their personal and educational backgrounds and their reflections on the ethics of Islamic finance (see chapter 5).

The third most numerous were representatives of governments and multilateral organizations. The government representatives were mostly regulators at central banks and securities commissions, including in Pakistan, Saudi Arabia, Malaysia, Oman, and Iran. The multilateral organizations where I conducted interviews included the Accounting and Auditing Organization for Islamic Financial Institutions (the largest international standard-setting body for Islamic finance), the Islamic Development Bank, and the Islamic Financial Services Board. I also attended a World Bank conference on Islamic finance and a Euromoney conference on Islamic-finance regulation. My primary concern in these interviews was to understand how states and multinational organizations shepherd Islamic finance, including by managing the stability of Islamic banks and their access to Islamic liquidity.

The smallest group of expert interviewees comprised observers who sat outside or adjacent to the industry, such as academics (excluding shariah scholars) and journalists. The academics were mostly university professors specializing in Islamic economics, Islamic finance, or business. They were the interviewees most likely to criticize the Islamic-finance industry, usually because they believed Islamic economic principles had the potential to help society but were failing to do so. Because they were critical yet well-informed, and because they readily understood my research agenda, academics provided useful correctives to opinions and claims I heard elsewhere. They also opened up to me an entire social world of academic scholarship in Islamic economics. The journalists I spoke with covered Islamic finance regularly for major generalist news sources such as Reuters, for national-level business newspapers, and for international publications specializing in Islamic finance. They provided global and comparative perspective, industry history, and contacts.

Throughout, I sought both breadth and depth. My interviewees ranged in rank from CEOs to bank tellers, in prestige from the governor of Saudi Arabia's central bank and many of the industry's dozen most famous shariah scholars to junior scholars and sales reps just starting out, and in age from a nonagenarian who established the world's first for-profit Islamic bank in 1975 to a teenager describing what he had learned about usury in middle school.

I targeted expert interviewees partly by snowball sampling and partly by hunting on my own for relevant contacts at each stage of my research, and in each locale. Snowball sampling involved discussing with existing contacts who could most knowledgeably answer the questions facing me at that moment and then requesting a connection. National Islamic-finance communities are small enough that prominent figures know one another; this accelerated the snowball once it got rolling. Hunting on my own involved poring over lists of conference speakers, examining quotes by experts in reliable news sources, and asking bankers, lawyers, and journalists to suggest appropriate experts.

Aspects of my biography helped me gain access to expert interviewees and lubricated our conversations. One advantage was my three years' experience working as a management consultant at the Boston and Dubai offices of a large international management consultancy before graduate school. There, I learned corporate strategy and operations, navigated balance sheets and profit-and-loss statements, and spent a year and a half working alongside middle- and upper-level managers at financial-services firms from Boston and Indianapolis to Dubai and Jeddah. Before that, I also interned at a boutique consultancy serving a large consumer-finance company and worked temp jobs at Putnam Investments and a law firm. Through these experiences working in finance and other white-collar service sectors, I absorbed the habitus, jargon, and sartorial norms of international business and learned to project polite confidence in chatting with C-level executives. The name of my past employer also conferred legitimacy upon my curriculum vita in the eyes of finance professionals, as did the presence of name-brand American educational institutions on my vita, my Anglo first and last name, my ethnoracial ambiguity (I am half Japanese, half white American), and my male gender.

My insider-outsider status and presentation of self—as someone who was not Muslim but who respected and studied fiqh-minded Islam, and who was familiar with Islamic finance and curious to learn more—seemed to lead many of my Muslim contacts to appreciate my interest and explain as much as they could. It also resonated with the many non-Muslims who work in the industry, many of whom themselves were quick to remark that they found the industry sociologically and anthropologically interesting. My knowledge of Arabic benefited me when I conducted interviews in that language, but even more so in allowing me to draw on news articles, Islamic legal texts, school textbooks, and online videos (such as of interviews with shariah scholars and business leaders) available in Arabic. Being a student of contemporary Islam granted me baseline familiarity with Islamic scriptures, Islamic legal concepts, and fiqh-minded practices and norms such as stock Arabic-Islamic verbal greetings. All of this helped me move smoothly in interviews, workshops, seminars, conferences, and talks I gave during fieldwork.

Despite these advantages, recruiting expert interviewees proved challenging at first—until I started building networks in the industry. When I began preliminary fieldwork in 2009, I was a doctoral student at Berkeley and struggled to find industry experts who would talk, especially in the Gulf region, where "corporate outreach" is less of a mantra than in North America or Western Europe. (The going was easier in Malaysia, where the state encourages academic research into Islamic finance.) I got a break when I attended a conference in Kuala Lumpur that invites brand-name shariah scholars from around the world. One of the speakers was Sheikh Nizam Yaquby, an internationally elite shariah scholar from Bahrain who sits on more Islamic-finance shariah boards than any other scholar in the world. To my surprise, Sheikh Nizam— whom I had seen being chased around the conference by hordes of professionals seeking his time and advice—sat with me in the hotel lobby and chatted energetically for over an hour. Thereafter, when I contacted other experts for interviews, I mentioned that I had interviewed Sheikh Nizam and watched my response rate rise. This reflected the weight that elite scholars' names have in the industry. As I accumulated interviews with other elite scholars and leading corporate figures, I tacked their names onto a running list that I would send to subsequent interview targets, and my hit rate continued to increase. Becoming a professor at Johns Hopkins also increased my legitimacy with expert interviewees, and I was soon being invited to give talks at their banks and other institutions.

Interviews with Mass-Market Customers and the General Public

The other half of the interviews conducted for this book comprised over 130 semi-structured interviews with members of the general public in Pakistan (2017) and Saudi Arabia (2020–21). Around half of the interviewees in each country were Islamic-banking customers: in Pakistan because I was permitted to recruit and interview at 14 branches spread across Karachi and Lahore of Meezan Bank, the country's oldest and largest Islamic bank; and in Saudi Arabia because Islamic banking has such high market share that any sample of the general public will hit upon many Islamic-banking customers. Interviews with customers and the general public typically lasted 20 to 90 minutes and probed attitudes and beliefs about Islamic banks, the shariah scholars who supervise them, and usury. I attended about half of the customer and general-public interviews in Pakistan in person but relied on my Urdu-speaking team of researchers, led by Pakistani Islamic banker Nasir Razak, to recruit interviewees, lead most of the interviews, translate and transcribe them, and code them using Dedoose qualitative-analysis software.

In Pakistan, around 30 percent of the people my team approached agreed to be interviewed; this hit rate did not vary much by gender. Our team was mixed-gender, with female interviewees usually being interviewed by a female interviewer. I trained all researchers and conducted sample interviews and coding sessions with them to maintain consistency. On the Saudi side, I led some of the general-public interviews via Zoom, but the majority were carried out one-on-one via Zoom or in person by my research assistant Faris Almaari, who is Saudi. I participated in all Zoom interviews at first to familiarize Faris with my approach; after around ten interviews, he proceeded on his own. Before and during his research in Saudi Arabia, I provided Faris with questions, trained him in interview procedure, and debriefed with him every night after he had conducted interviews. Faris and I coded the Saudi interviews in Dedoose using a combination of descriptive coding, in vivo coding, and versus coding.[3]

To recruit Saudis for Zoom interviews, we bought targeted ads on Facebook, Twitter, Instagram, and Snapchat. For the in-person interviews in Saudi Arabia, Faris approached people in parks, cafés, malls, and other public areas. Around 40 percent of the men and 30 percent of the women that Faris approached agreed to be interviewed.

Although it was infeasible to develop a random-sampling methodology, I diversified the sample in each country by gender, age, our rough assessment of interviewees' socioeconomic status (based on occupation and education), metropolitan area or region of the country, and in the Saudi case, Sunni or Shi'i sect. About half of the interviewees in Pakistan were Islamic banking customers approached at branches of Meezan Bank, the country's largest Islamic bank. The rest were approached at public places such as malls and coffee shops in the country's two largest metropolitan areas, Karachi and Lahore, and most turned out not to be Islamic-banking customers (which is no surprise given that Islamic banking's market penetration was around 8 percent when I conducted the research in 2017). In Saudi Arabia, our Zoom interviewees came from around the country and were mixed by gender and age. Most respondents to our ads were between 18 (our minimum age) and 35; later, we recruited middle-aged people and seniors to make up for this.

Thereafter, Faris conducted in-person interviews in the following cities to achieve diversity across geography, population, sect, and urban/suburban/rural setting: in north-central Saudi Arabia, ʿUnayzah and Buraydah; in the east, which has a significant Twelver Shiʿa population, Dammam, Khobar, and Sayhāt; in the south, Najrān, which has a plurality of Ismaili Shiʿa; and in the west, Jeddah and the fishing village Thuwal. Interviewees in Saudi Arabia received gift cards worth 100 Saudi riyals (US$27) to popular domestic retailers such as bookstores, cosmetics stores, and supermarkets. Interviewees in Pakistan received gift baskets containing mugs, pens, and chocolates worth around US$10. In both countries, I consulted with my native research assistants and other local acquaintances to offer gifts that would suffice to draw working-class and middle-class respondents to participate but that would not be so impressive that they elicited people to participate just for the gift. (We did encounter two clear cases of gift-seeking interviewees in our Saudi Zoom population who gave cursory responses; their data was not used.) Slightly over half of the Pakistan interviews with customers and the general public were in Urdu, which I do not speak; three-quarters of the Saudi interviews were in Arabic, which I do. The rest were in English.

Conferences, Trainings, Workshops, Visits, Document Analysis, and Ethnographic Observation

Secondarily to interviews, the research for this book included attendance at a wide range of organized events. Toward the beginning of my research, I worked as a summer intern at the Islamic-finance desk of Zaid Ibrahim & Company, a leading Malaysian law firm known for its strength in Islamic finance. There, under the tutelage of Aida Othman, who holds a PhD from Harvard in comparative law and Middle Eastern studies and is one of Malaysia's leading Islamic-finance lawyers, I learned the basic mechanics of Islamic finance as it works in practice. Over subsequent years, I participated in training courses around the world, including several one- and two-day trainings on Islamic contract law and Islamic financial regulation in Kuala Lumpur, a two-day course in London titled "Structuring Innovative Islamic Financial Products," and a three-day course at the Lahore University of Management Sciences that covered the divine economic logic, contracts, state regulation, and risk management (including Islamic derivatives) of Islamic finance, as well as Durham University's weeklong Islamic Finance Summer School, which offered detailed presentations by Islamic-finance practitioners, economists, and shariah scholars.

While interviews were my main research method, I employed others. During visits to over thirty branches of Islamic banks or headquarters and other financial institutions to conduct interviews, I took ethnographic notes on what I saw and heard outside my interviews. In Pakistan, Saudi Arabia, and the United Arab Emirates, my research assistants and I also went "mystery shopping": we pretended to be potential customers for Islamic financial services. This offered insights into banks' sales pitches for Islamic finance, the information they shared with and withheld from customers, and the look and feel of Islamic-bank branches.

I also familiarized myself with the secondary academic and business literature on Islamic finance and read the annual reports of the world's twenty largest Islamic banks. In addition, I supervised three cohorts of undergraduates in a seminar on Islamic finance at Johns Hopkins in analyzing television commercials for Islamic banks from around the world.

To develop a feeling for the breadth of Islamic finance, I visited institutions that lie outside the for-profit Islamic-finance industry. These included a day at the Wasil Foundation, a nonprofit Islamic-microfinance institution in rural Punjab, and a day at Kelantan Golden Trade, a government-sponsored enterprise in Malaysia's Kelantan state that seeks to popularize use of the gold dinar and silver dirham in Malaysia. To get a feel for Islamic education in Pakistan, I toured two of the country's best-known madrasahs for a day each: Darul Uloom Karachi and Jamia Binoria Aalamiya Karachi, spending a day at each. I was also given a private tour of a museum chronicling the life of Mohammed Alsubeaei, founder of one of Saudi Arabia's leading Islamic banks. Although details from these visits did not make it into this book, they strengthened my appreciation for the diverse visions of an Islamic financial system that Muslims around the world have brought to life.

NOTES

Preface

1. All names of consultants in this preface are pseudonyms.

2. During the age of stability in American banking—from the 1950s through the 1970s—American bankers spoke of the "3-6-3 rule": take deposits at 3 percent, lend at 6 percent, and be on the golf course by 3:00 p.m.

3. Compound annual growth rate. Pronounced "CAG-err."

4. Abderrahmane enounced "Emirati" as it is pronounced in Arabic: *imārātī*. Perhaps the latter sounds more Prada-esque.

5. As Gellner (1983) does.

6. After 2008, I directed these neurons' owners to Ibrahim Warde's *The Price of Fear: The Truth behind the Financial War on Terror* (2008), which dismantled any imagined associations between Islamic finance and terrorism.

7. The amygdala is a brain region responsible for fear and anxiety.

8. Said 1979.

Introduction

1. A genre called *nashīd*.

2. Shariah scholars are also known as muftis, maulvis, mullahs, maulanas, Islamic jurists (*fuqahā᾽*), *'ulamā᾽ al-sharī'ah* (literally "shariah scholars"), and sometimes simply "sheikhs" (*shuyūkh*).

3. This book will usually use terms like "internationally elite" and "global elite" instead of "rock stars." Despite the book's opening, celebrity is not what makes the internationally elite scholars essential to the commercial success of Islamic finance. Rather, their celebrity stems from their central position in transnational networks of capital (see Pollard and Samers 2013) and their role in certifying cross-border transactions (see chapter 4 of this book). On the geography and interlocking networks of the international scholarly elite, see Bassens, Derudder, and Witlox 2012; Cuypers et al. 2020; Gözübüyük, Kock, and Ünal 2020; Hasan 2015; Kok and Shahgolian 2023; Poon et al. 2017; and Ünal 2010.

4. Davies and Sleiman 2012.

5. There is a vast corpus of literature on *makhārij* and *ḥiyal*. Ḥawfānī 2023 treats these topics as they relate to Islamic finance.

6. Mahira (pseudonym), conversation with author, 20 April 2017.

7. Hawala (*ḥawālah*) has nothing to do with the Islamic-finance industry. It is a simple, unregulated technique for transferring money without any money physically changing hands.

8. Asutay 2012; El-Gamal 2006a; Pitluck 2012, 2016; Yousef 2004.

9. Roth 2007. Healy and Krawiec (2017) call on social scientists to explore how state and organizational actors manage repugnant transactions and the availability of repugnance-management tools—a mission this book pursues.

10. 2:275 ("aḥalla-l-lāhu-l-bayʿa wa-ḥarrama-l-ribā").

11. Unsecured loans are not backed by collateral; secured loans are.

12. Pitluck 2012.

13. Nousheen Imran (Premium Customer Relationship Manager, Meezan Bank), conversation with author, 14 April 2017.

14. See Maurer 2006, 2011; Tripp 2006.

15. *Fiqh al-muʿāmalāt.*

16. Ahmed 2018; Emon 2018b; Doumani 2006; Haj 2009; Johansen 1999, 2006; Vogel 2000; Zaman 2002.

17. Arabi 1998; Heck 2006; Labib 1969; Udovitch 1979, 1985; Vogel and Hayes 1998.

18. Ünal 2010.

19. Does shariah permit organ transplants (Hamdy 2012) or engineering the human genome? What does it say about oncofertility (Ahmed 2010)? Do forbidden food additives remain forbidden if we change their chemical structure? See, inter alia, the rulings of the International Islamic Fiqh Academy of the Organization of Islamic Cooperation.

20. Mitchell 2019; Spencer 1968.

21. Bowler 2013; García 2014.

22. Electronic record of prices at which investors will buy and sell. Pardo-Guerra 2019.

23. The *heter iska* (see chapter 2).

24. *Zauber.*

25. Max Weber's oeuvre is the locus classicus on enchantment and disenchantment. See, inter alia, Weber 1958b, 1958d. For critiques and reconceptualizations, see Horkheimer and Adorno 1947; Jenkins 2000; Josephson-Storm 2017; Schluchter 2017; Turner 2011.

26. Berger 1967.

27. On enchanted modernities, see Deeb 2006 and Morello 2021.

28. S. S. (anonymous), conversation with author, 13 September 2013.

29. Sukuk, sometimes called Islamic bonds, are technically not bonds because they represent the right to proceeds from an asset, not an interest-bearing loan. In practice, they are structured to behave very much like bonds.

30. Arabic for "all finished."

31. Nizam Yaquby, conversation with author, 2 November 2009.

32. Takaful (*takāful*).

33. Excluding Russia.

34. Calculations available from author upon request.

35. The GCC comprises Bahrain, Kuwait, Oman, Qatar, Saudi Arabia, and the United Arab Emirates.

36. McCormick and Kruger 2009.

37. Graeber 2011.

38. Biswas 2023.

39. Hanson 2023.

40. Ahmed 2018.

41. Kurzman 2002.

42. Ahmed 2018, 93.

43. Zaman 2002.

44. Royal Islamic Strategic Studies Centre 2018.

45. El-Gamal 2006a; Farooq 2007; Galloux 1999; Khalil and Thomas 2006; Mallat 1996; Nomani 2006; Skovgaard-Petersen 1997; Tripp 2006; Warde 2010.

46. Bourdieu 1990, 53.

47. E.g., Krippner 2011.

48. Arrighi 1994.

49. Arrighi 2004; Harvey 1982.

50. Suchman 1995.

51. Suchman 1995.

52. I thank Fulya Apaydın for this formulation.

53. Ali Hamdan Al Raisi, conversation with author, 15 December 2014.

54. Pistor 2019.

55. The Muslim ummah (*ummat al-islām*) is the community of all the world's Muslims.

56. Doumani 2006; Johansen 1999, 2006.

57. Ahmed 2018; McMillen 2007; Michael J. T. McMillen, conversation with author, 13 February 2013; Samuel Hayes, conversation with author, 17 November 2008.

58. Lytton 2013.

59. Bartley 2018.

60. Apaydın 2018, 2021; Asutay 2013; Henry and Wilson 2004; Lai 2015; Tobin 2020.

61. Wittgenstein 1998, 2009.

62. I thank Sarah Quinn for this formulation.

Chapter 1

1. Ghosh and Shetty 2007.

2. *Al-akhlāq.*

3. Saeed bin Ahmad Al Lootah, conversation with author, 18 December 2013.

4. Saeed bin Ahmad Al Lootah, conversation with author, 18 December 2013.

5. Sheikh Mohammed bin Rashid Al Maktoum, formally ruler of Dubai since 2006 but de facto ruler and the driving force behind the emirate's development since the 1990s.

6. Z/Yen and China Development Institute 2022. Dubai also placed #5 worldwide in the "Government & Regulatory" and "Fintech" sub-indexes.

7. Authors who highlight this diversity include Doumani 1995, especially chap. 4; Ghazanfar 2003; Islahi 2015; Joseph 2012; Siddiqi 1981; Tripp 2006; Wilson 1998.

8. Schrank 2022, chap. 5.

9. Hodgson 1974, 75.

10. Asad 1986; Aydin 2017.

11. See Gellner 1983 on "Muslim society" as sui generis.

12. Ahmed 2016, 105–9.

13. Mawdudi 1984; Pollard and Samers 2007; al-Ṣadr 1977; Tripp 2006.

14. Muslim intellectuals of the late nineteenth and early twentieth centuries who sought to understand why Islamicate societies seemed less commercially, financially, and scientifically advanced—and less politically and spatially orderly—than Western European ones. Islamic modernists viewed Western modernity as both a challenge and an inspiration. They therefore hoped to rejuvenate Islamic civilization (as they understood it) by embracing values such as rationality, science, constitutionalism, mass Western-style education, and women's rights; expressing them in Islamic idioms; and demonstrating their inherent consonance with Islam (Kurzman 2002).

15. Riḍā 1970, 84–86 (Fatwa #33: "Ṣundūq al-tawfīr fī idārat al-barīd wa-bayān ḥikmat taḥrīm al-ribā" (The postal savings fund and an elucidation of the rationale for the prohibition of *ribā*).

16. Mallat 1996, 286.

17. *Ḥikmah.*

18. "Izālat . . . al-ẓulm wa-l-muḥāfaẓat ʿalá faḍīlat al-tarāḥum wa-l-taʿāwun."

19. Riḍā 1970, 85.

20. Rose 2010, 68.

21. Rahardjo 1988, 139.

22. Ḥarb 1911.

23. Davis 1983, 53, 86, 98.

24. *Al-Jarīdah al-Rasmīyah* (1972), Laws 74 and 86.

25. Mayer 1979 on lotteries; Oliver 2014 on wagering.

26. Mayer 1979, 551.

27. Harris 2010, 2017.

28. Musso 2017; Stiansen 1999, 2004.

29. Al-Najjar 1987; Galloux 1999; Tripp 2006; Warde 2010.

30. El-Ashker 1987; Mayer 1985.

31. Warde 2010.

32. Kahf 2004, 20.

33. Kahf 2004, 20.

34. Galloux 1997, 22–23.

35. Schönenbach and Klöwer 2014, 27.

36. Henry 1996, 259.

37. Schönenbach and Klöwer 2014, 27.

38. Kahf 2004, 19.

39. Roff 1998, 222.

40. Kahf 2004, 18, 20.

41. Islamic Research and Training Institute 1995.

42. Tripp 2006, 136–37.

43. Hertog 2016.

44. Yergin 1993.

45. Hertog 2011.

46. Beblawi and Luciani 1987.

47. Amuzegar 1982, 819.

48. Peterson 2007, 28.

49. Ulrichsen 2015, 13–15.

50. Presley and Wilson 1991, 1.

51. Presley and Wilson 1991, 1.

52. Arrighi 2004; Harvey 1982.

53. Lubin 2018, 28.

54. Cassim Docrat, conversation with author, 13 November 2012.

55. Henry 1996; Tripp 2006; Warde 2010.

56. Hanieh 2011, 57–84.

57. Wilson 1983, 80.

58. Riba. Saeed bin Ahmad Al Lootah, conversation with author, 18 December 2013.

59. Saeed bin Ahmad Al Lootah, conversation with author, 18 December 2013.

60. Al-Dukheil 1995, 172–78; Wilson 1991, 93–97.

61. Prince Amr bin Mohammed Al Faisal Al Saud, conversation with author, 6 July 2020.

62. Prince Amr bin Mohammed Al Faisal Al Saud, conversation with author, 6 July 2020.

63. al-Ghulayqah 2007.

64. Wilson 1991, 186–88.

65. bin Bāz 1992/1993.

66. Kahf 2004, 23.

67. Kahf 2004.

68. Schönenbach and Klöwer 2014, 30; Galloux 1999, 484.

69. Waterbury 1985, 70.

70. Saeed 1995, 29.

71. Saeed 1995, 29.

72. Saeed 1995, 30.

73. Al-Najjar 1984, 1987.

74. Abdulkader S. Thomas, conversation with author, 7 December 2009; Abdulkader S. Thomas, correspondence with author, 20 November 2023.

75. Abdulkader S. Thomas, conversation with author, 7 December 2009; Abdulkader S. Thomas, correspondence with author, 20 November 2023.

76. Al-Ṣadr 1977, 1982; Siddiqi 1983, 1985; Chapra 1992.

77. Homoud 1985, 194–242, 246–55.

78. Nienhaus 1986, 10.

79. Nienhaus 1986, 4–5.

80. Wilson 1983, 80, 84.

81. Habib Ahmed, conversation with author, 4 July 2013.

82. Nienhaus 1983; Sarker 1999; for a contrasting view, see Ul Haque and Mirakhor 1986.

83. Akerlof 1970.

84. Jalaluddin 2007, 64.

85. Prince Amr bin Mohammed Al Faisal Al Saud, conversation with author, 6 July 2020.

86. Sulaiman Al Harthy, conversation with author, 15 December 2014.

87. Cronqvist and Nilsson 2005.

88. Iqbal and Mirakhor 1987, 25.

89. Sarker 1999.

90. Dar and Presley 2000, 5.

91. Bashir 1990.

92. Khan 1989, 28.

93. Bashir 1990.

94. Saeed bin Ahmed Al Lootah, conversation with author, 18 December 2013; Mohammed Ibrahim, conversation with author, 2 June 2013.

95. Al-Najjar 1986, 6.

96. Quoted in Abdul Alim 2014, 51.

97. Saeed 1995.

98. Saeed 1995.

99. Smith 2004, 173.

100. Mohamed Ali Elgari, conversation with author, 24 August 2019.

101. As per AAOIFI standards.

102. Hassan Jivraj, conversation with author, 12 June 2019; Hassan Jivraj, correspondence with author, 22 November 2023.

103. Fahad Ibrahim Alshathri, conversation with author, 27 August 2019.

104. Abdul Alim 2014, 29.

105. Abdul Alim 2014.

106. Smith 2004.

107. Wilson 1983, 91.

108. Smith 2004, 175–76.

109. Smith 2004, 175–76.

110. Sajid Siddiqui, conversation with author, 25 October 2016.

111. His works published in English Romanize his name as "Homoud," but others, such as Maali and Napier (2010), write "Hamoud." Short vowels in Arabic are usually unwritten, and pronunciation can vary.

112. Malley 2004, 192.

113. Maali and Napier 2010, 97.

114. Maali and Napier 2010 (unpublished draft of "Accounting, Religion, and Organisational Culture"), 7.

115. Maali and Napier 2010, 98–104.

116. Sultan and Ebrahim 2011, 2.

117. Abdul Alim 2014.

118. Hasan 2011, 318.

119. Fourcade et al. 2013, 602.

120. *Fuqahā'*.

121. *'Ulamā'*.

122. *Lā yumkin*.

123. *Sharṭ*.

124. Yusuf DeLorenzo, conversation with author, 10 August 2020.

125. Yusuf DeLorenzo, conversation with author, 10 August 2020.

126. Spiro 1999.

127. Muzammil Kasbati, conversation with author, 29 May 2017.

128. Zulkifli Hasan, conversation with author, 31 October 2014.

129. Stella Cox, conversation with author, 5 November 2013.

130. Stella Cox, conversation with author, 5 November 2013.

131. Stella Cox, conversation with author, 5 November 2013.

132. Samir Abid Shaikh, conversation with author, 29 July 2020.

133. Kahf 2002; author conversation with Prince Amr bin Mohammed Al Faisal Al Saud, 6 July 2020.

134. "Dato' Dr Abdul Halim Ismail," https://www.merdekaaward.my/the-award/past -recipients/education-community/dato-dr-abdul-halim-ismail.

135. Chapra 1985.

136. Ismail 1986.

137. Ismail 2002.

138. Al-Ghazālī (1058–1111 CE) described the protection of religion (*dīn*), life (*nafs*), intellect ('*aql*), progeny (*nasl*), and property (*māl*) as the public benefit (*maṣlaḥah*) guaranteed by shariah, and hence as shariah's higher objective (*maqṣad*, pl. *maqāṣid*). In the Ghazālian view, anything necessary to preserve or, in some cases, improve these five protected things falls within the higher objectives of shariah (*maqāṣid al-sharī'ah*); anything that harms them should be averted by shariah. Yet al-Ghazālī restricted the application of the maqasid doctrine to situations in which scriptural sources and analogical reasoning (*qiyās*) did not provide clear answers. He also required that to qualify as falling within this protected class of elements, something must be clearly derivable by analogy from an existing ruling supported by scripture. Since the nineteenth century, many reformers have used the maqasid concept more expansively and liberally, such as to assert that shariah guarantees human rights and women's rights. In the financial context, some have mobilized the concept to justify patronizing conventional finance, and others interest simulation.

139. Kitamura 2020, 88–89.

140. Kitamura 2020, 87–88.

141. Kitamura 2020, 90–91.

142. Warde 2010, 82.

143. Rudnyckyj 2017b, 274–76.

144. Rosly and Sanusi 2001.

145. Nagaoka 2007, 78–80.

146. Rudnyckyj 2019, 175–76.

147. Kahf 2004.

148. Babic 2023; Braunstein 2019; Ewers et al. 2018; Hanieh 2018, 2020a, 2020b; Kamrava 2020; Mogielnicki 2021; Qanas and Sawyer 2022; Seznec and Mosis 2019; Ulrichsen 2016, 103–29; Young 2014.

149. Arrighi 1994.

150. Hanieh 2020b.

151. Krippner 2011.

152. Bartley 2011.

153. Smith and Fischlein 2010.

154. Smith and Fischlein 2010; Silverman and Baum 2002.

Chapter 2

1. Quinn 2019, 1.
2. Asutay 2012; Ahmed 2004.
3. Choudhury and Abdul Malik 1992.
4. Asutay 2012; see Siddiqi 2006.
5. Shaikh, Ismail, and Shafiai 2017.
6. Abd Wahab and Abdul Rahman 2011.
7. Siddiqi 2004.
8. An Islamic endowment of property held in trust to be used for educational, religious, or charitable purposes. The property is typically a building or plot of land, but it can even be cash. Moral economists assert that the waqf can serve developmental purposes.
9. Marzban, Asutay, and Boseli 2014.
10. Baaquie, Bacha, and Abdul Hamid 2016.
11. Lie 1997, 346–47.
12. Stephens 2018.
13. al-Ghazali 2003, 184.
14. Beverley 2015.
15. Stephens 2018, 161.
16. Hamidullah 1955, 78.
17. Islahi 2014a, 35.
18. Hamidullah 1936.
19. Hamidullah 1936.
20. Stephens 2018, 156.
21. Silver and Arrighi 2003.
22. Mandaville 2007, 96.
23. Esposito 1999.
24. Mandaville 2007, 96.
25. Lapidus 1997, 447.
26. Chaudhuri 1985, 210–11; Kuran 2011, 48–62; Udovitch 1970.
27. Chapra 1992, 2000; Siddiqi 1981; Ahmad 1979; Naqvi 1981, 1994; see Asutay 2012, 94–95.
28. Asutay 2012; Ahmed 2016.
29. Haron 1996.
30. Bilkis Ismail, presentation at Durham Islamic Finance Summer School, 3 July 2013.
31. Usmani 2002, 12–13.
32. Siddiqi 1981; Anwar and Saeed 1987; Ariff 1988; El-Hawary, Grais, and Iqbal 2007; Iqbal and Mirakhor 2007; Khan 1986.
33. Diamond and Dybvig 1983.
34. Khan 1987; Ahmed 2002; Cihak and Hesse 2008.
35. Wright 2010.
36. *Mā naqdar nu 'akkid.*
37. Suad AlBibi, conversation with sales representative at Sharjah Islamic Bank, 20 November 2019.
38. Khan 2003, 46, 45.
39. Abdel Karim and Archer 2013; Grais and Pellegrini 2006; Htay and Syed 2013; Pitluck 2012; Sundararajan 2008; Taktak, Zouari, and Boudriga 2010; Taktak 2011; Wilson 2007.
40. Sayd Farook, conversation with author, 21 November 2013. See also Farook, Hassan, and Clinch 2012; Ismail and Be Lay 2002; Shahimi, Ismail, and Ahmad 2006; Sundararajan 2008; Taktak, Zouari, and Boudriga 2010; Zoubi and Al-Khazali 2007.
41. Hameed 2006.
42. E.g., Siddiqui 2012, 40–41.

43. Pervez Nasim, conversation with author, 7 January 2020.

44. Pervez Nasim, presentation at UFANA Conference Toronto, 30 March 2010 (recording accessed on YouTube).

45. Wright 2010.

46. Pervez Nasim, conversation with author, 15 January 2020.

47. I use the words *faqīh* and *fuqahā'* to refer generally to experts in *fiqh*. However, two caveats are in order. First, there are others—such as judges (*quḍāh*, singular *qāḍī*) and lawyers—who have significant knowledge of Islamic law (shariah) and jurisprudence but who may not have the credentials requisite for qualification as a *faqīh*. Second, there are multiple terms used to refer to experts in Islamic law and jurisprudence. A *faqīh* is an expert in *fiqh* (jurisprudence), whereas a *muftī* is a legal expert capable of *iftā'* (the issuance of *fatāwá* [singular *fatwá*], i.e., Islamic legal opinions). In many historical settings, there has been overlap between the meanings of the terms *faqīh* and *muftī*. Today, the waters are muddied by the fact that convention varies across world regions and some governments appoint state muftis. Also, it is rare to hear someone call herself or himself a *faqīh*, but others may use it as a deferential term.

Another still higher qualification is *mujtahid*, which is a religious jurist capable of *ijtihād*, i.e., creative independent judgment in a legal and theological question by application of *uṣūl al-fiqh*, or the principles of jurisprudence (the study of these constitutes a scholarly field in itself). *Ijtihād* is the establishment of new precedent and new legal thought. The term *muqallid* refers to someone who, in explicit contrast to a *mujtahid*, adheres to and applies the preexisting legal traditions of a school of jurisprudence.

48. Aquinas 1922.

49. Aquinas 1922, ST IIa–IIæ, Q. 78, Art. 2. By "justice," Aquinas means not distributive (i.e., social) justice but commutative (i.e., transactional) justice.

50. Al Zuhayli 2006, 25.

51. Aristotle 2010, 17.

52. Aquinas 1922, ST IIa–IIæ, Q. 78, Art. 1. Aquinas asserts here that money can be paid "only on account of something . . . that has been received, as . . . in buying and selling."

53. Ghazanfar 2003, 37. Al-Ghazālī evocatively writes that "in relation to other goods, dirhams and dinars [i.e., money] are like prepositions in a sentence—used to give proper meaning to words; or like a mirror reflecting colors but having no color of its own."

54. Neusner 1990.

55. Polanyi 2001, 71–79.

56. Usmani 2002, 77.

57. Usmani 2002, 12.

58. *Ẓulm*. Asif Iftikhar, conversation with author, 11 April 2017.

59. 2:279.

60. Aristotle, *Nicomachean Ethics*, V.1, 1129a–1134b.

61. Asif Iftikhar, conversation with author, 21 October 2016.

62. "Paisay ke paisa."

63. Anam (pseudonym), conversation with author, 19 April 2017.

64. "Baghair miḥnat muft men mil rahā hai." Hamza (pseudonym), conversation with author, 20 April 2017.

65. Zain (pseudonym), conversation with author, 21 April 2017.

66. Calder 2016, 246.

67. Roth 2007; Rossman 2014.

68. Weber 1978, 577.

69. Weber 1978, 587.

70. Noonan 1957; Wood 2002; Schumpeter 1954, 73–142; Neusner 1990; Ghazanfar 1991; Islahi 2014a.

71. Moosa 1998, 18.

72. Zelizer 1979.

73. MacKenzie 2006, 143–78.

74. Steensland 2010; see also Fourcade and Healy 2013.

75. Tawney 1998; Schumpeter 1954; Noonan 1957; see Bentham 2014.

76. Humayon Dar, conversation with author, 22 October 2013.

77. Al-Amine 2008; Bacha 1999; Dusuki 2009; Kamali 2007.

78. Sultan Al Nugali, conversation with author, 18 August 2019.

79. Richard Tredgett, conversation with author, 6 November 2013.

80. In late medieval and early modern Eastern Christendom, debates over usury were less acute and less universally negative than in the Latin West (Laiou 2003, 210).

81. For only then will the jurist's words have a proper climate in which to be appreciated. Witte 2002, 119.

82. Luther 1966 (1519–21), 213.

83. Tawney 1998; Nelson 1949.

84. Bentham 2014.

85. Hollander 1999.

86. Nonetheless, usury continued to be a charged issue for three centuries after Calvin, particularly as credit markets spread (Hawkes 2010; Valeri 1997).

87. Zimmermann 1996, 824–33; Matthews 1921.

88. Noonan 1957, 100–132.

89. Noonan 1957, 351.

90. Ramsey 2014.

91. Hill 2017.

92. Bowler 2013.

93. Looft 2014.

94. Su, Yan, and Harvey 2022.

95. SEI Catholic Values Funds, LKCM Aquinas Funds, Epiphany Funds.

96. Commerzbank Globale Aktien Katholische Werte Fonds.

97. Calculation from fund financials; available upon request.

98. Meislin and Cohen 1964. Historians have offered various explanations. Weber made a millitary-religious argument (1950, 267–68).

99. Gamoran 2008; Cohen 1950.

100. See, e.g., Soloveitchik 1970.

101. In a *heter iska*, the active partner ("borrower") effectively guarantees that the silent partner ("lender") will receive her investment principal back in full, plus an expected rate of profit (say 5 percent). Claiming a loss or a lower profit rate than expected is virtually impossible for the silent partner, requiring "complete documentation and halachically valid witnesses" (Orlian 2009).

102. Mudaraba savings accounts and term deposits typically advertise what looks like a fixed rate of return ("expected profit rate"), though they do not technically guarantee the principal or the rate of return.

103. Katz 2000, 55–58.

104. *Heter iska klali.*

105. Reisman 1995, 415–18.

106. Banks inside and outside Israel serving Orthodox Jews do sometimes draw up specialized *heter iska* contracts for particular transactions.

107. Marx 1992.

108. Hawkes 2010; Le Goff 1998.

109. Wherry 2012.

110. Wyrtzen 2020, 899.

111. Calder 2016.

Chapter 3

1. Hasan Faraz, personal communication, 23 September 2019.
2. 2:275 (Yusuf Ali trans.).
3. Sunan al-Nasā'ī 4455.
4. E.g., DeLorenzo 2006, 1.
5. Calder 2016.
6. Abū Dā'ūd 1996 (855/856 CE): Ḥadīth 3503 (Bk. 24, H. 88).
7. Saleh 1986, 85.
8. Rushd 1988; see Rittenberg 2014, 145.
9. 5:90, "min ʿamali al-shayṭāni"; see also 2:219.
10. Edbiz Consulting 2012, 76.
11. El-Gamal 2006a; Kuran 2005.
12. Calculation available upon request.
13. Bartley 2018, 176–80.
14. Ponte 2019; Eberlein et al. 2014, 11–12.
15. Mukund Bhatnagar, conversation with author, 17 August 2020.
16. Rifaat Ahmed Abdel Karim, presentation at Euromoney Qatar Conference, Doha, 10 December 2013. The IILM Corporation is a consortium of central banks and multilateral development institutions that aims to help Islamic financial institutions manage liquidity. It issues short-term shariah-compliant instruments denominated in major reserve currencies such as the U.S. dollar.
17. Mukund Bhatnagar, conversation with author, 17 August 2020.
18. Mukund Bhatnagar, conversation with author, 17 August 2020.
19. Including Bank AlJazira (Saudi Arabia; converted 1998–2002), National Bank of Sharjah (UAE; converted into Sharjah Islamic Bank in 2002), Dubai Bank (UAE; converted 2006–8), and Ahli United Bank (Kuwait; converted 2010).
20. National Commercial Bank (Saudi Arabia, announced conversion process in 2014).
21. Kuwait, Qatar, and Bahrain likewise show little change among incumbent banks, a spread of Islamic offerings, and the rise of Islamic banks in their top six.
22. Sultan Al Nugali, conversation with author, 18 August 2019.
23. Syarizal Rahim, conversation with author, 3 September 2020.
24. As in Malaysia and Bahrain, notes Muzammil Kasbati of Ernst & Young (conversation with author, 29 May 2017).
25. "The challenge of building a liquid market for domestic sukuk lies in generating a reliable secondary market," remarked Ayman Mohammed Alsayari, deputy governor of the Saudi Central Bank. This is difficult because Islamic banks and other Islamic financial institutions tend to buy and hold high-quality instruments. Ayman Mohammed Alsayari, conversation with author, 27 August 2019.
26. Eyal 2019.

Chapter 4

1. Weber 1978, 31–33.
2. Weber 1978, 36–38.
3. Weber 1978, 32.
4. Johnson, Dowd, and Ridgeway 2006, 57.
5. Dezalay and Garth 2016, 191.
6. Ahmed 2018, 93.
7. Zaman 2002.
8. Royal Islamic Strategic Studies Centre 2018.

9. Najeem (pseudonym), conversation with author's research assistant, 13 April 2017.

10. *Aslāf*.

11. DeLorenzo 2014.

12. Messick 1993; Hallaq 1984; Asad 1986; Zaman 2002; Zeghal 1996.

13. Moon and Wotipka 2006, 121.

14. Zeghal 2024 (quote from pre-publication overview).

15. Securities Commission Malaysia 2009.

16. State Bank of Pakistan 2004.

17. Badr Albadran of Al Rajhi Bank, correspondence with author, 14 February 2014.

18. Mohamed Ali Elgari, conversation with author, 24 August 2019.

19. Mohamed Ali Elgari, conversation with author, 24 August 2019.

20. Zulkifli Hasan, conversation with author, 31 October 2014.

21. Esam Ishaq, conversation with author, 23 November 2016.

22. Muhammad Imran Usmani, conversation with author, 28 October 2016.

23. Mohamed Ali Elgari, conversation with author, 25 August 2019.

24. Nizam Yaquby, conversation with author, 2 November 2009.

25. Esam Ishaq, conversation with author, 23 November 2016.

26. Adam 2023.

27. Daud Bakar 2017, 2019a, 2019b.

28. Daud Bakar 2017.

29. Sloane-White 2017, 4.

30. Peletz 2020.

31. Fischer 2016.

32. Nasr 2009.

33. Atia 2013; Awass 2019; Rudnyckyj 2010, 2017a, 2017b; Hefner 2012; Hoesterey 2015; Mohamad and Saravanamuttu 2015; Poon, Pollard, and Chow 2018; Samers 2015; Tobin 2016, 2020; Tuğal 2009; Adaş 2003.

34. Suchman 1995.

35. Ercanbrack 2020.

36. Suchman 1995, 579–82.

37. Kahf 2004; Prince Amr bin Mohammed Al Faisal Al Saud, conversation with author, 6 July 2020.

38. Prince Amr bin Mohammed Al Faisal Al Saud, conversation with author, 6 July 2020.

39. Calder 2020.

40. See Fourcade 2011.

41. Altaf (pseudonym), conversation with author's research assistant, 18 April 2017.

42. Eskandar Shah, conversation with author, 24 November 2016.

43. Small- and medium-sized enterprises.

44. See Schrank 2021 on how being self-interested versus publicly minded can affect the likelihood that governance agents will join transnational networks.

45. Salah (pseudonym), conversation with author, 19 August 2019.

46. Salah noted that a few of his Saudi customers wanted to know what Islamic contracts his banks used to structure their products—a characteristic of the Saudi market, where laypersons know more Islamic law on average than they do anywhere else (see chapter 7).

47. Muhammad Ehtisham, conversation with author, 14 April 2017.

48. Mukund Bhatnagar, conversation with author, 17 August 2020.

49. Paul McViety, conversation with author, 19 December 2013.

50. Burt 1995, 2004.

51. Suchman 1995.

52. Dezalay and Garth 1996.

53. Burt, Reagans, and Volvovsky 2021.

54. Ünal 2011.

55. Davies and Sleiman 2012.

56. Zelizer 2005, 2012.

57. See, inter alia, Bandelj 2012, 2020; Bandelj and Gibson 2019; Wherry 2016, 2017; Wherry, Seefeldt, and Alvarez 2019.

58. Schrank 2021.

Chapter 5

1. Rossman 2014.

2. On this type of reflexive economic consideration, see Rudnyckyj 2014.

3. Weber 1978, 819–20.

4. Schacht 1964, 70–71; Anderson 1976, 7; Gibb 1947, 13.

5. Hallaq 1984; Johansen 1999, 2006; Doumani 2006.

6. Turner 2010, 163.

7. Weber 1978, 821.

8. Crone 1999.

9. Cuno 2006; Doumani 2006.

10. Pirbhai 2008.

11. Kugle 2001.

12. Senturk 2007.

13. Behdad 1994.

14. Johansen 1999, 38–40, 65–66.

15. 2:275.

16. 2:173.

17. *Inshallah.*

18. Mohamad Daud Bakar, panel discussion, Kuala Lumpur Islamic Finance Forum, 21 November 2016.

19. Usman (pseudonym), conversation with author, 12 December 2013.

20. Zeeshan Ahmed, conversation with author, 30 October 2016.

21. "Innamā al-ʿilmu ʿindanā al-rukhṣatu min thiqatin fa-ammā al-tashdīdu fa-yuḥsinuhu kullu aḥadin."

22. "Yurīdu allāhu bi-kumu al-yusra wa-lā yurīdu bi-kumu al-ʿusra," 2:185.

23. Yusuf Talal DeLorenzo, conversation with author, 10 August 2020.

24. *Al-kutub al-ṣafrāʾ.*

25. *Ṭalāq.*

26. *Buyūʾ.*

27. *Fiqh al-muʿāmalāt.*

28. Nizam Yaquby, conversation with author, 2 November 2009.

29. Waterbury 2020, 131.

30. Aziz Ur Rehman, conversation with author, 16 December 2013.

31. *Muḍārib.*

32. *Rabb ul-māl.*

33. Zeeshan Ahmed, conversation with author, 31 October 2016.

34. Yusuf DeLorenzo, conversation with author, 10 August 2020.

35. Aziz Ur Rehman, conversation with author, 16 December 2013.

36. Zeeshan Ahmed, conversation with author, 30 October 2016.

37. Zeeshan Ahmed, conversation with author, 30 October 2016.

38. Irshad Ahmad Aijaz, conversation with author, 27 October 2016.

39. Hassan Jivraj, conversation with author, 7 January 2020.

40. Ashruff Jamall, conversation with author, 31 May 2017.

41. *Hibah.*

42. "SBP Directive: Islamic Banking Industry Required to Stop Offering 'Special Hiba,'" *Business Recorder* (Karachi), 6 January 2015.

43. The practice of Islamic legal institutions borrowing from, and patterning themselves after, secular ones is not unique to Islamic finance. Michael Peletz (2020, 26–30) shows that in recent decades, Malaysia's Islamic courts have come to rely more on written evidence and less on oral testimony, emphasized written precedent more because of the proliferation of English-language Islamic-law publications, grown more adversarial, and patterned their sartorial norms after those of Malaysia's civil courts.

44. Hassan Jivraj, correspondence with author, 8 November 2020.

45. Irshad Ahmad Aijaz, conversation with author, 27 October 2016.

46. Emon 2006.

47. Weber 1978, 819–20.

48. Hallaq 1984; Iqbal 1986.

49. Fadel 1996.

50. Jackson 1996.

51. Emon 2018a.

52. Abou El Fadl 2001; Emon 2006.

53. Coulson 1964, 202–17.

54. See Zaman 2012.

55. Mohammad Hashim Kamali, conversation with author, 25 November 2016.

56. Mohammad Hashim Kamali, correspondence with author, 24 November 2023.

57. Baaquie 2023; Bacha and Mirakhor 2018; Manzoor, Karimirizi, and Mostafavisani 2017; Mohamed and Mobin 2020.

58. Mohammad Hashim Kamali, conversation with author, 25 November 2016.

59. Lee 2019.

60. Al-Shāṭibī 1999, pt. 2, chap. 8.

61. "Al-ḍarūrāt tubīḥ al-maḥẓūrāt."

62. Al-Shāṭibī 1999, pt. 2, chap. 11.

63. See Quran 2:185, inter alia.

64. Zeeshan Ahmed, conversation with author, 30 October 2016.

65. Ghosh and Shetty 2007.

66. Dar 2021.

67. Shaharuddin et al. 2020.

68. Shaharuddin et al. 2020, 43.

69. Shaharuddin et al. 2020, 43.

70. Ibrahim 2015, particularly 178–81.

71. Masud 2009, 88.

72. Ahmed 2018, 50–52, 114.

73. Ahmed 2018, 50–52; Balchin 2009, 220; Rahman 1970, 326.

74. Hegazy 2007, 600.

75. Hegazy 2007, 601.

76. Hegazy 2007, 601.

77. Mansoori 2011, 404.

78. Mansoori 2011, 403.

79. Mansoori 2011, 403.

80. Irshad Ahmad Aijaz, conversation with author, 27 October 2016.

81. ʿIbādāt.

82. *Madhhab.*

83. Esam Ishaq, conversation with author, 23 November 2016.
84. Irshad Ahmad Aijaz, conversation with author, 27 October 2016.
85. "Illā ʿind al-ḥājah al-muliḥḥah." AAOIFI 2017, 207 (Std. 8, §3/1/3) (italics added).
86. Asad 1986; Masud 2009.
87. Yusuf DeLorenzo, conversation with author, 10 August 2020.
88. Yusuf DeLorenzo, conversation with author, 10 August 2020.
89. De Roover 1967, 258–59.
90. "Al-aṣl fī al-ashyāʾ al-ibāḥah."
91. Kamali 1999.
92. Nizam Yaquby, conversation with author, 2 November 2009.
93. Y. J., presentation at Structuring Innovative Islamic Financial Products course in London, 14 September 2013.
94. Irshad Ahmad Aijaz, conversation with author, 27 October 2016.
95. Esam Ishaq, conversation with author, 23 November 2016.
96. Hussein Hamid Hassan, Q&A after his presentation, Durham Islamic Finance Summer School, 1 July 2013.
97. Weber 1978, 1186.
98. See Ercanbrack 2015, 129–35.
99. Doumani 2006; Ahmed 2018.
100. Rushdi Siddiqui, conversation with author, 23 September 2013.
101. Dato' Mohammad Faiz Azmi, conversation with author, 6 September 2020.
102. Irfan 2014, 248.
103. Khnifer 2011.
104. El Baltaji 2011.
105. Irfan 2014, 251.
106. Irfan 2014, 250–51.
107. Irfan 2014, 251–52.
108. Irfan 2014, 246.
109. al-Bīshī 2012, author's translation.
110. Ercanbrack 2020.

Chapter 6

1. Goldstein 2018.
2. Muhammad Waseem Bari, conversation with author, 18 April 2017.
3. Marx and Engels 1978, 475.
4. F. I. (anonymous), conversation with author, 25 August 2019.
5. Quoted in McBain 2012.
6. Polanyi 2001.
7. Carruthers 2017.
8. Irfan 2014.
9. DeLorenzo 2007.
10. Yusuf DeLorenzo, conversation with author, 10 August 2020.
11. Yusuf DeLorenzo, conversation with author, 10 August 2020.
12. Stanton 2008.
13. DeLorenzo 2007.
14. Yusuf DeLorenzo, conversation with author, 10 August 2020.
15. Usmani 2007.
16. Mohamed Damak, conversation with author, 18 June 2017.
17. Atif Hanif, conversation with author, 6 November 2013.
18. Pauly 2009.

19. Paul McViety, conversation with author, 19 December 2013.

20. Parker 2017.

21. Usmani 2007.

22. Usmani 2007.

23. Usmani 2007, 7.

24. Usmani 2007, 8.

25. Usmani 2007, 8.

26. Usmani 2007, 8.

27. "Maqāṣid al-ʿuqūd." Sheikh Osaid Kailani, conversation with author, 8 June 2016.

28. Usmani 2007, 12–13.

29. Usmani 2007, 14.

30. Usmani 2007, 14.

31. Agency contract. The party with cash (*muwakkil*, the principal) deposits it with an agent (*wakīl*), who invests the funds in a pool of assets and then returns the profits to the principal, less a fee taken by the agent.

32. Power 1997; Strathern 2000.

33. Bilal (pseudonym), conversation with author, 12 December 2016.

34. Shoaib (pseudonym), conversation with author, 16 December 2013.

35. Members of the Faysal Bank Shariah Audit department at Karachi head office, conversation with author, 1 November 2016.

36. Members of the Faysal Bank Shariah Audit department at Karachi head office, conversation with author, 1 November 2016.

37. Yasser Dahlawi, conversation with author, 10 August 2020.

38. Yasser Dahlawi, conversation with author, 10 August 2020.

39. H. S., conversation with author, 7 December 2013.

40. Yasser Dahlawi, conversation with author, 10 August 2020.

41. Weber 1969, 7.

42. Nizam Yaquby, panel discussion at the Kuala Lumpur Islamic Finance Forum, 25 September 2013.

43. Esam Ishaq, panel discussion at the Kuala Lumpur Islamic Finance Forum, 25 September 2013.

44. Edbiz Consulting 2016, 300.

45. Vizcaino 2012.

46. Khan 2010.

47. "Al-kharāju bi-l-ḍamān."

48. Siddiqi 2007.

49. Obiyathulla Ismath Bacha, conversation with author, 22 November 2016.

50. Mahmoud El-Gamal, presentation at Harvard University Forum on Islamic Finance, Cambridge, MA, 26 April 2014.

51. El-Gamal 2006a.

52. Mahmoud El-Gamal, presentation at Harvard University Forum on Islamic Finance, Cambridge, MA, 26 April 2014.

53. Kahf and Habbani 2016.

54. Quoted in Liau 2010.

55. Zulkifli Hasan, conversation with author, 31 October 2014.

56. Al-Zuhayli 2006.

57. Al-Zuhayli 2006.

58. *Daʿwah*.

59. Shamsul Akmal Ahmad, conversation with author, 1 December 2016; Shamsul Akmal Ahmad, correspondence with author, 26 November 2023.

60. Anonymous conversation with author, 2016 (date withheld).

61. Islamic International Rating Agency 2021, 26.

62. Emirates Islamic Bank 2006, 36.

63. Esam Ishaq, panel discussion at the Kuala Lumpur Islamic Finance Forum, 21 November 2016.

64. Al-Shalhoob, n.d.; Al-Zuhaili, n.d.

65. Calder 2010.

66. Dubai Financial Services Authority 2019.

67. Stella Cox, conversation with author, 5 November 2013.

68. Mohammad Ali Qayyum, conversation with author, 25 October 2013.

69. Anonymous conversation with author, 7 December 2013.

70. Esam Ishaq, panel discussion at the Kuala Lumpur Islamic Finance Forum, 21 November 2016.

71. Hasan Faraz, conversation with author, 28 October 2016.

72. Usmani 2009, 25–26.

73. Lee 2011.

74. Dusuki 2010.

75. Muhammad Hasanan Yunus, conversation with author, 1 December 2016.

76. Lee 2011.

77. Shamsul Akmal Ahmad, conversation with author, 1 December 2016.

78. Paul Boots, conversation with author, 19 November 2013.

79. Paul Boots, conversation with author, 19 November 2013.

80. Paul Boots, conversation with author, 19 November 2013.

81. Nathaniel Armstrong, conversation with author, 7 April 2022.

82. Hassan Jivraj, correspondence with author, 13 December 2023; Shoaib (pseudonym), conversation with author, 16 December 2013; F. I. (anonymous), conversation with author, 25 August 2019.

83. Yusuf DeLorenzo, conversation with author, 10 August 2020.

Chapter 7

1. "Jamāʿat-e Islāmī kā mehengāʾī" 2019.

2. Al-Muṭlaq 2019.

3. CNN Arabic 2018; Al-Dānī 2018.

4. "Mithl alladhīna yalʿabūna al-qimār wa-l-maysir."

5. Apaydın 2018, 2021; Baskan and Wright 2011; Henry and Wilson 2004; Lai 2015; Lai and Samers 2017; Rethel 2010, 2018; Rudnyckyj 2013, 2019; Warde 2004; Wilson 2002a, 2011, 2015; Yousef 2004.

6. Buckley and Hanieh 2014; Calder 2019, 2022; Cham 2018; Seznec and Mosis 2019; Warde 2010; Wilson 1983.

7. Baskan 2004; Nomani and Rahnema 1994; Soliman 2004; Smith 2004; Stiansen 2004; Wilson 1983.

8. Ercanbrack 2015.

9. Nasr 2009.

10. Hanieh 2020a, 2020b; Wilson 1983.

11. Hoggarth 2016; Kuran 1997a; Pollard and Samers 2007; Wilson 2015.

12. Warde 2008, 2010.

13. Sloane-White 2017.

14. Abdul Alim 2014; Kitamura 2020, 2021; Seznec and Mosis 2019.

15. Çizakça 2011.

16. "State Bank ne sharaḥ sūd baṛhā dī."

17. Kazi 2017.

18. "Sūd ek laʿnat hai."

19. Sumayyah (pseudonym), conversation with author's research assistant, 26 May 2021.

20. Tabish (pseudonym), conversation with author, 20 April 2017.

21. Shafqat (pseudonym), conversation with author, 18 April 2017.

22. Shafqat (pseudonym), conversation with author, 18 April 2017.

23. Shakir (pseudonym), conversation with author, 20 April 2017.

24. Rona-Tas and Guseva 2018, 68.

25. Muhannad (pseudonym), conversation with author, 21 July 2020.

26. "Akhdh māl muqābil māl bi-ziyādah." Raha (pseudonym), conversation with author's research assistant, 30 May 2021.

27. "Paisa ke paisa." Pervez (pseudonym), conversation with author, 12 April 2017.

28. Rasheed (pseudonym), conversation with author, 19 April 2017.

29. Abdulaziz (pseudonym), conversation with author, 28 July 2020.

30. Amru (pseudonym), conversation with author, 29 May 2021.

31. Muneer (pseudonym), conversation with author, 23 May 2021.

32. Ministry of Education of Saudi Arabia 2020a, 130–32.

33. Ministry of Education of Saudi Arabia 2020b, 41.

34. Ministry of Education of Saudi Arabia 2020b, 32, 41, 47, 54, 250.

35. Ministry of Education of Saudi Arabia 2020b, 54.

36. Ministry of Education of Saudi Arabia 2020b, 68, see chap. 5.

37. Ministry of Education of Saudi Arabia 2020b, 40.

38. Ministry of Education of Saudi Arabia 2020a, 129.

39. Jamaldeen and Friedman 2012.

40. Muhammad (pseudonym), conversation with author's research assistant, 17 June 2021.

41. Abdul Muhsin (pseudonym), conversation with author's research assistant, 20 May 2021. Hadith source: Jāmiʿ al-Tirmidhī 1206 (14/3).

42. Sumayyah (pseudonym), conversation with author's research assistant, 26 May 2021.

43. Sarfraz (pseudonym), conversation with author's research assistant, 12 April 2017.

44. Tabish (pseudonym), conversation with author, 20 April 2017.

45. Ramiz (pseudonym), conversation with author, 12 April 2017.

46. Sanam (pseudonym), conversation with author, 21 April 2017.

47. Shozab (pseudonym), conversation with author, 13 April 2017.

48. Saqib (pseudonym), conversation with author, 12 April 2017.

49. Tabish (pseudonym), conversation with author, 20 April 2017.

50. Nawaz (pseudonym), conversation with author, 20 April 2017.

51. Ashfaq (pseudonym), conversation with author, 18 April 2017.

52. Amina (pseudonym), conversation with author's research assistant, 18 April 2017.

53. Syed Muhammad (pseudonym), conversation with author's research assistant, 13 April 2017.

54. Le Goff 1998; Hawkes 2010; Graeber 2011.

55. Ali Amir (pseudonym), conversation with author's research assistant, 20 April 2017.

56. "Miḥnat kar ke kamāʾūn."

57. Chiragh (pseudonym), conversation with author, 20 April 2017.

58. Faiza (pseudonym), conversation with author, 21 April 2017.

59. Faris Almaari, conversation with author, 20 October 2021.

60. Misbah Aamir and Zaid Ansari, conversation with author, 16 July 2021.

61. Abbasi 2014.

62. Mukhtar 2018, 38.

63. Al-Zahrvi et al. 2014, 73.

64. Qurʾān 2:278; Rahman and Khan 2020, 51.

65. Akram and Choudhary 2016, 64.

66. Hashmi et al. 2018, 86.

67. Akram and Choudhary 2016, 145.

68. Akram and Choudhary 2016, 238.

69. Pakistan Bureau of Statistics 2022.

70. Shirazi et al. 2016.

71. Chapra 2004; Islahi 2015b; Kuran 1995, 1996, 1997a; Mawdudi 2011; Nasr 1996, 103–5; Zaman 2021.

72. "Ṣāf suthrā aur istiḥṣāl se pāk muʿāsharah."

73. Mukhtar 2018, 38.

74. Askari and Naheed 2012, 8.

75. Khatoon and Sanya 2020, 11.

76. Akram and Choudhary 2016, 227–28.

77. Muhammad (pseudonym), conversation with author's research assistant, 17 June 2021.

78. "Idhā inta tadhallalta li-shakhṣ."

79. Abdulaziz (pseudonym), conversation with author, 28 July 2020.

80. LUMS Center for Islamic Finance training seminar, Lahore, 14 October 2016.

81. Imtiaz Ul Haq, conversation with author, 19 October 2016.

82. Sadia (pseudonym), conversation with author's research assistant, 21 April 2017.

83. Kainat (pseudonym), conversation with author's research assistant, 20 April 2017.

84. Roshana (pseudonym), conversation with author, 19 April 2017.

85. Bandar (pseudonym), conversation with author, 11 July 2021.

86. Adnan (pseudonym), conversation with author, 20 April 2017.

87. Agha (pseudonym), conversation with author's research assistant, 13 April 2017.

88. Dars-e Nizami is an eight-year curriculum of study in Islamic sciences with roots in eighteenth-century South Asia and specific to the Ḥanafī school of jurisprudence. Shaheen is using the term as a broad synonym for shariah scholarship in the South Asian context.

89. Shaheen (pseudonym), conversation with author, 18 April 2017.

90. Arshad (pseudonym), conversation with author, 13 April 2017. "Islamic jurist" is a translation here for maulvi.

91. Nasreen (pseudonym), conversation with author, 19 April 2017.

92. Baloch (1990–2016), celebrated by some Pakistani and international activists as a feminist icon (Khoja-Moolji 2022), was strangled to death by her brother in a so-called "honor killing."

93. Nasreen (pseudonym), conversation with author, 19 April 2017. The SBP is the State Bank of Pakistan.

94. Khurram (pseudonym), conversation with author, 20 April 2017. The SBP is the Securities and Exchange Commission of Pakistan.

95. US$1,200–1,300 in 2009, when Iqbal met the security guard.

96. Urdu: chaudharī.

97. Shahid Iqbal, conversation with author, 4 November 2016.

98. Weber 1958b.

99. Atia 2013, 1–5. In the rest of her book Building a House in Heaven, Atia demonstrates how, despite leading Egyptian shariah scholars' failure to support Islamic banking and finance, "pious neoliberalism" has flourished in Egypt via charities that redefine the "deserving poor."

100. Hawkes 2010.

101. "Allāhumma qanniʿnī bi-mā razaqtanī."

102. Muhammad Naeem, conversation with author, 6 November 2016.

103. Ghias 2013.

104. Not to be confused with Mufti Naeem's madrassah Jamia Binoria Aalamia.

105. Ghias 2013.

106. Bill 1984.

107. Hallaq 2009, 355–550.
108. Brown 2017.
109. Al-Rasheed 2007, 22–58.
110. Nizam Yaquby, personal communication, 4 November 2009.
111. Prokop 2003, 78.
112. Roy 2004, 93.
113. Commins 2012, 134–56; Macris 2015.
114. "Al-milk al-fardī wa-l-jamāʿī."
115. "Bi-l-ṭuruq al-ḥakīmah."
116. bin Bāz 2004/2005, 340, my translation.
117. Muslim World League Islamic Fiqh Council 2007, 51–52.
118. bin Bāz 2004/2005, 43.
119. Shaikh 2009.
120. Jalal 2014.
121. Shaikh 2008, 596.
122. Mawdudi 1960, 1984.
123. Nasr 1994.
124. Nasr 1994, 191.
125. Nasr 1994, 193.
126. Kennedy 1990, 63.
127. Kennedy 2004, 102.
128. Kennedy 2004, 101–2.
129. Nasr 1994, 191.
130. Council of Islamic Ideology 1980.
131. Kennedy 2004, 102; Janjua 2003.
132. Khan and Mirakhor 1990, 366.
133. Looney 1996.
134. Council of Islamic Ideology 1980.
135. Ahmed 1987.
136. Zaidi 1987.
137. M. S. Mufti, personal communication, 25 October 2016.
138. Khan 2008.
139. Evans 1986.
140. Evans 1986.
141. Evans 1986.
142. Ahmed Ali Siddiqui, conversation with author, 28 October 2016.
143. Evans 1986.
144. Kennedy 2004, 108.
145. Gargan 1992; Kennedy 2004, 107–8; Warde 2010, 117.
146. Mahmood-ur-Rahman Faisal v. Secretary, Ministry of Law and Others, 44 PLD 1 Federal Shariat Court (Pakistan) (1992, para. 255).
147. Seznec and Mosis 2019, 20–21.
148. Jean-François Seznec, conversation with author, 26 July 2019.
149. Saudi Arabia's central bank was known as the Saudi Arabian Monetary Authority (SAMA) from its establishment in 1952 until 2020, when its official name changed to the Saudi Central Bank.
150. Wilson 1991, 36–44.
151. Jean-François Seznec, conversation with author, 26 July 2019.
152. Seznec and Mosis 2019, 21–22.
153. Peterson 2018, 18–19.
154. Alsubeaei and Heck 2010, 99.

155. Wilson 1991, 95.

156. Abdulaziz and Nasser Alsubeaei, conversation with author, 26 August 2019.

157. Chaudhry 1997.

158. Mackie 1982.

159. See Seznec and Mosis 2019, 21.

160. Mouline 2014, 174.

161. Seznec and Mosis 2019, 21.

162. Jean-François Seznec, conversation with author, 26 July 2019.

163. Khan 2015, 121.

164. Khan 2015, 122–23.

165. Warde 2010, 118.

166. Janjua 2004.

167. Chaudhry 1997.

168. M. Aslam Khaki v. Syed Muhammad Hashim and 2 others, PLD 2000 SC 225 Supreme Court (Pakistan), Shariat Appellate Bench 2000.

169. Bilal (pseudonym), personal communication with author, 12 April 2017.

170. Mushtak Parker, conversation with author, 14 November 2013.

171. Ahmed Abdulkarim Alkholifey, conversation with author, 27 August 2019.

172. When I asked the governor if he considered the Saudi Islamic-banking sector's heavy reliance on organized tawarruq to be a problem, he replied, "No, from a regulatory point of view, I don't. Some critics probably say it's not the *real* tawarruq. But it's a perfect fit for retail." Ahmed Abdulkarim Alkholifey, conversation with author, 27 August 2019.

173. Apaydın 2018, 2021; Rethel 2018; Rudnyckyj 2013, 2019.

Conclusion

1. Ercanbrack 2015.

2. Wittgenstein 1998, 74, MS 136 16b: 21.12.1947.

3. El-Gamal 2000; Ghazanfar 2003; Islahi 2014a; Tripp 2006.

4. Wittgenstein 2009.

5. Das 1998.

6. Bourdieu 1977.

7. Ahmed 2018.

8. E.g., Schacht 1964.

9. Ahmed 2018, 57–59.

10. One of the special subset of hadiths that enjoy elevated status because Muslims attribute their content to God but their wording to the Prophet Muhammad. A *ḥadīth qudsī* therefore enjoys intermediate status between the Quran, which is the revealed word of God, and "ordinary" hadiths, whose content and wording are both attributed to the Prophet.

11. Suchman 1995, 582; italics in original.

12. Rudnyckyj 2014.

13. Wittgenstein 2009.

14. There are thought-provoking parallels between the way this type of effortful self-discipline and study lead to the formation of new types of piety in Islamic finance and, as examined by Lynne Gerber (2011), in evangelical Christian programs for weight loss and sexual reorientation. I thank Damon Mayrl for this insight.

15. Muhammad Aftab Athar, conversation with author, 18 April 2017.

16. The Karachi Interbank Offered Rate.

17. The State Bank of Pakistan.

18. Ni Putu Desinthya, conversation with author, 8 July 2023.

19. Jepperson 1991, 147.

20. Edgell, Miller, and Frost 2023.

21. Winchester 2008, 1754.

22. Sheikh Osaid Kailani, conversation with author, 8 June 2016.

23. Chazi and Syed 2010.

24. Al-Roubaie 2009.

25. Alrifai 2015.

26. Vogel and Hayes 1998.

27. Samuel Hayes, conversation with author, 17 November 2008.

28. Blake Goud, conversation with author, 19 October 2020.

29. Abdul-Muhmin 2008, 195.

30. Fligstein 2021, chaps. 4 and 8.

31. Mizruchi 2013.

32. Eyal 2019, 104–29.

33. Berger 1967, 129.

34. Charles Tripp (2006) leans in this direction after an erudite series of reflections on Islamic theorization about the economy through the nineteenth and twentieth centuries.

35. Polanyi 2001.

36. Casanova 1980.

37. Reynolds 2015.

38. Zelizer 1979, 1981.

39. Guhin 2014.

40. Rudnyckyj 2010.

41. Hill 2017.

42. Martí 2010.

43. Bowler 2013.

44. Hefner 2017, 269.

45. Hefner 2017, 265–73.

46. Gorski and Altınordu 2008.

47. Asad 1986, 7. I apply Asad's conceptualization of Islam as a discursive tradition to fiqh.

48. Zaman 2002, 2012; Zeghal 1996, 2013, 2024.

49. Abu-Lughod 1989; Salvatore 2021; see also Shaikh 2008.

50. Turner 2010.

51. See chapter 1.

52. Babb and Kentikelenis 2021, 533–34.

53. Nasr 2009, 14.

54. Bayat 2005.

55. Khan 2015.

56. Majid Pireh (secretary of shariah committee of the Iranian Securities and Exchange Organization), conversation with the author, 30 November 2019.

57. Tuğal 2009.

58. Davie 1994.

59. Bartley 2011, 446.

60. Durkheim 1984; Power 1997; Schluchter 2017; Vogel 1996; Weber 1958a, 209–39; Weber 1969.

61. Carruthers 2020, 151.

62. Hallaq 2012; see especially p. 152.

63. Alexander 2002; Asad 2011; Bellah 1967.

64. Asad 2003, 2011; Hurd 2015; Mahmood 2016.

65. Taylor 2007, 3.

66. Steve Bertamini served as CEO of Saudi Arabia's Al Rajhi Bank from 2015 to 2019.

Methodological Appendix

1. Six of the expert interviews were conducted on my behalf by research assistants who were in-country when I was not: four with Islamic-bank branch managers or deputy branch managers in Saudi Arabia, and two with Islamic-bank branch managers in the United Arab Emirates.

2. Also known as muftis, maulvis, mullahs, *fuqahā'*, and *'ulamā' al-sharī'ah*.

3. Saldaña 2009.

BIBLIOGRAPHY

Abbasi, Manzoor Ahmed. "Towards a De-Radicalization of Pakistani Society: The Need for a Balanced and Progressive Education System." *The Dialogue* 9, no. 3 (2014): 257–70.

Abd Wahab, Norazlina, and Abdul Rahim Abdul Rahman. "A Framework to Analyse the Efficiency and Governance of Zakat Institutions." *Journal of Islamic Accounting and Business Research* 2, no. 1 (2011): 43–62.

Abdel Karim, Rifaat Ahmed, and Simon Archer. *Islamic Finance: The New Regulatory Challenge*. Singapore: Wiley, 2013.

Abdul Alim, Emmy. *Global Leaders in Islamic Finance: Industry Milestones and Reflections*. Singapore: Wiley, 2014.

Abdul-Muhmin, Alhassan G. "Consumer Attitudes towards Debt in an Islamic Country: Managing a Conflict between Religious Tradition and Modernity?" *International Journal of Consumer Studies* 32, no. 3 (2008): 194–203.

Abdul-Rahman, Yahia. *The Art of Islamic Banking and Finance: Tools and Techniques for Community-Based Banking*. New York: Wiley, 2010.

Abou El Fadl, Khaled. *Speaking in God's Name: Islamic Law, Authority and Women*. Oxford: Oneworld, 2001.

Abū Dā'ūd, Sulaymān. *Sunan Abī Dā'ūd*. Beirut: Dār al-Kutub al-'Ilmīyah, 1996.

Abu-Lughod, Janet L. *Before European Hegemony: The World System A.D. 1250–1350*. New York: Oxford University Press, 1989.

"Accidental Deaths & Suicides in India" (2020 data). New Delhi: National Crime Records Bureau, Ministry of Home Affairs, Government of India, 2021.

Accounting and Auditing Organization for Islamic Financial Institutions (AAOIFI). *Shari'ah Standards*. Manama, Bahrain: Accounting and Auditing Organization for Islamic Financial Institutions, 2017.

Adam, Faraz. "Zakat in the World of Web3." Directed by IBF Net Group. YouTube, 2023. https://www.youtube.com/watch?v=PJj7OJWUpgc.

Adaş, Emin Baki. *Profit and the Prophet*. Urbana: University of Illinois Press, 2003.

Ahmad, Khurshid. *Economic Development in an Islamic Framework*. Leicester: Islamic Foundation, 1979.

Ahmad Tajudin Abdul Rahman. *Workings of an Islamic Bank: Case Study of Bank Islam Malaysia Berhad*. Kuala Lumpur: Bank Islam Malaysia, 2000.

Ahmed, Habib. "Maqāṣid al-Sharī'ah and Islamic Financial Products: A Framework for Assessment." *ISRA International Journal of Islamic Finance* 3, no. 1 (2011): 149–60.

———. *A Microeconomic Model of an Islamic Bank*. Jeddah: Islamic Research and Training Institute, 2002.

———. *Role of Zakāh and Awqāf in Poverty Alleviation*. Jeddah: Islamic Development Bank Group and Islamic Research & Training Institute, 2004.

Ahmed, Habib, and Nourah Mohammad Aleshaikh. "Debate on 'Tawarruq': Historical Discourse and Current Rulings." *Arab Law Quarterly* 28, no. 3 (2014): 278–94.

Ahmed, Rumee. "Sacred Bodies: Considering Resistance to Oncofertility in Muslim Communities." In *Oncofertility: Ethical, Legal, Social, and Medical Perspectives*, ed. Teresa K. Woodruff, Laurie Zoloth, Lisa Campo-Engelstein, and Sarah Rodriguez, 279–86. Boston: Springer US, 2010.

———. *Sharia Compliant: A User's Guide to Hacking Islamic Law*. Stanford: Stanford University Press, 2018.

Ahmed, Shahab. *What Is Islam? The Importance of Being Islamic*. Princeton: Princeton University Press, 2016.

Ahmed, Z. "Interest-Free Banking." *Journal of Islamic Banking and Finance* 4, no. 1 (1987): 8–30.

Akerlof, George. "The Market for 'Lemons': Quality Uncertainty and the Market Mechanism." *Quarterly Journal of Economics* 84, no. 3 (1970): 488–500.

Akram, Mian Muhammed, and Mehmood Ahmed Choudhary. *Economics* (12th Standard). Lahore: Punjab Curriculum and Textbook Board, 2016.

Alexander, Jeffrey C. "On the Social Construction of Moral Universals." *European Journal of Social Theory* 5, no. 1 (2002): 5–85.

Alrifai, Tariq. *Islamic Finance and the New Financial System: An Ethical Approach to Preventing Future Financial Crises*. Hoboken, NJ: Wiley, 2015.

Alsubeaei, Huda, and Gene W. Heck. *Mohammed Alsubeaei: A Journey of Poverty and Wealth*. Newport, Isle of Wight: Medina Publishing, 2010.

al-Tirmidhī, Muḥammad ibn ʿĪsá. *Jāmiʿ al-Tirmidhī*. Medina, Saudi Arabia: al-Maktabat al-Salafīyah, 1965.

Alvi, Ijlal Ahmed, Ahmed Rufai Mohammed, Ghazal Zahid Khan, Usman Mohammad Naseer, Babar Naseer, Mohammad Saqib Khan, and Sayyed Zarrar. *Sukuk Report: A Comprehensive Study of the International Sukuk Market*. Manama, Bahrain: International Islamic Financial Market, 2011.

Amengual, Matthew, and Tim Bartley. "Global Markets, Corporate Assurances, and the Legitimacy of State Intervention: Perceptions of Distant Labor and Environmental Problems." *American Sociological Review* 87, no. 3 (2022): 383–414.

Amine, Muhammad al-Bashir Muhammad al-. *Risk Management in Islamic Finance: An Analysis of Derivatives Instruments in Commodity Markets*. Leiden: Brill, 2008.

Amuzegar, Jahangir. "Oil Wealth: A Very Mixed Blessing." *Foreign Affairs* 60, no. 4 (1982): 814–35.

Anderson, J.N.D. *Law Reform in the Muslim World*. University of London Legal Series. Vol. 11. London: Athlone Press, 1976.

Anwar, Muhammad, and Mohammed Saeed. "Reorganization of Islamic Banking: A New Proposal." *American Journal of Islamic Social Sciences* 4, no. 2 (1987): 295–304.

Apaydın, Fulya. "Financialization and the Push for Non-State Social Service Provision: Philanthropic Activities of Islamic and Conventional Banks in Turkey." *Forum for Development Studies* 42, no. 3 (2015): 441–65.

———. "Governing Islamic Finance in the Muslim World." In *Civilization and Governance: The Western and Non-Western World*, ed. Boy Luethje, 175–92. Singapore: World Scientific, 2022.

———. "Islamic Finance and Development in Malaysia." In *The Oxford Handbook of Politics in Muslim Societies*, ed. M. Cammett and P. Jones. New York: Oxford University Press, 2021.

———. "Regulating Islamic Banks in Authoritarian Settings: Malaysia and the United Arab Emirates in Comparative Perspective." *Regulation & Governance* 12, no. 4 (2018): 466–85.

Aquinas, Thomas. *The Summa Theologica of St. Thomas Aquinas*. New York: Benziger Bros, 1922.

Arabi, Oussama. "Contract Stipulations (Shurūṭ) in Islamic Law: The Ottoman Majalla and Ibn Taymiyya." *International Journal of Middle East Studies* 30, no. 1 (1998): 29–50.

Ariff, Mohamed. "Islamic Banking." *Asian-Pacific Economic Literature* 2, no. 2 (1988): 48–64.

Aristotle. *The Politics*. Chicago: University of Chicago Press, 2010.

Aristotle, J.A.K. Thomson, Hugh Tredennick, and Jonathan Barnes. *The Nicomachean Ethics*. Rev. ed. London: Penguin Books, 1976.

Arrighi, Giovanni. *The Long Twentieth Century: Money, Power, and the Origins of Our Times*. London: Verso, 1994.

———. "Spatial and Other 'Fixes' of Historical Capitalism." *Journal of World-Systems Research* 10, no. 2 (2004): 527–39.

Arrighi, Giovanni, and Beverly J. Silver. "Capitalism and World (Dis)Order." *Review of International Studies* 27, no. 5 (2001): 257–79.

Arrighi, Giovanni, Beverly J. Silver, and Benjamin D. Brewer. "Industrial Convergence, Globalization, and the Persistence of the North-South Divide." *Studies in Comparative International Development* 38, no. 1 (2003): 3–31.

Asad, Talal. *Formations of the Secular: Christianity, Islam, Modernity*. Stanford: Stanford University Press, 2003.

———. "Freedom of Speech and Religious Limitations." In *Rethinking Secularism*, ed. Craig Calhoun, Mark Juergensmeyer, and Jonathan VanAntwerpen, 282–98. Oxford: Oxford University Press, 2011.

———. *The Idea of an Anthropology of Islam*. Washington, DC: Center for Contemporary Arab Studies, Georgetown University, 1986.

———. "Thinking about Religion through Wittgenstein." *Critical Times* 3, no. 3 (2020): 403–43.

Ashker, Ahmed Abdel-Fattah el-. *The Islamic Business Enterprise*. London: Croom Helm, 1987.

Askari, Hassan, and Nighat Naheed. *Pakistan Studies* (7th Standard). Lahore: Punjab Textbook Board, 2012.

Astor, Avi, and Damon Mayrl. "Culturalized Religion: A Synthetic Review and Agenda for Research." *Journal for the Scientific Study of Religion* 59, no. 2 (2020): 209–26.

Asutay, Mehmet. "Conceptualising and Locating the Social Failure of Islamic Finance: Aspirations of Islamic Moral Economy vs. The Realities of Islamic Finance." *Asian and African Area Studies* 11, no. 2 (2012): 93–113.

———. "The Development of Islamic Banking in Turkey: Regulation, Performance and Political Economy." In *Islamic Finance in Europe: Towards a Plural Financial System*, ed. Valentino Cattelan, 213–27. Cheltenham: Edward Elgar, 2013.

Atia, Mona. *Building a House in Heaven: Pious Neoliberalism and Islamic Charity in Egypt*. Minneapolis: University of Minnesota Press, 2013.

Awass, Omer. "Contending with Capitalism: Fatwas and Neoliberal Ideology." *Journal of World-Systems Research* 25, no. 1 (2019): 145–68.

Aydin, Cemil. *The Idea of the Muslim World*. Cambridge, MA: Harvard University Press, 2017.

Baaquie, Belal Ehsan. "Bonds with Index-Linked Stochastic Coupons in Quantum Finance." *Physica A: Statistical Mechanics and Its Applications* 499 (2018): 148–69.

———. "Sukuk with Index-Linked Coupons and Hedging: Case Study of Petronas." *World Scientific Annual Review of Islamic Finance* 01 (2023): 87–105.

Baaquie, Belal Ehsan, Obiyathulla Ismath Bacha, and Baharom Abdul Hamid. "Why Commodity-Linked Sukuks Should Be Introduced." *Asian Investor*, 28 September 2016. https://www.asianinvestor.net/article/why-commodity-linked-sukuks-should-be-introduced/430071.

Babb, Sarah, and Alexander Kentikelenis. "Markets Everywhere: The Washington Consensus and the Sociology of Global Institutional Change." *Annual Review of Sociology* 47, no. 1 (2021): 521–41.

Babic, Milan. "State Capital in a Geoeconomic World: Mapping State-Led Foreign Investment in the Global Political Economy." *Review of International Political Economy* 30, no. 1 (2023): 201–28.

Bacha, Obiyathulla Ismath. "Derivative Instruments and Islamic Finance: Some Thoughts for a Reconsideration." *International Journal of Islamic Financial Services* 1, no. 1 (1999): 9–25.

Bacha, Obiyathulla Ismath, and Abbas Mirakhor. "Funding Development Infrastructure without Leverage: A Risk-Sharing Alternative Using Innovative Sukuk Structures." *World Economy* 41, no. 3 (2018): 752–62.

Balchin, Cassandra. "Family Law in Contemporary Muslim Contexts: Triggers and Strategies for Change." In *Wanted: Equality and Justice in the Muslim Family*, ed. Zainah Anwar, 209–36. Petaling Jaya, Malaysia: Musawah, 2009.

Baltaji, Dana El. "Goldman Sachs Sukuk Row May Dent Industry Lure: Islamic Finance." Bloomberg, 21 December 2011. https://www.bloomberg.com/news/articles/2011-12-20/goldman-sachs-sukuk-row-may-dent-industry-lure-islamic-finance.

Bandelj, Nina. "Relational Work and Economic Sociology." *Politics & Society* 40, no. 2 (2012): 175–201.

———. "Relational Work in the Economy." *Annual Review of Sociology* 46, no. 1 (2020): 251–72.

Bandelj, Nina, Tyler Boston, Julia Elyachar, Julie Kim, Michael McBride, Zaibu Tufail, and James Owen Weatherall. "Morals and Emotions of Money." In *Money Talks: Explaining How Money Really Works*, 39–56. Princeton: Princeton University Press, 2017.

Bandelj, Nina, and Christopher W. Gibson. "Relational Work and Consumption." In *The Oxford Handbook of Consumption*, ed. Frederick F. Wherry and Ian Woodward, 151–66. New York: Oxford University Press, 2019.

Bartley, Tim. "Certification as a Mode of Social Regulation." In *Handbook on the Politics of Regulation*, ed. David Levi-Faur, 441–52. Cheltenham: Edward Elgar, 2011.

———. *Rules without Rights: Land, Labor and Private Authority in the Global Economy*. Oxford: Oxford University Press, 2018.

Bashir, Abdel-Hameed Mohamed. "Profit-Sharing Contracts with Moral Hazard and Adverse Selection." *American Journal of Islamic Social Sciences* 7, no. 3 (1990): 357–83.

Baskan, Birol, and Steven Wright. "Seeds of Change: Comparing State-Religion Relations in Qatar and Saudi Arabia." *Arab Studies Quarterly* 33, no. 2 (2011): 96–111.

Baskan, Filiz. "The Political Economy of Islamic Finance in Turkey: The Role of Fethullah Gülen and Asya Finans." In *The Politics of Islamic Finance*. Edinburgh: Edinburgh University Press, 2004.

Bassens, David, Ben Derudder, and Frank Witlox. "'Gatekeepers' of Islamic Financial Circuits: Analysing Urban Geographies of the Global Shari'a Elite." *Entrepreneurship & Regional Development* 24, no. 5–6 (2012): 337–55.

Bayat, Asef. "Post-Islamism at Large." In *Post-Islamism: The Changing Faces of Political Islam*, ed. Asef Bayat, 3–30. New York: Oxford University Press, 2013.

———. "Radical Religion and the Habitus of the Dispossessed: Does Islamic Militancy Have an Urban Ecology?" *International Journal of Urban and Regional Research* 31, no. 3 (2007): 579–90.

———. "What Is Post-Islamism?" *ISIM Review* 16, no. 1 (2005): 5.

Beblawi, Hazem, and Giacomo Luciani. *The Rentier State*. London: Croom Helm, 1987.

Behdad, Sohrab. "A Disputed Utopia: Islamic Economics in Revolutionary Iran." *Comparative Studies in Society and History* 36, no. 4 (1994): 775–813.

Bellah, Robert N. "Civil Religion in America." *Daedalus* 96, no. 1 (1967): 1–21.

Bentham, Jeremy. *A Defence of Usury*. Cambridge: Cambridge University Press, 2014.

Berger, Peter L. *The Sacred Canopy: Elements of a Sociological Theory of Religion*. New York: Anchor, 1967.

Beverley, Eric Lewis. *Hyderabad, British India, and the World: Muslim Networks and Minor Sovereignty, c. 1850–1950*. Cambridge: Cambridge University Press, 2015.

Bill, James A. "Resurgent Islam in the Persian Gulf." *Foreign Affairs* 63, no. 1 (1984): 108–27.

bin Bāz, ʿAbd al-ʿAzīz bin ʿAbdullāh. "Ḥukm al-bayʿ ilá al-ajal bi-l-taqsīṭ." In *Fatāwá Islāmīyah*, ed. Muḥammad bin ʿAbd al-ʿAzīz al-Musnad. Riyadh: Dār al-Waṭan li-l-Nashr, 1992/1993 (1413 A.H.).

——. *Majmūʿ fatāwá wa-maqālāt mutanawwiʿ, Vol. 1: Al-Tawḥīd wa-mā yataʿalliq bihi*, ed. Muḥammad bin Saʿd al-Shuwayʿir. Riyadh: Dār al-Qāsim, 2004/2005 (1425 A.H.).

Bīshī, Muḥammad al-. "ʿIstiʿānah muzayyafah' bi-asmāʾ ʿulamāʾ Saʿūdiyīn tuhaddid bi-inhiyār aḍkham iṣdār Amrīkī li-l-ṣukūk." *Al-Iqtiṣādīyah*, 18 January 2012.

Biswas, Partha Sarathi. "NCRB Report Shows Farm Suicides on Rise." *Indian Express*, 5 December 2023. https://indianexpress.com/article/cities/pune/ncrb-report-farm-suicides-rise -farm-labourers-covid-9055694/.

Brown, Nathan. *Official Islam in the Arab World: The Contest for Religious Authority*. Washington, DC: Carnegie Endowment for International Peace, 2017.

Bouheraoua, Said, Shamsiah Mohamed, Noor Suhaida Kasri, and Syahida Abdullah. "Shariah Issues in Intangible Assets." *Shariah Journal* 23, no. 2 (2015): 287–324.

Bourdieu, Pierre. *The Logic of Practice*. Trans. Richard Nice. Stanford: Stanford University Press, 1990.

——. *Outline of a Theory of Practice*. Vol. 16. Cambridge: Cambridge University Press, 1977.

Bowler, Kate. *Blessed: A History of the American Prosperity Gospel*. New York: Oxford University Press, 2013.

Braudel, Fernand. *Civilization and Capitalism, 15th–18th Century [Civilisation matérielle, économie et capitalisme]*. Berkeley: University of California Press, 1982.

Braunstein, Juergen. "Domestic Sources of Twenty-First-Century Geopolitics: Domestic Politics and Sovereign Wealth Funds in GCC Economies." *New Political Economy* 24, no. 2 (2019): 197–217.

Buckley, Michelle, and Adam Hanieh. "Diversification by Urbanization: Tracing the Property-Finance Nexus in Dubai and the Gulf." *International Journal of Urban and Regional Research* 38, no. 1 (January 2014): 155–75.

Burt, Ronald S. "Structural Holes and Good Ideas." *American Journal of Sociology* 110, no. 2 (2004): 349–99.

——. *Structural Holes: The Social Structure of Competition*. Cambridge, MA: Harvard University Press, 1995.

Burt, Ronald S., Ray E. Reagans, and Hagay C. Volvovsky. "Network Brokerage and the Perception of Leadership." *Social Networks* 65 (2021): 33–50.

Cabezón, José Ignacio. *Scholasticism*. Albany: State University of New York Press, 1998.

Calder, Ryan. "Before the Boom: Oil Wealth, Shariah Scholars, and the Birth of the Islamic Finance Industry." In *The I. B. Tauris Handbook of Sociology and the Middle East*, ed. Fatma Müge Göçek and Gamze Evcimen, 131–39. London: I. B. Tauris, 2022.

——. "God's Technicians: Religious Jurists and the Usury Ban in Judaism, Christianity, and Islam." *European Journal of Sociology* 57, no. 2 (2016): 207–57.

——. "How Religio-Economic Projects Succeed and Fail: The Field Dynamics of Islamic Finance in the Arab Gulf States and Pakistan, 1975–2018." *Socio-Economic Review* 17, no. 1 (2019): 167–93.

——. "Sharīʿah-Compliant or Sharīʿah-Based? The Changing Ethical Discourse of Islamic Finance." *Arab Law Quarterly* 34 (2020): 1–24.

——. "Short-Selling Replication in Islamic Finance: Innovation and Debate in Malaysia and Beyond." In *Current Issues in Islamic Banking and Finance: Resilience and Stability in the Present System*, ed. Angelo M. Venardos, 277–315. Singapore: World Scientific, 2010.

Calhoun, Craig J., Mark Juergensmeyer, and Jonathan VanAntwerpen. *Rethinking Secularism*. Oxford: Oxford University Press, 2011.

Camara, Mohamed Saliou, Thomas O'Toole, and Janice E. Baker. *Historical Dictionary of Guinea*. 5th ed. Lanham, MD: Scarecrow Press, 2014.

Carruthers, Bruce G. "Financial Decommodification: Risk and the Politics of Valuation in US Banks." In *Policy Shock: Recalibrating Risk and Regulation after Oil Spills, Nuclear Accidents and Financial Crises*, ed. Edward J. Balleisen, Lori S. Bennear, Kimberly D. Krawiec, and Jonathan B. Wiener, 349–70. Cambridge: Cambridge University Press, 2017.

———. "Law, Governance, and Finance." *Theory and Society* 49, no. 2 (2020): 151–64.

Casanova, José. *Public Religions in the Modern World*. Chicago: University of Chicago Press, 1980.

———. "Rethinking Secularization: A Global Comparative Perspective." *Hedgehog Review* 8, no. 1–2 (2006): 7–23.

Cham, Tamsir. "Determinants of Islamic Banking Growth: An Empirical Analysis." *International Journal of Islamic and Middle Eastern Finance and Management* 11, no. 1 (2018): 18–39.

Chapra, Muhammed Umer. *Islam and the Economic Challenge*. Islamic Economics Series. Vol. 17. Leicester: Islamic Foundation, 1992.

———. "Mawlana Mawdūdī's Contribution to Islamic Economics." *Muslim World* 94, no. 2 (2004): 163–80.

———. *Towards a Just Monetary System*. Islamic Economics Series. Vol. 8. Leicester: Islamic Foundation, 1985.

———. "Why Has Islam Prohibited Interest? Rationale behind the Prohibition of Interest." *Review of Islamic Economics* 9 (2000): 5–20.

Chaudhry, Kiren Aziz. *The Price of Wealth: Economies and Institutions in the Middle East*. Ithaca: Cornell University Press, 1997.

Chaudhuri, K. N. *Trade and Civilisation in the Indian Ocean: An Economic History from the Rise of Islam to 1750*. Cambridge: Cambridge University Press, 1985.

Chazi, Abdelaziz, and Lateef A. M. Syed. "Risk Exposure during the Global Financial Crisis: The Case of Islamic Banks." *International Journal of Islamic and Middle Eastern Finance and Management* 3, no. 4 (2010): 321–33.

Choudhury, Masudul Alam, and Uzir Abdul Malik. *The Foundations of Islamic Political Economy*. London: Macmillan, 1992.

Cihak, Martin, and Heiko Hesse. "Islamic Banks and Financial Stability: An Empirical Analysis." IMF Working Papers 2008, no. 016 (2008): A001.

Çizakça, Murat. *Islamic Capitalism and Finance: Origins, Evolution and the Future*. Cheltenham: Edward Elgar, 2011.

CNN Arabic. "ʿAḍū bi-hayʾat ʿulamāʾ il-Saʿūdīyah: Bītkūyin gharar ka-l-qimār lā yadhkul fīhi Muslim." 15 January 2018.

Cohen, Boaz. *Antichresis in Jewish and Roman Law*. New York: Jewish Theological Seminary of America, 1950.

Commins, David. *The Gulf States: A Modern History*. London: Bloomsbury, 2012.

Coulson, N. J. *A History of Islamic Law*. Edinburgh: Edinburgh University Press, 1964.

Council of Islamic Ideology. *Report on the Elimination of Interest from the Economy*. Islamabad: Council of Islamic Ideology, 1980.

Crone, Patricia. "Weber, Islamic Law and the Rise of Capitalism." In *Max Weber and Islam*, ed. Toby E. Huff and Wolfgang Schluchter, 247–72. London: Transaction Books, 1999.

Cronqvist, Henrik, and Mattias Nilsson. "The Choice between Rights Offerings and Private Equity Placements." *Journal of Financial Economics* 78, no. 2 (2005): 375–407.

Cuno, Kenneth M. "Contrat salam et transformations agricoles en basse Égypte à l'époque ottomane." *Annales* 61, no. 4 (2006): 925–40.

Cuypers, Ilya R. P., Gokhan Ertug, John Cantwell, Akbar Zaheer, and Martin Kilduff. "Making Connections: Social Networks in International Business." *Journal of International Business Studies* 51, no. 5 (2020): 714–36.

Dānī, ʿAbdullāh al-. "Al-Manīʿ liʾ ʿUkāẓ': 'Al-bītkūyin' min ḍurūb al-ribā wa-l-qimār." *Okaz*, 3 June 2018.

Dar, Aftab Ahmed. *Pakistan Studies* (10th Standard). Lahore: Gohar Publisher, 2018.

Dar, Humayon A. "Obituary: Sheikh Dr. Hussein Hamid Hassan." *Islamic Economist* (London), October 2021. https://www.islamiceconomist.com/obituary-sheikh-dr-hussein-hamid -hassan-prof-humayon-dar/.

Dar, Humayon A., and John R. Presley. "Lack of Profit Loss Sharing in Islamic Banking: Management and Control Imbalances." *International Journal of Islamic Financial Services* 2, no. 2 (2000): 3–18.

Das, Veena. "Wittgenstein and Anthropology." *Annual Review of Anthropology* 27 (1998): 171–95.

Daud Bakar, Mohammad. *Corporate Matrimony: How to WOO Clients into Long-Term Relationships*. Kuala Lumpur: Amanie Media, 2019a.

———. *I Have 25 Hours a Day: The Smart Way to Create More Time*. Kuala Lumpur: Amanie Media, 2017.

———. *Mindset Is Everything*. Kuala Lumpur: Amanie Media, 2019b.

———. *Shariah Minds in Islamic Finance*. Kuala Lumpur: Amanie Media, 2016.

Davie, Grace. *Religion in Britain since 1945: Believing without Belonging*. Making Contemporary Britain. Oxford: Blackwell, 1994.

Davies, Anjuli, and Mirna Sleiman. "'Rock Star' Scholars a Risk for Islamic Finance." Reuters, 12 February 2012.

Davis, Eric. *Challenging Colonialism: Bank Misr and Egyptian Industrialization, 1920–1941*. Princeton: Princeton University Press, 1983.

de Roover, Raymond. "The Scholastics, Usury, and Foreign Exchange." *Business History Review* 41, no. 3 (1967): 257–71.

Deeb, Lara. *An Enchanted Modern: Gender and Public Piety in Shiʿi Lebanon*. Princeton: Princeton University Press, 2006.

DeLorenzo, Yusuf Talal. "Introduction to Understanding Riba." In *Interest in Islamic Economics: Understanding Riba*, ed. Abdulkader Thomas, 1–9. New York: Routledge, 2006.

———. "The Total Returns Swap and the 'Shariah Conversion Technology' Stratagem." Unpublished paper. 2007. https://www.dinarstandard.com/finance/DeLorenzo.pdf.

———. "Understanding Modern Islamic Finance." Presentation to Irving Masjid (Irving, TX), 23 February 2014.

DePalm, Lindsay J. "The Separation of Economy and Sentiment: A Comparison of How Individuals Perceive Hostile Worlds." *Journal of Cultural Economy* 13, no. 4 (2020): 428–43.

Dezalay, Yves, and Bryant G. Garth. *Dealing in Virtue: International Commercial Arbitration and the Construction of a Transnational Legal Order*. Chicago: University of Chicago Press, 1996.

———. "'Lords of the Dance' as Double Agents: Elite Actors in and around the Legal Field." *Journal of Professions and Organization* 3, no. 2 (2016): 188–206.

Diamond, D. W., and P. H. Dybvig. "Bank Runs, Deposit Insurance, and Liquidity." *Journal of Political Economy* 91 (1983): 401–19.

Donnelly, John Patrick. *Calvinism and Scholasticism in Vermigli's Doctrine of Man and Grace*. Leiden: Brill, 1976.

Doumani, Beshara. "Le contrat salam et les relations ville-campagne dans la Palestine ottomane." *Annales* 61, no. 4 (2006): 901–24.

———. *Rediscovering Palestine: Merchants and Peasants in Jabal Nablus, 1700–1900*. Berkeley: University of California Press, 1995.

Dubai Financial Services Authority. "DFSA Takes Action to Protect the Integrity of Islamic Finance." 23 April 2019. https://www.difc.ae/newsroom/news/dfsa-takes-action-protect -integrity-islamic-finance/.

Dukheil, Abdulaziz M. al-. *The Banking System and Its Performance in Saudi Arabia*. London: Saqi Books, 1995.

Durkheim, Emile. *The Division of Labor in Society*. Trans. W. D. Halls. New York: Free Press, 1984.

———. *The Elementary Forms of Religious Life*. Trans. Karen E. Fields. New York: Free Press, 1995.

Dusuki, Asyraf Wajdi. "Can Bursa Malaysia's Suq al-Sila' (Commodity Murabahah House) Resolve the Controversy over Tawarruq?" ISRA Research Paper no. 10. Kuala Lumpur, 2010.

———. "Shari'ah Parameters on the Islamic Foreign Exchange Swap as a Hedging Mechanism in Islamic Finance." *ISRA International Journal of Islamic Finance* 1, no. 1 (2009): 77–99.

Eberlein, Burkard, Kenneth W. Abbott, Julia Black, Errol Meidinger, and Stepan Wood. "Transnational Business Governance Interactions: Conceptualization and Framework for Analysis." *Regulation & Governance* 8, no. 1 (2014): 1–21.

Ecklund, Elaine Howard. *Religion vs. Science: What Religious People Really Think*. New York: Oxford University Press, 2017.

———. *Science vs. Religion*. Oxford: Oxford University Press, 2010.

Edbiz Consulting. *Global Islamic Finance Report 2012*. London: Cambridge Institute of Islamic Finance, 2012.

———. *Global Islamic Finance Report 2016*. London: Cambridge Institute of Islamic Finance, 2016.

Edgell, Penny, Mahala Miller, and Jacqui Frost. "What Makes Life Meaningful? Combinations of Meaningful Commitments among Nonreligious and Religious Americans." *Sociology of Religion* 84, no. 4 (2023): 426–46.

"Elenco degli istituti finanziari islamici." *Oriente Moderno* 7 (68), no. 1/9 (1988): 405–8.

Emirates Islamic Bank. *Annual Report 2006*. Emirates Islamic Bank, 2006.

Emon, Anver M. "Conceiving Islamic Law in a Pluralist Society: History, Politics and Multicultural Jurisprudence." *Singapore Journal of Legal Studies* (December 2006): 331–55.

———. "Ijtihad." In *The Oxford Handbook of Islamic Law*, ed. Anver M. Emon and Rumee Ahmed, 181–206. Oxford: Oxford University Press, 2018a.

———. "Islamic Law and Finance." In *The Oxford Handbook of Islamic Law*, ed. Anver M. Emon and Rumee Ahmed, 843–60. Oxford: Oxford University Press, 2018b.

———. *Religious Pluralism and Islamic Law: Dhimmīs and Others in the Empire of Law*. Oxford: Oxford University Press, 2012.

Emon, Anver M., and Rumee Ahmed. "On Reading Fiqh." In *The Oxford Handbook of Islamic Law*, ed. Anver M. Emon and Rumee Ahmed, 45–73. Oxford: Oxford University Press, 2018.

Ercanbrack, Jonathan. "The Standardization of Islamic Financial Law: Lawmaking in Modern Financial Markets." *American Journal of Comparative Law* 67, no. 4 (2020): 825–60.

———. *The Transformation of Islamic Law in Global Financial Markets*. Cambridge: Cambridge University Press, 2015.

Ernst & Young. *Banking in Emerging Markets: GCC FinTech Play 2017*. ey.com. EYGM, 2017.

Esposito, John L. "Contemporary Islam: Reformation or Revolution?" In *The Oxford History of Islam*, ed. John L. Esposito, 643–90. Oxford: Oxford University Press, 1999.

Evans, Richard. "Pakistan's Interest-Free-Banking Law Is Still Adjusting to the Profit Motive." *Christian Science Monitor*, 13 March 1986.

Ewers, Michael C., Ryan Dicce, Jesse P. H. Poon, Jeffery Chow, and Justin Gengler. "Creating and Sustaining Islamic Financial Centers: Bahrain in the Wake of Financial and Political Crises." *Urban Geography* 39, no. 1 (2018): 3–25.

Eyal, Gil. *The Crisis of Expertise*. Cambridge: Polity, 2019.

Fadel, Mohammad. "The Social Logic of Taqlīd and the Rise of the Mukhataṣar." *Islamic Law and Society* 3, no. 2 (1996): 193–233.

Farook, Sayd, M. Kabir Hassan, and Gregory Clinch. "Profit Distribution Management by Islamic Banks: An Empirical Investigation." *Quarterly Review of Economics and Finance* 52, no. 3 (2012): 333–47.

Farooq, Mohammad Omar. "The Riba-Interest Equivalence: Is There an Ijma (Consensus)?" *Transnational Dispute Management* 4, no. 5 (2007). https://www.transnational-dispute -management.com/article.asp?key=1063.

Fischer, Johan. *Islam, Standards, and Technoscience in Global Halal Zones.* New York: Routledge, 2016.

Fligstein, Neil. *The Banks Did It: An Anatomy of the Financial Crisis.* Cambridge, MA: Harvard University Press, 2021.

Ford, Laura R. *The Intellectual Property of Nations: Sociological and Historical Perspectives on a Modern Legal Institution.* Cambridge: Cambridge University Press, 2021.

Fourcade, Marion. "Cents and Sensibility: Economic Valuation and the Nature of 'Nature.'" *American Journal of Sociology* 116, no. 6 (2011): 1721–77.

———. *Economists and Societies: Discipline and Profession in the United States, Britain, and France, 1890s to 1990s.* Princeton Studies in Cultural Sociology. Princeton: Princeton University Press, 2009.

Fourcade, Marion, and Kieran Healy. "Classification Situations: Life-Chances in the Neoliberal Era." *Accounting, Organizations and Society* 38, no. 8 (2013): 559–72.

Fourcade, Marion, Philippe Steiner, Wolfgang Streeck, and Cornelia Woll. "Moral Categories in the Financial Crisis." *Socio-Economic Review* 11, no. 3 (2013): 601–27.

Galloux, Michel. *Finance islamique et pouvoir politique: Le cas de l'Égypte moderne.* Paris: Presses Universitaires de France, 1997.

———. "The State's Responses to Private Islamic Finance Experiments in Egypt." *Thunderbird International Business Review* 41, no. 4/5 (1999): 481–500.

Gamal, Mahmoud El-. "An Economic Explication of the Prohibition of Riba in Classical Islamic Jurisprudence." In *Proceedings of the Third Harvard University Forum on Islamic Finance*, 31–44. Cambridge: Center for Middle Eastern Studies, Harvard University, 2000.

———. *Islamic Finance: Law, Economics, and Practice.* Cambridge: Cambridge University Press, 2006a.

———. "Short Selling and the Travesty of Islamic Finance." *Islam and Economics* (blog). 15 September 2006b. https://elgamal.blogspot.com/2006/09/short-selling-and-travesty-of -islamic.html.

Gamoran, Hillel. *Jewish Law in Transition: How Economic Forces Overcame the Prohibition against Lending on Interest.* Cambridge: Cambridge University Press, 2008.

García, Alfredo. "Relational Work in Economic Sociology: A Review and Extension." *Sociology Compass* 8, no. 6 (2014): 639–47.

Gargan, Edward A. "Islam Challenges Pakistan Economy." *New York Times*, 23 February 1992.

Gelbard, Enrique, Mumtaz Hussain, Rodolfo Maino, Yibin Mu, and Etienne B. Yehoue. *Islamic Finance in Sub-Saharan Africa: Status and Prospects.* Washington, DC: International Monetary Fund, 2014.

Gellner, Ernest. *Muslim Society.* Cambridge: Cambridge University Press, 1983.

Gerber, Lynne. *Seeking the Straight and Narrow: Weight Loss and Sexual Reorientation in Evangelical America.* Chicago: University of Chicago Press, 2011.

Ghazali, Muhammad al-. "Dr. Muhammad Hamidullah (1908–2002)." *Islamic Studies* 42, no. 1 (2003): 183–87.

Ghazanfar, Shaikh M. *Medieval Islamic Economic Thought: Filling the "Great Gap" in European Economics.* London: Routledge, 2003.

———. "Scholastic Economics and Arab Scholars: The 'Great Gap' Thesis Reconsidered." *Diogenes* 39, no. 154 (1991): 117–40.

Ghias, Shoaib A. "Juristic Disagreement: The Collective Fatwā against Islamic Banking in Pakistan." In *Contemporary Islamic Finance: Innovations, Applications, and Best Practices*, ed. Karen Hunt-Ahmed, 103–19. Hoboken, NJ: Wiley, 2013.

Ghosh, Sugata, and Mayur Shetty. "'All Arabs Will Prefer Islamic Banking.'" *Economic Times* (India), 3 December 2007, English edition.

Ghulayqah, Khālid bin ʿAbdullāh al-. "Hal kāna taḥrīm al-ʿulamāʾ li-l-bunūk al-taqlīdīyah saba-ban fī taʾakhkhur qiyām al-bunūk al-Islāmīyah." *Midād* (Saudi Arabia), 8 November 2007.

Gibb, H.A.R. *Modern Trends in Islam.* Chicago: University of Chicago Press, 1947.

Goldstein, Steve. "Here's the Staggering Amount Banks Have Been Fined since the Financial Crisis." *MarketWatch*, 24 February 2018.

Göle, Nilufer. "Islam in Public: New Visibilities and New Imaginaries." *Public Culture* 14, no. 1 (2002): 173–90.

———. "Manifestations of the Religious-Secular Divide: Self, State, and the Public Sphere." In *Comparative Secularisms in a Global Age*, ed. L. E. Cady and E. S. Hurd. New York: Palgrave Macmillan, 2010.

Gorski, Philip S., and Ateş Altınordu. "After Secularization?" *Annual Review of Sociology* 34, (2008): 55–85.

Gözübüyük, Remzi, Carl Joachim Kock, and Murat Ünal. "Who Appropriates Centrality Rents? The Role of Institutions in Regulating Social Networks in the Global Islamic Finance Industry." *Journal of International Business Studies* 51, no. 5 (2020): 764–87.

Graeber, David. *Debt: The First 5,000 Years.* Brooklyn, NY: Melville House, 2011.

Grais, Wafik, and Matteo Pellegrini. *Corporate Governance in Institutions Offering Islamic Financial Services: Issues and Options.* Washington, DC: World Bank Publications, 2006.

Guhin, Jeffrey. "Religion as Site Rather than Religion as Category: On the Sociology of Religion's Export Problem." *Sociology of Religion* 75, no. 4 (2014): 579–93.

Guthman, Julie. "The Polanyian Way? Voluntary Food Labels as Neoliberal Governance." *Antipode* 39, no. 3 (2007): 456–78.

Habib, Ghazi M. "A Note on the Banking Industry." In *Strategic Management of Services in the Arab Gulf States*, ed. M. S. Kassem and Ghazi M. Habib, 155–76. Berlin: De Gruyter, 1989.

Haeri, Niloofar. *Say What Your Longing Heart Desires: Women, Prayer, and Poetry in Iran.* Stanford: Stanford University Press, 2021.

Haj, Samira. *Reconfiguring Islamic Tradition: Reform, Rationality, and Modernity.* Stanford: Stanford University Press, 2009.

Hallaq, Wael B. *The Impossible State: Islam, Politics, and Modernity's Moral Predicament.* New York: Columbia University Press, 2012.

———. *Sharīʿa: Theory, Practice, Transformations.* Cambridge: Cambridge University Press, 2009.

———. "Was the Gate of Itjihad Closed?" *International Journal of Middle East Studies* 16, no. 1 (1984): 3–41.

Hamdy, Sherine. *Our Bodies Belong to God: Organ Transplants, Islam, and the Struggle for Human Dignity in Egypt.* Berkeley: University of California Press, 2012.

Hameed, Tariq. "Does the Diminishing Musharakah Reflect the Spirit of Sharia?" *Mortgage Finance Gazette*, 8 January 2006. https://www.mortgagefinancegazette.com/market-news/does-the-diminishing-musharakah-reflect-the-spirit-of-sharia-2-08-01-2006/.

Hamidullah, Muhammad. "Haidarabad's Contribution to Islamic Economic Thought and Practice." *Die Welt Des Islams* 4, no. 2 (1955): 73–78.

———. "Islam's Solution of the Basic Economic Problems: The Position of Labour." *Islamic Culture* 10, no. 2 (1936): 213–33, 245–46.

Hanieh, Adam. *Capitalism and Class in the Gulf Arab States.* New York: Palgrave Macmillan, 2011.

———. *Money, Markets, and Monarchies: The Gulf Cooperation Council and the Political Economy of the Contemporary Middle East.* Cambridge: Cambridge University Press, 2018.

———. "New Geographies of Financial Power: Global Islamic Finance and the Gulf." *Third World Quarterly* 41, no. 3 (2020a): 525–46.

———. "Variegated Finance Capital and the Political Economy of Islamic Banking in the Gulf." *New Political Economy* 25, no. 4 (2020b): 572–89.

Hanson, Melanie. "Average Student Loan Debt" (electronic report). Updated 22 May 2023. Education Data Initiative. https://educationdata.org/average-student-loan-debt.

Ḥarb, Muḥammad Ṭalaʿat. ʿIlāj Miṣr al-iqtiṣādī wa-mashrūʿ bank al-Miṣriyīn. Cairo: Maṭbaʿat al-Jarīdah, 1911.

Haron, Sudin. "Islamic Banking: A New Vehicle in Fostering Entrepreneurship." *Journal of Islamic Banking and Finance* 13, no. 3 (1996): 28–39.

Harris, Kevan. "Lineages of the Iranian Welfare State: Dual Institutionalism and Social Policy in the Islamic Republic of Iran." *Social Policy & Administration* 44, no. 6 (2010): 727–45.

———. *A Social Revolution: Politics and the Welfare State in Iran.* Berkeley: University of California Press, 2017.

Harvey, David. *The Limits to Capital.* Oxford: Blackwell, 1982.

———. "The Spatial Fix: Hegel, Von Thunen, and Marx." *Antipode* 13, no. 3 (1981): 1–12.

Hasan, Abul. "Globalisation of Islamic Financial Services and World City Networks." *Journal of Islamic Finance* 4, no. 1 (2015): 1–13.

Hasan, Aznan. *Fundamentals of Sharīʿah in Islamic Finance.* Kuala Lumpur: IBFIM (Islamic Banking & Finance Institute Malaysia), 2011.

Hashmi, Hassan Aldin, Mehboob Al-Rehman, Saeed Akhtar, Talmid Al-Hassan Rizvi, Anayat Ali Khan, and Abdul Rasheed Naumani. *Islāmīyāt* (11th Standard). Lahore: Punjab Curriculum and Textbook Board, 2018.

Hassan, Abdullah al-, May Khamis, and Nada Oulidi. *The GCC Banking Sector: Topography and Analysis.* Washington, DC: International Monetary Fund, 2010.

Hawary, Dahlia El-, Wafik Grais, and Zamir Iqbal. "Diversity in the Regulation of Islamic Financial Institutions." *Quarterly Review of Economics and Finance* 46, no. 5 (2007): 778–800.

Ḥawfānī, Asmāʾ. "Al-makhārij al-fiqhīyah fī al-muʿāmalāt al-mālīyah al-muʿāṣirah." PhD diss., University of Adrar (Algeria), 2023.

Hawkes, David. *The Culture of Usury in Renaissance England.* New York: Palgrave Macmillan, 2010.

Healy, Kieran, and Kimberly D. Krawiec. "Repugnance Management and Transactions in the Body." *American Economic Review* 107, no. 5 (2017): 86–90.

Heck, Gene William. *Charlemagne, Muhammad, and the Arab Roots of Capitalism.* Berlin: De Gruyter, 2006.

Hefner, Robert W. "Epilogue: Capitalist Rationalities and Religious Moralities—An Agonistic Plurality." In *New Religiosities, Modern Capitalism, and Moral Complexities in Southeast Asia,* ed. Juliette Koning and Gwenaël Njoto-Feillard, 265–85. Singapore: Palgrave Macmillan, 2017.

———. "Islam, Economic Globalization, and the Blended Ethics of Self." *Bustan* 3, no. 2 (2012): 91–108.

Hegazy, Walid S. "Contemporary Islamic Finance: From Socioeconomic Idealism to Pure Legalism." *Chicago Journal of International Law* 7, no. 2 (2007): 581–604.

Henry, Clement M. *The Mediterranean Debt Crescent: Money and Power in Algeria, Egypt, Morocco, Tunisia, and Turkey.* Gainesville: University Press of Florida, 1996.

Henry, Clement M., and Rodney Wilson. "Conclusion." In *The Politics of Islamic Finance,* ed. Clement M. Henry and Rodney Wilson, 286–95. Edinburgh: Edinburgh University Press, 2004.

Hertog, Steffen. "The Evolution of Rent Recycling during Two Booms in the Gulf: Business Dynamism and Societal Stagnation." In *Shifting Geo-Economic Power of the Gulf: Oil, Finance and Institutions,* ed. Matteo Legrenzi and Bessma Momani, 55–74. Farnham: Ashgate, 2011.

———. "The Oil-Driven Nation Building of the Gulf States after the Second World War." In *The Emergence of the Gulf States: Studies in Modern History,* ed. J. E. Peterson, 323–51. London: Bloomsbury, 2016.

Hill, Graham. "Enchanting Self-Discipline: Methodical Reflexivity and the Search for the Supernatural in Charismatic Christian Testimonial Practice." *Sociological Theory* 35, no. 4 (2017): 288–311.

Hirschman, Albert O. *The Passions and the Interests: Political Arguments for Capitalism before Its Triumph*. Princeton: Princeton University Press, 1977.

Hoang, Kimberly Kay. *Dealing in Desire: Asian Ascendancy, Western Decline, and the Hidden Currencies of Global Sex Work*. Oakland: University of California Press, 2015.

———. *Spiderweb Capitalism: How Global Elites Exploit Frontier Markets*. Princeton: Princeton University Press, 2022.

Hodgson, Marshall. *The Venture of Islam, Volume 1: The Classical Age of Islam*. Chicago: University of Chicago Press, 1974.

Hoesterey, James Bourk. *Rebranding Islam: Piety, Prosperity, and a Self-Help Guru*. Stanford: Stanford University Press, 2015.

Hoggarth, Davinia. "The Rise of Islamic Finance: Post-Colonial Market-Building in Central Asia and Russia." *International Affairs* 92, no. 1 (January 2016): 115–36.

Hollander, Samuel. "Jeremy Bentham and Adam Smith on the Usury Laws: A 'Smithian' Reply to Bentham and a New Problem." *European Journal of the History of Economic Thought* 6, no. 4 (1999): 523–51.

Homoud, Sami H. *Islamic Banking: The Adaptation of Banking Practice to Conform with Islamic Law*. London: Arabian Information, 1985.

Horkheimer, Max, and Theodor W. Adorno. *Dialectic of Enlightenment*. Trans. John Cumming. London: Verso, 1947.

Htay, Sheila Nu Nu, and Ahmed Salman Syed. "Practice of Profit Equalization Reserve and Investment Risk Reserve by Islamic Banks." *International Journal of Research in Social Sciences* 2, no. 2 (2013): 15–19.

Hung, Ho-fung. "The Global, the Historical, and the Social in the Making of Capitalism." In *Global Historical Sociology*, ed. Julian Go and George Lawson, 161–62. Cambridge: Cambridge University Press, 2017.

———. "Marx, Weber, and the 'Ceaseless Accumulation of Capital.'" In *Political Power and Social Theory*, vol. 23, ed. Julian Go, 303–10. Bingley: Emerald, 2012.

Hurd, Elizabeth Shakman. "Appropriating Islam: The Islamic Other in the Consolidation of Western Modernity." *Critique: Critical Middle Eastern Studies* 12, no. 1 (2003): 25–41.

———. *Beyond Religious Freedom: The New Global Politics of Religion*. Princeton: Princeton University Press, 2015.

———. *The Politics of Secularism in International Relations*. Princeton: Princeton University Press, 2008.

Ibn Rushd. *Bidāyat al-mujtahid wa-nihāyat al-muqtaṣid*. Vol. 2. Beirut: Dār al-Qalam, 1988.

Ibrahim, Ahmed Fekry. *Pragmatism in Islamic Law: A Social & Intellectual History*. Syracuse, NY: Syracuse University Press, 2015.

Iqbal, Muhammad. *The Reconstruction of Religious Thought in Islam*. Lahore: J. Iqbal, 1986.

Iqbal, Munawar, and Philip Molyneux. *Thirty Years of Islamic Banking*. New York: Palgrave Macmillan, 2005.

Iqbal, Zamir, and Abbas Mirakhor. *An Introduction to Islamic Finance: Theory and Practice*. Singapore: Wiley, 2007.

———. *Islamic Banking*. Washington, DC: International Monetary Fund, 1987.

Irfan, Harris. *Heaven's Bankers: Inside the Hidden World of Islamic Finance*. New York: Overlook Press, 2014.

Islahi, Abdul Azim. *Economic Thinking of Arab Muslim Writers during the Nineteenth Century*. London: Palgrave Macmillan, 2015a.

———. "'The Genesis of Islamic Economics' Revisited." *Islamic Economic Studies* 23, no. 2 (2015b): 1–28.

———. *History of Islamic Economic Thought: Contributions of Muslim Scholars to Economic Thought and Analysis*. Northampton, MA: Edward Elgar, 2014a.

————. *Muhammad Hamidullah and His Pioneering Works on Islamic Economics.* Jeddah: Scientific Publishing Centre, King Abdulaziz University, 2014b.

Islamic Financial Services Board. *Islamic Financial Services Industry Stability Report 2022.* Kuala Lumpur: Islamic Financial Services Board, 2022.

Islamic International Rating Agency. *Fiduciary Rating Report: Dubai Islamic Bank P.J.S.C. (January 2021).* Sanabis, Bahrain: Islamic International Rating Agency, 2021.

Islamic Research and Training Institute. *Tabung Haij as an Islamic Financial Institution: The Mobilization of Investment Resources in an Islamic Way and the Management of Hajj.* Jeddah: Islamic Development Bank, 1995.

Ismail, Abd Ghafar, and Adelina Tan Be Lay. "Bank Loan Portfolio Composition and the Disclosure of Loan Loss Provisions: Empirical Evidence from Malaysian Banks." *Asian Review of Accounting* 10, no. 1 (December 2002): 147–62.

Ismail, Abdul Halim. *The Deferred Contracts of Exchange: Al-Quran in Contrast with the Islamic Economists' Theory on Banking and Finance.* Kuala Lumpur: Institute of Islamic Understanding Malaysia, 2002.

————. *Islamic Banking in Malaysia: Some Issues, Problems and Prospects.* Kuala Lumpur: Bank Islam Malaysia Berhad, 1986.

Jackson, Sherman A. "Taqlid, Legal Scaffolding and the Scope of Legal Injunctions in Post-Formative Theory." *Islamic Law and Society* 3, no. 2 (1996): 165–92.

Jalal, Ayesha. *The Struggle for Pakistan: A Muslim Homeland and Global Politics.* Cambridge, MA: Harvard University Press, 2014.

Jalaluddin, AbulKhair. "Motivations of Australian Small Business Firms to Apply Profit-Loss Sharing Method of Finance." *Review of Islamic Economics* 11, special issue (2007): 53–66.

Jamaldeen, Faleel, and Joan Friedman. *Islamic Finance for Dummies.* Hoboken, NJ: Wiley, 2012.

Janjua, M. Ashraf. *History of the State Bank of Pakistan, 1977–1988.* Karachi: State Bank Printing Press, 2003.

————. *History of the State Bank of Pakistan, 1988–2003.* Karachi: State Bank Printing Press, 2004.

Jenkins, Richard. "Disenchantment, Enchantment and Re-Enchantment: Max Weber at the Millennium." *Max Weber Studies* 1, no. 1 (2000): 11–32.

Jepperson, Ronald L. "Institutions, Institutional Effects, and Institutionalism." In *The New Institutionalism in Organizational Analysis,* ed. Walter W. Powell and Paul J. DiMaggio, 143–63. Chicago: University of Chicago Press, 1991.

Jivraj, Hassan. "Faith in Finance: An Introduction to Sukuk Structures." *Debtwire* (special feature), 26 January 2017, 1–6.

Johansen, Baber. *Contingency in a Sacred Law: Legal and Ethical Norms in the Muslim Fiqh.* Leiden: Brill, 1999.

————. "Le contrat salam: Droit et formation du capital dans l'Empire abbasside." *Annales* 61, no. 4 (2006): 863–99.

Johnson, Cathryn, Timothy J. Dowd, and Cecilia L. Ridgeway. "Legitimacy as a Social Process." *Annual Review of Sociology* 32 (2006): 53–78.

Joseph, Sabrina. *Islamic Law on Peasant Usufruct in Ottoman Syria: 17th to Early 19th Century.* Leiden: Brill, 2012.

Josephson-Storm, Jason Ānanda. *The Myth of Disenchantment: Magic, Modernity, and the Birth of the Human Sciences.* Chicago: University of Chicago Press, 2017.

Kahf, Monzer. "Islamic Banks: The Rise of a New Power Alliance of Wealth and Shari'a Scholarship." In *The Politics of Islamic Finance,* ed. Clement Henry and Rodney Wilson, 17–36. Edinburgh: Edinburgh University Press, 2004.

————. "Strategic Trends in the Islamic Banking and Finance Movement." *Proceedings of the Fifth Harvard University Forum on Islamic Finance* (2002): 169–81. Conference held at Center for Middle Eastern Studies, Harvard University, 6–7 April 2000.

Kahf, Monzer, and Elhadi Idris Habbani. "Tawarruq Potential Risks: The Practices of Islamic Financial Institutions in Qatar." *Journal of Islamic Economics, Banking and Finance* 12, no. 4 (2016): 54–88.

Kamali, Mohammed Hashim. "Commodity Futures: An Islamic Legal Analysis." *Thunderbird International Business Review* 49, no. 3 (2007): 309–39.

———. "Ethics and Finance: Perspectives of the Shari'ah and Its Higher Objectives (Maqasid)." *ICR Journal* 3, no. 4 (July 2012): 618–36.

———. "Maqāṣid al-Sharī'ah: The Objectives of Islamic Law." *Islamic Studies* 38, no. 2 (1999): 193–208.

Kamrava, Mehran. "Cities, Globalized Hubs, and Nationalism in the Persian Gulf." *Middle East Journal* 74, no. 4 (2020): 521–37.

Katz, Jacob. *Tradition and Crisis: Jewish Society at the End of the Middle Ages.* Syracuse, NY: Syracuse University Press, 2000.

Kazi, Durriya. "The Writing on the Walls, Trucks and Autos: A Glimpse of Pakistani Visual Poetry." *Scroll.In,* 19 February 2017.

Kennedy, Charles H. "Islamization and Legal Reform in Pakistan, 1979–1989." *Pacific Affairs* 63, no. 1 (1990): 62–77.

———. "Pakistan's Superior Courts and the Prohibition of Riba." In *Islamization and the Pakistani Economy,* ed. Robert M. Hathaway and Wilson Lee, 101–17. Washington, DC: Woodrow Wilson International Center for Scholars, 2004.

Khalil, Emad H. "An Overview of the Sharia'a Prohibition of Riba." In *Interest in Islamic Economics: Understanding Riba,* ed. Abdulkader Thomas, 55–68. New York: Routledge, 2006.

Khalil, Emad H., and Abdulkader Thomas. "The Modern Debate over *Riba* in Egypt." In *Interest in Islamic Economics: Understanding Riba,* ed. Abdulkader Thomas, 68–94. New York: Routledge, 2006.

Khan, Feisal. "How 'Islamic' Is Islamic Banking?" *Journal of Economic Behavior & Organization* 76, no. 3 (December 2010): 805–20.

———. *Islamic Banking in Pakistan: Shariah-Compliant Banking and the Quest to Make Pakistan More Islamic.* New York: Routledge, 2015.

Khan, M. Mansoor. "Main Features of the Interest-Free Banking Movement in Pakistan (1980–2006)." *Managerial Finance* 34, no. 9 (2008): 660–74.

Khan, Mohsin. "Islamic Interest-Free Banking: A Theoretical Analysis." In *Theoretical Studies in Islamic Banking and Finance,* ed. Mohsin Khan and Abbas Mirakhor, 15–36. Houston, TX: Institute for Research and Islamic Studies, 1987.

Khan, Mohsin S., and Abbas Mirakhor. "Islamic Banking: Experiences in the Islamic Republic of Iran and in Pakistan." *Economic Development and Cultural Change* 38, no. 2 (1990): 353–75.

Khan, Muhammad Fahim. "Guaranteeing Investment Deposits in Islamic Banking System." *Journal of King Abdulaziz University: Islamic Economics* 16, no. 1 (2003): 45–52.

Khan, Salman. "Organised Tawarruq in Practice: A Shari'ah Non-Compliant and Unjustified Transaction." *New Horizon* (December 2010): 16–21.

Khan, Waqar Masood. *Towards an Interest-Free Islamic Economic System.* Markfield: Islamic Foundation, 1986.

———. "Towards an Interest-Free Islamic Economic System." *Journal of King Abdulaziz University: Islamic Economics* 1 (1989): 3–38.

Khatoon, Asma, and Miss Sanya. *Muṭāla'a-e Pākistān* (10th Standard). Peshawar: Leading Books/Khyber Pakhtunkhwa Textbook Board, 2020.

Khnifer, Mohammed. "Goldman Sucks?" *Islamic Business & Finance,* no. 69 (December 2011): 28–29.

Kitamura, Hideki. "Islamic Finance as an Ethno-Political Agenda in the 1980s: An Inquiry into the Role of Islamic Finance Pioneers." *Sojourn* 36, no. 1 (2021): 98–123.

———. "Who Pioneered Islamic Banking in Malaysia? The Background of the Pioneers of Bank Islam Malaysia Berhad." *Contemporary Islam* 14, no. 1 (2020): 75–93.

Kok, Seng Kiong, and Azar Shahgholian. "The Impact of Proximity within Elite Corporate Networks on the Shariah Governance-Firm Performance Nexus: Evidence from the Global Shariah Elite." *Emerging Markets Review* 54, no. 100998 (2023): 1–23.

Krippner, Greta R. *Capitalizing on Crisis: The Political Origins of the Rise of Finance.* Cambridge, MA: Harvard University Press, 2011.

Kugle, Scott Alan. "Framed, Blamed and Renamed: The Recasting of Islamic Jurisprudence in Colonial South Asia." *Modern Asian Studies* 35, no. 2 (2001): 257–313.

Kuran, Timur. "The Absence of the Corporation in Islamic Law: Origins and Persistence." *American Journal of Comparative Law* 53, no. 4 (2005): 785–834.

———. "The Discontents of Islamic Economic Morality." *American Economic Review* 86, no. 2 (1996): 438–42.

———. "The Genesis of Islamic Economics: A Chapter in the Politics of Muslim Identity." *Social Research* 64, no. 2 (1997a): 301–38.

———. *Islam and Mammon: The Economic Predicaments of Islamism.* Princeton: Princeton University Press, 2004.

———. "Islam and Underdevelopment: An Old Puzzle Revisited." *Journal of Institutional and Theoretical Economics (JITE)/Zeitschrift für die gesamte Staatswissenschaft* (1997b): 41–71.

———. "Islamic Economics and the Islamic Subeconomy." *Journal of Economic Perspectives* 9, no. 4 (1995): 155–73.

———. *The Long Divergence: How Islamic Law Held Back the Middle East.* Princeton: Princeton University Press, 2011.

———. "Why the Middle East Is Economically Underdeveloped: Historical Mechanisms of Institutional Stagnation." *Journal of Economic Perspectives* 18, no. 3 (2004): 71–90.

Kurzman, Charles. Introduction to *Modernist Islam, 1840–1940: A Sourcebook*, ed. Charles Kurzman, 3–27. Oxford: Oxford University Press, 2002.

Kusuma, Ketut Ariadi, and Anderson Caputo Silva. *Sukuk Markets: A Proposed Approach for Development.* Policy Research Working Paper. Vol. 7133. Washington, DC: World Bank Group, 2014.

Labib, Subhi Y. "Capitalism in Medieval Islam." *Journal of Economic History* 29, no. 1 (1969): 79–96.

Labīd, Abū ʿAqīl. "Muʿallaqa of Labīd." In *The Seven Odes: The First Chapter in Arabic Literature.* Trans. and ed. A. J. Arberry, 142–47. New York: Macmillan, 1957.

Lai, Jikon. "Financialised Ethics, Economic Security and the Promise of Islamic Finance." *Asian Journal of Comparative Politics* 7, no. 1 (2022): 45–57.

———. "Industrial Policy and Islamic Finance." *New Political Economy* 20, no. 2 (2015): 178–98.

Lai, Karen P. Y., and Michael Samers. "Conceptualizing Islamic Banking and Finance: A Comparison of Its Development and Governance in Malaysia and Singapore." *Pacific Review* 30, no. 3 (2017): 405–24.

Laiou, Angeliki E. "Economic Concerns and Attitudes of the Intellectuals of Thessalonike." *Dumbarton Oaks Papers* 57 (2003): 205–23.

Lapavitsas, Costas. *Profiting without Producing: How Finance Exploits Us All.* London: Verso, 2013.

Lapidus, Ira M. "Islamic Revival and Modernity: The Contemporary Movements and the Historical Paradigms." *Journal of the Economic and Social History of the Orient* 40, no. 4 (1997): 444–60.

Le Goff, Jacques. *Your Money or Your Life: Economy and Religion in the Middle Ages.* Trans. Patricia Ranum. New York: Zone Books, 1998.

Lee, Dana Elizabeth. "At the Limits of Law: Necessity in Islamic Legal History, Second/Eighth through Tenth/Sixteenth Centuries." PhD diss., Princeton University, 2019.

Lee, Georgina. "Commodity Murabahah: Better the Devil You Know?" *Islamic Finance News*, 3 August 2011.

Liau, Y-Sing. "Tawarruq Woes Driving More Equity Funding: Scholar." Reuters, 12 February 2010.

Lie, John. "Sociology of Markets." *Annual Review of Sociology* 23 (1997): 341–60.

Looft, Michael. *Inspired Finance: The Role of Faith in Microfinance and International Economic Development*. New York: Palgrave Macmillan, 2014.

Looney, Robert E. "Financial Innovation in an Islamic Setting: The Case of Pakistan." *Journal of South Asian and Middle Eastern Studies* 19, no. 4 (1996): 1–30.

Lubin, David. *Dance of the Trillions: Developing Countries and Global Finance*. Washington, DC: Brookings Institution Press, 2018.

Luther, Martin. *The Christian in Society (I)*. Ed. James Atkinson and Helmut T. Lehmann. Vol. 44. Philadelphia: Fortress Press, 1966.

Lytton, Timothy D. *Kosher*. Cambridge, MA: Harvard University Press, 2013.

Maali, Bassam, and Christopher Napier. "Accounting, Religion and Organisational Culture: The Creation of Jordan Islamic Bank." *Journal of Islamic Accounting and Business Research* 1, no. 2 (2010): 92–113.

MacKenzie, Donald A. *An Engine, Not a Camera: How Financial Models Shape Markets*. Cambridge, MA: MIT Press, 2006.

Mackie, Alan. "Saudi Arabia: New Problems Emerge in the Banking System—Some Key Areas of Banking Reform Are Now Complete." *Financial Times*, 26 April 1982.

Macris, Jeffrey R. "Population and Economic Activities in the Arab Trucial States: A 1901 Accounting." *Journal of the Middle East and Africa* 6, no. 2 (2015): 165–89.

Mahmood, Saba. *Religious Difference in a Secular Age: A Minority Report*. Princeton: Princeton University Press, 2016.

Mallat, Chibli. "Tantawi on Banking Operations in Egypt." In *Islamic Legal Interpretation: Muftis and Their Fatwas*, ed. Muhammad Khalid Masud, Brinkley Messick, and David S. Powers, 286–97. Cambridge, MA: Harvard University Press, 1996.

Malley, Mohammed. "Jordan: A Case Study of the Relationship between Islamic Finance and Islamist Politics." In *The Politics of Islamic Finance*, ed. Clement M. Henry and Rodney Wilson, 196–215. Edinburgh: Edinburgh University Press, 2004.

Mandaville, Peter G. *Global Political Islam*. London: Routledge, 2007.

Mansoori, Muhammad Tahir. "Is 'Islamic Banking' Islamic? Analysis of Current Debate on Shari'ah Legitimacy of Islamic Banking and Finance." *Islamic Studies* 50, no. 3/4 (2011): 383–411.

Manzoor, Davood, Majid Karimirizi, and Ali Mostafavisani. "Financing Infrastructure Projects Based on Risk Sharing Model: Istisna Sukuk." *Journal of Emerging Economies and Islamic Research* 5, no. 3 (2017): 72–84.

Martí, Gerardo. "Ego-Affirming Evangelicalism: How a Hollywood Church Appropriates Religion for Workers in the Creative Class." *Sociology of Religion* 71, no. 1 (2010): 52–75.

Marx, Karl. *Capital: A Critique of Political Economy*. Vol. 3. Trans. David Fernbach. London: Penguin, 1991.

———. *Capital: A Critique of Political Economy*. Vol. 1. Trans. Ben Fowkes. London: Penguin, 1992.

Marx, Karl, and Friedrich Engels. "Manifesto of the Communist Party." In *The Marx-Engels Reader*, 2nd ed., ed. Robert C. Tucker, 469–500. New York: W. W. Norton, 1978.

Marzban, Shehab, Mehmet Asutay, and Adel Boseli. "Shariah-Compliant Crowd Funding: An Efficient Framework for Entrepreneurship Development in Islamic Countries." Paper presented at the Eleventh Harvard Forum on Islamic Finance, Cambridge, MA, 27 April 2014.

Masud, Muhammad Khalid. "Ikhtilaf al-Fuqaha: Diversity in Fiqh as a Social Construction." In *Wanted: Equality and Justice in the Muslim Family*, ed. Zainah Anwar, 65–94. Petaling Jaya, Malaysia: Musawah, 2009.

Masuzawa, Tomoko. *The Invention of World Religions; or, How European Universalism Was Preserved in the Language of Pluralism*. Chicago: University of Chicago Press, 2005.

Matthews, Nathan. "The Valuation of Property in the Roman Law." *Harvard Law Review* 34, no. 3 (1921): 229–59.

Maurer, Bill. *Mutual Life, Limited: Islamic Banking, Alternative Currencies, Lateral Reason*. Princeton: Princeton University Press, 2011.

———. *Pious Property: Islamic Mortgages in the United States*. New York: Russell Sage, 2006.

Mawdudi, Abu al-Aʿla. *Economic System of Islam*. Reprint ed. Trans. Riaz Husain, ed. Khurshid Ahmad. Lahore: Islamic Publications, 1984.

———. *First Principles of Islamic Economics*. Trans. Ahmad Imam Shafaq Hashemi, ed. Khurshid Ahmad. Markfield: Islamic Foundation, 2011.

———. *The Islamic Law and Constitution*. Trans. Khurshid Ahmad. Lahore: Islamic Publications, 1960.

Mayer, Ann Elizabeth. "Islamic Banking and Credit Policies in the Sadat Era: The Social Origins of Islamic Banking in Egypt." *Arab Law Quarterly* 1, no. 1 (1985): 32–50.

———. "The Regulation of Interest Charges and Risk Contracts: Some Problems of Recent Libyan Legislation." *International and Comparative Law Quarterly* 28, no. 4 (1979): 541–59.

McBain, Sophie. "Islamic Finance's 'Scholar Problem': Why Are Shariah Scholars Paid So Much?" *Spears*, 26 April 2012. https://spearswms.com/islamic-finances-scholar-problem-why-are-shariah-scholars-paid-so-much/.

McCormick, Liz Capo, and Daniel Kruger. "Bond Vigilantes Confront Obama as Housing Falters." Bloomberg, 29 May 2009.

McGuire, Meredith B. *Lived Religion: Faith and Practice in Everyday Life*. Oxford: Oxford University Press, 2008.

McMillen, Michael J. T. "Islamic Project Finance." In *Handbook of Islamic Banking*, ed. M. Kabir Hassan and Mervyn K. Lewis, 200–239. Cheltenham: Edward Elgar, 2007.

Meislin, B. J., and M. L. Cohen. "Backgrounds of the Biblical Law against Usury." *Comparative Studies in Society and History* 6, no. 3 (1964): 250–67.

Messick, Brinkley Morris. *The Calligraphic State: Textual Domination and History in a Muslim Society*. Berkeley: University of California Press, 1993.

Millo, Yuval. "Making Things Deliverable: The Origins of Index-Based Derivatives." *Sociological Review* 55 (2007): 196–214.

Ministry of Education of Saudi Arabia. *Al-fiqh 1: Al-taʿlīm al-thānawī—Al-barnāmaj al-mushtarak*. Riyadh: Ministry of Education, 2020a.

———. *Al-fiqh 2: Al-taʿlīm al-thānawī—Masār al-ʿulūm al-insānīyah*. Riyadh: Ministry of Education, 2020b.

Mitchell, Matthew. "Borrowing from the Buddha: Buddhist Temples as Financial Centers in Premodern East Asia." *Education about Asia* 24, no. 2 (2019): 51.

Mizruchi, Mark S. *The Fracturing of the American Corporate Elite*. Cambridge, MA: Harvard University Press, 2013.

Mogielnicki, Robert. *A Political Economy of Free Zones in Gulf Arab States*. Cham: Palgrave Macmillan, 2021.

Mohamad, Maznah. "The Ascendance of Bureaucratic Islam and the Secularization of the Sharia in Malaysia." *Pacific Affairs* 83, no. 3 (2010): 505–24.

Mohamad, Maznah, and Johan Saravanamuttu. "Islamic Banking and Finance: Sacred Alignment, Strategic Alliances." *Pacific Affairs* 88, no. 2 (2015): 193–213.

Mohamed, Hazik, and M. Ashraful Mobin. "Debt Forgiveness and Debt Relief for Covid-19 Economic Recovery Financed through GDP-Linked Sukuk." *European Journal of Islamic Finance*, no. 16 (2020): 1–8.

Moon, Hyeyoung, and Christine Min Wotipka. "The Worldwide Diffusion of Business Education, 1881–1999: Historical Trajectory and Mechanisms of Expansion." In *Globalization and*

Organization: World Society and Organizational Change, ed. Gili S. Drori, John W. Meyer, and Hokyu Hwang, 121–36. Oxford: Oxford University Press, 2006.

Moosa, Ebrahim. "Allegory of the Rule (Ḥukm): Law as Simulacrum in Islam?" *History of Religions* 38, no. 1 (1998): 1–24.

Morello, Gustavo. *Lived Religion in Latin America: An Enchanted Modernity.* New York: Oxford University Press, 2021.

Mouline, Nabil. *The Clerics of Islam: Religious Authority and Political Power in Saudi Arabia.* Trans. Ethan S. Rundell. New Haven: Yale University Press, 2014.

Mukhtar, Shahid. *Tārīkh-e Islām* (9th Standard). Lahore: Punjab Curriculum and Textbook Board, 2018.

Muslim World League Islamic Fiqh Council. "Report of the Committee Assigned to Draft the Resolution of the Islamic Fiqh Council on Insurance (First Session, 1398 AH/1978 CE)." In *Resolutions of Islamic Fiqh Council (Makkah Mukarramah): From 1st to 18th Sessions*, 44–54. Mecca, Saudi Arabia: Muslim World League, 2007.

Musso, Giorgio. "Sudan and the Unbearable Lightness of Islamism: From Revolution to Rentier Authoritarianism." *International Spectator* 52, no. 4 (2017): 112–28.

Muṭlaq, ʿAbdullāh bin Muḥammad al-. *Istudiyū al-Jumʿah*. Nidāʾ al-Islām radio network. 105.0 MHz. Riyadh, 22 November 2019.

Nagaoka, Shinsuke. "Beyond the Theoretical Dichotomy in Islamic Finance: Analytical Reflections on Murabahah Contracts and Islamic Debt Securities." *Kyoto Bulletin of Islamic Area Studies* 1, no. 2 (2007): 72–91.

Najjar, Ahmad al-. *Bunūk bi-lā fawāʾid*. Jeddah: al-Dār al-Saʿūdīyah li-l-nashr wa-l-tawzīʿ, 1984.

——. "Islamic Banks and I.A.I.B." *Middle East Business & Banking* (1986): 6–8.

——. "Islamic Banks in Egypt: A Model and the Challenge." In *Readings in Islamic Banking*, ed. Ataul Hoque, 258–70. Dhaka: Islamic Foundation Bangladesh, 1987.

Naqvi, Syed Nawab Haider. *Individual Freedom, Social Welfare and Islamic Economic Order.* Islamabad: Pakistan Institute of Development Economics, 1981.

——. *Islam, Economics, and Society.* London: Kegan Paul, 1994.

Nasr, Seyyed Vali Reza. *Mawdudi and the Making of Islamic Revivalism.* New York: Oxford University Press, 1996.

——. *The Rise of Islamic Capitalism: Why the New Muslim Middle Class Is the Key to Defeating Extremism.* New York: Simon and Schuster, 2009.

——. *The Vanguard of the Islamic Revolution: The Jamaʿat-i Islami of Pakistan.* Berkeley: University of California Press, 1994.

Nelson, Benjamin N. *The Idea of Usury: From Tribal Brotherhood to Universal Otherhood.* Princeton: Princeton University Press, 1949.

Neusner, Jacob. "Aristotle's Economics and the Mishnah's Economics: The Matter of Wealth and Usury." *Journal for the Study of Judaism* 21, no. 1 (1990): 41–59.

Nienhaus, Volker. "Islamic Economics, Finance and Banking: Theory and Practice." In *Islamic Banking and Finance*, ed. Butterworths Editorial Staff, 1–17. London: Butterworths, 1986.

——. "Profitability of Islamic PLS Banks Competing with Interest Banks: Problems and Prospects." *Journal of Research in Islamic Economics* 1, no. 1 (1983): 31–39.

Nomani, Farhad. "The Dilemma of Riba-Free Banking in Islamic Public Policy." In *Islam and the Everyday World*, 193–223. New York: Routledge, 2006.

Nomani, Farhad, and Ali Rahnema. *Islamic Economic Systems.* London: Zed Books, 1994.

Noonan, John Thomas. *The Scholastic Analysis of Usury.* Cambridge, MA: Harvard University Press, 1957.

Oliver, Lissa. "Libya: It's Not So Long Ago That Racing Was Starting to Flourish Again." *Thoroughbred Racing Commentary*, 26 February 2014. https://www.thoroughbredracing.com/articles/1704/libya-has-big-ambitions-racing-regeneration-continues-apace/.

Orlian, Meir. "Heter Iska 101 (IPES)." *Jewish Press* (May 2009): 55.

Pakistan Bureau of Statistics. *Pakistan Labour Force Survey 2020–21*. Islamabad: Government of Pakistan, 2022.

Pardo-Guerra, Juan Pablo. *Automating Finance: Infrastructures, Engineers, and the Making of Electronic Markets*. Cambridge: Cambridge University Press, 2019.

Parker, Mushtak. "Towards 50pc Market Share." *New Straits Times*, 2 April 2017. https://www .nst.com.my/news/2017/04/226661/towards-50pc-market-share.

Pauly, Christoph. "Profits in the Name of Allah: Sharia Banking Comes to Germany." *Spiegel International*, 22 October 2009.

Paxton, John, ed. *The Statesman's Year-Book, 1987–1988*. London: Macmillan, 1987.

Peletz, Michael G. *Sharia Transformations: Cultural Politics and the Rebranding of an Islamic Judiciary*. Oakland: University of California Press, 2020.

Peterson, John E. "Rulers, Merchants and Shaikhs in Gulf Politics: The Function of Family Networks." In *The Gulf Family: Kinship Policies and Modernity*, ed. Alanoud Alsharekh, 21–36. London: Saqi, 2007.

———. *Saudi Arabia under Ibn Saud: Economic and Financial Foundations of the State*. London: Bloomsbury Publishing, 2018.

Petroleum, British (BP). *BP Statistical Review of World Energy 2006*. BP, 2006. http://www.bp .com/statisticalreview.

Pirbhai, M. Reza. "British Indian Reform and Pre-Colonial Trends in Islamic Jurisprudence." *Journal of Asian History* 42, no. 1 (2008): 36–63.

Pistor, Katharina. *The Code of Capital: How the Law Creates Wealth and Inequality*. Princeton: Princeton University Press, 2019.

Pitluck, Aaron Z. "Altering the Trajectory of Finance: Meaning-Making and Control in Islamic Investment Banks." In *Financialization: Relational Approaches*, ed. C. Hann and D. Kalb, 111–35. New York: Berghahn Books, 2020.

———. "The Convergence Paradox of Islamic Finance: A Sociological Reinterpretation, with Insights for Proponents of Social Finance." In *Routledge Handbook of Social and Sustainable Finance*, ed. Othmar M. Lehner, 364–80. London: Routledge, 2016.

———. "Islamic Banking and Finance: Alternative or Façade?" In *The Oxford Handbook of the Sociology of Finance*, ed. Karin Knorr Cetina and Alex Preda, 431–49. Oxford: Oxford University Press, 2012.

Polanyi, Karl. *The Great Transformation: The Political and Economic Origins of Our Time*. 2nd ed. Boston: Beacon Press, 2001.

Pollard, Jane, and Michael Samers. "Governing Islamic Finance: Territory, Agency, and the Making of Cosmopolitan Financial Geographies." *Annals of the Association of American Geographers* 103, no. 3 (2013): 710–26.

———. "Islamic Banking and Finance: Postcolonial Political Economy and the Decentring of Economic Geography." *Transactions of the Institute of British Geographers* 32, no. 3 (2007): 313–30.

Ponte, Stefano. *Business, Power and Sustainability in a World of Global Value Chains*. London: Zed Books, 2019.

Poon, Jessie P. H., Jane Pollard, and Yew Wah Chow. "Resetting Neoliberal Values: Lawmaking in Malaysia's Islamic Finance." *Annals of the American Association of Geographers* 108, no. 5 (2018): 1442–56.

Poon, Jessie P. H., Jane Pollard, Yew Wah Chow, and Michael Ewers. "The Rise of Kuala Lumpur as an Islamic Financial Frontier." *Regional Studies* 51, no. 10 (2017): 1443–53.

Power, Michael. *The Audit Society: Rituals of Verification*. Oxford: Oxford University Press, 1997.

Presley, John R., ed. *Directory of Islamic Financial Institutions*. London: Croom Helm, 1988.

Presley, John R., and Rodney Wilson. *Banking in the Arab Gulf*. London: Macmillan, 1991.

Prokop, Michaela. "Saudi Arabia: The Politics of Education." *International Affairs* 79, no. 1 (2003): 77–89.

Qanas, Jalal, and Malcolm Sawyer. "Financialisation in the Gulf States." *Review of Political Economy* (2022): 1–18.

Quinn, Sarah L. *American Bonds: How Credit Markets Shaped a Nation*. Princeton: Princeton University Press, 2019.

———. "The Transformation of Morals in Markets: Death, Benefits, and the Exchange of Life Insurance Policies." *American Journal of Sociology* 114, no. 3 (2008): 738–80.

Rahardjo, M. Dawam. "The Question of Islamic Banking in Indonesia." In *Islamic Banking in Southeast Asia*, ed. Mohamed Ariff, 137–63. Singapore: Institute of Southeast Asian Studies, 1988.

Rahman, Fazlur. "Islamic Modernism: Its Scope, Method and Alternatives." *International Journal of Middle East Studies* 1, no. 4 (1970): 317–33.

Rahman, Sajid, and Gohar Ali Khan. *Islāmīyāt* (11th Standard). Peshawar: Leading Books/ Khyber Pakhtunkhwa Textbook Board, 2020.

Ramsey, Dave. *The Legacy Journey: A Radical View of Biblical Wealth and Generosity*. Brentwood, TN: Ramsey Press, 2014.

Rasheed, Madawi al-. *Contesting the Saudi State: Islamic Voices from a New Generation*. Vol. 25. Cambridge: Cambridge University Press, 2007.

Reisman, Yisroel. *The Laws of Ribbis: The Laws of Interest and Their Application to Everyday Life and Business*. Brooklyn, NY: Mesorah, 1995.

Rethel, Lena. "Capital Market Development in Southeast Asia: From Speculative Crisis to Spectacles of Financialization." *Economic Anthropology* 5, no. 2 (2018): 185–97.

———. "Financialisation and the Malaysian Political Economy." *Globalizations* 7, no. 4 (2010): 489–506.

———. "The Imaginary Landscapes of Islamic Finance and the Global Financial Crisis." In *Handbook on the Geographies of Money and Finance*, ed. Ronald Martin and Jane Pollard, 562–79. Cheltenham: Edward Elgar Publishing, 2017.

———. *The Political Economy of Financial Development in Malaysia: From the Asian Crisis to 1MDB*. London: Routledge, 2020.

Reynolds, Amy. *Free Trade and Faithful Globalization: Saving the Market*. Cambridge Studies in Social Theory, Religion, and Politics. Cambridge: Cambridge University Press, 2015.

Riḍā, Muḥammad Rashīd. *Fatāwá al-Imām Muḥammad Rashīd Riḍā*. Ed. Ṣalāḥ al-Dīn al-Munajjid and Yūsuf Khūrī. Beirut: Dār al-Kitāb al-Jadīd, 1970.

Rittenberg, Ryan M. "Gharar in Post-Formative Islamic Commercial Law: A Study of the Representation of Uncertainty in Islamic Legal Thought." PhD diss., University of Pennsylvania, 2014.

Rodinson, Maxime. *Islam and Capitalism*. London: Allen Jane, 1974.

Roff, William R. "Patterns of Islamization in Malaysia, 1890s–1990s: Exemplars, Institutions, and Vectors." *Journal of Islamic Studies* 9, no. 2 (1998): 210–28.

Rona-Tas, Akos, and Alya Guseva. "Consumer Credit in Comparative Perspective." *Annual Review of Sociology* 44, no. 1 (2018): 55–75.

Rose, Mavis. *Indonesia Free: A Political Biography of Mohammad Hatta*. Jakarta: Equinox, 2010.

Rosly, Saiful Azhar, and Mahmood Sanusi. "Some Issues of Bay' Al-'Inah in Malaysian Islamic Financial Markets." *Arab Law Quarterly* 16, no. 3 (2001): 263–80.

Rossman, Gabriel. "Obfuscatory Relational Work and Disreputable Exchange." *Sociological Theory* 32, no. 1 (2014): 43–63.

Roth, Alvin E. "Repugnance as a Constraint on Markets." *Journal of Economic Perspectives* 21, no. 3 (2007): 37–58.

Roubaie, Amer al-. "Islamic Finance: A Bulwark against Contagion in the Global Banking System." *Islam and Civilisational Renewal* 1, no. 2 (2009): 303–21.

Roy, Olivier. *Globalized Islam: The Search for a New Ummah*. New York: Columbia University Press, 2004.

Royal Islamic Strategic Studies Centre. *The Muslim 500: The World's 500 Most Influential Muslims, 2019.* 10th ed. Amman: Royal Islamic Strategic Studies Centre, 2018.

Rudnyckyj, Daromir. "Assembling Islam and Liberalism: Market Freedom and the Moral Project of Islamic Finance." In *Religion and the Morality of the Market,* ed. Daromir Rudnyckyj and Filippo Osella, 160–76. Cambridge: Cambridge University Press, 2017a.

———. *Beyond Debt: Islamic Experiments in Global Finance.* Chicago: University of Chicago Press, 2019.

———. "Economy in Practice: Islamic Finance and the Problem of Market Reason." *American Ethnologist* 41, no. 1 (2014): 110–27.

———. "From Wall Street to Halal Street: Malaysia and the Globalization of Islamic Finance." *Journal of Asian Studies* 72, no. 4 (2013): 831–48.

———. *Spiritual Economies: Islam, Globalization, and the Afterlife of Development.* Ithaca: Cornell University Press, 2010.

———. "Subjects of Debt: Financial Subjectification and Collaborative Risk in Malaysian Islamic Finance." *American Anthropologist* 119, no. 2 (2017b): 269–83.

Ṣadr, Muḥammad Bāqir al-. *An Introduction to Principles of Islamic Banking.* Trans. Mehdi Marzban. Tehran: Bonyād Beʿthat, 1982.

———. *Iqtiṣādunā: Dirāsah mawḍūʿīyah tatanāwalu bi-l-naqd wa-l-baḥth al-madhāhib al-iqtiṣādīyah li-l-Mārkisīyah wa-l-Raʾsmālīyah wa-l-Islām fī ususihā al-fikrīyah wa-tafāṣīlihā.* Beirut: Dār al-Kitāb al-Lubnānī, 1977.

Saeed, Abdullah. "Islamic Banking in Practice: The Case of Faisal Islamic Bank of Egypt." *Journal of Arabic, Islamic and Middle Eastern Studies* 2, no. 1 (1995): 28–46.

Saldaña, Johnny. *The Coding Manual for Qualitative Researchers.* Los Angeles: Sage, 2009.

Saleh, Nabil A. *Unlawful Gain and Legitimate Profit in Islamic Law.* Cambridge: Cambridge University Press, 1986.

Sallaz, Jeffrey. *Lives on the Line: How the Philippines Became the World's Call Center Capital.* New York: Oxford University Press, 2019.

Salvatore, Armando. "The Sociology of Islam: Beyond Orientalism, Toward Transculturality?" In *Exploring Islam beyond Orientalism and Occidentalism: Sociological Approaches,* ed. Christel Gärtner and Heidemarie Winkel, 43–63. Wiesbaden: Springer Fachmedien Wiesbaden, 2021.

Samers, Michael. "A Marriage of Convenience? Islamic Banking and Finance Meet Neoliberalization." In *The Changing World Religion Map,* ed. Stanley D. Brunn, 1173–87. Dordrecht: Springer, 2015.

Sarker, Md. Abdul Awal. "Islamic Business Contracts, Agency Problem and the Theory of the Islamic Firm." *International Journal of Islamic Financial Services* 1, no. 2 (1999): 12–28.

Schacht, Joseph. *An Introduction to Islamic Law.* Oxford: Clarendon Press, 1964.

Schluchter, Wolfgang. "Dialectics of Disenchantment: A Weberian Look at Western Modernity." *Max Weber Studies* 17, no. 1 (2017): 24–47.

Schneiberg, Marc, and Tim Bartley. "Regulating or Redesigning Finance? Market Architectures, Normal Accidents, and Dilemmas of Regulatory Reform." *Research in the Sociology of Organizations* 30 (2010): 281–307.

Schönenbach, Rebecca, and Gerd Klöwer. "Ahmed El Naggar: The Pioneer of Islamic Banking." *Bulletin (European Association for Banking and Financial History),* no. 1 (2014): 26–31.

Schrank, Andrew. *The Economic Sociology of Development.* Hoboken, NJ: Wiley, 2022.

———. "Regulators without Borders? Latin American Labour Inspectors in Transnational Context." *Global Networks* 21, no. 4 (2021): 723–48.

Schumpeter, Joseph A. *History of Economic Analysis.* London: Routledge, 1954.

Securities Commission Malaysia. "Registration of Shariah Advisers: Guidelines." Issued/effective: 10 August 2009. https://www.sc.com.my/api/documentms/download.ashx?id=8202036e-aa42-44f0-ab62-1e6f448628d3.

Senturk, Recep. "Intellectual Dependency: Late Ottoman Intellectuals between Fiqh and Social Science." *Die Welt des Islams* 47, no. 3–4 (2007): 283–318.

Seznec, Jean-François, and Samer Mosis. *The Financial Markets of the Arab Gulf: Power, Politics and Money.* Abingdon-on-Thames: Routledge, 2019.

Shaharuddin, A., Aizul Aiman Musa, Fatin Syahirah Mohamed Nawi, Adi Hanif Mohamed Ahmad, and Mukarrami Ab Mumin. "Dual Agency Practices in Islamic Financial Institutions: A Fiqh Perspective." *Journal of Fatwa Management and Research* 21, no. 1 (2020): 38–48.

Shahimi, Shahida bint, Abd Ghafar B. Ismail, and Sanep B. Ahmad. "Panel Data Analysis of Fee Income Activities Islamic Banks." *Islamic Economics* 19, no. 2 (2006): 23–35.

Shaikh, Farzana. "From Islamisation to Shariatisation: Cultural Transnationalism in Pakistan." *Third World Quarterly* 29, no. 3 (2008): 593–609.

———. *Making Sense of Pakistan.* New York: Columbia University Press, 2009.

Shaikh, Salman Ahmed, Abdul Ghafar Ismail, and Muhammad Hakimi Mohd Shafiai. "Application of *Wakf* for Social and Development Finance." *ISRA International Journal of Islamic Finance* 9, no. 1 (2017): 5–14.

Shalhoob, Salah al-. "Organized Tawarruq in Islamic Law: A Study of Organized Tawarruq as Practised in the Financial Institutions in Saudi Arabia." Unpublished paper. Online collection of King Fahd University of Petroleum and Minerals, Dhahran, Saudi Arabia, n.d.

Shāṭibī, Ibrāhīm bin Mūsá Abū Isḥāq al-. *Al-muwāfaqāt fī uṣūl al-sharī'ah.* Beirut: Dār al-Maʿrifah, 1999.

Shirazi, Safdar Ali, Muhammed Hussain Choudary, Akhtar Hussain Sandhu, and Rehman Ullah Choudary. *Pakistan Studies* (5th Standard). Lahore: Punjab Curriculum and Textbook Board, 2016.

Siddiqi, Mohammad Nejatullah. *Issues in Islamic Banking.* Lahore: Islamic Foundation, 1983.

———. "Madrasa Students Need to Understand the World in Which We Live: Mohammad Nejatullah Siddiqui (Interview)." *TwoCircles.Net,* 2007.

———. *Muslim Economic Thinking: A Survey of Contemporary Literature.* Jeddah: International Centre for Research in Islamic Economics, King Abdul Aziz University, 1981.

———. *Partnership and Profit-Sharing in Islamic Law.* Vol. 9. Leicester: Islamic Foundation, 1985.

———. *Riba, Bank Interest and the Rationale of Its Prohibition.* Jeddah: Islamic Research and Training Institute, 2004.

———. "Shariah, Economics and the Progress of Islamic Finance: The Role of Shariah Experts." Paper presented at the Seventh Harvard Forum on Islamic Finance, Cambridge, MA, 21 April 2006.

Siddiqui, Shahid Hasan. "Anatomy and Critique of Islamic Banking." *Pakistan Horizon* 65, no. 3 (2012): 35–58.

Silver, Beverly J., and Giovanni Arrighi. "Polanyi's Double Movement: The *Belle Époques* of British and US Hegemony Compared." *Politics & Society* 31, no. 2 (2003): 325–355.

Silverman, Brian S., and Joel A. C. Baum. "Alliance-Based Competitive Dynamics." *Academy of Management Journal* 45, no. 4 (2002): 791–806.

Skovgaard-Petersen, Jakob. *Defining Islam for the Egyptian State: Muftis and Fatwas of the Dār Al-Iftā.* Leiden: Brill, 1997.

Sloane-White, Patricia. *Corporate Islam: Sharia and the Modern Workplace.* Cambridge: Cambridge University Press, 2017.

Smith, Kristin. "The Kuwait Finance House and the Islamization of Public Life in Kuwait." In *The Politics of Islamic Finance,* ed. Clement M. Henry and Rodney Wilson, 168–90. Edinburgh: Edinburgh University Press, 2004.

Smith, Timothy M., and Miriam Fischlein. "Rival Private Governance Networks: Competing to Define the Rules of Sustainability Performance." *Global Environmental Change* 20, no. 3 (2010): 511–22.

Soliman, Samer. "The Rise and Decline of the Islamic Banking Model in Egypt." In *The Politics of Islamic Finance*, ed. Clement M. Henry and Rodney Wilson, 265–85. Edinburgh: Edinburgh University Press, 2004.

Soloveitchik, Haym. "Pawnbroking: A Study in *Ribbit* and of the Halakah in Exile." *Proceedings of the American Academy for Jewish Research* 38/39 (January 1970): 203–68.

Spencer, George W. "Temple Money-Lending and Livestock Redistribution in Early Tanjore." *Indian Economic & Social History Review* 5, no. 3 (1968): 277–93.

Spiro, David E. *The Hidden Hand of American Hegemony: Petrodollar Recycling and International Markets*. Ithaca: Cornell University Press, 1999.

Stanton, Daniel. "Don't Fear the Riba." *Arabian Business*, 24 January 2008. https://www.arabianbusiness.com/gcc/uae/don-t-fear-riba-122012.

State Bank of Pakistan. "Fit and Proper Criteria for Appointment of Shariah Advisors." Islamic Banking Department Circular no. 3, 26 October 2004.

Steensland, Brian. "Moral Classification and Social Policy." In *Handbook of the Sociology of Morality*, ed. Steven Hitlin and Stephen Vaisey, 455–68. New York: Springer, 2010.

Stephens, Julia. *Governing Islam: Law, Empire, and Secularism in Modern South Asia*. Cambridge: Cambridge University Press, 2018.

Stiansen, Endre. "Interest Politics: Islamic Finance in the Sudan, 1977–2001." In *The Politics of Islamic Finance*, ed. Clement M. Henry and Rodney Wilson, 155–67. Edinburgh: Edinburgh University Press, 2004.

———. "Islamic Banking in the Sudan: Aspects of the Laws and the Debate." In *Credit, Currencies and Culture: African Financial Institutions in Historical Perspective*, ed. Endre Stiansen and Jane I. Guyer, 100–117. Uppsala: Nordiska Afrikainstitutet, 1999.

Strathern, Marilyn. "New Accountabilities: Anthropological Studies in Audit, Ethics and the Academy." In *Audit Cultures: Anthropological Studies in Accountability, Ethics and the Academy*, ed. Marilyn Strathern, 1–18. London: Routledge, 2000.

Su, Min, Wenli Yan, and Nicholas Harvey. "Pecking Order Theory and Church Debt Financing: Evidence from the United Methodist Church." *Nonprofit Management and Leadership* 33, no. 1 (2022): 179–201.

Suchman, Mark C. "Managing Legitimacy: Strategic and Institutional Approaches." *Academy of Management Review* 20, no. 3 (1995): 571–610.

Sultan, Hussam, and Muhammed-Shahid Ebrahim. "Murabaha." Unpublished manuscript, last modified 30 October 2011. https://ssrn.com/abstract=1923606.

Sundararajan, V. "Issues in Managing Profit Equalization Reserves and Investment Risk Reserves in Islamic Banks." *Journal of Islamic Economics, Banking and Finance* 4, no. 1 (2008): 1–11.

Suwailem, Sami al-. *Al-tawarruq . . . wa-l-tawarruq al-munaẓẓam: Dirāsah taʾṣīliyah*. Mecca: Presented to the Islamic Fiqh Council of the Muslim World League, 2003.

Swatos, William H. "Enchantment and Disenchantment in Modernity: The Significance of 'Religion' as a Sociological Category." *Sociological Analysis* 44, no. 4 (1983): 321–37.

Taktak, Neila Boulila. "The Nature of Smoothing Returns Practices: The Case of Islamic Banks." *Journal of Islamic Accounting and Business Research* 2, no. 2 (September 2011): 142–52.

Taktak, Neila Boulila, Sarra Ben Slama Zouari, and AbdelKader Boudriga. "Do Islamic Banks Use Loan Loss Provisions to Smooth Their Results?" *Journal of Islamic Accounting and Business Research* 1, no. 2 (2010): 114–27.

Tawney, R. H. *Religion and the Rise of Capitalism*. New Brunswick, NJ: Transaction, 1998.

Taylor, Charles. *A Secular Age*. Cambridge, MA: Harvard University Press, 2007.

Tobin, Sarah A. *Everyday Piety: Islam and Economy in Jordan*. Ithaca: Cornell University Press, 2016.

———. "Islamic Neoliberalism for Jordan's Islamic Action Front in Islamic Banking and Finance." *Politics and Religion* 13, no. 4 (2020): 768–95.

Tripp, Charles. *Islam and the Moral Economy: The Challenge of Capitalism*. Cambridge: Cambridge University Press, 2006.

Tuğal, Cihan. *Passive Revolution: Absorbing the Islamic Challenge to Capitalism*. Stanford: Stanford University Press, 2009.

Turner, Bryan S. "Max Weber on Islam and Confucianism: The Kantian Theory of Secularization." In *The Oxford Handbook of the Sociology of Religion*, ed. Peter B. Clarke. Oxford: Oxford University Press, 2011.

———. "Revisiting Weber and Islam." *British Journal of Sociology* 61, no. s1 (2010): 161–66.

Udovitch, Abraham L. "Bankers without Banks: Commerce, Banking, and Society in the Islamic World of the Middle Ages." In *The Dawn of Modern Banking*, ed. UCLA Center for Medieval and Renaissance Studies, 255–73. New Haven: Yale University Press, 1979.

———. "Islamic Law and the Social Context of Exchange in the Medieval Middle East." *History and Anthropology* 1, no. 2 (1985): 445–65.

———. *Partnership and Profit in Medieval Islam*. Princeton: Princeton University Press, 1970.

Ul Haque, Nadeem, and Abbas Mirakhor. "Optimal Profit-Sharing Contracts and Investment in an Interest-Free Islamic Economy." IMF Working Paper 86, no. 12 (5 November 1986).

Ulrichsen, Kristian Coates. *The Gulf States in International Political Economy*. London: Palgrave Macmillan, 2016.

———. *The Political Economy of Arab Gulf States*. Houston, TX: James A. Baker III Institute for Public Policy, 2015.

Ünal, Murat. *The Small World of Islamic Finance: Shariah Scholars and Governance: A Network Analytic Perspective, V. 6.0*. Kronberg im Taunus: Funds@Work, 2010.

Usmani, Muhammad Taqi. "Concept of Musharakah and Its Application as an Islamic Method of Financing." *Arab Law Quarterly* 14, no. 3 (1999): 203–20.

———. *An Introduction to Islamic Finance*. The Hague: Kluwer Law International, 2002.

———. "Sukuk and Their Contemporary Applications." Working paper prepared for the Accounting and Auditing Organization for Islamic Financial Institutions (Manama, Bahrain), 2007.

———. "Verdicts on at-Tawarruq and Its Banking Applications." Unpublished paper in the Islamic Economics & Finance Pedia (http://www.iefpedia.com), 2009.

Valeri, Mark. "Religion, Discipline, and the Economy in Calvin's Geneva." *Sixteenth Century Journal* 28, no. 1 (1997): 123–42.

Vizcaino, Bernardo. "Money Market Curbs to Challenge Islamic Banks in Oman." Reuters, 1 November 2012.

Vogel, Frank E. *Islamic Law and Legal System: Studies of Saudi Arabia*. Leiden: Brill, 2000.

Vogel, Frank E., and Samuel L. Hayes. *Islamic Law and Finance: Religion, Risk, and Return*. Cambridge, MA: Kluwer Law International, 1998.

Vogel, Steven Kent. *Freer Markets, More Rules: Regulatory Reform in Advanced Industrial Countries*. Ithaca: Cornell University Press, 1996.

von Pock, Alexander. *Strategic Management in Islamic Finance*. Frankfurt: Deutscher Universitäts-Verlag, 2007.

Wallerstein, Immanuel. *The Modern World System I: Capitalist Agriculture and the Origins of the European World Economy in the Sixteenth Century*. New York: Academic Press, 1974.

Warde, Ibrahim. "Global Politics, Islamic Finance and Islamist Politics before and after 11 September 2001." In *The Politics of Islamic Finance*, ed. Clement M. Henry and Rodney Wilson, 37–62. Edinburgh: Edinburgh University Press, 2004.

———. *Islamic Finance in the Global Economy*. 2nd ed. Edinburgh: Edinburgh University Press, 2010.

———. *The Price of Fear: The Truth behind the Financial War on Terror*. Berkeley: University of California Press, 2008.

Warner, Michael, Jonathan VanAntwerpen, and Craig J. Calhoun. *Varieties of Secularism in a Secular Age*. Cambridge, MA: Harvard University Press, 2010.

Waterbury, John. *Missions Impossible: Higher Education and Policymaking in the Arab World*. Cairo: American University in Cairo Press, 2020.

———. "The 'Soft State' and the Open Door: Egypt's Experience with Economic Liberalization, 1974–1984." *Comparative Politics* 18, no. 1 (1985): 65–83.

Weber, Max. "Bureaucracy." In *From Max Weber: Essays in Sociology*, 196–244. New York: Oxford University Press, 1958a.

———. *Economy and Society: An Outline of Interpretive Sociology*. Ed. Guenther Roth and Claus Wittich. Berkeley: University of California Press, 1978.

———. *General Economic History*. Glencoe, IL: Free Press, 1950.

———. "Religious Rejections of the World and Their Directions." In *From Max Weber: Essays in Sociology*, ed. H. H. Gerth and C. Wright Mills, 323–59. New York: Oxford University Press, 1958b.

———. "Science as a Vocation." In *From Max Weber: Essays in Sociology*, 129–56. New York: Oxford University Press, 1958c.

———. "The Social Psychology of the World Religions." In *From Max Weber: Essays in Sociology*, 267–301. New York: Oxford University Press, 1958d.

———. "The Three Types of Legitimate Rule." In *A Sociological Reader on Complex Organizations*, ed. Amitai Etzioni, 6–15. New York: Holt, Rinehart & Winston, 1969.

Wherry, Frederick F. "How Relational Accounting Matters." In *Money Talks: Explaining How Money Really Works*, 57–69. Princeton: Princeton University Press, 2017.

———. "Performance Circuits in the Marketplace." *Politics & Society* 40, no. 2 (2012): 203–21.

———. "Relational Accounting: A Cultural Approach." *American Journal of Cultural Sociology* 4, no. 2 (2016): 131–56.

Wherry, Frederick F., and Parijat Chakrabarti. "Accounting for Credit." *Annual Review of Sociology* 48, no. 1 (2022): 131–47.

Wherry, Frederick F., Kristin S. Seefeldt, and Anthony S. Alvarez. "To Lend or Not to Lend to Friends and Kin: Awkwardness, Obfuscation, and Negative Reciprocity." *Social Forces* 98, no. 2 (2019): 753–75.

Wilson, Peter W. *A Question of Interest: The Paralysis of Saudi Banking*. Boulder, CO: Westview, 1991.

Wilson, Rodney. "Arab Government Responses to Islamic Finance: The Cases of Egypt and Saudi Arabia." *Mediterranean Politics* 7, no. 3 (2002a): 143–63.

———. *Banking and Finance in the Arab Middle East*. London: Macmillan, 1983.

———. "The Contribution of Muḥammad Bāqir Al-Ṣadr to Contemporary Islamic Economic Thought." *Journal of Islamic Studies* 9, no. 1 (1998): 46–59.

———. "The Development of Islamic Finance in the Gulf Cooperation Council States." In *The Transformation of the Gulf: Politics, Economics and the Global Order*, ed. David Held and Kristian Ulrichsen, 146–64. London: Routledge, 2011.

———. "The Evolution of the Islamic Financial System." In *Islamic Finance: Innovation and Growth*, ed. Simon Archer and Rifaat Ahmed Abdel Karim. London: Euromoney Books, 2002b.

———. *Islam and Economic Policy: An Introduction*. Edinburgh: Edinburgh University Press, 2015.

———. *Islamic Finance in Europe*. Florence: Robert Schuman Centre for Advanced Studies, European University Institute, 2007.

Winchester, Daniel. "Embodying the Faith: Religious Practice and the Making of a Muslim Moral Habitus." *Social Forces* 86, no. 4 (2008): 1753–80.

Witte, John. *Law and Protestantism*. Cambridge: Cambridge University Press, 2002.

Wittgenstein, Ludwig. *Culture and Value: A Selection from the Posthumous Remains*. Trans. Peter Winch, ed. Georg Henrik von Wright, Heikki Nyman, and Alois Pichler. Oxford: Blackwell, 1998.

———. *Philosophische Untersuchungen/Philosophical Investigations*. Trans. G.E.M. Anscombe, P.M.S. Hacker, and Joachim Schulte, ed. P.M.S. Hacker and Joachim Schulte. 4th ed. Chichester: Wiley-Blackwell, 2009.

Wittgenstein, Ludwig, G.E.M. Anscombe, and G. H. von Wright. *On Certainty*. Oxford: Black-well, 1969.

Wittgenstein, Ludwig, G.E.M. Anscombe, G. H. von Wright, and Heikki Nyman. *The Collected Works of Ludwig Wittgenstein: Culture and Value*. Past Masters. Charlottesville, VA: InteLex Corporation, 1998.

Wood, Diana. *Medieval Economic Thought*. Cambridge: Cambridge University Press, 2002.

World Bank and Islamic Development Bank Group. *Global Report on Islamic Finance: Islamic Finance: A Catalyst for Shared Prosperity?* Washington, DC: World Bank, 2016.

Wright, Erik Olin. *Envisioning Real Utopias*. London: Verso, 2010.

Wyrtzen, Jonathan. "For a (Comparative?) Global Historical Sociology." *Cambridge Review of International Affairs* 33, no. 6 (2020): 896–901.

Yergin, Daniel. *The Prize: The Epic Quest for Oil, Money & Power*. New York: Free Press, 1993.

Young, Karen E. *The Political Economy of Energy, Finance and Security in the United Arab Emirates: Between the Majilis and the Market*. London: Palgrave Macmillan, 2014.

Yousef, Tarik M. "The Murabaha Syndrome in Islamic Finance: Laws, Institutions and Politics." In *The Politics of Islamic Finance*, ed. Clement M. Henry and Rodney Wilson, 63–80. Edinburgh: Edinburgh University Press, 2004.

Zahrvi, Qazi Mujeeb Ul Rehman al-, Allama Mirza Yusuf Hussain, Rasheed Ahmed, and Abdul Haie Noor. *Islāmīyāt* (9th Standard). Lahore: Punjab Curriculum and Textbook Board, 2014.

Zaidi, N. A. *Eliminating Interest from Banks in Pakistan*. Karachi: Royal Book Company, 1987.

Zaman, Arshad. "Maulānā Maudūdī and the Genesis of Islamic Economics." *Turkish Journal of Islamic Economics* 8, no. 2 (2021): 597–622.

Zaman, Muhammad Qasim. *Modern Islamic Thought in a Radical Age: Religious Authority and Internal Criticism*. Cambridge: Cambridge University Press, 2012.

———. *The Ulama in Contemporary Islam: Custodians of Change*. Princeton: Princeton University Press, 2002.

Zeghal, Malika. *Gardiens de l'Islam: Les oulémas d'al Azhar dans l'Égypte contemporaine*. Paris: Les Presses de Sciences Po, 1996.

———. "The Implicit Sharia: Established Religion and Varieties of Secularism in Tunisia." In *Varieties of Religious Establishment*, ed. Winnifred Fallers Sullivan and Lori G. Beaman, 107–30. New York: Routledge, 2013.

———. *The Making of the Modern Muslim State*. Princeton: Princeton University Press, 2024.

Zelizer, Viviana A. "How I Became a Relational Economic Sociologist and What Does That Mean?" *Politics & Society* 40, no. 2 (2012): 145–74.

———. *Morals and Markets: The Development of Life Insurance in the United States*. New York: Columbia University Press, 1979.

———. "The Price and Value of Children: The Case of Children's Insurance." *American Journal of Sociology* 86, no. 5 (1981): 1036–56.

———. *The Purchase of Intimacy*. Princeton: Princeton University Press, 2005.

Zimmermann, Reinhard. *The Law of Obligations: Roman Foundations of the Civilian Tradition*. Oxford: Oxford University Press, 1996.

Zoubi, Taisier A., and Osamah Al-Khazali. "Empirical Testing of the Loss Provisions of Banks in the GCC Region." *Managerial Finance* 33, no. 7 (2007): 500–511.

Zuhayli, Wahba al-. "The Juridical Meaning of Riba." In *Interest in Islamic Economics: Understanding Riba*, ed. Abdulkader Thomas, 26–54. New York: Routledge, 2006.

———. "*Tawarruq*, Its Essence and Its Types: Mainstream *Tawarruq* and Organized *Tawarruq*." Unpublished paper. Online collection of Islamic Economics & Finance Pedia, n.d.

Z/Yen and China Development Institute. *The Global Financial Centres Index 32*. London: Z/Yen Group, 2022.

INDEX

Page numbers in *italics* indicate figures and tables. As in the industry, honorifics are included for shariah scholars, Islamic-finance pioneers, and royalty.

Al Lootah, Saeed bin Ahmad (Hajj): charitable foundation of, 28; Dubai Islamic Bank (DIB), 37, 38, 40, 52; in history of Islamic finance, 28–29, 67; turning to shariah scholars, 69
"low" Islamic finance, 24, 120, 133, 249, 241, 271; low Islamic banking, 129–30
Luther, Martin, on usury ban, 94
Lutheran, 96
Luxembourg, 20, 174, 213; interviews, 271, 272; Islamic fund assets by domicile (2021), 15; offshore-finance jurisdiction, 11

"Magic Circle" law firms (London), 136
Mahathir Mohamad, on Islamic finance, 66
Mahmood, Saba, liberal secular states defining religion, 263
Maimunah, Raja Teh, on Bursa Suq al-Sila ʿ (BSAS), 197
Malaysia, 1, 33, 50, 68, 71, 72, 108, 111, 201; CIMB Bank,107, 109; corporate sukuk issuances (2021), 14; violations, 180; experiment, 34; institutions of higher education, 126, 132; interviewees, 20, 21; interviews, 271, 272; Islamic bank visit, 21; Islamic banking assets (2021), 13; Islamic finance in, 66, 117, 135, 141, 144, 187, 237, 239; Islamic finance industry in, 11; Islamic fund assets by domicile (2021), 15; Islamic interbank, 62; Ismail and Gulf model in, 64–66; palm oil in, 196–97, 198, 199, 254; profit smoothing, 81; shariah advisors, 124, 126, 128–29, 185, 189–90; toyyib concept in, 165
Maldives, Islamic banking assets (2021), 13
Mālik (Imam), Muwaṭṭaʿ of, 55
Mālikī school of Islamic jurisprudence, 106, 158, 159, 160, 247
al-Manea, Abdullah (Sheikh): on Bitcoin, 205; market mentality of, 127; sukuk issuance, 167
Maria Theresa thaler (silver coin), circulation in Saudi Arabia, 235

market-minded scholars, Islamic banks aligning with, 56–60
market mindset, of shariah scholars, 127–29
markup-sale contract. See murabaha
Marx, Karl: Capital and scholastic conception of riba, 89; formulas for capital, 97–99
Masud, Muhammad Khalid, on Islamic jurisprudence, 160
Mawdudi, Abu al-Aʿla: influence on Zia-ul-Haq's economic policies, 232; Islamic democracy, 231; neorevivalist economics, 218
Maybank, 165
maysir (gambling or games of chance), 92
McGill University, 126
McViety, Paul: on elite shariah scholars, 136; sukuk issuances, 174
Meezan Bank (Pakistan), 169, 173, 194, 215, 276
Mennonite/Anabaptist, 96
merchant ethics, Islamic, 86, 93, 190, 192, 194
MGSB. See Mit Ghamr Savings Bank
Mit Ghamr Savings Bank (MGSB), 33–34, 45, 46
Middle East and North Africa (MENA) region, 30
Middle East and South Asia, Islamic financial assets (2021), 12
Mill, J. S., Urdu translations of, 74
Ministry of Religious Endowments (Egypt), 43, 44
Mizruchi, Mark, on U.S. corporate elite, 256
modernism, Islamic, 31–32
Mennonite/Anabaptist, 96
Mohamad, Mahathir. See Mahathir Mohamad
Mohamad, Maznah, research of, 129
Moody's, 134, 152
Moosa, Ebrahim, on legal-moral epistemology, 91
moral economists, 5–6, 21, 57, 62, 172; auto finance based on diminishing joint venture, 84; case for profit-and-loss sharing

Shaikh, Samir Abid, birth of the shariah
board, 63

shariah board(s), 1–2, 7, 10, 20, 23–24, 29,
157, 160; banks', 102–4, 112, 116, 166; birth
of, 62–64, 69, 262; determining "Islamic"
in term "Islamic finance," 241–42;
Deutsche Bank, 171–73; fundamental
rules of Islamic banks and, 62–64; Goldman Sachs, 166; Gulf model, 42; Islamic
finance, 105–7, 130–32, 241; legalism of,
253, 264; legitimacy of, 123–25, 133, 135,
137; organized tawarruq, 191, 194–95;
Pakistan, 162, 169, 228, 238; people on,
127–28; policing, 179–80, 184–86

shariah restrictions. See restriction

shariah risk, 243

shariah scholars: accommodation as ethical
worldview, 144–49; aligning religion and
finance, 241; Aristotelian-scholastic critique of usury in Abrahamic sacred law,
87–88; autonomy in Saudi Arabia and
Pakistan, 226–28; bracketing social concerns, 161–64; departure from PLS
principle, 81; deploying legitimacy in
high Islamic finance, 132–34; deploying
legitimacy in low Islamic finance, 130–32;
elite, filling structural holes, 134–37; ethical progress, 118–19; gatekeepers of Islamic finance, 7; Gulf model of Islamic
finance, 42–43; higher education for, 124,
126; historical perspective of, 86–91; importance of, 138–39; institutions of
higher education by, 126; internationally
elite and global elite, 279n3; Islamic derivatives, 92–93; Islamic finance, 1–2,
24–25, 140–41; Islamic-finance industry,
8; Islamicity and legal compliance, 110;
Islamic law forming horizontal alliance,
69–70; legalism of, 264; legitimation of, 120;
market mindset of, 127–29; moral economists and, 73–76; pedigree of, 123–27;
pioneering financiers, 67; public attitudes
toward, 222–25; remuneration of, 137–38;
rock-star, 1, 24, 93, 279n3; Saudi Arabian,

insulated from contentious politics,
228–29; scholasticism, 99–100; scholastic
jurists preserving usury ban, 90–91;
scholastic views of money, 89–90;
sources of collective legitimacy, 121–22;
sources of individual legitimacy, 123–27;
treatment at conferences, 1. See also
legitimation

Sharia Investment Services, 38

Sharif, Nawaz: Benazir Bhutto and, 233;
Musharraf ousting, 237

Shariyah Review Bureau (SRB), Yasser
Dahlawi of, 183

Sharjah Islamic Bank, 81

al-Shāṭibī, on necessities, 155–56

al-Shaybānī, Muḥammad, watching market,
127

al-Shaykh, Muḥammad Khāṭir Muḥammad
(Grand Mufti), shariah board, 63

Sheikh Zayed Road, artery of New Dubai,
29, 30

Shia and Shiism: interviewees, 277; scholars, 226

Siddiqi, Mohammad Nejatullah, 80; on
conventional finance, 188; Islamic economist, 64; two-tiered mudaraba, 78–79;
vision of commercial Islamic banking, 51

Siddiqui, Rushdi, Islamic equity index, 165

simulating interest. See interest simulation

Singapore, 2, 11, 68, 199

site visits, methods, 21

Sloane-White, Patricia, on corporate Islam,
128

Smith, Adam, on usury, 94

socialism, 31, 32, 73, 74, 75

Social Security trust fund (United States), 11

social welfarism/social welfare/socioeco-
nomic welfare, 36, 147–48; 203; 225, 229,
233, 237, 243; Abdul Halim Ismail on,
64–66; Aijaz on, 162–63; Al Lootah, 29;
big picture of, 162; bracketing out, 161–4;
"Christian finance" and, 95; criticism of
Islamic-finance industry, 165; future of
Islamic finance and, 255, 258; government

A NOTE ON THE TYPE

This book has been composed in Arno, an Old-style serif typeface in the classic Venetian tradition, designed by Robert Slimbach at Adobe.

Milton Keynes UK
Ingram Content Group UK Ltd.
UKHW030732171124
451305UK00002B/4

9 780691 258300